The Failure of Democracy
in the Republic of Congo

The
Failure of
Democracy
—— in the ——
Republic of
Congo

John F. Clark

LYNNE
RIENNER
PUBLISHERS

BOULDER
LONDON

Published in the United States of America in 2008 by
Lynne Rienner Publishers, Inc.
1800 30th Street, Boulder, Colorado 80301
www.rienner.com

and in the United Kingdom by
Lynne Rienner Publishers, Inc.
3 Henrietta Street, Covent Garden, London WC2E 8LU

Library of Congress Cataloging-in-Publication Data
Clark, John Frank.
  The failure of democracy in the Republic of Congo / John F. Clark.
    p. cm.
  Includes bibliographical references and index.
  ISBN 978-1-58826-555-5 (hardcover : alk. paper)
  1. Congo (Brazzaville)—Politics and government—1960–
2. Democracy—Congo (Brazzaville) 3. Democratization—Congo
(Brazzaville) I. Title.
  JQ3406.A58C53 2007
  967.2405—dc22

                                                      2007037616

British Cataloguing in Publication Data
A Cataloguing in Publication record for this book
is available from the British Library.

Printed and bound in the United States of America

∞   The paper used in this publication meets the requirements
      of the American National Standard for Permanence of
      Paper for Printed Library Materials Z39.48-1992.

5   4   3   2   1

*For Samantha Jasmine Clark
and John Yann Sita*

Contents

Preface

On the morning of 5 June 1997, I was standing just outside the US Cultural Center on the Avenue Amilcar Cabral in Brazzaville when automatic-weapons fire rang out from the nearby Mpila district, less than one mile away. All of those walking along the avenue instinctively backed away from the street and turned to look north toward Mpila. Soon, several armored vehicles raced down the street in the direction of the firing. My friend François Sita emerged from the Cultural Center a few minutes later and said, "Well, John, I think we'd better go home." As we threaded our way through the streets toward Makélékélé, we noticed that partisans were beginning to gather materials to put up roadblocks. We later learned that the armed confrontation in Mpila had begun several hours before the gunfire we heard.

Minor rebellions by disgruntled soldiers are not uncommon in central Africa, and so we did not immediately conclude that a civil war had broken out. The context of the fighting was ominous, however; at the moment when it began, presidential elections were only a few weeks away, and the preparations were far behind schedule. Less than two weeks before, in the towns of Owando and Oyo, there had been clashes between armed supporters of former president Denis Sassou-Nguesso (then a prominent candidate in the scheduled elections) and those of the sitting president, Pascal Lissouba. Sassou had created a militia from his former presidential guard after he gave up power in 1992, and he had increased the militia over the ensuing years. In the days following the events of 5 June, the fighting spread throughout other parts of the city, and some neighborhoods were purged of those belonging to minority ethnic groups. Despite multiple efforts to mediate the conflict, the fighting gradually became more intense, including the use of mortars and artillery by each side.

Following the evacuation of most foreigners, including me, during the first week of the war, the fighting grew still more intense. A full-scale civil war raged throughout Brazzaville and its environs during the summer and early fall (the dry season in the Congolese capital). The war ended with Sassou's return to power by force of arms and with the support of Angolan invaders in October. Some ten thousand Congolese died in the conflict. Sadly, the civil war of 1997 not only ended Congo's fragile experiment with competitive multiparty democracy, but also set the stage for even bloodier civil wars in 1998–1999 and in 2002–2004. In this study of Congolese politics, I explore the reasons for the failure of the country's democratic experiment.

*   *   *

In pleasant contrast to the disreputable behavior of many Congolese politicians, the Congolese people have shown me generosity, warmth, and kindness during my visits to their country. I honor the citizens of Congo for these qualities, as well as for the suffering they have endured. A number of fellow scholars from both Congos have displayed the same qualities, demonstrating to me that the generosity of the Congolese extends to the intellectual sphere. Among the Congolese scholars who have been of the greatest assistance are Rémy Bazenguissa-Ganga, Didier Gondola, and Brice Massengo. Their kindness and patience reminds me of an important reason why I chose to make the study of Africa a major part of my career. The challenge of getting a glimpse beneath the layers of mystery that obscure the workings of Congolese society and politics is daunting, and no Westerner will succeed without the assistance of Congolese collaborators.

Aside from these colleagues, virtually all of those in the very small fraternity/sorority of Congo specialists have helped me in my research on the country. This group includes Florence Bernault, David Eaton, Pierre Englebert, Victor Le Vine, Phyllis Martin, Patrick Quantin, and I. William Zartman. A larger group of scholars have helped me to sharpen my thinking about issues of political culture, political economy, democratization, and France's role in Africa; these include Edouard Bustin, Robert Fatton, Joshua Forrest, John Harbeson, Staffan Lindberg, Will Reno, Michael Schatzberg, Nicolas Van de Walle, Leonardo Villalón, and Crawford Young. The intellectual diversity of this group no doubt reflects my own eclecticism.

Before his death in October 2000, my dear friend and colleague Chris Gray generously shared his impressive knowledge of central African history and geography with me, and I continue to miss his bright mind and warm friendship. I have also learned a great deal about central African society and religion from my dear friend Terry Rey, now at Temple University. I owe a special thanks to four colleagues who read all or part of the manuscript while I was in the process of revisions; these include Pierre Englebert, David Gardinier, Phyllis Martin, and James Swan. Two anonymous readers for Lynne Rienner Publishers also provided valuable criticism and suggestions to which I have tried to respond. I surely have forgotten a number of others who helped me, and to them, my apologies. Finally, none of these kind friends and colleagues bears any responsibility for errors of fact or interpretation in the book.

The two Africana librarians at the University of Florida (UF) have been consistently helpful to me since I began my career at Florida International University in 1991. Peter Malanchuk and Dan Reboussin have been of great assistance, both during my frequent visits to UF's wonderful library and from afar. I owe a substantial debt of gratitude to both.

My first trip to Congo was as a US Department of State intern at the US Embassy in Brazzaville in the summer of 1990. That summer, I met Roger Meece, then deputy chief of mission, with whom I have been in contact ever since; he has consistently been supportive of my research on Congo. Ambassador Meece also introduced me to François Sita, my closest Congolese friend. Ambassador David Kaeuper and his former deputy, James Swan, were kind and helpful to me during my visits to Congo in 2001 and 2002. My 2001 trip was undertaken under the auspices of the International Foundation for Elections Systems (IFES), to which I am grateful.

This book was partly written while I was serving as chair of my department at Florida International University, and I was only able to complete it because of one semester and several briefer periods of leave from my duties. During those leaves, Lisa Prugl and then Paul Kowert served as acting chair of the department. Each also served, in turn, as director of graduate programs in the department while I was chair. I am deeply grateful to these two collegial friends who "minded the shop" while I was on leave and temporarily relieved me from the pressures of administration to pursue my research.

My greatest debt for the completion of this book is owed to my friend François Sita, a former professor and director of the Institut Superieur de Gestion at Marien Ngouabi University in Brazzaville. For more than ten years, François has been my host, my guide, my translator, my source of contacts, my sounding board, and my inspiration. During Congo's many travails over that time, he has displayed immeasurable courage, strength, and selflessness. I admire him greatly for his detachment, capacity for forgiveness, irrepressible optimism, hope, enthusiasm, love, and patience. His goodness and force of will remind me that Congo's future is not predestined, and that many Congolese will seek to heal and rebuild Congo's shattered society. François has an admirable disinterest in politics and has never sought to influence me about Congolese politics in any partisan way. The youngest of his four sons, John Yann Sita, was born amidst the chaos of the 1997 war, just before the Sita family had to temporarily flee their home (and, alas, not for the last time).

In the course of completing the manuscript for this book, I married Esther Alonso. I am grateful to her for her tolerance of my obscure intellectual interests, as well as for her love and encouragement. Esther's discipline, determination, thoughtfulness of others, and devotion to her family inspire me. Our daughter, Samantha Jasmine Clark, was born 5 April 2006, and she is now the joy of our life. Thanks to Oilda for watching the baby. This book is dedicated to Samantha and to John Yann Sita.

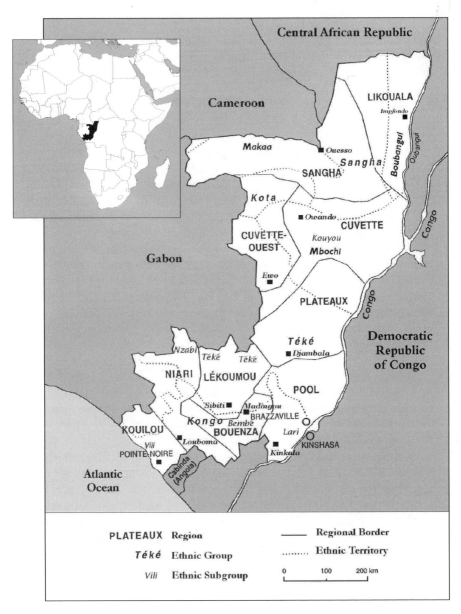

Central African Republic

Cameroon

LIKOUALA

Impfondo

Makaa

Ouesso

Sangha

SANGHA

Boubangui

Oubangui

Kota

Owando

CUVETTE

Gabon

CUVETTE-
OUEST

Kouyou

Mbochi

Congo

Ewo

PLATEAUX

Congo

Téké

Democratic
Republic
of Congo

Nzabi

Téké

Téké

Djambala

NIARI

LÉKOUMOU

POOL

Sibiti

Madingou

BRAZZAVILLE

Kongo

Bembé

KOUILOU

BOUENZA

Lari

Vili

Louboma

KINSHASA

POINTE-NOIRE

Kinkala

Cabinda
(Angola)

Atlantic
Ocean

PLATEAUX	Region	——— Regional Border
Téké	Ethnic Group	········ Ethnic Territory
Vili	Ethnic Subgroup	0 100 200 km

Republic of Congo: Regions and Ethnic Groups

*Map courtesy of Jennifer Gebelein, adapted and reprinted with permission
from Philippe Frank, "Ethnies et partis: Le cas du Congo," Afrique Contemporaine,
no. 182 (2nd trimester 1997): 4, De Boeck University, www.cairn.info.*

1

The Republic of Congo: Failure of a Democratic Experiment

This book is an exploration of a specific, concrete question about the social world: why did the experiment in multiparty democratic government in the Republic of Congo[1] fail in 1997? As with most questions about the social world, the answer can be either a simple, straightforward one or an elaborate dissertation. The more the striking complexity of the social world is appreciated, the more likely a detailed exposition is valued. The careful examination of the Congo case can, in the first instance, provide accurate information to theoretically minded scholars examining a phenomenon across many cases. Yet, this case study is intended to do more: it also seeks to remind us explicitly that each case is unique, and that each can only be understood fully in the terms that the actors themselves used, that is, from the inside out.

I pay close attention in the study to theoretical work in several areas related to democratization, including political culture, political economy, ethnic and regional identity formation, and constitutional design. Congo, like better-studied African cases, has something to tell us about the theoretical debates in each of these areas of inquiry, and I seek to highlight those lessons, whether Congo emerges as a case in point or a difficult anomaly. I also make a serious effort to situate the Congolese experiment with democracy within the country's historical context. Few aspects of Congo's economy, political values, or ethnic sensibilities can be deeply appreciated without abundant allusion to their historical roots.

In this introductory chapter, I undertake four tasks. The first is to present a barebones overview of the democratic experiment in Congo. Every significant aspect of this historical review will be explored in more detail in the following chapters. The overview is a necessary prerequisite of a second immediate task, a further explication of the research question. This task involves in particular a specification of the terms used with reference to the Congo case. Third, I take up the question of the relevance of the research question, leading in turn to a brief discussion of some other bodies of literature in relation to that on democratization. Finally, I provide an outline of the remainder of the book. Although the logic of the organization will only become fully apparent in Chapter 2, some readers will inevitably want to know immediately how the study will unfold.

■ An Overview of the Democratic Experiment in Congo

The multiparty experiment in the Congo Republic began in 1991, along with a wave of other similar such experiments that began sweeping the African continent in 1989. In the case of Congo, a military dictator operating under the ideological cover of Marxist-Leninism, Denis Sassou-Nguesso, was forced to cede power to an interim regime following a three-month national conference ending in mid-1991 (Clark 1993).[2] In August of the following year, Sassou stood against several other challengers in a presidential election, but failed to secure enough votes to proceed to the second round. A new president, Pascal Lissouba, a scientist, former UNESCO official, and veteran Congolese politician, finished first in the first round with 36 percent, and won a majority (61 percent) in the second.

Over the course of its short life, the Congolese experiment with multiparty politics underwent a series of severe challenges, the first coming during the transition period. One crisis involved efforts by the transitional government to rein in the army, accompanied by alleged coup plots; a second involved alleged cheating by the transitional government in the local and municipal elections of May 1992 (*Africa Confidential,* "Characteristic Ambiguity," 6 March 1992: 5; *Africa Confidential,* "Testing the Waters of Democracy," 19 June 1992: 6–7). Congo later experienced fierce fighting among militia groups and the army in 1993 and early 1994. The experiment essentially came to an end in mid-1997 when a full-blown civil war broke out only weeks before scheduled national elections.

Soon after the election of Lissouba in 1992 a crisis far more serious than those of the transition erupted. This one was occasioned by the collapse of the president's coalition in Parliament. Lissouba had won the second round of the elections by forging a partnership with former president Sassou and his party, the Parti Congolais du Travail (PCT).[3] Through this alliance, Lissouba not only won the presidency, but also controlled a majority in the National Assembly. His own Union Panafricaine pour la Démocratie Sociale (UPADS) party held thirty-nine seats and Sassou's PCT held eighteen after the legislative elections; with the cooperation of some smaller parties, Lissouba's coalition commanded a majority in the 125-seat body. When Lissouba announced the formation of his first government in September, however, Sassou's PCT only received three minor cabinet posts. Insulted, Sassou abandoned the coalition, and made an alliance with Lissouba's strongest competitor, Bernard Kolélas. Kolélas himself had finished second in the presidential balloting, winning 39 percent in the second round, while his Mouvement Congolais Pour le Développement et la

Démocratie Intégrale (MCDDI) party had won twenty-nine seats in the Assembly, the second highest total. When the new coalition was formed,[4] it controlled a majority in the Assembly.

Rather than naming a prime minister from this opposition coalition, as the constitution required, however, Lissouba dissolved the Assembly and ordered the holding of new elections the following year. When the opposition did not concede to this "solution," a major confrontation ensued. Opposition partisans demonstrated outside the office of the president in December, and Lissouba's presidential guard fired on them, killing three. Toward the end of the year, the crisis was temporarily resolved when Lissouba was persuaded to appoint a "national unity" government, headed by a neutral prime minister.

The rerun of the legislative elections in May 1993 marked the beginning of an even more serious crisis, a round of fighting that the Congolese later called their first civil war. In the presence of international observers, Lissouba's new coalition of his UPADS and many smaller parties won a total of sixty-two seats in the Assembly.[5] Even with eleven seats still undecided because of a lack of majority in the first round, it was clear that Lissouba's coalition had won a majority. Citing "monstrous frauds and irregularities," however, the opposition rejected the results of the election (*Marchés Tropicaux et Méditerréens*, "Congo," 21 May 1993: 1321).

At this point, Congo's notorious militia groups began to make their first appearance on the scene.[6] A group loyal to Kolélas, the Ninjas, took control over the Brazzaville neighborhoods of Bacongo and Makélékélé, those largely populated by the Lari people who looked upon Kolélas as their leader. This militia began to purge the neighborhoods of residents from the regions of Niari, Bouenza, and Lékoumou (Nibolek), those that had overwhelmingly supported Lissouba in the elections. Meanwhile, Lissouba's own militia, the Zoulous, began to purge their own neighborhoods (Diata and Mfilou) of Lari residents. When the second round of voting was held on 6 June, the opposition boycotted. In the aftermath of these elections—later struck down by the Supreme Court—the fighting between Kolélas's Ninjas and the government forces reached the point of civil war. Meanwhile, cooler heads organized mediation efforts led by neutral Congolese political figures, international diplomats, and Gabonese president Omar Bongo throughout the months of June and July. On 4 August 1993, these efforts reached fruition in the Libreville Accords, an agreement that arranged for the arbitration of the disputed seats by an international jury and specified procedures for the rerun of elections to fill the contested seats (Zartman and Vogeli 2000: 273–276).

In October, the elections for the remaining eleven seats were again contested, sparking another round of violence. When the election results confirmed Lissouba's majority in the Assembly, the opposition groups boycotted the opening of the new Assembly session, leading to a renewal of fighting. The carnage was worse this time, with incredible violence aimed at the representatives of rival ethnoregional constituencies. The worst of the killing took place between November 1993 and January 1994, at which point Lissouba ordered the shelling of Bacongo and Makélékélé. During both of these rounds of fighting, Sassou and his Cobra militia mostly stayed on the sidelines.

This time it was entirely the Congolese themselves who restored the peace, chiefly through an interregional committee in the Assembly, composed of deputies from the two warring sides (Zartman and Vogeli 2000: 278). By 31 January the basic accord was in place, and peace returned gradually to the country, though marked with periodic outbreaks of fighting. In January 1995, a new agreement was reached between Lissouba and Kolélas in which the latter's MCDDI gained cabinet posts, including the Interior Ministry, in a new government. Relative peace prevailed in Congo from the middle of 1994 through the first months of 1997, at which time the start of the next presidential election campaign got under way.

Sadly for Congo, the country's fragile civil peace—and democratic experiment—was destroyed soon after the 1997 presidential election campaign began. The peace was first broken in the northern region of Cuvette, whence hailed both Sassou and Joachim Yhombi-Opango, another former president (1977–1979). The latter had joined the Lissouba government as prime minister in 1993, at the height of the first electoral standoff. In early May 1997, when Sassou sought to be carried into Yhombi's hometown of Owando on a traditional chief's chair, violence broke out between Yhombi's (mostly Kouyou) supporters and Sassou's (mostly Mbochi) bodyguards. A bout of fighting between the supporters of Yhombi and Sassou in the towns of Oyo and Owando ensued, leaving twelve persons dead (*Le Semaine Africaine,* "Une douzaine de tués et des sinistrés," 29 May 1997: 1, 3; Pourtier 1998: 18). Before the fighting went too far, however, outside mediators again intervened. In this instance, UNESCO Director-General Federico Mayor persuaded the feuding politicians to sign a pledge on 31 May 1997 to refrain from any further violence during the campaign.

Although the partisans of peace in Congo breathed a sigh of relief, their hopes were soon dashed. Two days after the signature of this new agreement, four members of Yhombi's bodyguard were killed while trying to pass through a roadblock near Oyo, Sassou's hometown (Pourtier 1998: 18). In the early morning of 5 June 1997, government forces surrounded Sassou's residence in Mpila, apparently with the mission of arresting two of Sassou's associates implicated in the Oyo incident and of seizing the arms of the Cobras.[7] As Sassou's Cobras had already organized the residence as a virtual armed camp, however, the arrests could not be effected, and fighting erupted once again. The struggle soon spread to the surrounding neighborhoods, and eventually to all of Brazzaville. What followed was a four-month-long civil war between the well-armed militia of Sassou and the militias and army forces loyal to Lissouba. Many elements of the regular army either joined forces with Sassou's fighters or simply abandoned their posts. Kolélas and his militia remained neutral until Lissouba persuaded him to join his government in September. Before his forces could have any impact on the stalemate, however, the Angolan army made a decisive intervention. In apparent revenge for Lissouba's embrace of the National Union for the Total Independence of Angola (Mabeko-Tali 2000), Angola sent thousands of its troops into Congo on behalf of Sassou, allowing him to seize the country's key installations in October.

With Sassou's return to power through force of arms, Congo's experiment with a democratic system was suspended. The senior members of the previous government (including Lissouba and Kolélas) fled into exile, and were later accused of "genocide" by the Sassou regime. Several were later tried and convicted in absentia. Since 1997, the country has seen two more rounds of civil war, the deadliest taking place between December 1998 and November 1999. The second broke out in the Pool region shortly after the deeply flawed elections of 2002 and continued in sporadic fashion for more than a year. See further discussion in Chapter 10.

■ The Research Question

Having briefly reviewed some details of the case, let us specify the question that is being posed in this study: what accounts for the failure of the democratic experiment? Two concepts in the question require further explanation, namely, "democratic experiment" and "failure." Why was the cumbersome phrase "democratic experiment" chosen rather than the simpler term "democracy" (a shorthand that I use for "democratic experiment" elsewhere in this study)? The answer is that the Congolese democratic experiment had not been "consolidated" before its collapse in 1997, although a transition *had* taken place in 1992. This reply, in turn, compels us to consider more fully the meaning of the terms "transition," "consolidation," and—most problematic of all—"democracy" itself.

Fortunately, this study does not require a deep foray into the minefield of the meaning of the term "democracy." It is enough to specify that in this study the term "democracy" refers to the limited, formal definition of the concept. One scholar (Plattner 1998) has labeled this form of the concept "liberal democracy," to distinguish it from other, broader varieties of democratic rule, such as "constitutional democracy" or "social democracy" (also see Ottemoeller 1999). To distinguish narrowly between formal democracies and other types of regimes, one may usefully follow Przeworksi et al. (2000: 14–20). These scholars begin by proclaiming that (formal) democracy is "a regime in which those who govern are elected through contested elections" (15); they go on to specify that both the executive and the legislature must be elected, and that multiple parties must legally contest the elections (18–20).[8] They logically stipulate that the executive may be indirectly elected, so as not to exclude parliamentary regimes (19).

After extended consideration, Przeworski et al. add one further criterion for a formal democracy to exist: alternation (2000: 27). If a constitutionally *new* regime is in power, but the ruling party has not lost an election, one cannot know whether or not that regime would cede power were it to lose an election. These authors cite empirical evidence to show, however, that in most cases new regimes that control a large percentage of the legislature do *not* in fact experience peaceful, electoral alternation. Accordingly, they decide not to code regimes that have not experienced alternation as "democracies" for purposes of their study. To illustrate the kinds of cases they have in mind, they cite Botswana. This state has had regular, relatively fair elections for both the executive and legislature in which multiple parties competed. Does Botswana thus deserve to be called a democracy? For Przeworski et al., it does not, because the same party (the Botswana Democratic Party [BDP]) has prevailed in each postindependence election and the regime has therefore not experienced alternation. According to the operational rules of these authors, then, Botswana is coded as a nondemocracy, though one might fairly consider it an unconsolidated proto-democratic regime. Przeworksi et al. acknowledged that Botswana is neither fish nor fowl, but decided to err on the side of conservatism by excluding such regimes from the list of democracies on the ground they historically do *not* tend to consolidate democratic governments.

This discussion is useful when we consider the case of Congo, for the Lissouba regime falls into the same category as the BDP regime in Botswana. Lissouba's presidency clearly was the result of a "democratic transition," as defined by Bratton and van de Walle (1997), and was recorded as such in their study of democratic transitions. Both Lissouba himself and the Congolese legislature certainly came to power by virtue of free and fair elections contested by multiple candidates and parties. The regime was never consolidated, however, by alternation of a new party into the governing role. Following these definitions, I have chosen to refer to the 1992 to 1997 period in Congo as one of "democratic experiment." The collapse of the experiment in 1997 was not a case of "democratic breakdown," as referred to by Linz (1978), because no democratic regime had yet been consolidated. Rather, it was a regime that resulted from democratic transition, but was not yet a consolidated democracy.

The other term in need of specification in the research question posed here is "failure." In the case of Congo, the use of the term is uncontroversial because the collapse of the democratic experiment was accompanied by a much larger breakdown in civil order. The second regime of Sassou (II), which came to power in October 1997, did so by force of arms rather than by election. Likewise, the legislature that Sassou put in place in January 1998 was appointed, not elected. Most would agree that the 2002 elections in Congo were so manipulated that they do not represent a return to democratic experimentation, but, in any case, these took place under a new constitution. Even if the collapse of the democratic experiment had been less dramatic, any breakdown in the constitutional change of power by free multiparty elections should be considered a failure of a democratic experiment, or a breakdown of a democratic regime. Such failures obviously do not exclude the launching of new democratic experiments or the eventual emergence of new democratic regimes.

Many studies of democratization find it useful to admit a third category of political regime, besides democracies and nondemocracies, namely the intermediate category of "quasi-democracies" or "semi-democracies." In the African setting, such terms have been used to describe the Abdou Diouf regime in Senegal (Vengroff and Creevey 1997) and the Henri Konan Bédié regime in Côte d'Ivoire (Mundt 1997). Such regimes are characterized by the legal existence of multiple parties and by the regular holding of elections, but also by serious irregularities in those elections or in other social controls that keep a dominant party in power. Some of these regimes have recently been called "electoral authoritarian" regimes (see Chapter 10). Such was the case with Mexico, in the era when the Partido Revolucionario Institutiónal (PRI) dominated the political scene, and in India before the Congress Party opened the political space sufficiently to allow other parties to take power. Such systems often give essentially authoritarian regimes a cover of democratic legitimacy, and sometimes a genuine mandate of popular support. In post–Cold War Africa, such regimes have become commonplace. For the postdemocratic experiment regime in Congo, "electoral authoritarian" is a better label than "semi-democracy" by far.

■ Why the Failure of Formal Democracy Matters

It is fair to ask whether the consolidation of (formal) democracy in Congo would really matter to the country's inhabitants. Many categories of observers think not, and if they are right, the analysis of its failure would not matter much either. The critics range from those who think that formal democracy does not go far enough, to those who believe it is irrelevant, to those who actively oppose it on grounds of its impracticality. Indeed, since the outcomes of failed democratic experiments seem to include civil war accompanied by mass killing, there is good reason to be cautious about advocating such experiments. The critics are unlikely to be convinced by the brief rejoinders that are offered here, but the case should be made that the consolidation of formal democracy would matter to the Congolese. If it does matter to them, Congolese and others ought to care about why the experiment failed. In any case, the Congolese are likely to try again to introduce formal democracy into their country, in which case the lessons of the past will be important.

One argument against the interest in formal democracy for African states is that it does not go far enough. As I have argued elsewhere, democratic systems that were limited in certain ways, but that meet the definition used here, would have the best chance of survival in Africa (Clark 1994a). Some scholars, particularly those on the left, have explicitly rejected this view, however (Longman 1998: 77; Fatton 1992). Like-minded thinkers have instead often called for social democracy or "popular democracy" (Saul 1997; also see Mengisteab and Daddieh 1999). Such "deeper" varieties of democracy would charge the state with both meeting people's fundamental economic needs, without which political participation is (putatively) not possible, and empowering them with the "positive liberty" that allows their participation to be meaningful.[9] After all, these critics implicitly argue, what meaningful political choices can hungry peasants or illiterate workers make?

Three important things may be said in reply. First, social democracy is simply not an option for Congo now, and even less so for poorer African states. The most Congo can reasonably aspire to in the short term is the kind of formal democracy defined above. Desirable though the satisfaction of socioeconomic needs is, this could not be accomplished without the huge, wholesale commitment of the international community, a commitment that is hardly in the cards. Likewise, the redistribution of existing wealth within in a country like Congo would not go far toward the goal of fulfilling social and economic needs. Second, the establishment of formal democracy in no way precludes the subsequent emergence of a welfare state, if and when the economy and society ever gain the capacity to support such a state. Indeed, this is a laudable goal for the future. Third, Saul (1997), at least, has great difficulty giving concrete meaning to the vague phrase "popular democracy." For many on the left, popular democracy has been a euphemism for dictatorship in the name of the oppressed. But Congo Republic endured twenty years as a "popular republic" during which time the Congolese enjoyed neither the negative liberty of formal democracy nor the positive liberty promised by popular democracy.

Another argument against formal democracy is that it would make no difference, that it would be irrelevant, because current global economic forces dictate all significant policies to African states.[10] Such authors as Mkandawire (1999) and Ould-Mey (1998: 51–54) have specifically argued that the ubiquity of structural adjustment programs (SAPs) in Africa makes the formal democratization of African states meaningless. (Many analysts of globalization now make similar claims.) These authors argue that the internal policies that really matter are economic policies; these, in turn, *must* be reformed along liberal lines because structural adjustment (and now, more generally, globalization) requires it. Thus, regardless of whether a state is formally democratic, the policies that matter will be the same.

Although it is true that the scope of economic action for African states is severely circumscribed by their limited economic means, such arguments should not be accepted as the last word. Sincere though such arguments may be, they underestimate the choices that African leaders have.[11] For African state leaders, the dimension of economic crisis that matters in this context is the possibility of not being able to meet debt obligations. These are the economic circumstances that force state leaders to confront the conditionalities associated with debt relief. In such situations, state rulers have at least three options, each of which has been exercised from time to time. First, they can agree to such programs and then attempt to implement them as Ghana and Uganda have done. Second, they can agree to the SAPs in principle, and then proceed to negotiate them in every detail, seek extensions on the grounds of economic and political crisis, and otherwise delay implementation of real (and painful) reforms. A great many African states, including Zambia, Congo, and many others have followed this course (Van de Walle 2001). Third, they can opt simply to default on their debts. In this case, however, they would become even more disconnected from the world economy and also suffer a loss of future aid and access to credit. Among the states that have opted not to participate in the programs of the international financial institutions (IFIs) at one time or another are Angola, the DRC, Sudan, and Zimbabwe. Those interested in formal democracy implicitly argue that, in a time when many African states face tough choices such as these, state leaders should be more accountable to their citizens, not less. African political parties should be debating such issues and taking positions on them, so that African citizens can have an impact on such state choices.

Still other scholars stress, through the focus of their research, the need for democratic practices among local populations in a decentralized state (Crook and Manor 1998). Nothing in such projects inherently contradicts the limited goal of formal democracy, and, indeed, the rooting of democratic ideals in local and peripheral areas can be quite complementary to formal democracy. At the same time, successful formal democracy mostly depends on the commitment of elites to play by the (democratic) rules of the game. Even in the long-established democracies of the West, substantial minorities of citizens maintain essentially undemocratic attitudes. This is evident in the large percentage of votes often gained by quasi-fascist or communist parties in many European countries.

In the African context, scholars such as Schaffer (1998) suggest that formal democracy cannot possibly work because the bulk of the population of many African states (Senegal, in this case) does not have democratic values. Schaffer demonstrates that when Senegalese citizens use the French word *démocratie,* or the Wolof word *demokaraasi,* they often have in mind social realities that are quite different from those evoked by cognate words in the minds of Europeans or Americans. Fortunately for the West, the successful practice of democracy does not require all citizens to have a deep appreciation for the liberal roots and meanings of the concept. Likewise, in Senegal, the country's recent political trajectory suggests that formal democracy may be able to proceed even when sizable swaths of the population miscomprehend its intentions or smaller groups actively oppose it. This study ultimately finds, with Schaffer, that undemocratic values are central to understanding democratic failure in Congo, but it neither assumes nor concludes that such values *determined* the trajectory of the experiment.

Those who value formal democracy must admit that it does not ensure every political value that a liberal-minded person might desire. Indeed, in the United States, formal democracy existed side by side with social and racial oppression for generations. This fact begs two other questions, however. First, was the long denial of the civil and political rights of US citizens a product of formal democracy or, rather, a set of social ills that existed *despite* it? Although a nondemocratic social revolution might have corrected such monstrous social injustices much sooner, likely it would have been accompanied by massive civil war with an unforeseeable outcome. In many such social revolutions, the original injustices have gone uncorrected while additional social and political prices have been paid. Second, would a much earlier extension of civil rights in the United States have been incompatible with the continuation of formal democracy? The experience of the 1960s suggests not. On the contrary, that experience suggests that once the social values of the population had evolved to a point of respect for civil rights across racial lines, the democratic system could serve to extend those rights.

Hence, we arrive at the importance of formal democracy. First, it is a morally sound and potentially stable way of communicating social needs and aspirations from a state's people to their government. Although no such system is even close to perfect in this regard, none other, to paraphrase Churchill, seems to work better. Second, and as important, formal democracy is fully compatible with, and generally supports, the extension of deeper social rights and privileges to the population. In many cases the establishment of formal democratic systems in former authoritarian polities has led to an immediate improvement in the enjoyment of civil and political rights. Even the extension of social and economic rights can be a logical outcome of formal democratization, as the cases of Portugal and Spain suggest.

Still other arguments suggest that the establishment of formal democracy should be actively opposed. Some are not opposed to the practice of formal democracy in the abstract, but suggest (implicitly or explicitly) that the establishment of formal democracy *in African states* is currently impossible. Important preconditions must exist before democracy can be established, and any premature attempt to establish democracy of any kind is likely to have dire consequences.

One such argument entails the prediction of severe conflict between ethnic, regional, and other identity communities. Indeed, few can have failed to notice that liberalization around the world has often been accompanied by nationalist or ethnic violence, and scholars have certainly taken notice (e.g., notably, Snyder 2000). In Africa, Congo, Zaire, and Rwanda all experienced little if any violent conflict among ethnoregional or identity communities during the 1980s, when all three states were forthrightly authoritarian. In the early 1990s, all three were launched on the path of political reform, and all three experienced significant outbreaks of intercommunal violence.[12] Researchers studying other African states have expressed the fear that political liberalization may lead to intercommunal violence and social breakdown (Azevedo 1999; Ottaway 1999). Both at the level of case study and at the broader continental level, other analysts suggest that intercommunal bloodshed and state decay is not a necessary outcome of liberalization. Writing of Rwanda, Longman argues that excessive state strength, rather than state weakness, was the true cause of the 1994 genocide (1998: 77). Having carried out a systematic study of forty-seven sub-Saharan African states, however, Smith rejects the hypothesis that gains in civil liberties lead to increases in ethnic tensions. In fact, his study "has provided some compelling evidence that just the opposite is the case" (e.g., Senegal, Ghana, and Zambia) (2000: 34). While Smith's study hardly resolves this issue, it at least challenges the claim that liberalization leads inevitably to intercommunal violence.

As indicated here, one of the main reasons that premature democratization efforts are thought unwise is that they may lead to state breakdown or collapse. Many of the African states analyzed in the edited work of Zartman (1995), including Somalia, Zaire, and Angola, all began to experience an acceleration of state decay after they began a process of liberalization in the early 1990s. Huntington (1968) had already made an early and powerful statement that state capacity and stability mattered more than the mode of rule. Country studies of African states followed this important work by analyzing the modes of the extension of state power into the peripheral regions of state territory (e.g., Callaghy 1984). More recently, Reno (1998) has shown that one of the consequences of deteriorating state capacities may be "warlord politics," or a form of power seeking aimed not at increasing bureaucratic capacity, but at realizing short-term economic gains without state reconstruction. In turn, the practice of warlord politics further accelerates the process of the deterioration of state power, often to the point of state collapse. With dynamics such as these in mind, a seasoned and capable scholar of African politics, Jeffrey Herbst, has recently turned his attention to the structural prerequisites of state control and authority (2000). Herbst's study, in contrast to Longman, implicitly assumes that effective state control over territory is the prerequisite for other forms of social progress. The importance of his work lies in demonstrating the link between effective state control and the demographics of the national territories.

Given this compelling imperative of the need for state control, should one be interested in the processes of democratization in Congo? The answer is yes, for two reasons. First, the Congolese state only lost effective control over the national territory for a brief period during the 1997 civil war. Since then, the state has periodically lost control over portions of the country, but its authority has been rapidly reasserted. Thus, basic control over the national territory has rarely been an issue in Congo, as it chronically has been in African states such as Angola, the DRC, Liberia, the Sudan, and Somalia. That the Congolese state's capacities are meager is incontestable, given its limited legitimacy and financial resources, but this does not mean that it has ever completely collapsed.[13] Moreover, basic civil order and state authority have now been reestablished. Second, a large contingent of Congolese have not given up on the idea of multiparty politics in their country. Even President Sassou pays lip service to the idea and allows legal political competition under the constitution adopted in 2002. Thus, if we accept the arguments that democratization may stimulate ethnic conflict or state disintegration, the reasons for studying the previous democratization effort are even more compelling. Perhaps the lessons of the past will be a guide to the future return of real democracy to Congo.

What all of these related bodies of literature show is that both economic development and political development are connected to democracy and democratization efforts. In this light, whether or not one thinks formal democracy would be good for the Congolese, the issue is important. The Congolese will certainly face the prospect of democratic experimentation in the future. When they do, their success or failure will have important implications for the extension of state power into new domains of social life, for economic development, for the expansion or contraction of human rights, and for civil peace among Congo's multiple communal constituencies.

■ Organization of the Study

Chapter 2 sets out the main epistemological challenge of this study, namely, to explore the extent to which the failure of democracy in Congo can be *explained,* in the narrow sense, and to what extent it can be *understood.* In the most direct sense, a specific act by one of the principals in the Congolese drama ended the democratic experiment. When President Lissouba dispatched troops to Sassou's residence in Mpila on the morning of 5 June 1997, a series of events was set in motion that destroyed any hope of a continuation of the democratic experiment then in place. This reality became clear later, following other events that made a return to civilian rule under the existing constitution impossible.

Of course, no serious historian or policymaker—much less social scientist—would possibly be satisfied with this answer alone. Our curiosity demands that we know about the structural circumstances of Lissouba's decision: What conditions may have forced, or at least prompted, him to act as he did? What was the larger context in which he acted? What historical forces made his action unsurprising in some way, if not predictable? In short, what structural conditions created the web of significance in which the Congolese president acted? Such questions point us to the existence of a dialectical interaction of agents and structures that perpetually give rise to new social contexts. Chapter 2 is devoted to laying out this agent-structure dialectic as a way of understanding the trajectory of democratic experiments. It presents the hypothesis that, despite all of the structural constraints on his action, Lissouba could have chosen a different course on 5 June 1997. In turn, had he chosen differently, there is some possibility that democracy might have been consolidated in Congo. If agency does indeed matter, and there was scope for agency in the Congolese experiment, then the goal of explaining the outcome, as opposed to understanding it, is in question. Chapter 2 ends with a discussion of the value of comparative analysis.

Chapter 3 begins a series including five others that serve a dual purpose. On the one hand, each presents an alternative hypothesis to the one just stated. These alternative hypotheses come in a variety of forms, but all point to the structural features of Congo's internal society or international position that put constraints on the behavior of Congo's posttransition leaders. All suggest that the trajectory of Congo's democratic experiment was largely predetermined. On the other hand, each of these six chapters helps us to understand the context within which Lissouba and other Congolese leaders acted. They aid us in understanding the varying degrees to which each was constrained, or was forced to act in specific ways, by the structural context in which they operated. Chapter 3 presents an overview of Congo's postcolonial institutions and culture, culled from the country's late-colonial and postcolonial culture. An undemocratic political culture is often blamed for the failure of democratic experiments, while the pretransition institutions are also thought to exert a determining influence. This chapter also provides important historical background to the study.

Chapter 4 focuses on several aspects of the Congolese economy and their impact on the course of the democratic experiment. The chapter establishes the rentier nature of the Congolese economy and the resulting economic class divisions in the society. It further takes notice of the structural adjustment programs that have been introduced into the country and their impact on tolerance among the Congolese population. In essence, this chapter examines the contention of many scholars that structural economic adjustment and simultaneous democratic consolidation are not possible. It also asks whether the class structure of Congo made successful democratization impossible, specifically, whether or not the presence of a large urban lumpen proletariat in the country fueled the rise of the militia groups that eventually tore the country apart.

Chapter 5 explores the constraints, arising from the country's ethnic and regional cleavages, that hindered democratic consolidation. The political entities that emerged in posttransition Congo primarily spoke for and answered to ethnic and regional constituencies rather than ideological or class constituencies. The alternative hypothesis is that Congo's democratic experiment was doomed from the start by these deep identity conflicts. The chapter explores some of the following questions: Was this outcome inevitable, or did it merely reflect the choices made by the political class? If it was inevitable, did the practice of ethnoregional politics make the consolidation of democracy impossible? In what ways did ethnoregional politics constrain the behavior of political agents?

Chapter 6 studies the closely related question of the Congolese army and militia groups. The Congolese army that President Lissouba inherited in 1992, and particularly its officer corps, was thoroughly dominated by northern elements. Some percentage of these officers no doubt resented the fact that they had become answerable to a civilian president and, worse still, one from the south. Likewise, the same officers no doubt looked forward to the return of a northerner, like Lissouba's three predecessors, to the presidency. The behavior of the army during the civil war of 1993–1994 showed that it was indeed not entirely at the command of President Lissouba. Perhaps the rise of the militia groups, then, was inevitable given the structural relationship of the army to the state.

Chapter 7 turns to the nature of the transition itself and to the institutional design of the new regime. There is prima facie evidence that Congo's poorly chosen posttransition constitution may have doomed the experiment from the start. Did the possibility of president and prime minister issuing from different political families make conflict and democratic failure inevitable? Did the nature of the transition make the shape and character of the constitution inevitable? This chapter explores these questions with a focus on the nature of the constitution and Congo's constitutional crisis in late 1992.

Chapter 8 considers the impact of Congo's relations with other states on the outcome of the democratic experiment. Since independence, Congo has had an intensive and close relationship with France, even in the days of the Marxist experiment. Although most have referred to such relationships as neocolonial, in the case of France and Congo they are more appropriately termed interstate patron-client relations. The Franco-Congolese relationship became rocky during the period of the democratic experiment. Many observers, especially exiled Congolese observers, have been keen to put the blame on France for many of Congo's problems, including the failure of the democratic experiment. In the end, a foreign power other than France was directly responsible for ending the Congolese civil war of 1997: Angola. Was this intervention ultimately to blame for the democratic failure in Congo?

Chapter 9 returns to the problem of agency in the democratic failure, again taking up the epistemological question. While Chapters 3 through 8 make abundant reference to the role of agency, this chapter identifies several specific decisions of Congolese leaders that either kept the democratic experience going, caused it harm without destroying it, or ultimately caused it to fail. In each case, the weight of the structural constraints and pressures on the decisionmaker is closely examined. In turn, this chapter evaluates the impact of each decision on the reshaping of structural circumstances that provided a context for future action. It suggests that Congolese leaders always had some scope for choice, though the range of choices available tended to close tighter and tighter over time. The path dependency of the democratic experiment created by the earlier choices is also evident; choices that were made late in the democratic experiment were conditioned not only by the structural forces that existed in 1992, but also by new structural realities that were created by earlier choices. This chapter also suggests that political culture is the one structural feature under which many other causes of the democratic failure can be subsumed. Political culture is thus at the center of a "thick description" of the failure of the experiment.[14]

In order to understand more fully the meaning of the Congolese experiment for the future, Chapter 10 presents an overview of politics in Congo since Sassou's "second coming." The review of his record shows that President Sassou slowly prepared the country for a return to constitutional rule in a manner that assured the outcome of the 2002 elections. Sassou's course after 1997 was to establish an electoral autocracy that allowed for multiparty elections without jeopardizing his personal rule. The elections gave a facade of legitimacy to his regime. This chapter also shows that Sassou's behavior in the 2002–2006 period, when he was securely in power, reinforced the undemocratic aspects of Congolese political culture. Congo's post-1997 politics show that the country has not yet overcome its deeply antidemocratic history and culture. They also show that the country's recent leaders have done little to alter that culture and thus to open a genuinely new chapter in Congo's political history.

■ Notes

1. The "Congo" analyzed in this study is the state officially named the Republic of Congo, but it most typically goes by the names Congo-Brazzaville or Congo Republic. It is to be distinguished from the former Belgian Congo across the

Congo River, whose official name is now the Democratic Republic of Congo. The Democratic Republic of Congo, called Zaire from 1971 to 1997, is often referred to simply as the DRC or, now less commonly, Congo-Kinshasa. In this study, "Congo" refers to the Republic of Congo, while its larger neighbor is referred to as the DRC.

2. Denis Sassou-Nguesso's first presidency (1979–1991) is now often referred to as "Sassou I." His second period of rule, which began in 1997, is referred to as "Sassou II."

3. For translations of the names of parties in this volume, see the list of acronyms.

4. The coalition actually went under the name Union pour le Renouveau Démocratique–Parti Congolais du Travail (URD-PCT). The URD was an umbrella organization that included the MCDDI as its most important constituent party.

5. By this time, Lissouba's coalition had expanded to include several other smaller parties and had been renamed Mouvance Présidentielle (Presidential Domaine).

6. On militia groups in the 1993–1994 war, see Bazenguissa-Ganga (1994) and Chapter 6 of this volume.

7. For a short overview of the start of the war, see Clark (1998); for a more detailed account, Pourtier (1998). The actual intentions of those who went to Sassou's residence on that day are disputed. The controversy is discussed at more length in Chapter 6 of this volume.

8. Przeworski et al. seem to have neglected to stipulate that universal suffrage is a criterion of their operational definition of democracy, but their discussion appears to assume it.

9. The language of "positive" and "negative" liberty comes from Berlin (1969).

10. The label "irrelevant" is given by Ake (1998), cited in Van de Walle (1999: 96).

11. In fact, all states in the international system, even the most powerful, face limits on the scope of action that they may choose to take. Sometimes these can be quite severe, even for great powers—France in 1939 comes to mind.

12. On Congo, see Clark (1997a); on Zaire, see Clark (1995); on Rwanda, Longman (1997, 1998).

13. Even at the height of the 1997 war, life was continuing fairly normally in some of the country's secondary cities, including Pointe Noire, and even in some suburbs of Brazzaville for most of the war.

14. "Thick description" is, of course, a phrase coined by Clifford Geertz (1973). Its meaning here is somewhat different, but the allusion is intended and meaningful.

2

Structure, Agency, and the Collapse of Democracy

This chapter has three closely related purposes. First, it asks what kind of answers might be given to the master question of this study, that is, why did the democratic experiment in the Republic of Congo fail? This discussion will necessarily be circumscribed, for any deep venture into the field of epistemology would quickly come to consume the study. Here, I only seek to lay my cards on the table with respect to this question. Second, this chapter presents, explains, and justifies the research design for answering the question at hand, given the epistemological assumptions outlined. Third, the chapter discusses one specific problem of the research design in more detail, namely the problem of comparative analysis. This discussion serves to justify further the research design that has been chosen.

■ What Kind of Answer to the Question Is Possible?

Before considering how to answer the question posed in this study, let us begin by asking to what extent the question can be answered at all, and what kinds of answers are possible. In the introduction, reference was made to a possible inferential description that might be offered for the case of the failure of democracy in Congo. One trio of prominent social scientists (King, Keohane, and Verba 1994) has suggested that descriptive inference should, in fact, be the goal of most qualitative research in the social sciences. Specifically, it should be the goal of case studies of social phenomena, like the one chosen for this study. According to these authors, descriptive inference involves "using observations from the world to learn about other unobserved facts" (1994: 9). They distinguish this form of reasoning from causal inference, which they define as the process of "learning about causal effects from the data observed" (9). This latter mode of reasoning is much more demanding and can only apply when examining multiple cases of a phenomenon in ways that meet other logical requirements for reaching scientific conclusions. It does not apply to individual case studies.

In most regards, King, Keohane, and Verba are broad-minded in their view of what counts as social science and in what kinds of studies make a contribution. Unlike many other social science methodologists, they do not use description as a term of condemnation; on the contrary, they identify description both as intrinsically valuable and as indispensable as a (preliminary) step in more theoretical scientific inquiry: "Even if explanation—connecting causes and effects—is the ultimate goal, description has a central role in all explanation, and it is fundamental in and of itself" (1994: 34). As they present it, careful descriptive inference is the yeoman's work of social science. To determine the general "causes" of democratic consolidation in the developing world, the facts of many cases must be carefully analyzed. Such facts may be difficult to perceive, but they may be discovered through descriptive inference. Thus, the theoretical social scientist must depend on the accuracy of the facts determined about all of the cases. Further, because all of the cases used cannot be examined in intimate detail, the social scientist must rely on the careful descriptive work of those doing case studies. Accordingly, if the social "facts" about the Congo case could be determined, this might prove invaluable to social scientists studying democratization in Africa (e.g., Bratton and Van de Walle 1997) who attempt to generalize across many cases. For this reason, King, Keohane, and Verba repeatedly point to the great value of understanding cases "from the inside."

These authors do distinguish, however, between "good descriptive history," as they put it, and descriptive inference. The former involves merely the collection of facts in a presentable way and in a delimited area, whereas the latter entails the systematic examination of data in a way that yields descriptive "facts" about a case (King, Keohane, and Verba 1994: 34). Further, these scholars specify that interpretation must be understood as part of the social scientific process, and not as an alternative paradigm for understanding (1994: 37). Although they accept that interpretivist work can be useful in generating hypotheses, they claim that the processes of reaching "valid scientific inferences" are universal. Accordingly, they reject the idea that "thick description" of the sort discussed by Geertz (1973) could contribute to scientific knowledge of the social world (38–43). These authors argue that all social analysis involves simplification of an infinitely complex social world, and only rigorous, systematic simplification can lead to inference and ultimately to the testing of hypotheses.

Despite this liberal interpretation of what counts as social science, it is far from clear that the sort of answers they seek can be found for the question posed here. It would be most satisfying, for instance, if some single cause for the failure of the democratic experiment in Congo could be identified. Such a cause might either be a structural condition, which prevented the consolidation of democracy from the start, or an action or set of actions that actively caused it to fail. If a cause for the democratic failure could be identified, the logical course of action would be to consider a series of logical hypotheses. Each would either be rejected or could tentatively be confirmed as a possible answer to the question of why democracy failed. If logical reasoning confirmed what the evidence suggested, a tentative claim of validity for the given hypothesis might be ventured. In this case, social scientists studying many cases of democratization in hopes of achieving causal inferences would know where to put the Congo case; it could be classified as a case of democratic failure for reason "x," and not any other. If such is the requirement for qualitative analysts studying cases like Congo in pursuit of the answers to larger social science questions, they are unlikely to realize their goal.

To use the language of a different pair of scholars (Hollis and Smith 1990), can one hope to "explain" the Congo case, or merely to "understand" it?[1] In the opinion of this researcher, it is too much to ask that such a social phenomenon as the failure of a democratic experiment be *explained* (with scientific certainty). The reasons for this judgment are multiple. First, as I have argued in a study on the source of Ugandan foreign policy (Clark 2001), in the social world even hypotheses that are rejected as *the* cause of a policy may provide great insight in helping us to understand it. In the case of Uganda's involvement in the second (1998 to 2002) war in the Democratic Republic of Congo (DRC), consider the "fact" that the Ugandan government had a tacit alliance with the United States and Britain. To some national-minded policy analysts working from the French foreign ministry in Paris, this reality appeared to be directly related to Uganda's reckless lack of regard for sovereign prerogatives in its invasion of the DRC. On the other hand, the systematic analysis that I attempted of Uganda's motives suggested that the most important "efficient cause" of Uganda's policy was probably something else. Nonetheless, I conceded that US support for Uganda was an important contributing, and perhaps necessary, condition for Uganda's foreign behavior.[2]

As I considered other hypotheses about the sources of Ugandan behavior, I similarly discovered other political realities that conditioned the context of the decision. For instance, what about the notion that presidents Paul Kagame of Rwanda and Yoweri Museveni of Uganda conspired in an ethnic (Tutsi and Hima) plot to put their ethnic kinsmen in power throughout the Great Lakes region? Although most have rejected the idea of an ethnic conspiracy as the source of the war in the DRC, most would concede that one source of the original Kagame-Museveni friendship was probably ethnic fealty. Here is another rejected hypothesis that is relevant to a "thick description." Given this daunting challenge of understanding, one must often settle for finding the contingent realities that should go at the center of the thick description.

This example leads us to a (first) general point about the social world: the decisions of individuals are virtually always taken in the context of multiple conditioning social realities. In the case of Uganda's invasion of Congo, President Museveni appears to have made the decision himself, probably after seeking the advice of only a few close associates (Clark 2001: 262). It also appears that he made the decision that he did, however, only in the presence of many accompanying political conditions: among them, he expected the support, or at least acquiescence, of the Ugandan people; he expected not to be harshly criticized by the United States; and he expected that Parliament, which was not consulted, would vote to authorize the funds to pay for the war.

Let us now suppose that Museveni's contemporary alliance with Kagame was the efficient cause of his action. This picture brings to mind a myriad of counter-factual questions: Would Museveni have decided similarly in the absence of US support? Would he have acted similarly if his domestic situation were less secure? And would he have acted similarly if he feared a hostile reaction from Parliament? No one can possibly know the answer to such questions for sure. Even putting the question directly to Museveni himself would not reveal the answer since, as his country's chief policymaker on a matter of great international sensitivity, he could scarcely afford to be honest. Accordingly, one cannot ever explain Museveni's decision with scientific precision. What we face is not an event that has one or more discreet causes, but rather social action undertaken by a willful individual enmeshed in a web of social meaning. Although a plausible interpretation of events may be constructed to help us understand the political outcome, this is not the same as having established a social "fact," the term that is used by King, Keohane, and Verba (1994: 34–35).

An explanation of the democratic failure is also unlikely because, secondly, the social conditions themselves are so contingent. The conditions of the social environment are not much like those of the physical environment. These conditions are neither immutable nor necessary, but are rather the result of human creation, or construction. We may grant that the social conditions were relatively stable at a moment in time, as when Museveni made his decision to invade the DRC. Nonetheless, students of African politics are all too aware of the great volatility of political expectation and "reality." While political liberalization was scarcely on the agenda of any African rulers at all in 1987, virtually every one was seized with the issue by 1990. Let us imagine that we determine that the probable acquiescence of the United States weighed heavily in Museveni's calculus regarding his invasion of the DRC. If this were so, then we would need to investigate the source of the US-Ugandan entente in great detail. Were we to do so, we would find that the reality of the entente itself was subtle and contingent. Would the United States actually support Uganda in the event of war? What if the war quickly began to go badly? Such questions call for probabilistic answers that cannot be accurately calculated by either human beings or machines. Likewise, how sure could Museveni be of the support of the

Ugandan people? Of the officer corps of his army? Of his support in Parliament? Perhaps he could be reasonably sure, but not entirely sure, for significant political events such as the 11 September 2001 terror attacks have a way of turning seemingly firm political realities on their heads.

Third, it is a daunting challenge to assess the influence of personality on social and political outcomes. Typically, this challenge is answered by assuming the rationality of human agents who make the fateful choices that become the proximate causes of democratic consolidation or failure, or of war and peace. The huge variation in actual behavior of African leaders under similar circumstances, however, belies the notion that rationality or rational choice provide a blueprint to explain their actions collectively. Leopold Senghor gave up power with virtually no pressure to leave, while Mathieu Kérékou gave it up reluctantly and under great pressure, and Mobutu Sese Seko held on to the bitter end. Such commonplace observations as these often lead us to conceive typologies for personality types or leadership styles, such as the useful categories conceived by Jackson and Rosberg (1982). Knowing that a given ruler has acted in the past more as a prophet, prince, autocrat, or tyrant is certainly useful in understanding his behavior and provides important clues about likely future behavior. Nonetheless, accurate categorization of rulership type does not allow us to predict with certainty, nor to *explain,* a ruler's actions in the past.

To return to the problem of Museveni's decision to invade the DRC in August 1998, does his "operational code," or personality type, tell us anything about his decision? Certainly, but it does not provide a simple explanation of the decision. Rather, the decision has to be understood in the political context in which it took place. Let us imagine that psychiatrists determined that Museveni has a personality that makes him prone to leading his state into foreign wars. Such a determination may well help us to understand his fateful decision in August 1998. But we would need to know a variety of other things about the contingent sociopolitical circumstances of the decision, such as those mentioned above. A mere propensity to use of force outside the borders of a leader's state does not explain a given invasion. Why did Museveni's Uganda not invade Sudan during its long years of conflict with that country? Or why did Museveni not invade Rwanda in the late 1980s? Or why did Museveni not order an invasion of the DRC sooner, say in 1994, when Mobutu's vulnerabilities were becoming apparent and his international support evaporating? To answer questions, we have to ask questions about the internal and international political context of Museveni's decisions at those prior moments in history. Likewise, Lissouba's personality and that of a few other prominent Congolese are keys to understanding the collapse of the democratic experiment in Congo. But they are not the only keys.

In accord with these epistemological evaluations, it appears impossible that we can conclude with an explanation of the collapse of democracy in

Congo. Rather, we would do well to provide a convincing understanding of it. To claim that the democratic collapse could be explained suggests that something in either the structural circumstances of Congo or the personality of the key leaders made it inevitable. On the contrary, however, there is no good analytical reason to believe that the democratic collapse was inevitable, as will become clear in the course of this book.

Of course, I make no pretense of having presented a comprehensive argument on this monumental issue of praxis in the study of the social world. It is most unlikely that any of the dedicated partisans of "explanation" of social phenomena will be convinced by this short exposition. But the forgoing analysis makes clear my own sense of the instability of the facts we might like to know about the social world and our limited ability to apprehend them. Moreover, I do not regard these constraints with anything other than a sense of frustration. Accordingly, I intend to be as rigorous and careful as possible in presenting an understanding of the democratic collapse. If social scientists on the other side of the epistemological divide are able to develop and test new hypotheses to explain democratic collapse, or if they are better able to categorize the Congolese case on the basis of this study, then they may find it useful, despite my own reservations about the kinds of intellectual enterprises in which they engage. In that sense, the epistemological stand taken here is paradoxical: it doubts severely our ability to establish facts about the social world, but it calls upon us to be as systematic and rigorous as possible in reaching an understanding of social events. The position is likely to annoy those along wide stretches of an epistemological continuum, but it represents an honest effort to be fair and clear about my perceived limits on and possibilities of social knowledge.

Given these limits, probably the best kind of answer that could be given to the question posed in this discussion could be called an "analytical description." The analytical description of this study examines sociopolitical conditions and events from the outside, but often depends upon some inside understanding of the political values and sensibilities of the actors whose behavior ultimately led to the collapse of the democratic experiment in Congo. This process certainly involves "using observations from the world to learn about other unobserved facts," as called for by King, Keohane, and Verba in their specification of descriptive inference. Yet, it surely falls short of their demand for the identification of social and political facts that might lead to scientific explanation. At the same time, it can and will go well beyond the "good descriptive history" that seeks only to present some relevant events in a relatively systematic way. Each part of the study begins with hypotheses posed in a careful way; in turn, each hypothesis is evaluated in as objective a manner as possible. Accordingly, I hope to provide an answer somewhat different from the valuable "thick descriptions" provided by anthropologists, who seek primarily to describe social patterns using the terms of the social participants themselves.

■ A Framework for Analytical Description

Given these perceived limits on our ability to comprehend political events, coupled with a real desire to describe political realities with precision, how can we best proceed to answer a question like the one posed here? As suggested above, the key to understanding the collapse of the democratic experiment in Congo lies in grasping the interaction between the key agents and most important social structures relevant to the case. Many scholars would wish to refer to such a technique as an application of structuration theory, à la Giddens, or as an example of constructivism in comparative analysis as in Green (2002). Indeed, it is the case that the agents and structures on the Congolese scene did "co-constitute" one another and evolve together through a dialectical process. But one really need not resort to such social science vocabularies to undertake usefully the strategy of understanding deployed here, for the strategy itself long predates the invention of such terms as structuration theory and constructivism. Moreover, a long detour into the analysis of such theories would serve chiefly to divert and delay us from analyzing the case.

Nonetheless, the awareness of the criticality of agent-structure dynamics has informed the work of numerous democratic analysts, including Linz and Stephan (1996: chapter 5). Many of these important analysts have not resorted to prolonged references to the arcane epistemological debates of social theorists. Likewise, we will lay out simply a strategy for understanding the case of democratic failure in Congo with relatively little reference to such debates. To begin with the structural conditions in which the Congolese experiment took place, we should ask which of these structures were most vital to the outcome. The existing theoretical literature on democratization, especially on democratic consolidation, is a useful guide. In surveying that literature, five sociopolitical structures emerge as the key to success or failure of democratic experiments. These include the following types: psychological structures of politics; economic structures; ethnic and regional identity structures; constitutional and institutional structures; and international structures. Only the first of these might be slightly obscure to political scientists, but psychological structures are meant here merely as another rendering of what we normally call political culture. By economic structures, I mean both the internal structure of the Congolese economy and Congo's structural position in the global economic system. A specific chapter is devoted to the analysis of each of these structures and, in each instance, I refer to the theoretical literature on the relationship between the structure and democratization.[3]

While considering such structural features of the context of a country's democratic experiment, it is important to be alert to their perpetually evolving nature. Although the word "structure" conjures up images of solid and immutable edifices, the sociopolitical structures discussed here exist primarily in the minds of the observers who contemplate the Congolese situation. Accordingly, they are subject to rather dramatic and sudden changes as the thinking of human beings evolves.[4] This may be relatively easy to grasp in the case of political culture, and harder to grasp in the case of a state's position in international economy. But either can evolve, or be "restructured," over time. Just as most of us think that Germany's contemporary political culture is far different from that of the 1930s, the international economic position of some states, like China or Japan, has changed just as dramatically; these shifts are psychological, as well as materially grounded. With regard to the evolution of a country's economic structure, both internal and international, it is recorded in its economic performance over shorter periods of time. Economic performance, in turn, is thought to be closely linked to the probability of democratic consolidation, as we shall see below. Thus, the chapters that examine the structural conditions of Congo's democratic experiment pay heed to their evolution in Congo's social and political realities over the short time period that the experiment went on.

Chapter 6 does not reflect any of the five fundamental aspects of social and political structure identified above: it discusses the role of the army and militias in the Congolese democratic experiment. These civil-military relations are analytically positioned between the broadly structural features of a society and the contingent actions taken by individual agents on a daily basis that constitute the dialectic that drives politics. This is true because civil-military relations can quite easily be viewed as a product of these larger structures. Civil-military relations are what they are because of the deep political values that the main political actors hold; in most African countries, they are highly conditioned by the arraying of various ethnic and regional constituencies against one another, and the emergence and suppression of nonstate militia groups is also a product of a country's political economy. The roles of the army and militias easily merit a separate chapter to discuss their impact on the collapse of the democratic experiment in Congo. Indeed, the analytical juxtaposition of civil-military relations between broad structures and individual action makes them particularly interesting. Many theorists have identified civil-military relations as a crucial variable in the formula that may lead to the collapse or survival of democratic experiments.

Some other structural features of Congo are not accorded a separate chapter for analysis, based on my judgment that such structural variables are either insufficiently important to merit sustained consideration, or are better subsumed under some other structure. Consider, for instance, the questions of geography and demographic distributions of population. These structural features of various state-societies are not normally thought to be the key determinants of democratic transition or consolidation. Although these variably have recently been identified in a major scholarly effort as the key determinants of state building and the consolidation of power in African societies (Herbst 2000), they do not so obviously affect democratization.

Another, related, structural variable not given systematic treatment in this study is that of population size. Diamond (1999: 117–121) has observed in one instance that there is a negative statistical correlation between the population size of states and the incidence of democracy among all of the world's states. This suggests, in turn, a negative correlation between state size and the ability to consolidate a new democratic regime. Diamond's point is not simply to bemoan the difficulty of democratic consolidation for larger states; rather it is to give policy advice for agents seeking to promote democratization. In this context, he makes a case for decentralization, arguing that the rooting of democratic practices at all local levels of government has beneficial effects on the consolidation of democracy at the national level (121–132). The thrust of his analysis serves as the starting point for the study of Crook and Manor (1998), who sought to investigate democratic practices in local settings; in their study, however, the issue of the strong centralization of state authority in Congo is dealt with as an issue of political culture. In this book, Lissouba's putative effort to decentralize the Congolese state is dealt with as a facet of the problem of institutional design.

A seriously complicating issue in the consideration of the structural constraints of democratic consolidation is that structural change or evolution in one area affects other structures, as well as acting directly on the overall context in which agents act. There is a sense in which structures co-constitute one another, just as agents and structures do. Among the most important reasons for Congo's undemocratic political culture, for instance, are the country's underdevelopment and its history as a colony of France. In turn, Congo might be said to remain stuck in a state of stagnant underdevelopment partly because of its defective political institutions. Thus, the two structures "cause," or mutually reinforce, one another. Although the neo-Marxist analyst will inevitably take the country's political economy as primary, and other structures as secondary, cultural anthropologists may reverse the order of causation. Only the truly detached observers can perceive that neither culture nor economics is primary, and that each perpetually acts to recreate the other. Processes of democratic transition and reform necessarily entail the disruption of the negative cycles in which nondemocratic culture and inequitable, exploitative economics reinforce one another. For our purposes, one must recognize these patterns of mutual reinforcement in order to understand the failure of the democratic experiment.

If the first step in a good analytical description is to identify the most important structures that provide the context for democratic experiments, the second step is to identify the most important agents and analyze their actions relevant to such experiments. Several of the most important actions of the key principals in Congo's democratic experiment are analyzed in Chapter 9. Yet this chapter only represents the culmination of the discussion of the role of agency, which is found throughout the book. Indeed, it is not possible to understand the saga of Congo's failed democratic experiment without abundant references to the key agents and their actions throughout the discussion.

Often, it is the unpredictable actions of agents that impede the value of theoretical models that seek to explain the success or failure of experiments in democracy. Because major change is often slow, at best, in the social structures that condition the possibilities for democratic consolidation, social scientists are often tempted to take them as determinative in the socio-analytic equations that would explain social phenomena. In so doing, the influence of individual agents and their actions is often slighted or ignored; for the scientific theorists, the variables whose influence cannot be estimated across cases are better left aside. As the comparative analysis of different states demonstrates, however, the variable actions of agents in similar structural circumstances do have an influence on social outcomes.

The most typical way to deal with the maddening problem of unpredictable agents is simply to assert that individuals behave in a consistent, rational way. The temptation to make this claim is universal and it afflicts constructivists (e.g., Onuf 1998), as well as devoted positivists, in their social claims. Although the claim of human rationality has a great many different meanings, it usually implies that human beings behave in a predictable way, given the structural social circumstances in which they find themselves, and given their own preferences.[5] As Morgenthau (1946) pointed out long ago, however, human beings respond to instinctual drives dwelling "below" the rational self, as well as to spiritual drives swelling "above" it. Human beings act to realize rational goals, but also to satisfy nonrational biological needs and spiritual aspirations. One cannot *explain* acts of pure passion or instances of unexpected altruism, but those familiar with the elemental biological and psychological drives of humans can certainly *understand* them. Likewise, in our pursuit of an accurate analytical description of the democratic experiment in Congo, the goal should be to try to understand the actions of the key agents at various critical junctures along the way.

The challenges of integrating the actions of agents into a good analytical description of a social phenomenon are multiple. One is to identify the agents that genuinely matter in the social outcome. In this case, these agents include actors outside of Congo itself, as well as the most prominent

Congolese political figures, and can be corporate as well as individual. In Congo, the Congolese army can be usefully seen as a corporate agent that has acted to reinforce or change civil-military relations in the country; meanwhile, those interested in political economy are quite used to analyzing the actions of classes and unions as corporate agents. In the Congolese context, France may be considered an important corporate agent. Another challenge is to discern *when* the actions of the various agents may have an important impact on social outcomes. Villalón and Hustable refer to such moments as "critical junctures" in the trajectories of state politics (1998). Recognizing such junctures, and the impact of specific actions during them, is a key to understanding social outcomes.

More daunting still is to understand how the actions of agents affect the contextual social and political structures for a country at the critical junctures when their actions matter most. A great many analysts have identified agent-structure interaction as the key to real understanding of outcomes in democratic experiments (e.g., Bratton and Van de Walle 1997: 20–27; Diamond 1999: 66; Linz 1978: 4–5; Przeworski 1998: 47–50; Young 1999: 34). Such outcomes are never predictable because of the impact of human will in the equation. This would be true even if one could fully comprehend all of the structural givens of a situation, hardly possible in itself. Although Lissouba's action of sending a military detachment to arrest Sassou on the morning of 5 June 1997 was not irrational, or beyond our understanding, it was also not predictable.[6] He might have chosen differently. Since he acted as he did, however, we are left to try to understand why he acted as he did, given the social context. To understand this one action, though, is not to understand entirely the failure of the democratic experiment. To move toward that goal, a series of other actions that preceded it and shaped the sociopolitical context for future decisions and choices must be examined. The impact of some such actions—as when members of a special committee draft a new constitution—will be relatively apparent. In other cases, as when the unlawful actions of a president undermine the confidence of the political class, the impact on social and political structures is subtler.

Given the method described here for providing a strong analytical description of the Congo case, what kind of conclusions are possible for a study of this kind? As argued above, there can be no claims of having scientifically identified *the* cause, or of having assigned a number to the weight of various causes, in the case of democratic failure in Congo. Nonetheless, a number of conclusions of value to the social analyst might be reached. First, it should be possible to identify which of the structural impediments to democratic consolidation were most important and which were of less significance. Second, it should be possible to discern something about the overall possibilities for democratic consolidation, given the structural conditions. Third, it should be possible to discover a relatively short list of critical acts by key players whose choices eroded the structural conditions for the consolidation of democracy. And fourth, it should be possible to describe how structural conditions changed as a result of the actions of key agents, leading up to the final demise of the democratic experiment.

In the course of this kind of analysis two specific techniques are particularly valuable. The first is that of counterfactual analysis, which allows us to consider hypothetical alternative trajectories for the democratic experiment if various actions had been different. This technique is particularly useful for analysts seriously considering the choices of agents as forces for democratic consolidation or failure. In the kind of analysis undertaken here, it is frequently useful to ask the question, "What impact would a different choice made at this juncture have had on the structural political context of the democratic experiment?" One is unlikely to be able to conclude that a different action at some moment in time would certainly have led to a different outcome in the democratic experiment. Nonetheless, such experiments suggest that the chances for a longer survival of a democratic experiment would have been likely if different choices had been made. This matters greatly since the important short-term goal for democrats during democratic experiments must be regime survival, as well as democratic consolidation.

A second technique has already been employed in our preliminary efforts, that is, the method of comparative analysis, which is discussed in more detail below. While comparative analysis is a typical technique for rigorous, scientific study, it can be of equal value in the kind of qualitative and epistemologically skeptical study undertaken here. The comparative aspect of this study demonstrates that the effort it is not merely to understand Congolese politics "from the inside." Rather, this study seeks to put Congo in the context of a great wave of new democratic experiments undertaken since the end of the Cold War.

■ The Importance of Comparison in Analytical Description

In what ways and with which countries might Congo be most usefully compared in a good analytical description of the country's democratic experiment? The aspects of comparison are directly suggested by the methodology sketched just above: the structural conditions for the democratic experiments, the actions of key agents, the dynamics of the agent-structure dialectic, and, most importantly, democratic outcomes. In fact, it is the great variability in the outcomes of the democratic experiments of the "third wave" that makes them an interesting object of study.[7] If all the countries that had experimented with democracy since 1974 had either succeeded or failed, then we would be more inclined to take the causes of the outcomes for granted. Moreover, the structural nature of the global political system, or some such other macrovariable, would doubtless be assigned most of the causal weight.

Of particular interest to students of Congo would be cases that show broad structural similarities with Congo, but experienced different outcomes in their democratic experiments. If no such cases existed, then the strength of the structural determinants of democratic outcomes would be confirmed. If cases with broadly similar structural conditions exist, with different outcomes, though, then benefit may be derived from a particularly close comparison with these cases. If we pair Congo with other such cases, then formerly obscure structural differences between the cases may become clear. Another possibility is that variation in the behavior of the key agents at critical junctures may become apparent. Being alert to other similar cases is generally useful when intriguing hypotheses about the democratic failure, based on both logic and evidence, have been identified. For instance, if, in studying the Congo case, the institutional design of the constitution seems to have put all political elites in a difficult situation, reference to other cases with similar institutional designs, but different outcomes, is a natural recourse.

In briefly examining the entire universe of states' experiments with democracy in the so-called third wave, there is noticeable variation in outcomes generally, and especially within regions. While most of the Latin American states experimenting with democracy since 1974 have experienced consolidation, the cases of Peru and Venezuela, among others, give us pause.[8] Democratic systems in these countries have barely survived and appear to be fragile. In Eastern Europe, where the wave only began after the demise of communism, outcomes have also been noticeably variable. Insofar as Vladimir Putin's regime represents a perpetuation of that of Boris Yeltsin, Russia has not experienced consolidation. Likewise, the former Soviet republics in central Asia have generally not experienced democratization. Meanwhile, the Eastern European countries that were not formerly part of the Soviet Union have all gone much further in democratic consolidation, most satisfying the formal definition laid out in Chapter 1.

Certainly, there is enough uniformity of the outcomes within subregions to suggest that the structural conditions for democratization play a huge role in the trajectory of democratic experiments. The fact that democratic consolidation has fared much better in the industrialized states of Eastern Europe than in the less industrialized states of central Asia is an observation easily made without benefit of formal models. Some of the central Asia republics never even launched democratic experiments, much less consolidated them. Such outcomes were not unpredictable given the weakness of democratic culture, the lack of strong civil society, the low levels of income and literacy, and other such social variables. Intriguingly, however, there is variation in outcome even when structural conditions are somewhat similar. The more successful cases suggest that the structural determinants alone do not provide us with a full understanding of the reasons for democratic outcomes, either within or across any region.

There is some value in comparing Congo with cases in these extra-African regions, but not nearly so much as there is in comparison with other African cases. Since Congo was nominally Marxist-Leninist between 1970 and 1991, comparison with the formerly communist states of Eastern Europe seems logical. In fact, though, Marxist was only one of many labels that applied to the pretransition regime in Congo, and certainly not the most important. Among the other labels that applied to the pre-1991 Congo regime were "military," "personalist," "Northern," "Mbochi," and—most accurately of all, perhaps—"neopatrimonialist." Marxism never went very deep in largely unindustrialized Congo.[9] Although Congo nationalized most foreign businesses during the 1970s, and maintained a wide array of state-owned enterprises into the 1990s, the same could be said of most other African states, including ones of a putatively capitalist orientation. Overall, Congo had and has much more in common with Gabon, the Central African Republic, and Cameroon, for instance, than it does with the formerly communist states of Eastern Europe. In terms of levels of development, Congo is more comparable to some Latin American cases. In general, however, Congo is more similar to other African cases and the comparative effort is reasonably concentrated on African cases.

The utility of comparing Congo chiefly with other African cases is reinforced by the diversity of outcomes in democratic experiments on the continent. To return briefly to the era of transitions in Africa, powerful movements in favor of democratic reform sprang up throughout Africa following the end of the Cold War. While some of these certainly predated the collapse of Eastern European communism, few garnered enough domestic and international support to challenge the regimes existing in 1988. Prior to 1988, only a very few states (Botswana, Gambia, Nigeria, Senegal) had experimented with democracy since the 1960s, and none had consolidated a democratic regime as defined in Chapter 1. Studying forty-two cases that were not experimenting with multiparty democratic systems prior to 1989, Bratton and Van de Walle (1997: 116–122) determined that sixteen African states, including Congo, experienced "democratic transitions" by 1994.[10] Twelve states experienced "flawed transitions," and fourteen others either "blocked" or "precluded" transitions. Thus about 38 percent of Africa's authoritarian states experienced a democratic transition, about 29 percent a flawed transition, and about 33 percent no transition at all.

The sixteen African states that experienced democratic transitions have also experienced a diversity of outcomes in terms of consolidation so far

(Villalón and VonDoepp 2005). It bears emphasizing that most of the experiments are still in an intermediate stage, and the medium-term outcome is not yet known. Of the sixteen, Congo has endured the most catastrophic failure, in that the democratic collapse was accompanied by a major civil war, followed by ongoing civil strife in subsequent years. Among the other fifteen cases, four have experienced severe civil disorder and the replacement of elected regimes by unconstitutional governments. These cases were the Central African Republic (CAR), Guinea-Bissau, Lesotho, and Niger. In each of these cases, however, there was eventually a return to democratic experiment, though none has subsequently experienced regime alternation.

In eight of the sixteen cases the democratic experiments are ongoing and have not been disturbed by unconstitutional changes of power but, again, are not yet consolidated in the formal sense of having experienced regime alternation. These cases include Malawi, Mali, Mozambique, Namibia, São Tomé, Seychelles, South Africa, and Zambia. Some of the regimes in these states may survive as unconsolidated quasi-democracies for many years. Such was the status of the regime in Senegal until that country's 2000 presidential elections, and such is the ongoing status of Botswana, which is yet to experience an alternation of regimes. Some have experienced military intervention (Clark 2007) and may well revert to authoritarianism. Thus the overall impact of the third wave of democratization in Africa cannot be finally judged for some time to come.

Among this set of states, however, there are many hints about how democracy is faring and its ultimate prospects. For instance, the democratic experiment in the CAR appeared to be most fragile from the beginning, and few were surprised when the constitutional regime succumbed to military—and foreign—intervention. Before those events in 2002, the regime in power had resorted to repressive acts to stave off public demonstrations of disapproval (Mehler 2005). Meanwhile, in Zambia, the elections of 2001 were of dubious fairness and were not accepted by the opposition. These followed a long period in which the regime of Frederick Chiluba openly manipulated the system in quasi-legal ways to ensure the outcome his party sought (Simon 2005). In Mozambique, elites in opposing parties have found mechanisms for sharing power that have less to do with the constitution than with informal arrangements among themselves (Manning 2005), which also does not bode well for democracy. In Mali, the record is more ambiguous. In general, the regime elected in 1992 has followed the rule of law, but the country's Supreme Court annulled the results of the 1997 legislative elections, which were "botched," and opposition parties subsequently boycotted the rerunning of the elections (Smith 2001: 73). On the other hand, other cases seem much more promising. In the case of Malawi, the judiciary has proven to be an escape valve for the pressures that have built up among opposition forces that have lost elections since 1994 (VonDoepp 2005). The prospects for democratic consolidation in South Africa and Namibia seem better still.

In only three cases have democratic systems been consolidated in the formal sense of having experienced alternation through democratic means: Benin, Cape Verde, and Madagascar. Of the three, Madagascar is the most troubling case from the perspective of democratic partisans. Although Madagascar has experienced three posttransition elections and alternation in the rulers in power, the rules of the game are not being widely accepted by the political elites (Marcus 2005). Accordingly, Madagascar meets the formal definition of democratic consolidation, but a qualitative assessment suggests that its democratic institutions are still quite fragile. The country experienced a contested alternation of power in 2001 following disputed national elections. Benin and Cape Verde, on the other hand, appear to have gone the furthest in both a technical and a real consolidation of democratic institutions among the countries experiencing transition between 1989 and 1994.[11]

Of all of the African cases with which one might compare that of Congo, the case of Benin is certainly the most fascinating. The Benin-Congo dyad is marked by utterly divergent outcomes of the democratic experiments over their first ten years. The Congolese experiment lurched from crisis to crisis from the moment of its inception. Benin, on the other hand, led the way among all of the new African democracies of the third wave (Decalo 1997; Magnusson 1999). It was the first of the Francophone African countries to have a national conference and the first to hold transitional, founding elections. In 1996 Benin was the first of the post-1989 "class" to experience alternation, when the former military ruler, Matheiu Kérékou, was reelected to office. None of which is to say that Benin's new course has been without difficulty. As Decalo noted six years after the transition, on the economic front, civilian rule initially proved to be a "disenchantingly harsh experience" for most Beninois (1997: 57). Magnusson, another keen observer of Beninois politics, has marveled that the new regime has survived the "domestic insecurity" of the new period (2001). Nonetheless, Benin navigated yet another successful election in 2006, and its population now enjoys some benefits of a democratic regime, including vastly improved human rights and civil liberties.

What makes the Benin-Congo dyad fascinating, however, is that the singularly dissimilar outcomes of the democratic experiments can be juxtaposed with the strikingly similar structural conditions for the two countries at the time the experiments were launched (Magnusson and Clark 2005). Both countries have small populations, with Benin at less than 5 million and with Congo just under 3 million. Both states are former French colonies that experienced relatively intensive contact with France. Dating to colonial times, both countries developed influential intellectual classes among the national elite. Although there was more intensive contact with Europeans along the Beninois coast in the precolonial period, Congo became a center for French colonial activity after Brazzaville was made the headquarters for Free France during World War II. The postcolonial trajectories are even more strikingly similar. Congo became an officially Marxist-Leninist state in 1970, and Benin followed in 1974. Accordingly, both chose an etatist path to development, featuring nationalization and huge public employment rolls.

The informal political patterns were equally parallel. In both Benin and Congo the more populated parts of the country are in the south, and the coastal regions of both countries experienced more contact with Europeans than the remote northern regions. As a result, levels of educational attainment have traditionally been higher in the south of each country. Meanwhile, disproportionate numbers of northerners were recruited for service in the colonial armies. In this context it is interesting that both countries were ruled by northern military rulers with Marxist leanings after Kérékou's rise to power in 1974.[12] Both Kérékou and Sassou are from relatively small ethnic groups that represent less than 15 percent of their respective states. Before the rise of the Marxist military leaders, neither country enjoyed any political stability, each enduring a period of political turmoil and coups in the 1960s. When the hour of democratic reform arrived, Congo followed the pattern of holding a national conference pioneered by Benin (Clark 1993). Even the new, posttransition institutions set up by the two countries were broadly similar, though there were key differences. Another political pattern common to both countries—neopatrimonial modes of political economy—were widespread throughout Africa and are of less interest in explaining the variation in democratic outcomes.

The structural similarities of Benin and Congo, and their diverging outcomes, have particular relevance to the analysis of the Congo case. On the face of the comparison, the Benin example seems to suggest that the survival of a democratic system in Congo was more than just theoretically possible: it was actually accomplished in a rather similar case. This naturally directs our attention to the agents and their decisions. Of course, we must not forget the entire set of African cases with more mixed records. Moreover, there is one rather apparent structural difference between Benin and Congo, namely, the latter's large petroleum endowment and the politico-economic patterns that come with it. Congo's oil income has allowed the state to become detached from its citizenry to a far greater extent than states that are not faced with the "curse of resources." Congolese oil also raises the stakes for Congo's relations with France, as discussed in Chapter 8.

A comparison between Congo and countries *not* undertaking democratic experiments after 1989 can also be fruitful. Gabon, for instance, shares a number of structural features with Congo, including a small population and large petroleum endowment. It also shares a common pattern of "rentierism" as a result (Yates 1996). The two countries have sometimes been studied together because of their somewhat parallel colonial experiences (Bernault 1996). Yet the political reform movement in Gabon was sidetracked by the country's wily ruler, Omar Bongo, before it could result in a political transition (Gardinier 1997a). Bratton and Van de Walle (1997) fairly judge Gabon to have had a "flawed transition," since, despite the constitutional changes allowing multiparty politics, Bongo illegally manipulated events to remain in power. Despite their structural similarities, the post-1990 experiences of the two countries contrast sharply.

Essentially, then, the general strategy of this study is targeted comparison rather than the systematic analysis of data across numerous cases. Where such comparisons are useful, data from the Congo case will certainly be compared with African continental averages, or the averages of all states experimenting with democracy. For the most part, however, more is to be learned about the case from comparing how different countries with similar problems dealt with them. Accordingly, as each different facet of the Congolese case is studied, the most relevant cases for comparison vary, and these other cases are introduced where they shed light on the situation in Congo.

■ Conclusion

It is doubtful that a single cause for the failure of democracy in Congo can ultimately be identified. Nor could all of the variables that contributed to the failure of the democratic experiment be identified and assigned a precise weight as to the importance of each. Rather, the most that we can hope for is to reach an *understanding* of the Congo case. To do so, we have to describe a great deal about the structural constraints on (and opportunities for) democratic consolidation that Congo faced after its transition in 1991. Further, we must examine at some length the actions of the critical agents and how their behavior worked to reshape the country's political structures over time. Together, these activities will lead us to an appreciation of the nature of the agent-structure dynamic of politics that Congo experienced over the period of its democratic experiment. Throughout all of these analytical activities, we will benefit from the targeted comparison of the agents actions and structures of Congo with those of other states. Indeed, a preliminary comparison of Congo with Benin suggests that there were real possibilities for democratic survival in Congo. If this is true, then the human and institutional agents who made decisions bearing on the survival of democracy can be said to be responsible for having destroyed the experiment, and Congo's civil peace along with it. On the other hand, we may discover a more tragic situation in which the most important actors tried to behave in a democratic way but were forced by exogenous forces to act in a manner that ultimately destroyed the country's fragile democratic institutions.

■ Notes

1. This distinction was made by a social scientist of considerable standing: Max Weber in his *Economy and Society,* cited in Hollis and Smith (1990: 71).

2. I take the distinction between efficient causes and necessary conditions from the work of Waltz (1959).

3. As a result, the theoretical literature on democratization, or democratic consolidation, is not reviewed within the confines of one single chapter, as might be typically thought to be required.

4. Perhaps it should be noted that natural evolution does not necessarily proceed as a result of tiny, incremental steps occurring in a constant fashion. More modern theories suggest patterns of "punctuated equilibrium," in which evolution occurs in fits and starts. Likewise, in the evolution of human political institutions the processes of change can be characterized by long periods of relative stability punctuated by periods of great transformation. Kuhn (1962) has famously argued for just such a pattern in the evolution of scientific thinking about natural phenomena.

5. Even to acknowledge that human beings only act rationally according to their preferences is a concession from a more demanding rationalist position. A more vigorous form of rationalism might claim that all human beings respond in predictable ways to social challenges, without regard to individual preferences. For instance, crude realism might argue that all individuals seek to maximize their power or social standing; crude materialists might claim that all individuals seek to maximize their wealth. But the counter-examples to such positions are so abundant that such claims are typically reduced to heuristic devices for the purposes of hypothesis generation.

6. It is not clear that Lissouba himself gave the order; the fractious advisers surrounding him often acted independently of presidential wishes. See Pourtier (1998: 18).

7. Both the wave metaphor and the designation of the wave (which began in 1974 and continues to the present) as the third since the beginning of the nineteenth century is that of Huntington (1991).

8. This date, 1974, marks the beginning of the third wave of democratization for Huntington.

9. Among the studies that seem to take Congo's Marxism seriously are Allen (1989) and, to a lesser extent, Young (1982).

10. Of forty-seven countries in sub-Saharan Africa, Bratton and Van de Walle excluded Botswana, Gambia, Mauritius, Senegal, and Zimbabwe from their study because these five states already had multiparty systems in 1989. The other fifteen experiencing a democratic transition were Benin, Cape Verde, Central African Republic, Guinea-Bissau, Lesotho, Madagascar, Malawi, Mali, Mozambique, Namibia, Niger, São Tomé, Seychelles, South Africa, and Zambia.

11. Some other African states not among the sixteen experiencing a transition during this period also seem to be doing well. Senegal, which was already experimenting with a democratic system in 1989, met the formal definition of consolidation in March 2000. At that time Senegal's Parti Socialiste (PS) lost both the presi-

dential and legislative elections to the Union Progressive Senegalaise (Galvan 2001). Ghana, which was judged by Bratton and Van de Walle to have undergone a "flawed transition" during the 1989 to 1994 period, saw both the continuation of a democratic system and the alternation in power of the ruling party during its elections in 2001.

12. In Congo, there was a succession of three northern military rulers: Marien Ngouabi (1968–1977), Jacques Yhombi-Opango (1977–1979), and Sassou-Nguesso (1979–1991).

3

History and Political Culture as Context

Political history is no mere epiphenomenon or dependent variable.
　　　　　　　　　　　　　　　　　　　—Vansina 1990: 251

Democracy is above all a culture, a new spirit that fundamentally changes human relations.
　　　　　　　　　　　　　　　　　　　—Okoko-Esseau 1995: 159

Did the democratic experiment in Congo fail because of the continuity of antidemocratic ideas and habits in the practice of Congolese politics? In this chapter, I explore the weight of history and ideas in the Congolese democratic experiment. The first section presents a number of general problems for the assessment of the role of political culture in democratization. Although there is insufficient space here to provide elaborate arguments for the positions taken on matters of theoretical controversy, my own conclusions on these issues are indicated. This sections ends with a discussion of the importance of critical junctures in the evolution of political culture. The second section provides a chronological description of the accretion of the main norms of Congolese politics from the precolonial period through the end of the single party era. This section serves the secondary purpose of providing an overview of Congo's political history. The third section analyzes the impact of the 1991 transition on Congo's political culture. The fourth section evaluates the role of political culture in Congo's democratic experiment in comparative perspective.

■ Theoretical Issues of Political Culture and Democratization

Political culture refers to the political values and preferences held by any population. The population in question may represent a subset of a national population or a much wider set including parts of many national populations. Thus, the majority of citizens in all of the developed Western states now hold a preference for democratic governance over other modes of rule. Here it is more relevant to note that a single polity may contain a plurality

37

of "populations" with regard to political culture. Of course, one may slice a national population along a number of lines of cleavage, particularly including the lines represented by social class, region, or ethnic group. In the African context, one may also usefully refer to the "political class" to signify that section of the population that has the volition, economic means, and social standing to "play politics."[1] Within these population subsets may be detected relatively distinctive attitudes about appropriate forms of governance and rule.

Political culture is a normative and psychological concept that exists only in the consciousness of human beings. It is reflected and recorded in important documents of state including constitutions, political declarations, laws, and edicts, as well as in ordinary political speech. Moreover, political culture is not only normative in the sense that it stands as a symbol of "normal," or usual, political behavior; it embodies the moral preferences and expectations of a population for certain kinds of political practice. The majority of people will not perpetually play political games that they believe are morally wrong. They eventually either denounce the game and quit playing it, or convince themselves that it is morally acceptable, if not desirable. While such normative political convictions may be the result of psychological delusion, and rarely result from sustained normative reflection, they are nonetheless real and heartfelt.

Political culture often trumps material variables in influence. In the abstract, the political culture of politically relevant sections of the population is directly determinative of political outcomes. No matter what the material conditions of a given country, if the political class or general population has no regard for democratic modes of rule, then the form of government can scarcely be democratic. If, on the other hand, the large majority of a country's population is fervently devoted to democratic norms, it is hard to imagine it long remaining an autocracy. This is true of impoverished states as well as developed ones, and helps us understand how industrialized Germany could fall into the grip of fascism while destitute India has evolved an apparently durable democracy.

This observation would be more significant, however, were it not for the fact that political values are partly a result of material conditions as well as a producer of political forms. Political culture may be viewed as the last link in a long chain of causation that leads from social structures to political outcomes.[2] History and material conditions are best viewed as deeper variables that exercise a heavy influence on the contemporary values of political classes and populations at large. Thus, contemporary political culture is best seen as a proximate variable in long causal chains. As such, social theorists often assign it a marginal place in the explanation of political outcomes. Yet economic development need not precede successful democratization. As Dahl points out (1997: 36–37), three possible sequences of successful democratization are possible with regard to relations between material development and political culture: in the Western model, "democratization and a democratic culture precede and ultimately favor socioeconomic development"; in the authoritarian-modernization model "socioeconomic development precedes and favors democratization and a democratic culture"; and, in a mixed model, "democratization occurs incrementally as economic, social, and political developments mutually reinforce one another."

Political culture also exists in a dialectical and mutually reinforcing relationship with political practice and speech. On the one hand, the practice of politics necessarily reflects the political values of some key part of a polity's population. This is not to say that political practice necessarily mirrors closely the overall, or "net," political preferences of an entire population, however. There are cases in which unrepresentative, fringe groups take control of states and rule them for extended periods. They do not normally do so, though, without the active or tacit support of some critical section of the population. On the other hand, the practice of politics tends naturally to reinforce the political values of a population. This explains the high degree of inertia that one witnesses in a society's dominant mode of rule. Absent some kind of crisis or critical moment, virtually all polities will retain their existing form of governance. Hence, authoritarian states remain authoritarian and democracies remain democratic in the absence of some form of widespread social reconsideration of prevailing political norms. But all political systems do "sooner or later confront severe crises" (Dahl 1997: 34).

These assertions about the nature of political culture represent a stand on the first matter of controversy about the concept, namely, whether or not it is an autonomous political variable in the great, unquantifiable political calculus that leads to specific forms of rule. For strict materialists, political culture is but epiphenomenon, or a product of more fundamental material forces that shape political values. Marx famously dismissed such psychological and ideal forces as a "superstructure," just as Hegel famously took the opposite view. The stand taken above is one that rejects either extreme position, but insists that we view political culture as an autonomous variable. To deploy Hegel's ubiquitous epistemological device, material and ideal forces are locked in a perpetual social dialectic that drives an uncertain evolution of political forms over time.

Contra both Hegel and Marx, however, the dynamic interaction of political ideals and material forces need not lead predictably to any universal outcome in terms of domestic political forms. This is true because of the constantly intervening element of individual choice, which can push the ever-evolving material-ideal dialectic of history in unforeseeable directions. Because of the element of choice, which involves nonrational as well as rational drives, history cannot conceivably come to an end.

For our rather more circumscribed analytical purposes, we only need to clarify two positions taken in these grand epistemological debates in the philosophy of history. First, the position taken here is that ideal forces—political values—exert an autonomous influence on political evolution. Second, this position argues that political values result not only from material forces of history but also from moral reflection, social interaction and debate, and the accumulation of previous political choices made over time.

Besides this grandest consideration about the role of political ideals, three other, less philosophical problems arise in the literature on the relationship between political culture and democratization. These philosophical problems all represent debates about the nature and role of political culture, but, surprisingly, they only occasionally emerge as the conscious objects of controversy among scholars. Typically, individual scholars take a position one way or the other on these issues, then proceed with their research rather than confront these issues directly. Hence, works are found representing one view or the other, but there is relatively little direct debate in the applied literature of social science.

The first of these further debates about political culture and democracy concerns the possibilities for change in the values of various populations. When studying a political culture at a moment in time, scholars tend to treat it as if it were static. Treating political culture in this way may suggest a conscious or unconscious belief that it is highly resistant to change. For instance, in his excellent study of politics in Senegal, Schaffer (1998) pays virtually no attention to the either past or future evolution of Senegalese political culture. The author presents an utterly convincing argument that the Senegalese have in mind political norms that Westerners would not recognize as democratic ones when they use the French word *démocratie* or the Wolof word *demokaraasi*. In the final chapter of his study Schaffer further suggests that the use of cognate words for "democracy" in many other cultures have meanings that have little or nothing to do with such Western norms as majority rule, individual rights, and representative government. Yet Schaffer has nothing to say about whether Senegalese political culture is now more favorable to democratic politics than it was in the past, or whether it might become even more favorable in the future. Despite all of the deeply undemocratic attitudes in Senegal culture concealed by the use of cognate words there, the country did experience the spectacle of peaceful alternation in political power in 2000. Over time the practice of multiparty politics may be slowly changing Senegalese perceptions of *démocratie* and *demokaraasi*.

A rich and important recent work on Congo also argues for a basic continuity in the country's political culture (Bazenguissa-Ganga 1997). Interestingly, this work traces the origins of contemporary culture to the late colonial period, including the reign of Congo's first president, Fulbert

Youlou (1958–1963). Although it is written mostly as a narrative, and with only a short interpretive introduction, the continuities of basic political practice are the clear theme of the book.[3] This study lucidly describes the succession of outward changes in political form that mask the underlying continuities of political practice across the various postcolonial regimes. Other astute Congolese observers saw the war of 1997 as a reverberation of the past violence in Congo, particularly that which accompanied the state's founding in 1959 (Yengo 1998). This perspective seems to confirm that the political patterns established in the late colonial era survived into the contemporary era.

Many other studies of political culture demonstrate deep awareness of the possibilities for change in political culture, as well as its continuities.[4] Haugerud, for instance, exhibits an appreciation for both the inertia *and* dynamics of the political culture of Kenya. Having acknowledged the continuities of culture, she goes on to argue that "national political culture is not a stable 'text,' but something these historical actors [i.e., important public speakers] create, transform, and enact in everyday struggles and practices, starting from positions of unequal power and authority" (1993: 10). Haugerud emphasizes the role of public forums known by their Swahili name *baraza* as the settings in which political culture is reinforced or changed. Her study includes two cases of upheaval in Kenya's political culture: one springing from the reanimation of opposition politics in the early 1990s, and another, more muted transformation, following Daniel arap Moi's rise to power in the early 1980s.

Much more apparently schizophrenic in his position regarding the question of continuity and change in political culture is Robert Putnam in his famous work on Italian political culture (1993). This highly regarded study examines the differing political cultures of northern and southern Italy, respectively, and connects them convincingly with the contemporary politics and development in the two regions. Putnam "traces the roots" of the civil cultures in the respective regions back some nine hundred years to the late medieval period. In the south he found an imperial monarchy headed by a Norman conqueror who adopted somewhat liberal policies in religion and a strong bureaucracy. "In its social and political arrangements, however, the South was, and would remain, strictly autocratic" (123). In the north, by contrast, Putnam discovered a more egalitarian social arrangement and more republican political forms; these he perceived to be the roots of effective and modern democratic governance (124–129). Putnam suggested that the contemporary high levels of economic development and civic politics in northern Italy and the clientelism, stagnation, and authoritarianism of the south are connected by continuous historical chains to these medieval roots. If we focus on this key argument, the book represents a pessimistic assessment of the possibilities for democratization in the developing world on the grounds of their "defective" political cultures. The argument makes a strong case for continuity in the basic forms of political culture and for the extreme difficulty of implanting a democratic system in an inhospitable environment.

The contradiction in Putnam's work appears when one compares this basic argument with that of an earlier part of his study, in which he had asked whether politics could change in response to a change in the institutional rules of the game (1993, chapter 2). Here he looked for signs of change in Italian politics at the national and regional levels following the installation of new and powerful regional assemblies in the country beginning in 1970. He found that political practices did change among elites in significant ways at both the regional and national levels over the ensuing decades. Notably, for instance, politics was "depolarized," with a weakening of extremist parties and a steady movement toward the pragmatic center (29–33). Elites began to view politics as much more consensual and less conflictual (34–35). Reviewing several hypotheses, Putnam concludes that most of the change in political culture was caused by "institutional socialization," that is, in response to the new institutional set up (37–38).

How can we explain the apparent contradiction of this important work, and what does it have to tell us? First, although Putnam does not study the matter intensively, the *rate* of change in the political cultures of north and south varied. For instance, in his study of public satisfaction with the regional governments' performance between 1977 and 1988, public satisfaction in the north increased at about twice the rate as in the south (1993: 55).[5] This suggests that political cultures that have deeply rooted, prodemocratic elements, as in northern Italy, are more likely to respond positively to institutional changes. Less culturally democratic populations will respond less dramatically. A second lesson of Putnam's work is that there may be layers of politico-cultural values and practice. That is, some elements of political culture are fundamental, and perhaps highly resistance to change, while others are more contingent or superficial, and thus prone to transformation in response to crisis or institutional change.

A corollary to the broad problem of change in political culture is the question of mechanisms. For those who acknowledge the possibilities for change in political culture, what sort of social events are capable of bringing it about? The most obvious candidate would be a thoroughgoing social revolution, though even these hardly managed to erase existing political cultures. Consider, for example, France after 1789, Russia after 1917, China after 1949, or Iran after 1979. In more proximate ways, however, each revolution had a deep impact on political thought and practice. Short of revolution, other political crises or "critical junctures" in states' political trajectories can also alter the political culture of populations. As Putnam's work shows, even a mere change in institutional form, not accompanied by crisis, can have a surprisingly large impact.

The second general problem of political culture and democratization concerns the relevant population that must possess prodemocratic values for democratization to occur. Specifically, must an entire national population hold democratic values for democratic institutions to be consolidated, or is it enough for elites to acquire and maintain them? Virtually all studies of political culture, including all of those examined above, invoke the mass-elite distinction at some stage. In general, those who believe that the voting masses must exhibit devotion to democratic practices, like Schaffer (1998), are more pessimistic about the prospects for democratic consolidation where democratic experiments are ongoing. On the other hand, those who emphasize the role of elite culture, and its possibility of filtering down into the popular consciousness, stress the need for a change in elite consciousness as a first step toward democratization. This problem takes on another dimension when one couples it with the problem of change in culture: must an undemocratic culture change at both levels before the grounds for democratization are prepared?

In response to these generic problems, it becomes clear that it demands too much to insist that the overwhelming mass of a national population must consciously exhibit democratic values for a democratic experiment to begin, or to ultimately succeed. The generally democratic cultures at the mass level in the industrialized West developed slowly over many centuries. Even today, one finds *un*democratic attitudes among many groups within the United States. These include particularly certain ethnic groups with a dominant political experience outside the United States in authoritarian cultures and those among poorly educated sections of other ethnic communities long established in the country. Likewise, Austria has its neo-Nazis and France its fascist National Front, each of whom has polled distressingly well in recent years. Yet devotion to democratic rules of the game does not seem urgently threatened in any of these states. Similarly, for African states, the key is to develop a political class that is committed to operate by democratic rules of the game. If such a class emerges, habituation to democratic rules of the game will gradually seep into the broader population, even if there is never universal acquiescence to democratic norms.

A third problem of political culture is where, or to what historical period, to go to find the real roots of political culture. While some analysts may go back hundreds of years (Putnam 1993), others may choose to start their historical searches in the twentieth century (Fernandez 2000). Others say little of the historical origins of political culture but seek simply to document its contemporary forms (Haugerud 1993; Schaffer 1998). Whatever the case, this problem is relevant to democratization because conflicting patterns and norms of politics at different stages of a country's history may be found. One period of history may be characterized by republican practices while another is deeply authoritarian.[6] These are often reflected in conflicted feelings about democracy among the contemporary strata of the population of states. In turn, these mixed political cultures with regard to democratic norms may lead to long periods of fluctuation between democratic and nondemocratic forms of rule. This has been the pattern in such states as Argentina, Brazil, Pakistan, and Thailand.

One Africanist scholar has logically delineated the periods that matter most for the study of political culture in African states: the precolonial, the colonial, and the anticolonial periods (1945–1960) (Chazan 1994: 69–76). Chazan should have also included the more recent postcolonial period as well, where "new dimensions appeared in the physiognomy of power" (Young 1994a: 283). Africa's very young populations are much more familiar and responsive to these postcolonial experiences, even if the older elites still remember fondly the satisfaction of leading their countries to independence.[7] Again, most scholars signal their intellectual instincts as much by their choice of what to study as by explicit argumentation. Observing the terrible repression of authoritarian rule in postcolonial Africa, the majority of Africanists have fixated on the colonial past. This colonization of most African populations[8] was both utterly repressive and totally alien in the early years, so most Africanists conclude that this experience is at the root of undemocratic political norms that characterize so many African populations. The finest expression of this view is to be found in the work of Crawford Young, worth citing at length:

> The colonial state during its phase of construction in most cases created entirely novel institutions of domination and rule. Although we commonly described the independent polities as "new States," in reality they were successors to the colonial regime, inheriting its structures, its quotidian routines and practices, and its more hidden normative theories of governance. Thus, everyday reason of state, as it imposed its logic on the new rulers, incorporated subliminal codes of operation bearing the imprint of their colonial predecessors. (1994a: 283)[9]

Young simultaneously credits colonialism with fundamentally altering the precolonial patterns of political thought and action and with passing on its authoritarian habits of rule to postcolonial populations.

Other serious scholars, however, propose that important elements of political culture are located at other junctures along the historical continuum. Herbst (2000) has posed a major challenge to Africanists by arguing that many of Africa's precolonial political patterns have persisted into the present. He believes that such patterns condition the possibilities for state consolidation among Africa's contemporary polities. On the other hand, institutionalists pursuing a line of inquiry similar to that of Putnam, have asked whether postcolonial political institutions condition the possibilities for democratic transition or consolidation. Studying the first of these topics, Bratton and Van de Walle find that the nature of an African state's postcolonial institutions was correlated with the probability of a given state experiencing political protest and, ultimately, a transition to democracy during the 1989 to 1994 period (1997: 139–149, 183). They also speculated that "institutional legacies" would bear on the prospects for democratic consolidation (243–255). Since these institutions reflected the (varying) political cultures of different African societies, then, their work suggests that postcolonial political experiences do also condition the possibilities for democratization.

This review leaves the question open: how far back in history should we search for the roots of political culture and which historical legacies have relevance for contemporary politics? The best answer is that all past periods are relevant as long as the social arrangement and political practices of that era are still visible in contemporary political behavior; only if political norms of the past have been completely eliminated do they lose relevance, as with cases of complete discontinuity in political practices. For instance, there was a complete break between the political practices of the ancient Inca and the subsequent political entities that have occupied the same geographical space. Accordingly, there is little to learn about modern Peruvian politics through the study of the political practices of the Inca.

The same could not be said to be true of most contemporary African states. To be sure, colonialism was a shattering social experience for the polities—and their inhabitants—that existed at the moment of European conquest. But did this conquest utterly obliterate the forms of politics then being practiced in Africa? Although the experiences were highly variable, the short answer is surely not. In some cases, the degree of colonial penetration and control was astoundingly light,[10] particularly where colonial authorities ruled indirectly, through an existing political structure. This was the case in British Africa, where "indirect rule" through existing authorities was consistently practiced; but the differences between direct and indirect rule have been highly exaggerated (Kirk-Greene 1995). The French, too, employed local political authorities as instruments of their alien rule, even when they imbued them with metropolitan titles. Accordingly, just as ethnopolitical identities that did not correspond with those of the colonial state survived into the postcolonial era, so did many political norms and practices from the precolonial era.

At this point, let us sum up the positions taken on the key questions of political culture as they relate to democratization. On the question of change in political culture, it is acknowledged that the continuities in the political practices of polities are highly resistant to change. This is a lesson that surprised revolutionaries have had to confront in many postrevolutionary societies. It is far more common for another layer of cultural political practice to be added to an existing core than for a complete transformation to occur. Having said so, however, it is important to avoid the trap of believing cultural practice to be an absolute determinant of political possibilities. On the question of elites versus the mass and political culture, the best observation is that elites tend to matter most in the short term, and the mass of society in the longer term. To have a transition, or even a political transition, it is quite often enough for a society to experience a change of heart of the political class; but to have a social revolution—or a consolidation of democracy—changes in the normative political expectations must sink more deeply into the population. Even then, a democratic polity can tolerate a sizable percentage of undemocratic spirits in its midst. Finally, on the question of the origins of political culture, we argue that one should try to understand contemporary political norms, and then look into the past to try to see where such norms might have their origins. Insofar as continuities of practice across the divisions of various critical junctures can be discerned, the real origins may lie deep in the past.

■ The Accretion of Congolese Political Culture

This section sketches several of the main elements of Congolese political culture as they have accreted and evolved over time and seeks to show how the practices from each preceding era were affected by subsequent political events. Political norms that relate to the possibilities for democratic politics—or those that impede it—are highlighted.

Political Norms from the Precolonial Era

Have any of the political practices and norms from Congo's precolonial past survived to the present? Are they in any way reflected in the current modes of Congolese politics? If so, were there any proto-democratic practices in the precolonial cultures that might support democratization in a later period? The answers to these questions are difficult, but some have frequently taken a position out of political interest or ideological conviction. African leaders such as Julius Nyerere and Jomo Kenyatta have made claims of strong strains of egalitarianism and proto-democratic practices in the African past and further claimed that these were extinguished by colonialism (Simiyu 1988: 49–50). Some African scholars have supported these claims, asserting the presence of democratic assemblies that moderated the rule of precolonial gerontocracies (Kizerbo 1972: 176). Others have argued somewhat persuasively that the idea of democratic practice in traditional African societies is a myth (Simiyu 1988). France's leading student of African politics views this as the consensus view among Western scholars, observing that while precolonial politics was deliberative, "this deliberation was carried out in an exclusive fashion, in the context of a strong hierarchy of rules where only certain social categories (notably older men) had the right to speak and decide" (Bayart 1991: 6).

Most scholars prefer not to confront these questions at all, though the historical starting points of their analyses usually reveal their preconceptions. This is as true for the most acute observers of Congolese politics as for students of other polities. For instance, the sociologist Bazenguissa-Ganga (1997) begins his study of Congolese political culture in the late colonial period. Likewise, the historian Bernault (1996), writing on both Congo and Gabon, chose to cover the late colonial period through the reigns of the first presidents in her study. These choices surely signal these scholars' view that the late colonial period was the critical one in Congo's political evolution.

One is cautioned in any claim about the continuity of political practice in Congo from the precolonial era by the monumental work of the great historian-anthropologist of central Africa, Jan Vansina.[11] In his masterwork on political tradition in equatorial Africa (1990), the culmination of some forty years' work, the author makes breathtaking claims about the region's political history and backs them with evidence painstakingly compiled over a long career. The first claim is that the modern western Bantu peoples of the entire equatorial forest region "are the heirs of a *single ancestral society and culture* whose carriers expanded into the area four or five millennia ago" (6).[12] Vansina's second claim is entirely implicit, but it is an important subtext of his work: he argues that precolonial culture had important elements of equality, individual autonomy, and social commitment to the welfare of others. This is particularly true of the period before the advent of the region's three great kingdoms, which Vansina estimates most likely occurred in the fourteenth century (156). Finally, in only a few scant pages, Vansina unequivocally argues that European colonialism utterly demolished this tradition during the forty-year period over which it was established. In his words, "The only concession to the equatorial way of life was to preserve some cultural flotsam and jetsam, and to erect a structure labeled customary law, which was utterly foreign to the spirit of the former tradition" (239).

Vansina's position on the egalitarianism and individual autonomy in precolonial equatorial culture appears only indirectly in the text, and accordingly it must be teased out. For Vansina, these elements of social equality and autonomy in the equatorial traditions are subtle but unmistakable. First, in describing the social unit of the "House" (as discussed below), Vansina says that its ideology "was based on the fiction that it was a family" (1990: 75). Accordingly, the head of the house had a paternal responsibility for the welfare of his "family." Second, because of the lack of a lineage system, "free men had a wide choice as to the establishment they cared to join" (75). Here (and elsewhere; see 1990: 252–253) Vansina emphasizes a degree of individual autonomy, at least among certain classes of residents.[13] Autonomy also existed higher up the ladder in that local political leaders often escaped the demands of their superiors, particularly through migration in a setting of relatively low population density. Intriguingly, and unexpectedly, Vansina finds an important expression of social equality in the practice of witchcraft:

> Witches were those people, women or men, who had the ability to kill others out of envy by wishing them evil, consciously or unconsciously. Such killings were thought to occur frequently, and witchcraft was suspected on the occasion of every death. Witchcraft incorporated the notion of absolute, malicious evil, and held that pure evil always was the work of humans, and only humans. A corollary of this belief was that one should never give cause for envy. One should never stand out, one should always share. *In sum witchcraft was an ideology of equality and cooperation.* . . . The ideology was in tune with the stress on equality between social units and on the need to pretend at least superficially (as in the use of kinship terminology) that social inferiors were equals. (1990: 96–97, emphasis added)

Vansina returns to this point in his description of colonialism's destruction of the equatorial African political tradition (253).

There are two important qualifications to this basic position. One can be discerned in Vansina's implicit distinction between two great phases in the history of equatorial Africa, the first prevailing from ancient times until the advent of three great kingdoms in the region. During both phases, the elemental unit of social organization was the House, usually composed of ten to forty people, and headed by a "big man" (1990: 74–75). The main purpose of a House was to organize food production, and it included the wives and kinfolk of the big man, "but also friends, clients, and various dependents as well" (75). The next highest level of sociopolitical organization was the village, which was "an aggregate of Houses. . . . The village was led by the big man who founded it, assisted by the big men of the other Houses who made up its council" (78). A cluster of villages located in a relatively close environment, but separated from other constellations of villages, was perceived as the next highest level of organization, but in this time, "the district had no chief and need not have a principal village" (81). Accordingly, the village was the largest unit of political order and these maintained a segmentary, or acephalous, relationship among themselves, while the district was a conscious unit of social order during this first phase.

Vansina's description of the advent of ever-larger sociopolitical units at a later time is classic in that it might describe the evolution of human societies in many settings. The first step was the emergence of "chiefs" to rule at the level of the district. According to Vansina, this step was occasioned by the "unfolding of a more complex economic system by or after the sixth century AD" (1990: 147). Once one chiefdom was established, its existence threatened the security of surrounding acephalous districts, which then rapidly all acquired chiefs in response (148). In succession, two other larger political units subsequently arose as this basic process continued to unfold. The next larger political entity bears the label "principality"—as translated by Vansina—and was led by a paramount chief. Naturally, the construction of these units was achieved by the subordination of some collection of (district) chiefdoms by more powerful rulers. Following the development of the social practice of matrilinearity, kingdoms ultimately appeared in the equatorial forest region (152–158). Three kingdoms that arose sometime around the fourteenth century persisted in one form or another until the advent of European colonial rule in the area. These three kingdoms included the Loango kingdom, north of the Congo River along the Atlantic coast; the famous Kongo kingdom, centered mostly south of the Congo River into modern Angola; and the Tio kingdom, located on the plateau area northwest of the other two. The Loango and Tio kingdoms occupied major parts of the contemporary state of Congo Republic, whereas the Kongo kingdom occasionally extended its suzerainty across the Congo River into the area that is now part of Congo's modern state. Over their five-hundred-odd years of existence, these kingdoms grew and shrank over time, particularly in response to the economic impact of European trade, especially the slave trade, along the Atlantic coast.[14] This era was a second phase in equatorial Africa's precolonial history.

For Vansina, the emergence of these kingdoms is of tremendous historical interest, but he also stresses that they did not, in his view, extinguish the prevailing sociopolitical patterns that existed before. For instance, the House remained an important unit of social organization within chiefdoms, principalities, and even kingdoms. Indeed, much of the internal politics of the kingdoms was driven by the rivalries among the various Houses. Moreover, none of the kingdoms ever achieved a high level of centralization, and a great deal of local autonomy continued to exist at the local level. Certainly, Vansina would concede that some level of social equality was lost in the growth of these kingdoms, for he describes the accumulation of wealth (e.g., 1990: 145, 232–233) that resulted mostly from a monopoly on trade with Europeans but also on internal extraction. The advent of matrilinearity also reduced the degree of individual autonomy in the second phase. Hence, his minor qualification would be that some equality was lost with the rise of the kingdoms. Nonetheless, his insistence that European colonialism, not the rise of the kingdoms, destroyed the prevailing social norms of the region emphasizes the high degree of continuity in sociopolitical practices that he perceived across the two great eras.

Another important qualification of Vansina's position is that he was highly aware of the elements of social hierarchy in the equatorial systems, both before and after the rise of the kingdoms. The following interjection was excised from the quotation above on witchcraft: "Quite paradoxical for societies built on competition between big men and on the inequality of status!" (1990: 96). In his penultimate chapter Vansina returns to the theme of paradox, stating, "Right from the outset two ideologies coexisted: one that extolled and explained the success of big men and one that stressed the ideal equality of all, which underlines the suspicion of witchcraft" (253). Thus, Vansina was aware of the deeply inegalitarian and authoritarian aspects of precolonial societies, even if he preferred not to stress them.

Interestingly, the authoritarian and hierarchical aspects of precolonial culture also present a paradox: they are so obvious that we often take them for granted. This is partly the case because they are omnipresent in all traditional societies, including those of premodern Europe. Such negative patterns of political behavior, from the standpoint of democratic development, are quite evident in the descriptions of the equatorial African societies by Vansina and most other historians. Moreover, it is equally evident that these have survived into contemporary times, albeit in modified form, as they have been molded by the subsequent modes of political practice over time.

What were some of the authoritarian and hierarchical patterns of politics and rule in the precolonial societies that pose an obstacle to the development of democracy as long as they persist? At the most intimate level, the "big man" represented an arbitrary power from which members of the "family" could have no appeal. Citing the record of a puberty ceremony for boys in one equatorial community, Vansina indicates that what allowed an individual male to become a "big man" included the possession of wealth, fame, numerous wives and children, heroism in war, and a gift for persuasion in speech (1990: 73). There is absolutely no indication that they were selected by any community of peers, or that they achieved power through reputation for qualities of fairness, good judgment, or demonstrations of concern for the public welfare. If they enjoyed the social autonomy from superior levels of authority that Vansina claims, then they also enjoyed the privilege of behaving arbitrarily toward others in the "families" that they controlled. Accordingly, the enjoyment of any rights by such social inferiors as slaves, women, minors, and even adult males who were not "big men" would have been entirely at the discretion of the leader. Leaders who controlled the political units at higher levels—the villages, districts, principalities, and kingdoms—exercised similarly arbitrary authority over those beneath them.

Another deeply, but perhaps not so obviously, antidemocratic feature of precolonial society was the utterly ubiquitous connection of earthly political authority with supernatural powers. MacGaffey (1970) showed long ago that Bakongo big men were believed to possess supernatural powers and were more powerful than earthly witches. Vansina acknowledges that this view was widespread in the whole equatorial area in citing MacGaffey's work (Vansina 1990: 97 and n. 86). According to Vansina, the big man's own charms helped him "repel the attacks of witches" whereas he used his own supernatural powers to kill competitors and subjects.

Rulers at the higher echelon political units enjoyed parallel powers. Vansina says of the chiefs that "their followers attributed their success to supposed links with occult powers, especially to charms" (146). Of the paramount chiefs, Vansina notes that one pillar of their earthly powers was "an ideological link with a specific nature spirit, or *nkira*" (151).

What was true for the chiefs and paramount chiefs in this regard was true all the more so for the kings. For instance, the Maloango, king of Loango, was perceived by his people to have quasi-divine powers. His subjects believed that he controlled the rain and other natural phenomena. Writing of the early Maloango, Martin claims that "the spiritual and ritual significance of the Maloango's office and person can hardly be overemphasized" (Martin 1972: 20). The nature of the Maloango as a divine figure is equally emphasized in other works on Loango; Obenga (1985) refers to them as the "king-gods" in his analysis. In turn, the Maloango carefully cultivated the perception that he possessed divine powers through a series of rituals and behaviors designed to impress his subjects (Martin 1972: 19–21; Obenga 1985). A rather similar situation prevailed with the Tio kings of the same early period, who were believed to have returned to earth from the spirit world (Vansina 1969: 36). In his study of Tio during the early colonial period, Vansina found that the Tio still had a real fear of the king's magical powers. Among them was an ability to dispatch lions to kill any enemies of the kingdom (Vansina 1973: 377–378). In the case of the Kongo kingdom the situation is much more complicated because the king, "the Manikongo," was converted to Christianity by Portuguese voyagers at the early date of 1491. Later, Manikongo sought to use Christian spirituality as a means of ideological control (Thornton 1983: 44–45, 64–68). Clearly, those who possessed otherworldly powers could not be appropriately or justly checked by the political institutions fashioned by mere mortal human beings.

In these matters of the occult, symbolism was of paramount importance to the rulers. For instance, the possession of boxes bearing sacred charms *(nkobi)* was one key to holding offices among the Tio (Vansina 1973: 324–338). The use of animal symbolism was another, apparently universal instrument of ideological authority. The leopard, in particular, was a ubiquitous symbol of royal power throughout the equatorial region (Vansina 1990: 74; Martin 1972: 21).[15]

The rulers of these kingdoms also possessed virtually unchecked powers to make law and adjudicate cases in the earthly realm.[16] With regard to the Maloango's earthly powers, Martin avers that "the administration was strictly hierarchical: all power derived from the Maloango who appointed officials" (1972: 21). The Maloango kept all of his local adjuncts firmly under his control and served as "Supreme Judge in the kingdom" (22). He "wielded an all-pervasive authority, his position being reinforced by his semi-divine nature" (158). In the case of the seventeenth century Manikongo, this king ruled partly through the instrument of a "royal council." This body, in turn, was appointed at the will of the king and here "only a handful even within the council would have real power" (Thornton 1983: 45). The situation in early Loango was remarkably similar (Martin 1972: 161).[17] Although the Kongo kingdom was vast, and transportation and communications were poor, the Manikongo possessed the military force to crush those who would rise against him, often with Portuguese assistance. As a result, the rural notables "rather than attempt to secede from Kongo, or to become 'overmighty subjects' . . . sought to bind themselves as much as possible to the king and to the [capital city]" (Thornton 1983: 43). Although the Tio kingdom was more decentralized, the Tio kings enjoyed considerable arbitrary power in both the early and later periods (Vansina 1969: 29; Vansina 1973: 390–394), though less than the rulers of the other two kingdoms.

Yet another inegalitarian and authoritarian aspect of political life in the kingdoms was the existence of a hierarchical class of "nobles." Although the historians of the central African kingdoms sometimes prefer to emphasize the differences from European feudalism, the parallels are clear, and the historians reveal their own sense of rough comparability through their use of terms. Martin's description of the seventeenth century Loango notables is revealing: "The traditional aristocracy apparently exploited their position in society to the full. Land belonged to the community, but the local ruler enjoyed the right of usufruct. As the Maloango received tribute on a national level, so the *mfumu nssi* [literally, "lords of the earth"] were the local recipients" (Martin 1972: 26). She goes on to describe the impressive social and economic privileges of this class. Describing the situation in nineteenth-century Tio, Vansina identifies two classes of aristocracy, which he calls "lords" and "squires." The former were "chiefs-of-the-crown," who controlled a number of squires, and the latter were "chiefs-of-the-land," who ruled over territorial subdivisions of the empire (Vansina 1973: 311). The earthly powers of both "squire" and "lord" were related to the links of individual officeholders with *nkira,* or "nature spirits." Lords built great houses, kept numerous wives, and maintained a retinue of retainers (330–336). Naturally, lords possessed and displayed great wealth. Although the patterns of succession were enormously complex, they were generally hereditary (322, 337). Among the Bakongo, too, there existed a durable nobility, although the occupants of noble office were appointed rather than inherited (Thornton 1983: 39).

To describe the myriad details of the politico-economic relations among the kings, nobles, and free citizens in these various kingdoms, especially as they evolved over time, is not possible here. Nonetheless, the label "feudal" does not do undo violence to the social reality. In general, free peasants provided tribute to the nobles, who in turn paid tribute to the king or his representatives. In both sets of relationships a basic "patron-client" rapport existed between the superior and inferior classes. In return for their tribute payments to their social superiors, the peasants generally received physical protection and the rendering of judgments in disputes among them. For their part, the nobles were recognized by the kings as the legitimate local authorities—and as the legitimate exploiters of local labor—as recompense for their payments to the king. The possession and display of wealth were both a standard by which social recognition was gained and the social prerogative of the occupation of established offices. Of course, the "big men," be they kings, nobles, or local chiefs, were also expected sometimes to spend part of their wealth on other occasions for the well-being or status maintenance of their inferiors (Vansina 1990: 125). But this redistribution must have represented a small portion of what was extracted. Once the European slave trade was under way, the "big men" in Loango and Kongo who took control of the collection of slaves from the interior greatly increased their own wealth, further exacerbating social inequality (Martin 1972: chapter 8).

A counterpart to the rise of ruling classes in the equatorial kingdoms was the advent of the practice of indigenous slavery in the region. The institution of indigenous slavery was extremely complex and bore little resemblance to the chattel slavery of the Western hemisphere. Notably, slaves were typically seen as part of a family and often regained their freedom over time—or at least their children became free. In addition to becoming slaves as a result of defeat in battle, free men and women could become slaves as a result of the commission of crimes or by becoming indebted (Vansina 1990: 155; Martin 1972: 167). The coming of the European slave trade increased the number of slaves held locally for purposes of their eventual sale (Rodney 1966). Although slaves did not constitute a permanent "class" in the equatorial societies, another group did: the indigenous peoples living in the area before the gradual movement of Bantu-speaking peoples into the region. Many of these indigenous people ("autochthons"), typically hunter-gatherers rather than agriculturalists, were forest-dwelling "pygmies." Those that have survived into the current age retain an inferior status vis-à-vis the Bantu, including in Congo.

Yet another "class" of generally disenfranchised residents of the equatorial kingdoms was women, although again the social reality is extraordinarily complex. Nonetheless, writing of precolonial African women in the broadest terms, Coquery-Vidrovitch indicates that the distinction between the social and economic duties of a free woman and a slave was "tenuous" (1997: 26).[18] The general status of women was no higher in the equatorial part of the continent. Women normally had no say about whom they would marry, and they could be given away (as a political offering) or paid as tribute by men. Women were accused of witchcraft disproportionately and suffered as a result (Vansina 1990: 97, 159). Women were valued for their childbearing capacity, and men often had to make a "bridewealth" payment to the families of women they wished to marry (Vansina 1990: 103–104).[19] Thornton, however, describes the gender division of labor in rural areas as being quite equitable (1983: 29). Moreover, he indicates that at the king's court, the widows of dead kings or noblemen "were quite active politically." Women even served in prominent positions on the royal council (48). Likewise, Martin describes a remarkable office occupied by a female relative of the king called the Makunda. This female official "had special responsibility for Vili women, especially when their husbands abandoned them or physically mistreated them" (1972: 24–25). These exceptional cases notwithstanding, the social standing of women in general in the precolonial kingdoms was undeniably inferior to that of males.

Nearly all of the social inequities and oppressive political conditions prevailing in the precolonial kingdoms persisted into the colonial and postcolonial periods. To these, the colonial authorities added new repressive political norms. Although their actions served to transform substantially most of the political patterns of the precolonial period, these were hardly obliterated. Perhaps Vansina is correct to suggest that the egalitarian aspects of these societies were completely destroyed; if so, however, the socially oppressive habits—those that he describes well but does not emphasize—were maintained or deepened. Of course, the institutions of slavery and a formal class of nobleman may have vanished with the coming of colonial rule. But other precolonial political patterns are still visible to this day in Congo and other central Africa states: the use of magic and the occult in political practice; the prominent presence of the "big men" in public life based on their wealth and military prowess; the persistence of patron-client patterns in the regulation of class relationships; and the effort to maintain the sociopolitical marginalization of women by a male-dominated establishment. We shall see how colonialism altered these original political patterns, supplemented them with far more deadly and repressive ones, and how the resulting hybrid patterns have subsequently reverberated throughout Congo's history.

The Colonial Period to 1930

In examining the colonial period, it is important to recognize two radically different phases of the colonial experience. The first phase began in 1880 when Pierre Savorgnan de Brazza gained the signature of the king of the Tio (the "Makoko") on a "treaty" granting France protectorate rights in the local territory. The French only slowly established their commercial and administrative presence there and faced frequent revolts through the end of the 1910s. Effective control of most of the territory was achieved by 1890. All of France's equatorial African possessions were originally known as "French Congo," but these were organized into four separate territories between 1906 and 1910: Moyen-Congo, Oubangui-Chari, Gabon, and Chad. The first of these later became the Republic of Congo and the second the Central African Republic. The four were administrated collectively under the umbrella of the Afrique Equatoriale Française (AEF), a federation of the four colonies. This period was marked by brutal colonial administration and economic rapine at the hands of French concessionary companies until 1930. The second period began with France's occupation by Nazi Germany in 1940, at which time the AEF, with its headquarters at Brazzaville, became the headquarters of Free France. Following the war, France gradually extended political rights to the territories. This took place in a series of short stages, and led first to Congo's autonomy within the French Union in 1958, and then to its complete independence in 1960.

In fact, the long period of European contact and trade in Equatorial Africa had already dramatically altered local societies, including their political cultures, in myriad ways before formal colonization. Indeed, the Portuguese had actually established their own colony among the Mbundu people of northern Angola in 1571, a colony that initially lasted for some twenty years (Birmingham 1981: 26–37). Although this colony failed in its main goals of mining silver, establishing a permanent settler presence, creating plantations, and Christianizing the population, it did serve as an effective slave gathering depot. During the 1560s, the Portuguese had also established a presence in the Kongo kingdom and interfered perpetually in its politics, including restoring ousted Christian monarchs to power (34–35). This was only the beginning of a pattern of European interference in the politics of all of the kingdoms near the Atlantic coast. Likewise, the Portuguese initiation of the slave trade along the equatorial coast only represented the beginning of the three-hundred-year-long Atlantic slave trade. Besides slaves, European traders exported equatorial forest products, ivory, and many other commodities, while also introducing not only European technological innovations—notably firearms—but also new plant species like cassava and maize.

Trade with Europeans was apparently very important in the centralization of the Loango and Kongo kingdoms; the inland Tio kingdom had much less direct contact with Europeans and remained more decentralized. Even more obviously, the massive slave trade had an enormous impact on political norms in the region. The incentive to capture slaves surely increased the amount of intercommunal fighting, led to constant migration, exacerbated inequalities of wealth, and led to the dehumanization of captors and captured alike. Indeed, Martin's study (1972) of the impact of European trade on the Loango kingdom records all of these results.

Nonetheless, the process of formal European penetration and "pacification"—to use the contemporary euphemism—of the indigenous kingdoms and autonomous areas constituted an unprecedented shock to the normative worldview of equatorial Africans. The actual offices of the old political forms were first diminished and then eliminated, being replaced with the very different institutions and offices of the colonial state. The impact of colonization, however, went far beyond the outward destruction of political institutions—psychological universes were upended, as well. As Vansina argues, "The peoples of the rainforests began first to doubt their own legacies and then to adopt portions of the foreign heritage. But they clung to their own languages and to much of the older cognitive content carried by them. Thus they turned into cultural schizophrenics" (1990: 247). Equatorial Africa, therefore, experienced not so much the death of its tradition but its transformation into a harsh, dehumanizing hybrid of precolonial and colonial praxis.

The nature of the colonial administration in AEF was complex, and evolved over time. During the initial phase of colonization, de Brazza himself served as the commissioner general (governor) of the colony and the impact of the growing French presence was relatively mild. The most brutal phase, from 1898 to 1930, came about when the French government turned over effective administration to forty "concessionary companies" (Coquery-Vidrovitch 1972). Thirteen of these operated in the territory of the contemporary Congo Republic. The French government created the concessions after other methods of developing and exploiting the natural resources of Congo had failed. According to the original terms, the companies were given a thirty-year lease during which they enjoyed exclusive rights to forestry, agriculture, and industry, though not to mining. In return, the companies paid an initial deposit of 8,000 to 100,000 francs, depending on the size of the concession. In addition, each company was to pay an annual rental charge of 500 to 50,000 francs, "depending on the case"; the charge was to increase after the fifth and eleventh years. Finally, each was to pay a tax of 15 percent of its profits (51).

Although the companies were not accorded sovereign rights over the territories of their concessions, they came to exercise the rights of colonial authority in practice. Their main aim was to extract as much wood, rubber, ivory, and other natural resources from their territories as they could, as cheaply as possible. To create a labor force for the companies, the colonial administration imposed a head tax. Often the tax was payable in the form of goods, including ivory or rubber gleaned from the forests (Coquery-Vidrovitch 1972: 119). Thus, the tax became the link between the official administration and the concessionary companies (117–141). In addition to creating unspeakable abuses, the tax did not raise enough funds for the construction of a viable internal infrastructure. The agents of the companies often whipped those who failed to gather a sufficient quota of rubber. As frequently, they made hostages of the wives and children of workers who failed to turn over a specified quantity of goods. Porters and other forced laborers were sometimes simply worked to death (177–180).

These abuses were brought to the attention of European authorities by daring journalists, and de Brazza was dispatched on a mission of inquiry in

1905, but he died before he could fulfill his charge. Meanwhile, the abuses continued unabated through the 1910s. When the writer André Gide made his famous voyage through Congo in 1927, the scale of the abuses continued to be huge (Gide 1994). The numerous revolts against European abuses that occurred throughout the whole period were brutally suppressed by the colonial authorities (Coquery-Vidrovitch 1972: 197–219). In some cases, whole ethnic groups were virtually wiped out (Vansina 1990: 244).[20] The construction of the Chemin de Fer Congo–Océan (CFCO), the railway linking Brazzaville with the Atlantic port at Pointe Noire between 1922 and 1934 was carried out largely through forced labor. The conditions in the workers' camps caused incomprehensible misery and death. Over 127,000 workers were recruited from throughout AEF for work on the railway over the years of its construction, and over 14,000 died according to official colonial figures (Coquery-Vidrovicth 1972: 194–195; Moukoko 1999: 81–82).

What effects did such monstrously inhumane modes of rule have on the political culture? What were the political "lessons" of colonialism for the local populations? Many of these can be logically deduced, but they also show through in the behavior of the Congolese populations themselves, as are recorded in the reports of colonial administrators, journalists, and other outside visitors. We should note, too, that those who became the collaborators of the Europeans, on the one hand, and those who were essentially victims, on the other, learned rather different lessons. First, the instrument of social terror as tool for rule was introduced into the country's politics. French colonial rule demanded utter submission to its demands, and protests were most likely to bring swift and brutal retaliation. This was an innovation compared to the far more banal oppression of the precolonial polities. Second, the colonial situation disconnected the population from their ruling political authorities. The state viewed the population as a source of labor and an object of domination, and not as a community to whom it owed protection or social welfare. In turn, the population sought only to avoid the state or, where possible, to resist it.[21] Third, those who collaborated came to see the state as an instrument of the people's economic exploitation for the benefit of the rulers, while the population at large came to see it as a force for economic extraction that provided little in return. Finally, all Congolese must have absorbed the lesson that a major role for the state is the organization of the exploitation of the country's natural resources. All of these political patterns reverberate in Congo's postcolonial politics.

The Colonial Period After 1930

With the end of the concessionary system, Congo became a "normal" colony of the French state, allowing the colonial subjects to address themselves directly to state authorities. Later, after World War II, the French began to enact political reforms to Congo that would allow for representation of the indigenous people in local and metropolitan political institutions. These reforms would also gradually extend civil rights to the population more generally. The French undertook these reforms partly because of changing sentiment about the legitimacy of colonialism itself in the post-Nazi era and also in fulfillment of promises to the populations of their African colonies made during the war. In the case of AEF, France had a particular debt of gratitude since the French territories, then under the leadership of Félix Éboué, had rallied to France in the painful early hours of Nazi occupation. French colonial governors specifically made such promises at the famous Brazzaville Conference of January 1944. As a result, most analysts of French-colonial Africa formally begin their studies with the World War II period (e.g., Bernault 1996), but they are inevitably drawn back at least into the 1930s where the basic patterns of postwar politics began. The year 1930 carries specific significance as the date of the end of de facto rule by concessionary companies.

The patterns of politics that emerged in Congo in the late colonial period are strikingly different from those of the earlier period. Beginning in the 1930s a new, more consciously political and less localized form of resistance to colonialism began to appear. Postwar political figures co-opted the movements from this era and deployed them in the new arena of politics created by the new French-mandated institutions. In order of their appearance, the following political patterns emerged in the specified period: the blending of messianic and supernatural forms of social "escapism" with anticolonial and opportunistic political movements; the emergence of new movements based on the leadership of charismatic leaders; the consolidation of ethnic and regional constituencies as the most important social bases of support for the various movements; the co-optation of rival political figures through access to political office and to state-extracted wealth; the manipulation of the rules by those in power to maintain or reinforce their control of political institutions; and the occurrence of ethnopolitical violence as a result of the perceived stakes of politics. Interestingly, all of these patterns were related to French manipulation of the political scene, but none were the results of a specific, conscious effort of French authorities to create them.[22] Rather, these patterns reflect a syncretism of precolonial and early colonial political patterns being played out in an environment created by the delineation of an artificial territorial unit and by the imposition of alien political institutions. All of the patterns that emerged during this time endured to the postcolonial period.

The first pattern to become evident was the blending of supernatural belief with political activism and resistance. This pattern doubtless reflects the precolonial association of political leaders with esoteric, magical powers of control. Two cases from the late colonial era demonstrate how the spiritual and political worlds came together to form an integrated complex of belief relevant to both.

One is the singular case of the movement spawned by André Matsoua's political activism; its power resonates in Congolese politics to this very day.[23] The remarkable Matsoua began his political voyage as a secular figure, not a spiritual leader. Matsoua was a Lari born in the Pool region of Congo in 1899. He was educated at a Catholic mission school in the same region, but he joined the customs service in Brazzaville in 1919 (Sinda 1978). After World War I Matsoua traveled to France, where he eventually joined the French army and then fought in the Rif war of Morocco from 1924 to 1925. In 1926, back in Paris, Matsoua founded a "mutual aid society" *(association amicale)* for AEF residents living in France. Using this platform, he began calling on French authorities to undertake reforms in their colonial policies, notably reforms in the colonial penal code known as the *indigénat*. Meanwhile, he dispatched two envoys into the Pool region of Congo to raise money among the Lari people for his cause, and these representatives raised a remarkable 100,000 francs by the end of 1929 (Bernault 1996: 72).[24] Rightly fearing these activities, French colonial officials arrested Matsoua and several associates in late 1929. The following year they deported him to Brazzaville, put him on trial, and sentenced him to three years of prison and then ten additional years of exile in Chad. Matsoua's sentencing sparked the mobilization of the Lari community, which then ceased all cooperation with colonial authorities. For instance, the Lari refused to accept official bonuses, to participate in official demonstrations, or to join in the campaign to increase peanut production (Bernault 1996: 73; Gauze 1973: 5).

In 1935 Matsoua escaped from his Chadian exile and eventually made his way back to Paris. There he again took up his organizing activities, this time in a clandestine fashion. Rather oddly, Matsoua enlisted in the French army under an assumed name in 1939 but was discovered and arrested again in 1940. This event led to an attack by a Lari commando group on a territorial guard unit in Pool (Gauze 1973: 5). Matsoua was again transferred to Brazzaville, and then condemned to a life sentence at hard labor in February 1941 (Bernault 1996: 73). The following January, Matsoua died in prison under mysterious circumstances, though the colonial authorities named bacillary dysentery as the cause of death (Gauze 1973: 5). Many suspected that Matsoua was murdered. Whatever the case, the Matsouaist movement soon became imbued with messianic and supernatural elements. Some of Matsoua's followers refused to believe that he was dead, while others expected him to be resurrected and return to earth as a savior for the oppressed Lari people. Thus, in the minds of some followers, he became a Christ-like figure whose return promised both personal salvation and earthly liberation (Gauze 1973: 6).

In the meanwhile, the Lari remained politically passive over the following fourteen years. They maintained their passive resistance to colonial initiatives, and no new Lari political leaders emerged. Given the chance to vote in the territorial elections later organized by colonial authorities, larger percentages of Lari indicated their preference for Matsoua, either by spoiling their ballots or by writing in Matsoua's name. This was true in the elections for the territorial assembly in 1946, for the French National Assembly in 1951, and again for the territorial assembly in 1952. For instance, in a 1951 poll, some 24 percent of Congolese voters cast blank ballots, which would have been a large majority of voters in the Pool region (Gauze 1973: 14). In the elections for the territorial assembly the following year, a living candidate polled 15,572 votes against 15,075 in favor of Matsoua (16). Matsoua's spell was not broken until the Abbé Fulbert Youlou, Congo's first president, was able to claim the mantle of Matsoua and reawaken the political passion of the Lari in 1956. Both Bernard Kolélas, prime minister of Congo at the time of the democratic collapse, and Frédéric Bitsangou (see Chapter 10) have capitalized on Matsoua's legacy in more recent times.

Another more clearly religious sect that took on a political meaning was that of the N'Zambie Bougie. This sect was launched by one Zepherin Lassy in July 1948, at which time Lassy claims to have been "visited by the Holy Spirit." Lassy had a charismatic personality; a varied professional background, including a stint as a soldier in World War II; and much experience traveling in Europe and Africa. Membership in his sect grew slowly, and its existence did not come to the attention of colonial authorities until 1953 (Gauze 1973: 18). A large part of the sect's success owes to Lassy's sponsorship by Félix Tchicaya, Moyen-Congo's deputy to the French National Assembly after 1946. Tchicaya paid for Lassy's maintenance and financed the construction of his first chapel in the Kouilou region. Lassy was essentially a clever conman who convinced his followers of his ability to perform miracles while collecting monetary donations from them in return (19). The theological doctrine of the cult had a Christian basis, but blended in local elements and suggested that Lassy himself was a prophet. Lassy called upon followers to shun local fetishes and to follow an ethical code based on the Bible and Koran. Thus, the religious content of the doctrine was not dissimilar to that of the much better known Kimbangouist sect in Belgian Congo, which had itself spread to French Congo in the late 1930s.

The political significance of the N'Zambie Bougie sect lay in the need for the various local politicians to mobilize the population of the Kouilou region for electoral purposes. From 1953 to 1956 Tchicaya patronized Lassy's cause and Lassy repaid the former by urging his followers to support Tchicaya in his electoral bids. This support was critical to Tchicaya in his bid to remain Moyen-Congo's representative to the French Assembly in the elections of January 1956. In this contest, Tchicaya managed to beat his nearest rival by only 2,000 votes in an election that brought over 154,000 to the polls (Gauze 1973: 21). Later in the same year, Lassy decided to withdraw his support for Tchicaya and to throw it behind another Vili politician, Stéphane Tchitchellé (Gauze 1973: 38; Bernault 1996: 274). This act of political realignment both recorded and hastened Tchicaya's eclipse as an important Congolese politician. Tchitchellé thereafter continued to rely on the N'Zambie Bougie as an important base of local support.

Aside from these two important religio-political movements in Congo, each with a distinctive ethnoregional base, a number of other such movements have appeared in colonial times. Kimbangouism was brought to Congo Republic by a certain Simon-Pierre M'Padi, who claimed to be the heir of Kimbangou. There the religion became known as Kakism, or N'Gounzism, and was practiced by many Bakongo. Yet another fascinating cult, the *fétiche Ngol,* celebrated the power of General de Gaulle while incorporating rituals designed to counteract the force of evil spells. While this movement holds great interest as a sociological phenomenon, political actors were apparently not able to bend it to their purposes (Bernault 1996: 187–195). A great number of other such cults became popular in Congo during the 1940s and afterwards, but none had the political significance of Matsouanism or N'Zambie Bougie.

Two further features of late colonial political movements may be discussed together: personalistic politics and ethnoregional patterns of political support. What links the two phenomena is that ethnic and regional groups sought to identify "big men" to represent their interests in the national political institutions and in the (French) metropolitan institutions. Since no great ideological issues divided Congo's early politicians, the political parties that they created never came to represent distinctive ideological positions. On the most obvious ideological issue that might have divided them—the pace of decolonization—there was never serious division; for instance, all parties enthusiastically supported an affirmative vote in the referendum on the French Community (Gauze 1973, chapter 7). In this regard the psychological effects of colonization were entirely successful. Instead, all of Congo's politicians started with an ethnic or regional base of support. Contests among politicians of the same ethnic group or region depended chiefly on their charisma, articulation, and confidence. Colonial authorities sought to manipulate these choices, but their efforts sometimes backfired, as in the case of Matsoua. Once an ethnic or regional basis of support was established, individual politicians sought to maintain it while also seeking alliances with other ethnic and regional leaders, trying always to keep them in a subordinate position. Or, with a secure ethnic or regional base, a politician might assay an ideological position designed to appeal across such parochial lines of social cleavage.

Congo's two earliest political leaders each emerged with an ethnic base, and neither ever managed to gain substantial influence in the rival ethnic communities. One, Tchicaya, counted on the solid support of the Vili people and subsidiary support of other southern peoples, especially in Kouilou. Tchicaya, a nephew of the contemporary Malongo (Moukoko 1999: 332), came from an elite Vili family in Libreville, Gabon, and acquired higher education in Senegal prior to becoming an accountant and journalist. After fighting with the Free French in World War II, Tchicaya became the deputy for Gabon and Moyen-Congo in the French Assembly. He was reelected to the same post, each time with a narrower margin, in 1951 and 1956. He only founded his political party, the Parti Progressiste Congolaise (PPC) in 1946, after his first election. Until 1957, the PPC was the local affiliate of the transterritorial party of Félix Houphouet-Boigny, the Rassemblement Démocratique Africain (RDA). Tchicaya began to lose support rapidly in the mid-1950s when it was perceived that he had been "bought" by the French administration and had also lost touch with his local base while residing permanently in Paris (Bernault 1996: 210; Gauze 1973: 4, 18). When his party failed completely in the 1957 territorial assembly elections, Tchicaya was replaced by Tchitchellé. The RDA then sought a new local affiliate.

Congo's other early important politician, Jacques Opangault, had a parallel ethnic base among the Mbochi people in northern Congo. Both the older, official accounts (Gauze 1973: 1–2) and the more modern ones (Bernault 1996: 179–180) described Opangault and his Mouvement Socialiste Africaine (MSA) party as being primarily ethnically based.[25] Indeed, Opangault emerged on the political scene as a founding member of the Comité Mbochi, a self-help organization for the northern Congolese group, in 1938. This committee's first important political action was to vigorously protest the replacement of the Mbochi language with Lingala, a vehicular language of northern Congo, by the Catholic vicariate of Brazzaville (Bernault 1996: 179; Gauze 1973: 2).[26] That the committee chose *this* issue as the one on which to confront local authorities reveals much about its ethnic orientation. Yet in the 1952 elections for the territorial assembly, Opangault, the strongest candidate in his party, chose to run in the Brazzaville circumscription against the PPC candidates (Gauze 1973: 16). This was a (failed) effort to try to capture the Lari and Bakongo vote of Pool for his party.

The political strength of the Lari people was reawakened by another charismatic personality, Félix Youlou, Congo's eventual first president. As with the other politicians, Youlou's first task was to secure his own ethnic base of support. Fortunately for him, his most important rival in this regard was the long-dead Matsoua. Since Youlou received his secondary education outside of Congo, he had to reinvent himself as an authentic Lari once ordained as a priest in 1946. As Bernault brilliantly shows (1996: 244–246), he did this by connecting himself with various Lari cultural organizations and by reaching out to the Matsouanists after returning to Brazzaville. Having consolidated that base, Youlou next successfully undertook to establish his credentials as a scholar of broader Congolese and African customs and politics (246–248). This Youlou accomplished without alienating his base, essentially posing in different forms before different audiences. Youlou then burst dramatically onto the political stage in 1956 as a candidate for deputy in the French Assembly.[27] For the first time since the death of Matsoua, the Lari were united behind a living candidate. With his base established Youlou immediately sought to broaden the appeal of his party among all of the country's ethnic groups (Gauze 1973: 31; Bernault 1996: 276–277). In November 1956 he was elected mayor of Brazzaville. In the following year, his Union Démocratique pour la Défense des Interêts Africains (UDDIA) party eclipsed the PPC in the territorial assembly elections, winning a near-majority twenty-two seats in the forty-five seat body. Even the waning local European party had rallied to the UDDIA.

The pattern of the voting in these crucial elections reflected all of the patterns described above: the importance of ethnic and regional loyalties, the dominant role of personalities, and the significance of alliances made among rival politicians. The UDDIA prevailed in the Bakongo and Lari circumscriptions of Pool, Djoué, and Bouenza, which were Youlou's base. It also prevailed in Kouilou where Tchitchellé had abandoned the PPC in its dying hours and aligned himself with Youlou and the UDDIA. The MSA prevailed strongly in the Mbochi region of Likouala-Mossaka and in the Téké region of Alima-Lefini, a region neighboring Opangault's fiefdom. The far northern districts of Likouala and Sangha also went to the MSA, though less definitively. The MSA's chief rivals here, however, were not the UDDIA, but local parties. Prevailing in Niari was another local politician, Simon Kikounga N'Got, who had created his own party, the Groupement pour le Progrès Economique et Social (GPES). Kikounga N'Got had a last-minute conversion and switched his allegiance from the UDDIA to the MSA, believing that Opangault would emerge as the leader of the territorial assembly (Bernault 1996: 263). Thus we see that each of the two major parties was animated by personalities far more than ideals, that each had a distinctive ethnoregional base, and that each depended on alliances with other, less important, regional leaders. The three political groups represented by Opangault, Tchicaya, and Youlou in 1956 had been reduced to two.[28]

One can observe the other three features of late colonial politics most clearly in the final years before independence. This period was one in which Youlou sought first to seize, then to consolidate, his grip on power. His main tactics were the co-optation of rival political figures, and the manipulation of the rules to reinforce his control of political institutions.

A dangerous setting for the deployment of such tactics was created by the extremely even division of political forces following the March 1957 territorial assembly elections. After these elections the MSA-GPES alliance held twenty seats, and the PPC one, to the twenty-two held by the UDDIA, with two further seats held by independents. When the independents joined with the MSA, GPES, and PPC in an alliance in May, they held the narrowest possible margin of one seat. Given the split nature of the Assembly, however, the colonial governor opted for a unity government with equal ministries for each side. The governor himself was president of the government council, but Opangault became vice president, as leader of the largest bloc, under the terms of the Loi-Cadre (Overseas Reform Act) of 1956 (Gauze 1973: 35). The tensions were exacerbated later in the year when an MSA deputy from Niari, Georges Yambot, defected from his own party to the UDDIA, giving Youlou's forces a majority in the Assembly. According to Bernault (1996: 278), Yambot had been "bought" by Youlou's European allies. Again the colonial governor intervened to keep peace between the parties.

The following January 1958 saw the first in a series of rounds of political violence in Congo related to the UDDIA-MSA standoff (Bazenguissa-Ganga 1997: 59–64). Like so many subsequent ethnopolitical confrontations, all of these took place in Congo's burgeoning urban areas, where representatives of differing ethnoregional constituencies came together.[29] Youlou and several delegates from the UDDIA traveled to Dolisie, capital of Niari region, to spread his political message and consult with local supporters. There the UDDIA delegation was attacked by partisans of Kikounga N'Got, sparking a larger confrontation between the partisans of the UDDIA and GPES. At least one person was killed and several others wounded (Gauze 1973: 40; Bernault 1997: 279).

The following year political attention was focused on the referendum to decide Congo's participation in the French Community, but violence followed in the aftermath. In September 1958, the Congolese voted overwhelmingly (by 99 percent!) to join the French Community as an autonomous state.[30] In November, the territorial assembly met in the (then) capital of Pointe Noire to form the new government. Since this spelled Youlou's investiture as prime minister, however, the MSA supporters were desperate to stop the event. Accordingly, MSA and PPC leaders in Pointe Noire recruited local supporters to disrupt the first seating of the Assembly of the new republic on 28 November. Only the intervention of local police and gendarmes allowed the Assembly to proceed, after the hall was cleared. After a short debate, the Assembly unanimously declared Congo a republic and Youlou was invested as the prime minister based on his one-vote margin. After calling on the governor, Youlou and his supporters then left Pointe Noire for Brazzaville, where they proceeded to establish a new seat of government for the country. Meanwhile, back in Pointe Noire, three days of fighting between the two sides left five dead and twenty others seriously wounded (Bernault 1996: 280–282; Gauze 1973: 64–65).

Although the MSA acquiesced in the transfer of the government to Brazzaville, tensions remained high. The following February 1959 saw yet another round of violence, this time between Mbochi partisans of the MSA and Youlou supporters in Brazzaville. This time the outcome was some one hundred dead and two hundred wounded (Gauze 1973: 69–70). For the third straight time, MSA or GPES partisans initiated the fighting, and each time Youlou's supporters responded. Each time the scale of the violence escalated. After this third round of ethnopolitical confrontations, Opangault was arrested.

Youlou's manipulation of the rules to his own political advantage became evident in the next set of Congolese elections. By this point, the government was well enough under his control that he could determine the timing and manner of elections. The ethnopolitical fighting in February 1959, however, was launched by MSA militants, who demanded fresh elections for the now autonomous republic. Youlou finally obliged in June 1959, after reorganizing the electoral district boundaries and allocation of seats to the advantage of his party. He also increased the size of the Assembly from forty-five to sixty-one. In the poll, his UDDIA took fifty-one seats to only ten for the MSA, these being the only two remaining parties. Under the rules and districts of the 1957 elections, the UDDIA would have won only thirty-one seats to fourteen for the MSA. The UDDIA's majority benefited tremendously from the electoral rules, as revealed by the fact that it had won only 58 percent of the popular vote (Gauze 1973: 75). Opangault had remained under arrest for his role in the earlier violence during this time. At a later time, when his power was consolidated, Youlou again changed the rules, ramming through a constitutional amendment in March 1961 that allowed him to extend his presidential term. The constitutional changes also made the regime much more presidentialist (100 and 103).

Ironically, the first major challenge to Youlou's rule after the 1959 elections actually came from Matsouanist hardliners. Youlou used the episode to further consolidate his power. Although a great many Lari initially, and then a great number of non-Mbochi Congolese of many other ethnic groups, had rallied to the UDDIA, a hard core of Matsouanists continued to avoid all collaboration with the state, including the payment of taxes. From late June through August, Youlou moved to suppress their movement and to bring them into conformity with state regulations. In August, the legislature granted Youlou's request for exceptional powers and for the declaration of a state of emergency (Gauze 1973: 78). During the same time, Opangault was released from prison and Youlou made an effort to reconcile with the MSA; the party received two posts in Youlou's next cabinet. In November 1959 Youlou orchestrated a surprise move to have the Assembly elect him president of the republic, which it did unanimously.

Youlou's behavior over the next three years became a dismal model for the practice of politics throughout the postcolonial era. Before the name of Mobutu was widely known, Youlou was brilliantly practicing the technique of co-opting his political enemies through the cycle of arrest, rehabilitation, and corruption. This process unfolded in turn for Opangault and then for Kikounga N'Got (Bernault 1996: 308–309). Opangault was eventually made vice president of Congo in 1961 and then, as his influence waned, was later demoted to minister of public works. Kikounga N'Got was put under arrest for four months in 1960. Then, he was named minister of economic affairs in January 1961, and finally minister of labor in May 1963. Given the impossibility of regaining their former political stature, each leader consoled himself with the not inconsiderable monetary benefits that ministerial posts brought. Once Youlou was sure that Tchitchellé's influence was marginalized in 1960, he was stripped of his important post at the interior ministry and given a harmless one as minister of foreign affairs (Gauze 1973: 102). While he co-opted the leaders of other ethnoregional constituencies in this way, Youlou was packing the police, customs, and education services with his fellow Lari coethnics (Gauze 1973: 138–139), trying to create a longer-term basis of power.

Meanwhile, Youlou continued to consolidate power in both the legal and popular arenas in the name of "national unity." Like many other African leaders since, Youlou proclaimed this principle to be a reflection of authentic African political culture, as opposed to the competitive politics practiced in the West. In March 1961, Youlou staged a presidential election with himself as the sole candidate, winning 97 percent of the vote. This move certainly assured the appearance of an overwhelming popular mandate, but also helped Youlou achieve a personal cult of power extending beyond that of his own party. In August 1962, Youlou declared the three existing political parties (UDDIA, MSA, and PPC) dissolved and proclaimed the impending formation of a single-party state. By that time, the handful of MSA deputies had rallied to the unity government and had ceased effective opposition. When the Assembly finally adopted this principle as a law the following year, it was Opangault—symbolically—who made the speech in favor of the adoption of the momentous measure (Bernault 1996: 309). The Congolese political class clearly had no conception of a "loyal opposition" at this juncture, or later.

Hence, the period of late colonial politics in Congo one again reshaped the country's culture without destroying what had come before. The social hierarchy and the cult of the big man that prevailed in precolonial times persisted, and the essential alienation of political authorities from the needs of the people, so characteristic of the early colonial period, was scarcely bridged. A new set of political patterns not at odds with those of the earlier eras grew out of the authoritarian patterns of the past. Among these were the following: the apotheosis of the ethnoregional big man in the context of a heterogeneous new polity; the struggle for preeminence among such big men at a higher level of politics through the instruments of patronage and co-optation; the manipulation of legal rules to concentrate power in the person of the president in the name of national unity; and the paradoxical extension of social favors to one's own ethnic or regional community. Such patterns of politics were a constant of the entire postcolonial period, including the portion that following the transition of 1991. The durability of the political patterns established in Congo during the Youlou era explains why so many analysts began with this period, even if their roots can be traced to earlier periods.

To consider several counterfactual questions at this point can be revealing: Could the early political leaders of Congo in the postwar period have played a different game than they did? Might they have created a national political movement rather than ethnic and regional ones? Might they have shunned the co-optation of messianic movements for political purposes? Might they have created parties founded on ideological principles rather than their personal charisma? A fair review of this historical period suggests that such alternatives would not have been easy, but also that such an approach was not tried. Certainly such West African figures as Kwame Nkrumah and Sékou Touré made much stronger efforts in these regards; they sought with some success to imbue the parties that they created with ideological commitments that went beyond their own ethnic groups and personalities. The case of Julius Nyerere and Tanzania also suggests that the example of inspiring leadership can blunt, if not transform, the authoritarian and "tribalist" instincts of a unintegrated, nondemocratic, and ethnically rooted political culture. Whatever their other postindependence problems, neither Ghana, nor Guinea, nor Tanzania has yet seen a civil war or widespread ethnic violence. In Congo, by contrast, figures like Matsoua rooted their appeals in specific ethnic communities, rather than trying to forge a national consciousness. Likewise, President Youlou, traditionalist that he was, made little effort to transform Congo's political culture. Rather, he manipulated the population's occult beliefs and ethnic consciousness as political tools (despite finally reining in the Matsouanists). The large crowds that overthrew Youlou were more politically progressive than their president, even if some were equally motivated by ethnicity.

Still, it must be acknowledged that more democratically minded leaders would have found it a daunting challenge to transform Congo's authoritarian culture sufficiently for democracy to take root right away. Such a transformation was achieved nowhere in Africa during the late 1950s or 1960s. It is telling that Matsoua sought to create a secular and political movement, with some nationalist potential, but his followers transformed it into a Lari ethnic movement drawing on supernatural, occult beliefs. Moreover, Congolese leaders of a later period *did* try to create such movements and parties like those of Nkrumah and Touré, but with only limited success. This suggests that the political culture of the masses will often trump elite efforts to create a new political consciousness. The structure of political culture, though it exists only in the consciousness of a people, is remarkably durable and resistant. Such cultures can be transformed, but only with great and sustained effort.

The Postcolonial Period

There was a further accretion of new, hybridized political habits during the postcolonial period, as well. These were generally variations on the politico-cultural themes established by Youlou. Four important variations on the established themes are discussed in the following four chapters. The first is the patron-client economic relationship that grew up across the hierarchy linking the rulers and the ruled. For now, let us simply observe that the economic dependency of the political class is a state of mind, a psychological condition, as well as a material one. These relations became part of the country's elemental political economy, as discussed in the next chapter. Second, Congo continued to experience ethnoregional politics, though the course of the confrontations involved was hardly predictable. The myriad different forms of ethnic and regional politics of Congo are shot through with paradox and contingency. Third, the militarization of Congolese politics only appeared somewhat later, in 1968, but it continued without interruption through the end of the single-party period. The aspect of military control in Congolese politics echoes most directly the early colonial period, for control through military force was most evident then. Fourth, the Congolese dependence on France was a psychological, as well as an economic, phenomenon. Virtually nowhere in the world except in the consciousness of Francophone Africans does France remain a great power. France's enduring status in the minds of the Congolese remains a psychological condition from which they still require liberation.

It is useful to mention a number of other politico-cultural features of the Congolese polity that emerged during the post-Youlou years. This permits a picture of Congolese politics in the 1963–1990 period to emerge, which will be fleshed out in the next four chapters.

The great constant of the Congolese polity for the first thirty years of its postcolonial history is monopartyism. This reality is so apparent that it is usually taken for granted. Although the experience of monopartyism was certainly common in postcolonial Africa, it was not everywhere so rigorously required. In many other African states, the nominal democracies bequeathed by the departing colonials lasted longer, or a revival of multipartyism occurred sooner. In Congo, however, the practice of the single party was a reality from 1963 until the national conference in 1991. This outward institution mirrors the inner need of the Congolese to realize unity amidst their diversity in an environment of perpetual economic scarcity. Crystallizing into a psychological reality during the last two years of the Youlou regime was a distinctive politico-psychological complex that would define politics for the next generation of Congolese. This complex had a number of related elements including: a cult of youth that celebrated the right of the younger generation to seize control of the state and build a new political destiny;[31] a rhetorical—but scarcely real—commitment to the welfare of urban dwellers and particularly urban workers; a radical outlook in domestic and foreign affairs that emphasized the possibilities for domestic social transformation and change in the world system; a momentary deference to those with formal education and intellectuals (or intellectual posers); and a belief that the potential for economic development and prosperity depended chiefly on the action of the state. The cult of youth and the urban bias evident in Congo reflected to some extent a demographic reality of the country: it had become heavily urbanized early in its history, and relatively well educated—and politically sensitized—males made up an important section of the urban population. Psychological dependence on the state derives heavily from the impacts of colonialism, the role of the centralized state in France's political consciousness, and the fact that Brazzaville was the administrative capital for all of AEF. In his survey of 141 prominent personalities from the 1946–1963 period, Bazenguissa-Ganga found sixty-five administrative assistants and forty-eight teachers, but only five traditional chiefs (1997: 32).

The rapid crystallization of this politico-psychological complex goes far to explain the sudden, dramatic overthrow of Youlou during three days in August 1963, known as *les trois glorieuses*. Of course this complex was closely linked, too, with the nature of the postcolonial economy. Unindustrialized and antimarket Congo produced nothing like the number of jobs needed to absorb the swelling ranks of secondary school leavers who flooded the urban centers in the early 1960s. Moreover those absorbed into the state administrative services and in the public companies (like the CFCO) were thoroughly unionized and radicalized (Bazenguissa-Ganga 1997: 37–39). While these social forces caused the political environment to become highly charged, Youlou pursued a conservative line in foreign policy, notably one supporting the most reactionary forces in the Congo-Kinshasa civil conflicts, and an anticommunist line at home, while his ministers indulged in flagrant conscious consumption (Bazenguissa-Ganga 1997: 63–70; Gauze 1973: chapter 16). Sékou Touré's visit to Brazzaville in June 1963 proved to be the spark in the powder keg. Two months after his visit, the main union bosses all called for a general strike to begin on 13 August. For good measure, these union leaders went to a local cemetery to make a pact to "place themselves under the protection of the ancestors" (Bazenguissa-Ganga 1997: 72). The general strike led to arrests, to the killing of some demonstrators by police, and finally to street riots and mass protests that forced Youlou to resign on 15 August 1963, the third anniversary of Congo's independence.

The ages, backgrounds, and manner of appointment of the cabinet members of the first post-Youlou government reveal much about Congolese political culture at this time. The provisional government was chosen in front of a public crowd, filled with applauding unionists (Bazenguissa-Ganga 1997: 85–86). Those chosen included Alphonse Massamba-Débat (prime minister), forty-two years old, a former teacher; Germain Bicoumat (interior), then fifty-seven, a former CFCO accountant; David-Charles Ganao (foreign affairs), thirty-five, a former school inspector; Bernard Galiba (health, labor, and education), a young (age unknown) medical doctor; Pascal Lissouba (agriculture, etc.), thirty-two, with a doctorate in agricultural engineering; Paul Kaya (economics; planning, mines, and transport) thirty, with a doctorate in economics; and Edouard Ebouka-Babackas (finance and budget, and posts), thirty, a former customs inspector.[32] The last four of these had received their higher education in France, but all were well educated except Bicoumat; all had been public servants. By the end of the year, Massamba would be president of the republic and Lissouba would be prime minister, while Bicoumat, the oldest and least educated, rapidly lost influence.

Over his five years in power, Massamba never managed to satisfy the political demands of his more radical supporters, despite the perpetual leftward drift of the succession of governments he assembled. Meanwhile, the main beneficiaries of his economic policies were members of the political class lucky enough to receive official posts. By the end of 1963, Massamba had created a new, state-affiliated party, the Mouvement National de la Révolution (MNR).[33] A youth wing of the party, the Jeunesse of the MNR (JMNR), was created and remained highly influential in politics throughout Massamba's reign. The JMNR even gained de facto control over the army in 1965. By the end of 1964, the independent labor unions, notably the Christian-based one, were absorbed into a new, state-organized labor movement, the Confédération des Syndicats Congolais (CSC) (Gauze 1973: 160). In the economic sector, many foreign-owned businesses were nationalized, and an organization for the control and expansion of the state industrial sector was created. Only in foreign policy did Massamba and Lissouba (as prime minister) exert a moderating influence (161).

The succession of events through which Massamba's power gradually slipped away during the summer of 1968 is long and complicated (Gauze 1973: 165–168; Bazenguissa-Ganga 1997: 133–138). Instead of being felled in a coup d'état, his power was gradually usurped by a special military committee in the midst of complex political crisis. He had come to be opposed, however, by both Marxist forces and conservatives as he tried to follow an

African socialist path, à la Nyerere. Among the most important institutions that opposed him in the end was the radical students union, which had organized a provocative congress in Brazzaville in July. Both radicals and conservatives in the army lost faith in Massamba and began to campaign against him. He remained the nominal president of the republic until finally resigning in disgust on 29 August, having lost real power a month earlier. On his resignation Massamba tried to hand over power to a moderate, southern army officer, August Poignet, but this figure was soon replaced by the far more popular and dynamic Captain Marien Ngouabi.

Like his predecessor, Ngouabi was in many ways a reflection of Congo's evolving political culture. He initially took power in Congo at the age of twenty-nine, reflecting the continuing cult of youth in Congo. Although his training was for service as a military officer, he took that training in France, and he projected himself as an aspiring intellectual.[34] Ngouabi exhibited more charisma than either of his two predecessors, lived quite simply, and enjoyed the admiration of many of his countrymen for his populist habits. For all that, however, he was also a military man who took power illegally, and his actions marked the beginning of long military involvement in Congolese politics.

Ngouabi created a nominally Marxist-Leninist party, the Parti Congolais du Travail (PCT), that came into being on 31 December 1969. The party's main organs, its politburo and central committee, outwardly mirrored those of the Soviet Union's communist party. The country adopted a new official name, the République Populaire du Congo (People's Republic of the Congo), a name that it bore until 1991. The country's flag was changed to an amusing copy of the Soviet flag: a red field with crossed hammer and hoe in the corner. The habit of addressing fellow citizens as *camarade* (comrade) was successfully encouraged, a habit that still existed in 1990. Aspiring members of the PCT were officially supposed to have renounced any religious faith, as well as the belief in traditional fetishes, before joining the party.[35] State control over the economy continued to deepen, and the corporatist mass organizations for youth and labor of the 1960s remained.

In retrospect, however, it is remarkable how little impact the heroic symbols, stirring Marxist rhetoric, and apparent commitment to social egalitarianism really had on Congo's basic political culture. Just as it may be observed that Leninists and Stalinists never created the "Soviet man," Congolese Marxism proved to be no more than a superficial layer covering the ingrained beliefs and habits of previous eras. As in Poland, the Catholic Church remained strong in Congo throughout the Marxist period, even though some priests were arrested and even tortured (Okoko-Esseau 1995). Likewise, practitioners of the nkobi (or ndjobi) cult, whose practices harkened back to use of magic charms by the precolonial Téké community, continued to thrive in the revolutionary environment of 1970s Congo.[36]

Marxism in Congo was much more a perpetuation of existing patterns of authoritarianism in a new guise—even if it paid lip service to egalitarianism—than it was a transformative ideology creating a new social order. As Decalo observed, "for all its radical rhetoric and Ngouabi's stress on ideological militancy and purity, only the superficial, trivial and structural aspects of Marxism were imposed on Congo" (1981: 216).

Not only did Congolese Marxism prove incapable of social transformation under Ngouabi, but it was even more transparently a cover for repressive rule by a clique of northern military officers under the two follow-on regimes of Joachim Yhombi-Opango (1977–1979) and Denis Sassou-Nguesso (1979–1991). One sardonic observer scoffed at the Marxist label for the Congo regimes of this period, dismissing it as "kindergarten fascism" (Wiseman 1990: 605). Even Ngouabi's own demise apparently resulted from inside, ethnic scheming rather than ideological struggle, though the facts of his assassination in 1977 remain unclear. Whatever the case, his successor, Yhombi, lacked his charisma, his self-discipline, and his popularity with ordinary people. He also lacked anything other than the most superficial commitment to scientific socialism, which became one excuse for his (bloodless) overthrow in a meeting of the PCT politburo in 1979. On his demise, Sassou became the third and final northern military officer to rule Congo before the 1991 transition. Although his rise was interpreted at the time as a reinvigoration of the Marxist experiment, Sassou was (and remains) a warlord politician without any great vision for his country. His taste for expensive French tailoring and champagne belie any commitment to ordinary Congolese, and his rise only confirmed the eclipse of revolutionary potential in Congo.

*   *   *

In this fashion Congolese political culture has accrued over the course of the last several centuries. Returning to the precolonial era, social hierarchy and the authoritarian rule of monarchs are the most evident aspects of the political culture, despite Vansina's emphasis on putative social equality. In the colonial era, the imposition of a deadly, alien, and crushingly powerful state atop existing political practices occurred. Locals were drawn into the colonial system (for purposes of keeping costs down) and trained in the methods of bureaucratic rule, unconsciously absorbing the habits of authoritarian control. When this elite launched their own political careers in the late colonial period, they employed the most functional forms of social mobilization at their disposal: appeals to followers on the basis of ethnic kinship, potential regional advantage, and solidarity with supernatural beliefs. All of these patterns continued unabated in the postcolonial period, despite the radical efforts to eliminate them and unify the country around a nonsectarian vision. Instead, the revolutionary movements in Congo simply imbued the urban and formal sector classes with a profound sense of economic entitlement without creating any economic basis for the realization of the promises made. To contain these restless social forces, state authorities strived to maintain their monopoly of the instruments of force. They also created a network of repression to identify and neutralize those who would seek to overthrow the ruling cliques of northern officers. Meanwhile, the same authorities quieted the political ambitions of emergent ethnic and regional leaders through access to sinecures and state offices, offering the opportunity to divert public money to private use.

■ Congolese Political Culture and the Democratic Transition

This section investigates the impact of the transition to multiparty rule on Congolese political culture. The main instrument of the transition was the national conference that took place between 25 February and 10 June 1991. The conference marked a critical juncture in the evolution of Congolese political culture and offered a rare opportunity for the emergence of new, democratic elements. Mounting political and economic crises forced President Sassou to allow the conference. This analysis draws on the conclusions about political culture reached in the first section of this chapter, and takes account of the outline of political culture as it evolved over time.

The final crisis that led up to surrender of the Sassou regime to forces calling for political change had both political and economic dimensions (Clark 1993). Although the economic crisis in Congo was long-standing, having been initiated by the collapse of oil prices in 1985, the timing of the crisis makes clear the influence of world events outside of Congo. Crises can endure for long periods of time, and the crisis in Congo Republic probably would not have led to a crystallization of the political opposition in 1990 were it not for the end of the Cold War and the collapse of communism in Eastern Europe. Nonetheless, it was a general strike by Congolese workers in September 1990 that finally drove the Sassou regime to accept the idea of a national conference (Bazenguissa-Ganga 1997: 364–367). The strike leaders called for economic relief for workers, as well as political reform. These actions both reflected and reinforced the Congolese culture of looking to the state as a source of prosperity and welfare. Further, they created a false belief among Congolese workers that political reform would lead to a simultaneous improvement in their standards of living.

The conference did have significant potential to break the cycle of political culture in which violence and oppression reinforced an authoritarian culture. First, the conferences in all of the Francophone African countries that began democratic experiments in the early 1990s gave rise to new, apparently vital institutions of civil society. Second, they created an environment for the enunciation of new political norms and the public commitment of the political class to new modes of political behavior. Accordingly, the potential of the conferences to create long-term changes in political culture was far more important than their immediate role as instruments of transition (Clark 1998c). One Francophone African was particularly eloquent in expressing the hope represented by the conferences, referring to the conference phenomenon as "an unexpected breach in the wall of necessity, of determinisms and of fatalisms, which opens the possibility of freedom of action. It is not, therefore, a matter of fantasy, but rather the exercise of that which is the essence of humanity, the capacity for renewal" (Boulaga 1993: 167). In the case of Congo, the conference did prove to be an instrument of transition, as in Benin. Elsewhere, in Gabon, Togo, and Zaire, manipulative rulers stymied their work and prevented the conferences from becoming sovereign (Clark 1998c: 110). Thus, the conference dismantled the outward institutions of the single-party era, put in place a transitional regime that stripped Sassou of real power, began the process of constitutional reformation, and set a timetable for elections.

Yet most Congolese observers were disappointed in the results of the conference, precisely because it did not succeed in "cleaning the mentalities so impregnated with the culture of the previous system" (Nsafou 1996: 85). At the end of the conference, the Catholic prelate who had heroically presided over it declared, "The change, the break with the past has not taken place, the dream nurtured by thousands of men and women has not seen the slightest realization in daily life" (Kombo 1992: 52, cited in Okoko-Esseau 1995: 158).[37] Meanwhile, the keenest student of Congolese political culture later characterized the conference in a chapter title as "the disorder that restored the former order" (Bazenguissa-Ganga 1997: 349; see also Weissman 1993). These judgments were reached despite some impressive achievements of the conference that owed particularly to the sensitive leadership of Monsignor Ernest Kombo. Among the achievements were a public confession by Sassou of his misdeeds, the public embrace of Sassou and former president Yhombi, and a ritual (and literal) washing of the hands by the important political leaders in a public ceremony at the end of the conference.

The perpetuation of Congo's existing political culture was manifest in a quite a number of ways in the conference. First, the conference was almost entirely an affair for urban elites and specifically those involved in politics, that is, the political class. As soon as the idea of the conference was vetted, new political parties—and most with very few real members—began springing up in Brazzaville like mushrooms. Some sixty-seven of these participated in the conference, each represented by eight delegates. Hence, delegates from parties represented nearly one-half of the total number of delegates, some twelve hundred. Other delegates represented some forty scientific associations, ninety civil society organizations, eleven non-governmental associations (all represented by two members each), and four religious confessions (seven members each). The remainder represented labor unions, national institutions, state companies, the civil service, international organizations, the press, and other such groups. A scant five delegates represented the National Chamber of Commerce and Agriculture of Congo (Bazenguissa-Ganga 1997: 375–376). Thus private business and peasants were virtually unrepresented while the political class dominated all aspects of the proceedings. Even the civil society groups were mostly very recent creations of the politically minded.[38]

Second, the conference did not mark any great reduction in the ethnoregional aspect of Congolese politics. Bazenguissa-Ganga (1997: 380) noted that, at the end of each day, the groups from various regions and ethnic groups would meet under the direction of a community leader. More generally, the politics of the conference was partly a three-way contest among leaders from Pool region, former PCT stalwarts from the north (mostly Mbochi), and non-Lari southern groups collectively. The constitution of the conference's presidium (headed by André Milongo, a Mukongo from Pool) and executive structures represented a victory for the residents of Pool, heavily represented there, as did the ultimate selection of Milongo as the transitional prime minister (390–394). Subsequent events demonstrated the exasperating resilience of ethnoregional consciousness among the Congolese.

Third, there was also a generational struggle at the conference between the old guard, who gained entry into the political field in the 1960s, and a new generation. At the beginning the younger members of the conference and their allies among older cadres were active in pushing for the emergence of a new generation. By the end of the conference the forces favoring the new generation had been completely outmaneuvered, as was reflected in the choice of Milongo (b. 1935) and his transitional cabinet (Bazenguissa-Ganga 1997: 398–399). This cabinet featured the notable presence of many 1960s-era politicians in its key posts. Milongo's leading contender for the transitional leadership job was Pascal Lissouba, another who had begun his career in the 1960s.

Finally, the confrontation with the past at the conference was very selective. Some sins of the past, particularly those committed in the single-party era, were paraded before the public, but others were left buried. Most notably, Sassou was implicated in the assassination of the popular Ngouabi, and Lissouba connected with the murders of three southern politicians in 1965, while sins committed under Youlou were not mentioned. More broadly, there was an effort to rewrite Congolese history to the advantage of the then-triumphant southern politicians (Bazenguissa-Ganga 1997: 388–390).

Even those things that united the delegates reflected Congo's enduring political culture. Interestingly, all of the opposition forces insisted that Congo's new leadership must be technocratic, unlike the political barons and military men of the past. And indeed, no military personnel figured in the conference presidium or in Milongo's cabinet. This reflected the great esteem endowed upon those with formal education in the Congolese political class. Likewise, the selection of Kombo resonated with the deep religiosity of the Congolese, elite and common. Kombo's deployment of religious-style rituals of confession, absolution, and reconciliation were among the most helpful aspects of the conference because they were understood at a deep emotional level by all strata in Congolese society. Some, however, perceived them to be not Catholic rituals around which most Congolese could unite, but crypto-Kongolese rituals designed to celebrate the reemergence of that ethnic group (Bazenguissa-Ganga 1997: 390). After the conference, in the multiparty era, many Congolese perceived that their politicians continued to rely on fetishes to augment their political power, and they sometimes posed as messianic figures as a method of drawing political support (Gruénais, Mbambi, and Tonda 1995).

The failure of the political class to transform Congo's political culture at the national conference, despite the magnificent example provided by Monsignor Kombo, boded badly for the country's future. The moment represented a crucial moment at which Congo could have been pointed down a different path. At that moment, it was up to the country's elite to make a more significant break with the past, and begin the slow process of transforming the consciousness of the mass of Congolese. Could they have done otherwise? There is every reason to believe that they certainly could have done better. In addition to Kombo, President Sassou also behaved in a patriotic manner at this juncture, allowing the conference to convene, establish its sovereign rights, and to dismantle the old regime. Despite the common interpretation, he did have other options, as we will see in Chapter 9.

■ The Weight of Political Culture in Congo's Experiment

This section will make a preliminary analysis of the weight of political culture in the failure of Congo's democratic experiment. It compares briefly Congo's political culture with that of other African states that have varying degrees of success with democratization. Chapter 9 of this volume explores the linkage of political culture with other structures of Congolese politics and the impact of the decisions of Congolese leaders on its evolution.

The comparative analysis of African political cultures and democratic outcomes raises questions about the level of variation in historical experience in the key time periods: Were there any essential constants in the precolonial political experiences of African states, despite the breathtaking range of different political arrangements employed then? And was the variation in the colonial experiences of different African states, created by the colonial partition, great enough to explain any of the variation in postcolonial political trajectories? Finally, have postcolonial experiences reinforced or undermined the earlier accretions of political culture in such a way as to fundamentally recondition the prospects for successful democratization?

With regard to precolonial political cultures, historians and anthropologists intensively studying individual cases are certain to be struck by the great range of variation in political practice. Some precolonial societies were acephalous or segmented, while others were highly centralized. This was the case in the equatorial region of precolonial Africa as elsewhere. The question that most interests the political scientist, however, should be the level of variation in any proto-democratic structures of politics during this era. In this regard, scholars have sometimes noticed apparently proto-democratic structures and have sometimes tried to connect them with later political trajectories. A notable example is that of the *kgtola,* or assembly, in the case of Botswana. One anthropologist has observed that traditional Tswana chiefs often relied on votes in the *kgtola* to decide important political matters (Schapera 1970: 190–225). Yet, while such institutions may have put some limits on chiefly power, they "played a veto function at best, and this was not easily done, since those who opposed [the chief] had to fear reprisals from their leader" (Holm 1988: 182). Holm concludes that "the [precolonial] Tswana political systems had little semblance of democracy" (183). I have noted a few other such apparently proto-democratic practices elsewhere (Clark 1997a: 32), but it is clear that these were heavily outweighed by nondemocratic and even tyrannical political patterns in all precolonial African societies. As suggested by Simiyu (1988) and Bayart (1991) there is precious little in African precolonial traditions on which to build a modern democracy, and the egalitarian patterns noted by Vansina (1990) in equatorial Africa were hardly the basis for modern democracy.

The experience of colonial rule in Africa also represents a considerable amount of uniformity, which provides for a competing explanation for the great degree of convergence in the postcolonial experiences of African states. Scholars as ideologically divergent as Mahmood Mamdani (1996) and Crawford Young (1994a) both take the colonial experience as the critical one for all African states. Yet here, there is more evidence that the variation in colonial experiences did in fact point various African states along diverging postcolonial political trajectories. First, there are the deeply troubling cases of Ethiopia and Liberia, both of which Young and Mamdani are loath to mention. Ethiopia was the only contemporary African state to avoid colonialism (except briefly), and yet its patterns of politics are even more undemocratic than the African norm. If colonialism accounts for all of the authoritarianism in Africa, how is this case to be explained? Meanwhile, Liberia, essentially colonized by Americans of African descent at an early date, has hardly fared any better. None of which gainsays the overwhelmingly negative impact of the European colonial experience on the development of African political cultures.

On the issue of variations in the colonial experience and subsequent outcomes, some patterns do stand out. Most notably, those states that experienced the most brutal and dehumanizing modes of colonial rule have had the lowest degree of civil peace since their independence. Civil peace, in turn, is a prerequisite for the evolution of democratic political institutions. These same colonial states experienced the least degree of elite development, especially access to education. The states in question here are those that were colonized by Belgium and Portugal. In the early colonial phase, the Belgian Congo experienced perhaps the single most ghastly and miserable experience of any colony, knowing decades of terror, relentless economic extraction, and constant dehumanization of the population (Hochschild 1998). In the nationalist phase, the Belgians did nothing to prepare their colony for an independence that they scarcely envisioned (Young 1965). As a result, virtually no educated elite existed to take charge of the country's postcolonial institutions. In Rwanda and Burundi, the Belgians were more lightly implanted, as there were many fewer resources to exploit, and their rule took the form of indirect control through the collaboration with the Tutsi in each country. The consensus of academic opinion today, however, is that the rigidification of identity group consciousness in Rwanda by Europeans is primarily responsible for those countries' postindependence nightmares (e.g., Newbury 1988; Mamdani 2001). Similarly, in the Portuguese African colonies the cruelty of colonial rule there seems to be mirrored in the brutality and authoritarianism of the postcolonial polities. Angola and Mozambique endured interminable civil wars, while all three followed a nominally Marxist-Leninist political course. Although Guinea-Bissau and Mozambique have recently begun experimenting with democratic systems, both regimes are fragile in the extreme, and neither has consolidated a democracy.

On the other hand, those colonial states that suffered somewhat less brutal oppression, developed larger elites classes earlier, and had more practice with democratic forms have all had more positive postcolonial experiences. The African states that come to mind in this regard are Ghana and Senegal. The distinctiveness of the Senegalese cases lies in the development of the autonomous four communes of Saint Louis, Dakar, Gorée, and Rufisque, well-known to most Africanists. By 1922, some 18,000 voting African citizens with extensive political and civil rights were residing in these communes (of a population of some 1.2 million). As noted by Coulon, "However limited this experience was in terms of the numbers of people concerned, it clearly had an important impact on Senegalese political life. It fostered the habit of political competition, mobilized social forces . . . around political clans, and, above all, allowed a few Africans to be members of consultative bodies" (1988: 142). While Ghana's democratic background is less impressive, the Gold Coast colony did develop a relatively large, educated elite compared with the Belgian or Portuguese colonies. As a result, Ghana was at the forefront of the independence movement for colonized Africa. Moreover, it hardly seems coincidental that Senegal and Ghana each experienced longer periods of multiparty competition than most of their hinterland neighbors before 1990. In recent years, of course, each has returned to multiparty politics, and each has known an alternation of the parties in power due to the outcomes of well-managed electoral processes.

What then of the intriguing case of Benin, that compares so directly with Congo in so many regards? Benin's colonial experience was neither as brutally harsh as that of Congo nor as "enlightened" as that of Senegal, but was rather somewhere in between. If the degree of difference between the forms of colonialism imposed on Benin and Congo was significant, however, it did not show in the two countries' immediate postcolonial trajectories; as noted above, these were remarkably parallel. Accordingly, one should not attribute the divergence in their political courses since 1991 to these older, and only marginally different, political experiences.

These last observations allow us to come to a conclusion about the overall impact of political culture on the course of recent democratic experiments in Congo and elsewhere: the weight of the past is exceedingly heavy, but it does not *determine* the possibilities for democratic transition or consolidation. Virtually all forms of politics in Congo prior to 1991 were anathema to the kind of civil, open, democratic politics that high-minded persons like Monsignor Kombo hoped his country could develop. There was precious little in the country's past upon which to build in terms of a liberal political consciousness. All of the actors who participated in the national conference, and all of those who subsequently stood in elections for the new offices created by the new constitution, were products of the country's authoritarian past. Yet even those coming from the worst neighborhoods have plenty of choices about how to behave toward others. In Benin, politicians who were the products of an equally harsh political environment have behaved with enough civility for the democratic experiment to continue. The longer it continues, the more political values will likely change. In Congo, by contrast, the politicians gave in to the brutish habits that were so much a part of their past. In so doing, they have reinforced those habits for a new generation. The Kombos of Congo's future can now only await the next window of opportunity for change and reflect on the best strategies for promoting less power-hungry leaders when another such juncture occurs.

■ Notes

1. For one useful definition of the political class in Zaire, see Callaghy (1987: 347 and note 29).

2. Inglehart and Welzel (2005) make a powerful case for this idea.

3. Specifically, the author deploys Bourdieu's concept of "habitus." The author's final chapter is tellingly entitled: "La conférence nationale ou le désourdre qui a restauré l'ordre ancien" ("The National Conference or the Disorder That Restores the Old Order") (Bazenguissa-Ganga 1997: 348).

4. Besides the work examined in this paragraph, on Cuba, see the study of Fernandez (2000), especially chapter 5, where he describes some possibilities for change in political culture.

5. Interestingly, however, as Putnam is concerned with making the point that the new institutions created change in political culture, he stresses in the text that "in the South as in the North, the standing of regional governments in the eyes of their constituents was higher than ever before" (1993: 56). The points made in this paragraph are my interpretations, and not Putnam's.

6. Whatever other historical political experiences the population of northern Italy may have had, these regions experienced over twenty years of fascism between 1922 and 1943, within the living memories of many Italians. One may wonder why this political experience is less relevant to their contemporary political outlook than the sociopolitical practices of the 1100–1300 period.

7. For a similar view about the generational gap in political culture between certain older elites and the youth in Cuba, see Fernandez (2000: 82).

8. Ethiopia and Liberia might be excluded since neither experienced colonialism in the same ways as other European-created African polities. Ethiopia was only briefly occupied by the Italians between 1935 and 1941; Liberia was colonized by free or freed African Americans who returned to Africa beginning in the 1820s to found an independent African state.

9. In fairness to Young, his next sentence reads: "The legacy of the colonial state, however, is far from the sole determinant of political system and process in the era of independence."

10. According to Lemarchand (1970: 59) a mere ten German colonial officials were presiding over the state of Rwanda in the early 1910s. They could exert control over the country because that had the full cooperation of the upper "caste" Tutsi segment of the population. While this situation was exaggerated, it was not unique.

11. Vansina is a true giant in the field of African history, having been at the forefront of the effort to convince his fellow historians that Africa's precolonial history could be gradually pieced together through a combination of documentary evidence of European observers, linguistic evidence, oral testimonies, and archaeological artifacts. He insisted that this initial appointment at the University of Wisconsin be a joint one, however, in history and anthropology. See Vansina's autobiography (1994: 88).

12. The area in question covers the southernmost portions of Cameroon and the Central African Republic, all of the contemporary states of Gabon and Congo Republic, and a major part of the contemporary Democratic Republic of Congo as far south as northern Kasai. Emphasis added.

13. One may be reminded here of Samuel Huntington's argument that Jacksonian America represented one peak in the level of sociopolitical equality in the United States. Of course, de Tocqueville famously made similar observations about US equality in the subsequent decade of the 1840s. One might logically ask, of course, how one could speak of "equality" in a society that actively practiced slavery and denied women the right to vote, among other inequalities.

14. On the Loango kingdom during most of its history, see Martin (1972); on the Kongo kingdom in the seventeenth and eighteen centuries, see Thornton (1983); and on the Tio kingdom after the advent of colonialism, see Vansina (1973). For a

more succinct description of politics and culture of the Tio kingdom going back to the seventeenth century, see Vansina (1969). The expansion and contraction of the empires is recorded in a variety of maps found in all of these works.

15. The fact that Mobutu Sese Seko of Zaire chose to wear a leopard-skin hat can hardly be coincidental and speaks to the continuity of certain cultural symbols from precolonial to postcolonial times.

16. The historians who have studied these kingdoms undoubtedly wish us to take note that the kings often had considerably less capacity to have their decrees actually enforced in the far-flung, often decentralized kingdoms they ruled.

17. These broad brushstrokes of description obscure a huge amount of change, detail, and variation. For instance, Martin describes how the power of the king declined vis-à-vis his own council in the eighteenth century due to the slave trade (Martin 1972: 163).

18. The title of this chapter section is "Was Every Woman a Slave?" (1997: 26). She adds here, "A slave man was an individual made to do a job that a woman would normally do. There is no clearer way to describe the condition of women, slave or free, at the dawn of colonization."

19. This is another precolonial tradition that exists to this day in central Africa. The inverse relationship between monetary exchange and the "transfer" of women from their families to husbands in India and Africa is interesting in this regard.

20. Vansina writes of the Tsayi people in Congo. He reports that of their 135 villages only three remained after the imposition of colonial rule in their region from 1912 to 1916.

21. According to the psychological analysis of Mamdani (2001), writing about a different colonial situation, some colonized people may have developed a secret desire for (counter)genocide toward their rulers.

22. As an example of unintended consequences, one might consider the actions of AEF's governor from 1941 to 1944, the renowned French Guianan Félix Eboué. According to Thompson and Adloff's introduction to Gauze (1973: xvi), Eboué slowed the process of detribalization in Congo and "strengthened indigenous African institutions by upgrading the chieftaincy and Notables." Although intended as administrative reforms to augment local autonomy, such movements strengthened the ethnic consciousness that would later plague Congolese politics.

23. In late May of 1997, in the heated political atmosphere that preceded the aborted election then planned for the following month, I was confronted with Matsoua's continuing political presence first hand. At that time I encountered an elderly man in the Makélékélé neighborhood of Brazzaville wearing a photograph of Matsoua in a tiny frame around his neck on a chain. When I questioned this gentleman about the meaning of the photograph to him, he described it as a kind of amulet and indicated that he wore it as an expression of his political commitment to Matsoua. Further, he suggested that Bernard Kolélas, the most prominent Lari candidate in the election, bore in him the spirit of the deceased Matsoua.

24. According to Bernault, Matsoua also had a (presumably much weaker) following among the Bakongo at large, of which the Lari are a relatively distinctive subgroup.

25. The MSA was affiliated with a metropolitan French socialist party, the SFIO (Section Française de l'Internationale Ouvrière). In her work, Bernault refers to Opangault's party as the SFIO.

26. Thereafter, the party long maintained an anticlerical reputation, which hurt it in Congolese politics (Bernault 1996: 179).

27. Youlou had actually run unsuccessfully for the territorial assembly in 1946, but thereafter maintained his political quietude until the timing was right for his

reemergence in 1956. In the 1956 context, Youlou finished a close third, just behind Tchicaya and then Opangault.

28. A number of paradoxes and nuances of the ethnic and regional dimensions of Congolese politics are further explored in Chapter 5.

29. On the important issue of urbanization in Congo, see the special issue of *Politique Africaine,* no. 31 (October 1988) given the title, "Le Congo: Banlieue de Brazzaville."

30. Congo's formal and full independence from France passed off as a virtual afterthought on 15 August 1960. Oddly, the initiative for the final separation did not come either from Congo or France, but rather unfolded almost automatically as a result of the zeitgeist of colonial liberation then embracing the world.

31. What defines the "youth" in this context is not chronological age, but a political mindset of opposition to the older generation. On this question, and the diverse organizations into which the Congolese youth of the 1960s were divided, see Bazenguissa-Ganga (1997: 79–82).

32. This information is compiled from Bazenguissa-Ganga (1997: 86) and Gauze (1973: 155), while the ages can be found in Decalo, Thompson, and Adloff (1996).

33. It should be noted that the MNR did not legally become the sole legal party until 1966.

34. In a tour of the Ngouabi Museum in Brazzaville that I took in July 1990, the guide was careful to point out Ngouabi's (rudimentary) chemistry equipment and modest library. He assured us that Ngoaubi spent all of his leisure hours reading Marxist theory, as well as science and philosophy.

35. This was far from the case, however, as one might imagine. Many officials of the single-party era believed in the efficacy of magic and supernatural rituals, and some of the "adepts" of occult practices even served as officials of government. See, for example, Tonda (1988, especially 78–79).

36. On the roots of this cult, see Bernault (1996: 193); on the cult's influence in the PCT era, see especially Tonda (1988).

37. Monsignor Kombo repeated this view to me during an interview in late May 1997 and expressed his general disappointment in the comportment of the Congolese political class.

38. For instance, in 1990 Martin Mberi, who was later Lissouba's ruthless minister of interior, created—ironically—a human rights organization that gained representation at the conference.

4

Political Economy and the
Trajectory of Multiparty Politics

Did Congo fail to consolidate its democratic system because of the structural nature of the economy? Alternatively, did Congo fail to consolidate its democracy because of the structural nature of class relations in the country? Did Congo fail to consolidate its democracy because of its economic performance during the years of the democratic experiment? If so, was Congo's economic performance during this time the inevitable outcome of the structure of the economy or was it due to poor economic policies and ineffectual management?

The first section of this chapter reviews some of the most important theoretical literature on the relationship between economic development and democracy. This review orients the subsequent analysis of the relationship between economics and the failure of democracy. The second section describes the development of the Congolese economy and its classes from the late colonial period through the 1980s, that is, up until the eve of the democratic transition. The third section begins by describing Congo's economic performance over the period of the democratic experiment. It then offers an analysis of the extent to which this performance was the result of structural givens and the extent to which it was the result of policies adopted by the government. The final section makes a comparison between Congo and other African states undergoing democratic experiments in the 1990s and then examines the relationship between the forces and events that destroyed Congo's democratic experiment and the country's economic circumstances, underlying and proximate. This analysis permits an overall conclusion about the relationship between Congo's political economy and the outcome of the democratic experiment.

■ Theories of Economic Development
and Democratization

This overview of the theoretical literature on the relationship between development and democracy surveys those issues that are relevant to the Congo case and is composed of four sections. The first examines the general relationship between development and democratization as it has been revealed by systematic analysis at the global level. The second explores the somewhat more specific issues of class and income distribution as predictors of successful democratization. The third examines the impact of economic performance after democratic transitions on the course of democratic experiments. Finally, the fourth section discusses the special problem of democratization for rentier economies, such as those based largely on mineral extraction, of which Congo is a definitive example.

The General Relationship of Development and Democracy

That there exists a relationship between the economic development of states and the tendency to develop or sustain democratic forms of governance is obvious to even the most casual observers. Yet the nature and meaning of that relationship are far less apparent and, indeed, have been matters of great controversy. According to Przeworski et al. (2000: 78–79), since Seymour Martin Lipset first demonstrated the linkage between development and the likelihood of democracy through statistical analysis in 1959, his findings have "generated the largest body of research on any topic in comparative politics." That being the case, there is no prospect that one could meaningfully engage that entire body of theoretical literature here. Fortunately, a number of wonderful summaries of the progressive research on the relationship between development and democracy are available. Two in particular are exploited here: the fine overview produced by Diamond in 1992 of the theoretical literature that followed Lipset's pathbreaking 1959 study, and the systematic study by Przeworski et al., cited above. These two sources provide some of the clearest and most definitive answers to debates generated by those issues.

A first debate about the development-democracy linkage was whether the relationship was in fact a causal one, and, if so, in which direction the causation ran. Is the relationship between development and democracy a spurious one, actually caused by unrelated social variables, or does one lead directly to the other? If the relationship is causal, is it development that causes the subsequent observation of democracy in the relevant states, or is it the reverse? This issue was salient in the 1960s because the pathbreaking study of Lipset had showed only an association. Examining a large number of studies appearing from the late 1960s into the 1970s, however, Diamond (1992: 103–107) presents a number of methodologically precise studies that did demonstrate a causal relationship between development and democracy. Moreover, they showed that it was development that, over time, led to the subsequent appearance and persistence of democracy, and not the reverse. More recent studies confirm the same relationship between these variables using even more rigorous testing (e.g., Inglehart and Welzel 2005). These subsequent studies controlled for a variety of other variables that might have been the actual causes of democracy. Several also introduced a "lag" between the achievement of a certain level of development and the subsequent appearance of democracy. These studies thus showed the progressive impact of development over time, rather than merely capturing a "snapshot" relationship. Finally, the studies introduced a number of intervening variables, examined below.

The relationship was only demonstrated to be a statistical one, rather than an automatic or necessary one. All observers are aware of cases of less developed countries (such as India) that have lasting democracies, and of high income countries (notably several oil producers) that have *never* experimented with democracy. Furthermore, there were a number of other qualifications, some of which become relevant in the Congo case, as we shall see. For instance, there was a certain amount of regional variation. Even Lipset's original study showed regional variation between Europe and Latin America, for instance. Lipset's work showed that more developed European countries were more likely to be democratic than lesser developed European ones, and that more developed Latin American countries were more likely to be democratic than lesser developed Latin American states. As Diamond reinterpreted the data, however, it could also be used to show the ten European dictatorships in Lipset's sample had slightly higher levels of development than five Latin American democracies (1992: 95). Some regional variation across the statistical generalization certainly continues to persist to the present.

A second problem of the development-democracy linkage concerns whether development serves more to generate democratic transitions or democratic consolidation. In the literature on modernization theory that grew out of Lipset's original work, transitions to democracy were often presented as an inevitable by-product of socioeconomic development. But Lipset's most famous summary phrase does not make this connection. In his words, "The more well-to-do a nation, the greater the chances it will *sustain* democracy" (1959: 56; emphasis added). This suggests that development helps states experimenting with democracy consolidate it, however the transition occurred. Likewise, having investigated these relationships carefully, Przeworski et al. find that "wealthy countries tend to be democratic not because democracies emerge as a consequence of economic development under dictatorships but because, however they emerge, democracies are much more likely to survive in affluent societies" (2000: 137). Indeed, among all of the possible causes of democratic survival, these authors find that "per capita income is by far the best predictor of the survival of democracies. Democracies survive in affluent societies whatever may be happening to them. They are brittle in poor countries" (137). This statistical conclusion accords well with intuitive reflection on the trajectories of development and democratization in Asia and Africa.

Democracies did not emerge automatically in such countries as Taiwan or South Korea as they achieved relatively high levels of development. Once democracies did emerge, though, they have survived and indeed prospered. On the other hand, many democratic experiments were launched in Africa at the moment of independence, but most soon failed. Likewise, most of the democratic experiments of the 1990s have either failed outright or faced great difficulties (Villalón and VonDoepp 2005). All of these findings have been recently confirmed in the most sophisticated analysis of the democracy-development linkage to date (Inglehart and Welzel 2005).[1]

A third area of repeated inquiry has concerned the problem of whether development must reach a certain threshold before it could exert any positive impact on the democratic political development of a state. Among the first to be explicit on this issue was Dahl (1971: 67–68), who posited both upper and lower thresholds. Above the upper threshold "the chances of polyarchy [i.e., democracy] . . . are so high that any further increases in per capita GNP . . . cannot affect the outcome in any significant way." Likewise, below the lower threshold "the chances for polyarchy . . . are so slight that differences in per capita GNP or variables associated with it do not really matter" (68). This formulation implies that there is a middle range of development that allows for the possible consolidation of democracy, but does not ensure it.

This issue of thresholds is actually one variety of question related to the broader question of linearity in the relationship of development and democracy. That is, does successful democratic consolidation become progressively more likely as development reaches higher and higher levels? Dahl's early analysis cited above suggests not a straight line, but a series of three steps in an upward direction of likelihood for democratization as development progresses. The work of O'Donnell (1973), however, suggested a far more radical criticism of the model first suggested by Lipset and developed by others. O'Donnell, studying several Latin American cases, argued that a certain form of development—"dependent development"—led in the short term not to democratization, but to dictatorship. This author linked dependent development to the emergence of radical labor movements, which were in turn suppressed by the military governments of Latin America. The political and economic trajectories of the states he studied seemed to confirm this point of view; notably, Argentina, Brazil, and Chile all saw a return to authoritarianism in the 1960s and 1970s after enjoying a period of rising levels of income, education, and health. Diamond appears to have agreed with this assessment in the following summary of his position of this issue:

> The relationship between socioeconomic development and democracy is not unilinear but in recent decades has more closely resembled an "N-

curve"—increasing the chances of democracy among poor and perhaps lower-middle-income countries, neutralizing or even inverting to a negative effect at some middle range of development and industrialization, and then increasing again to the point where democracy becomes extremely likely above a certain high level of economic development. (1992: 109)

The sophisticated tests of Przeworski et al. (2000), however, do not bear out this thesis, although they do point out that the relationship between development and democratic consolidation cannot logically be "linear" in the strict sense.[2] Przeworski et al. argue that the cases of Argentina and Uruguay were essentially anomalies (2000: 99–101). They also point out that these two countries are the only ones with annual per capita incomes over US$4,000 to have experienced a transition from democracy to dictatorship between 1951 and 1990. The results of their comprehensive test of the relationship between per capita income and the incidence of transition from democracy to authoritarianism in all states over the same period provide convincing evidence for their claims. The table below shows that with every incremental increase in income, the likelihood that a state would experience a transition from democracy to authoritarianism in a given year declines (see Table 4.1). For countries at the lowest income levels, those below US$1,000 (at PPP [purchasing power parity], 1985 dollars), the likelihood of a democratic collapse was over 12 percent per year; for those at the US$1,001–2,000 level, the likelihood of democratic collapse declined to 5.5 percent per year. The likelihood of democratic collapse in the wealthiest states was zero over the time period covered. In fact, at every single increment of income increase, the likelihood of a transition from democracy to authoritarian rule (democratic collapse) declined in percentage terms. Thus, these data show that democratic collapse is progressively less likely as income levels rise, and they do not indicate any clear thresholds.

Table 4.1 Probability of Democratic Collapse, by Income Level, 1950–1990 (all 141 countries)

Income Level	Probability of a Transition to Authoritarian Rule
0–1,000	0.1216
1,001–2,000	0.0556
2,001–3,000	0.0428
3,001–4,000	0.0278
4,001–5,000	0.0185
5,001–6,000	0.0090
6,001–7,000	0.0080
7,001–	—

Source: Adapted from Przeworski et al. (2000: 93).
Note: Income level is in 1985 constant purchasing power parity dollars.

Another controversial area of debate concerns the intervening variables that link development to successful democratization. Most scholars
recognize that income levels per se are not the direct cause of democratic
consolidation. Rather, they are well aware that certain intervening
sociopolitical variables are most directly related to the success of democratic experiments in countries experiencing economic development. This
is true even when scholars chose to use income levels as the best (most
easily measurable) surrogate variable to indicate the level of socioeconomic development, as Przeworski et al. do (2000: 81, n. 2). They found that
education levels are also closely correlated with democratic survival, however (101). Other surrogate indicators for overall development have
included energy consumption per capita and industrialization, among the
many socioeconomic variables available. Diamond preferred to use the
Physical Quality of Life Index developed by Morris (1979) or the United
Nations Development Programme's (UNDP) indicator, the Human
Development Index (HDI), as better indicators of development. The former of these instruments is a composite of literacy, infant mortality rates,
and life expectancy; the latter combines measures of literacy and life
expectancy with the log of per capita GDP. That so many different indicators for socioeconomic development are used is testimony to the indirect-
ness of the development-democracy relationship.

Diamond usefully identifies four different sociopolitical consequences
of economic development that serve as a bridge to successful democratic
consolidation. Interestingly, as he starts the discussion, he quickly leaves
behind the world of statistical precision and plunges into the domain of theoretical speculation. Diamond first suggests that rising incomes and education levels lead to important changes in political culture (1992: 117–119).
Following the seminal study of Almond and Verba (1963), he argues that
more educated people are better informed, more politically engaged, more
trustful of others, and more tolerant. A number of other aspects of political
culture were discussed in Chapter 3, where the debate over the possibility
for change in political culture was reviewed. Inglehart and Welzel (2005)
make an impressive case, through both statistical demonstration and logical
analysis, that rising income and development reinforce what they called
"self-expression values," or, essentially, liberal politico-economic norms.
These norms in turn make both successful democratic transitions and successful consolidations possible.

Diamond next discusses the development of socioeconomic classes,
and particularly of a "commercial and industrial bourgeoisie" as a linkage
between development and democratization (1992: 119). Diamond specifically identifies the national bourgeoisie's awareness of, and esteem for, the
Western consensus about the value of democracy as an important pillar of
democratic stability (121). Third, under the vague subheading "State and

Society," Diamond discusses the reduction in corruption as "the chief instrument of upward class mobility" that accompanies the economic development of the private sector (122). Finally, Diamond identifies growth in the number and vitality of civil associations as an important bulwark of democracy in societies achieving higher levels of development (123–125). These bridging phenomena speak to the broader question of the causal mechanisms that link development with successful democratization. Although these issues continue to be debated, Inglehart and Welzel (2005) have for now made the most impressive arguments that changing political values across all classes, and not civil society or the development of a bourgeoisie, account for most democratization in the world.

Diamond's list shows how interconnected the structural features of society are that condition the probability of successful democratization. Diamond has argued indirectly that prodemocratic political culture, class development, and a vital civil society are functions of rising incomes and education levels. Inglehart and Welzel (2005) are even more explicit on this point. In turn, the new social givens that begin to appear at a certain level of development have an impact on the perpetuation of a developmental trajectory. In other words, the good social effects produced by development may create the conditions that allow further development to proceed. Thus, a positive cycle in which improving social conditions and attitudes lead to further economic development sometimes takes hold in a given society. Moreover, the various social variables are "causing" each other, as well as "causing" more economic development. For instance, an open, prodemocratic political culture reinforces the development of a vibrant civil society, and vice versa. Although rising incomes may be perceived to be at the heart of such positive cycles, one might equally ask what stimulates the initial advances in incomes in the first place. In a given case, the salutary actions of well-intentioned agents cannot be ruled out as the stimulus to such positive cycles.

For our purposes, the insights of general studies on development and democratization are most important. This literature shows that development is more linked to the consolidation phase of democratization than to the transition phase. It further shows that incrementally higher levels improve the chances for democratic consolidation in incremental ways. Thus, to the extent that Congo enjoyed relatively high levels of income, human welfare, and education, its chances for democratic consolidation should have been better than the African average.

Class Cleavages, Income Distribution, and Democratization

Another set of theories about democratization suggests that successful democratic consolidation may depend on either the development of specific socioeconomic classes in society or, relatedly, on changes in the distribution of income in society. The class theory, growing out of Marxian analysis of the industrial West, suggests that the emergence of democracy depends on prior emergence of a bourgeoisie. This class must be independent of state control even while the state directly serves its interests. The most important modern proponent of this theory has been Barrington Moore, who ultimately boiled down this argument to his famous dictum, "No bourgeoisie, no democracy" (Moore 1966: 418). The reasons why a bourgeoisie would favor formal democracy as a mode of rule have always remained vague, however. The most typical reasons offered are that formal democracy gives capitalism a cover of legitimacy and that it provides a mechanism for the resolution of intraclass disputes.

A great many non-Marxian analysts have subsequently come to associate the rise and consolidation of democracy, more vaguely, with the development of a bourgeoisie (Diamond 1992: 119–121) or, also vaguely, a "middle class" (e.g., Bates 1999). The economic basis for any middle class could naturally be much broader than those of a classic bourgeoisie. This broader formulation is much more relevant and interesting for the contemporary, postindustrial world. Even in such heavily industrialized emergent democracies as South Korea and Taiwan, the basis for the middle class is markedly different from that of Industrial Revolution–era Europe. In these countries, of course, the state has controlled much of the capital needed for industrial development. Meanwhile, such groups as professionals, managers, intellectuals, civil society leaders, and traders all form part of the more amorphous middle class.

Although such a theory as this one is hard to test, it is intuitively appealing, logical, and anecdotally supported by casual observation of the functioning of new democracies. The rise of some sort of middle class is the corollary to the general process of development itself. If levels of education and health are improving, for instance, classes of educators and health care professionals must necessarily be emerging at the same time to provide the services that lead to such increases. Meanwhile, rising income levels are necessarily linked to rises in the amount of productive economic activity taking place, which necessitates the emergence of a managerial class, if not a classic bourgeoisie. Since democratic consolidation is clearly supported by development, as Przeworski et al. demonstrate, then the rise of a middle class is a necessary correlate to the persistence of democracy in societies experiencing real development. In short, then, the existence of a proportionately large middle class surely signals increased prospects for the consolidation of democracy.

Another plausible and related theory about income distribution and democracy is that successful democratization depends on a relatively egalitarian distribution of income within a society. According to Przeworski et al. (2000: 117), the theory would suggest that in nascent democracies "dominant social groups may seek recourse to authoritarianism when the exercise of political rights by the poor—whether in the form of suffrage or freedom of association—results in egalitarian pressures." On the other hand, in societies that were already relatively egalitarian, the poor would presumably be much more content with their lot and put less pressure on the political system for redistribution of income. Accordingly, democratic norms could be consolidated without the destructive forces of class conflict putting elected officials in untenable political positions.

The statistical data, however, does not at all show that a society need be relatively egalitarianism as a prerequisite for a democratic experiment to succeed. In fact, the general patterns of all states at varying levels of income are similar whether they develop as democracies or as dictatorships. Measured by the well-known Gini index, the poorest societies (those with incomes below US$1,000 measured at PPP in 1985 dollars) were relatively egalitarian, as were those with incomes over US$5,000 per capita, using the same measure (Przeworski et al. 2000: 118). Meanwhile, societies at intermediate levels of development were less egalitarian, whether they were democracies or not. In fact, the democratic states at the intermediate levels of income were *less* egalitarian than the dictatorships. Thus, rising inequality appears to be a side effect of development up to a certain point, at which societies again become more egalitarian as they continue to become wealthier. Relating this finding to class, the emergence of a middle class seems to make societies initially less egalitarian, but then makes them more egalitarian again as the growth of the middle class continues. Accordingly, for a country like Congo, relatively wealthier than most of the African cohort, one should not be troubled to find that it was also less egalitarian, nor think that such inequality doomed the democratic experiment from the start.

Economic Performance and Democratic Consolidation
Another important variable conditioning a country's chances of democratic consolidation is economic performance *after* the transition. Przeworski et al. (2000) point out that some poor democracies survive against the odds, and they wondered why this was the case. India, whose democratic system has persisted from 1947 until today, is perhaps the most notable example of such a phenomenon. Hypothesizing that economic performance may be part of the answer, the authors systematically tested those countries that had democratic experiments lasting over twenty years in the period since 1800. In some cases democratic systems have endured to the present. They found that democratic experiments are highly sensitive to economic performance as measured by growth of per capita income. In fact, they found that a democratic regime is approximately twice as likely to "die" when economies are shrinking as when they are growing in a given year (2000: 109). Examining the results over long periods of time, they found even more

striking connections. When a democracy was growing economically over three consecutive years, its chance of dying was only 1 in 135; when its economy was shrinking over any two consecutive years, its chance of collapsing was a much larger 1 in 13 (109). Not surprisingly, they also found that poor democracies are much more vulnerable to the "growth effect"; richer democracies can often survive several years of decline intact, but poor democracies that experience shrinking economies in a given year fail at a rate of about 1 in 10 (111).

In an earlier study, the same four authors identified high inflation as another important aspect of economic performance that bore on the survival of new democracies. Interestingly, their findings showed that moderate inflation is *not* a threat to democratic experiments. Specifically, they found that a democratic regime has a 2.3 percent probability of dying in a given year when it experiences inflation below 6 percent, a 1.4 percent annual probability of failure when inflation ranges between 6 and 30 percent, and a 6.4 percent annual probability of failure at inflation rates over 30 percent (Przeworski et al. 1997: 298). Although the authors do not interpret the findings there, the reason that moderate inflation is helpful may be that debtors are better able to meet their obligations in such an environment. Taking into account both growth and inflation, the authors conclude, "Economic performance, then, is crucially important for the survival of democracy in less-affluent countries. When the economy grows rapidly with a moderate rate of inflation, democracy is much more likely to last even in the poorest lands" (298).

Przeworski et al. also inquire into the effects of changes in income distribution, using a variety of different measures for the independent variable, including the Gini coefficient and the ratio of income of the top 20 percent against that of the bottom 20 percent. In general, they find that changes in distribution ratios matter much less for democratic consolidation than do absolute incomes (2000: 120). In other words, an economy that is growing strongly, but becoming somewhat less egalitarian, has a better chance of consolidating a democratic system than one that is not growing overall but is becoming more egalitarian. Nevertheless, they find that a trend of growing inequality does threaten democratic experiments to some degree, and particularly in poorer societies. In particular, they note that, "democracy is vulnerable when the poor get relatively poorer" (121). When they examine the impact of welfare, as opposed to income, they find a bigger effect: either kind of regime, authoritarian or democracy, is more likely to fail when the average welfare level of the population declines.

With such ideas as these in mind, Pereira, Maravall, and Przeworski (1993) advocated policies of "social democracy" for the newly democratizing states of Eastern Europe, South Europe, and Latin America in the early 1990s. These authors clearly felt that the application of harsh, neoliberal policies uncushioned by welfare supports would throw the survival of democracy in the fragile new regimes into question. I had the same preoccupation about Congolese democracy soon after its establishment in the early 1990s (Clark 1993). Accordingly, one must examine the performance of the Congolese economy after the transition carefully to see whether the democratic failure appears to be linked to the social consequences that result from poor performance.

If poor economic performance is behind the failure of many democratic experiments, to what causes might such poor performances be attributed? One of the leading candidates for poor economic performance in the short term is structural adjustment. Adekanye (1995) has produced one of the more articulate and clear studies linking the effects of structural adjustment to both rising ethnic tensions in African countries and to democratic failure. Characteristic of those critical of structural adjustment, Adekanye begins by pointing out that the short-term effect of structural adjustment is nearly always social pain. That is, citizens suffer as their governments cut back on social services, reduce government budget deficits, increase taxes, privatize state-owned enterprises, and meet other conditions of debt rescheduling. This social suffering, in turn, leads to ethnic conflict as impoverished groups scramble to take control of dwindling resources. Such ethnic conflict, in turn, renders the consolidation of democratic regimes virtually impossible. Thus, when one observes a poor economic performance, an initial question should be whether structural adjustment policies are partly or wholly responsible for that outcome.

The Special Problem of Rentier Economies

Another, more particular aspect of Congo that necessarily concerns the student of its democratic experiment is that the country has a "rentier" economy. The "rentier state" originally referred to seventeenth- and eighteenth-century European states (like the Netherlands) that loaned money to other states and prospered on the interest (or rents). The modern usage was apparently first cited in reference to Iran by the scholar Hussein Mahdavy (Ross 2001: 129). Many other scholars have used the term since then, imbuing it with a spectrum of various nuances. Ross credits Hazem Beblawi with a particularly useful refinement of the term (129). Under Beblawi's definition, a rentier state is one that gains income directly from foreign clients through the sale of some good that is generated by a relatively small number of citizens in the state (Beblawi 1987: 51). This understanding fits the oil-producing states perfectly and it might also apply to other mineral-producing states where only a small number of workers are involved in mineral extraction. The definition definitely applies well to Congo, whose export economy has been thoroughly—and increasingly—dominated by oil revenues. Although scholars have most frequently used the term to describe the oil-rich states of the Persian Gulf, one Africanist scholar (Yates 1996) has used the term with reference to Gabon, where it is aptly applied. It could apply to states that export large amount of minerals, as well, if the mineral production does not involve a large workforce.

The recent work of Ross (2001) comprehensively reviews prior work on the rentier state and carries out careful statistical tests that explore the relationship of rentierism and democratization. Ross's results were sobering for advocates of democratization in the world's poor oil states. Ross found, first, that the "antidemocratic properties" of both oil and mineral wealth were "substantial" (2001: 342). Moreover, he found even relatively low levels of oil exports could hurt the chances for democratization in poor countries, as much or more than extraordinarily high levels. Since most oil-rich states are in Africa or the Middle East, and one could argue that these regions are not susceptible to democratization in any case, Ross controlled for region, and he still found the oil exports have a negative impact on poor states. He also controlled for other such variables as lag time following the onset of oil production, size of the state, and other commodity exports. He found that the connection between oil rent dependency and authoritarianism persisted in all cases. In fact, states that exported nonmineral commodities tended to be more democratic than those that did not—just the opposite of the case for oil exporters (344–345).

Despite the great care that Ross put into his research design to test the relationship between rentierism and authoritarianism, as well as to examine the causal mechanisms, his study is limited in at least one key regard: it does not distinguish between democratic transition and democratic consolidation, except in the deployment of a lag time between the observation of the independent variable and the dependent variable (i.e., "regime type"). But this does not provide for an adequate distinction at all for the causal mechanisms. In fact, it is clear from Ross's emphasis that he really has in mind the effects of these mechanisms on regime *transitions*. Specifically, the rentier and repression effects he describes would only be applicable to authoritarian regimes that were seeking to avoid a transition to democracy. Repression and patronage could be used by autocratic governments to stifle dissent, but they are not relevant to transitional, or unconsolidated, democratic regimes. Qualitative research on one African rentier state, Gabon, shows that precisely these two mechanisms have been used to suppress a transition to democracy there (Yates 1996; Gardinier 1997a). Ross also seems to have thought that the modernization effects of development—presumably muted in rentier regimes—might lead to democratic transitions. Przeworski et al. (2000: 137), however, decisively showed that the modernization effects have no bearing on transitions, but only on consolidation.

Thus, Ross's overall conclusion that oil does indeed hinder democracy—the answer to his titular question—should be carefully specified. While high oil-producing and other rentier states may be unlikely to experience democratic transitions, whether or not such states will have more or less success in consolidating democracy remains an open question. In practice, the number of high-production oil states in the developing world that have experimented with democracy is too low to create a testable sample. Most of the Persian Gulf and Arabian Peninsula states have *never* experimented with democracy, while most of the African oil producers had only brief democratic experiments following independence. But the collapse of democratic systems in Africa during the 1960s was near continentwide, and occurred before most of states in question (Nigeria, Angola, Gabon, Cameroon, and Congo) produced large amounts of oil. Despite the putatively antidemocratic qualities of large oil producers, two have managed to experiment with democratic systems in recent years, Nigeria and Congo. Nigeria's current experiment with democracy is ongoing, but not at all encouraging. Thus, in accord with these theoretical considerations on the impact of oil on the prospects for democratization, the effects of oil revenues on Congo's sociopolitical and economic development must be observed with care.

■ The Development of the Congolese Economy and Its Classes

Although Congo remains a poor, developing country by world standards, it is one of the wealthier and more developed societies of sub-Saharan Africa. In fact, Congo was already one of the more developed countries of the subcontinent at the time of formal independence in 1960. In that year, Congo's HDI score as calculated by the UNDP stood at .241.[3] Among all of the countries of sub-Saharan Africa, excluding South Africa, only Gabon (.259), Zimbabwe (.284), Lesotho (.245), and Zambia (.258) ranked higher in 1960.[4] This assessment will not surprise most students of Congolese history and development, who know that the country was relatively favored by some colonial policies after the end of the brutal concessionary system of rule in 1930. Like other French colonies with access to the sea, Congo received considerably more industrial and educational investment than landlocked Chad and the CAR (in Central Africa), or Mali, Niger, and Upper Volta (in West Africa). Moreover, once Brazzaville was selected to be the administrative capital for all of the AEF, it enjoyed particular investment by the French. A relatively large educated population and a burgeoning group of intellectuals were already present in Congo by independence. It is also noteworthy that Senegal, with an HDI score of only .146, and Côte d'Ivoire, with a score of only .168, were less developed by this measure than Congo in 1960, though these states are generally thought to have been favored by more sustained contact with metropolitan France.

Also interesting is that Congo had a much higher rate of per capita income growth, and a faster face of overall development, than the (rather dismal) African average. Although Congo's average rate of growth in per capita income between 1960 and 1995 was a modest 1.6 percent, this rate was far above the African average. Only Swaziland, Lesotho, and Equatorial Guinea (another oil state) had higher average growth rates over that long period, whereas Kenya and Uganda matched Congo's rate of 1.6 percent (United Nations Development Programme 1998: 144–145). By 1995, Congo's HDI index score was .519, putting it in the category of Medium Human Development, along with only a handful of other African states (South Africa, Botswana, Swaziland, Zimbabwe, Gabon, Namibia, and Mauritius). Thirty-five other African states for which data were available remained in the category of Low Human Development. The rate of growth in Congo's HDI score over the thirty-five years was also one of the best on the continent. By 1995, per capita GDP measured by PPP (in 1987 dollars) was US$906 (having fallen from US$1,066 in 1990, when oil prices were higher). This rate of income was again higher than all other African states except the island states, South Africa, Namibia, Botswana, and Gabon (141–142). Congo's rate of adult literacy stood at nearly 75 percent by 1995, far above the African average of only 57 percent, and even above the rates for the Arab and South Asian states (138, 206). Congo's life expectancy of only fifty-one years was only slightly above the African average, but the relatively low figure partly records the fact that Congo had one of the higher rates of AIDS infection on the continent.[5] In short, then, Congo's level of development was notably higher than a very low African average in 1960, and it more than kept pace with increases in development levels over the years to 1995. Accordingly, Congo should have had better prospects for democratization, on these scores, than its neighbors.

A large part of Congo's relatively more rapid development owed to the impressive revenues of its petroleum exports. The effects of these revenues on the country's social development were magnified by the fact of the country's small population. Congo's population was a mere 766,000 in 1959 (Wagret 1963: 123). This increased to approximately 1.4 million in 1975, and then to about 2.7 million in 1997 (United Nations Development Programme 1999: 199). The larger oil revenues of Nigeria, Cameroon, and Angola were offset by these countries' much larger populations. Accordingly, the per capita level of oil revenues for Congo was exceeded only by that of Gabon, which has had higher oil production levels and a smaller population. During these years Gabon and Congo also had the highest per capita income levels as a result.

The first commercial oil was produced in Congo in 1957, but the first major offshore deposits only began to be developed in the late 1960s. Congo began producing petroleum in large quantity in the early 1970s, just as the first Marxist government, that of Marien Ngouabi, was consolidating its power. In the 1970s production fluctuated between 30,000 and 55,000 barrels per day (bpd), before increasing suddenly in the early 1980s to about 110,000 bpd in 1984. Production increased gradually during the 1980s, just surpassing 150 million bpd in 1989, where production remained for 1990 and 1991. Following another increase in 1992, production averaged 173 million bpd for 1992 through 1995. Production then jumped again, to just over 200,000 bpd (some 16 percent) in 1996 when the Nkossi field came on stream, and again to 240,000 bpd (another 20 percent) in 1997. Congo's output reached an all-time high of 283 million bpd in 2000; since then, production has declined back below 250 million bpd.[6] Thus, oil output during the democratic experiment was at a historically high level, but it was also flat during the critical years of 1992 to 1995.

Meanwhile, world oil prices experienced striking jumps in price in 1973 and again in 1979, before collapsing to a much lower level in 1985 (see Table 4.2). Since the beginning of the 1980s, oil revenues have consistently represented over 90 percent of export earnings and a large fraction of government budget revenues. Average world oil prices have only recently regained their 1981 peak of over US$66 per barrel (in 2006 dollars). Until very recently, Congo enjoyed its highest levels of oil revenues in the 1980 to 1985 period, one that many Congolese recall fondly as their economic heyday. Low oil prices in the late 1980s contributed significantly to the disgruntlement with the first Sassou regime and even to its overthrow in 1991. Even lower oil prices in the 1992 to 1997 period, accompanied by stagnant production levels, served to reduce economic welfare during this period, and thereby harm the prospects for the democratic experiment.

Whereas Congolese oil production and world oil prices can be reliably tracked, the actual state revenues from this production cannot, partly because all of Congo's governments have sought to conceal them. Moreover, the costs of extracting Congo's offshore oil have also not been inconsiderable. These costs have been recouped by the main producers, including Elf-Congo, a subsidiary of France's former state-owned Elf-

Table 4.2 Average World Oil Prices in Constant 2006 Dollars

Time Period	Price[a]
1970–1973	15.83
1974–1979	27.76
1980–1985	51.87
1986–1991	23.95
1992–1997	19.68

Source: US Department of Energy.
Note: a. Dollars per barrel of oil.

Aquitaine, and Agip Recherches, a subsidiary of the Italian multinational oil producer ENI.[7] The fragmentary and anecdotal figures are hard to interpret. For instance, Okoko-Esseau (1995: 152) claimed that revenues dropped from a peak of 200 billion CFA francs in 1985 to a low of only 39 billion francs in 1989. If such a huge drop did take place, it was not due to falling prices alone. Some of the differences are due to the debts the Congolese state has accumulated against future oil revenues (the *dette gagée*). Since such debts, often kept out of official accounting records, are repaid directly from oil sales, this obscures the actual amount of the revenues. *Jeune Afrique* ("La guerre du pétrole est-elle finie?" 9–15 September 1993: 53) reported that Congo anticipated earning 45 billion CFA francs in 1993 (about US$90 million at that time), but that 21 billion of the revenues would go directly for the dette gagée. Thus, in 1993, nearly half of the petroleum revenues went to repay such debts. The same source further reported that another 90 billion CFA francs were already "mortgaged" against future oil earnings through 1999.

Nevertheless, it is certain that the development of its petroleum resources has had a profound impact on the nature of Congolese society and politics. Some of the wealth generated by petroleum revenues did trickle down to the population at large and the country's small middle class did expand considerably. Congo's overall levels of development increased particularly during the oil boom years (1973–1985). While Congo's HDI increased impressively between 1970 and 1992, partly due to oil wealth, that of most other African countries grew much more slowly (United Nations Development Programme 1998: 136–137). Increased Congolese government spending on health care, education, and infrastructure development during the years of high oil incomes accounts for much of this increase. This development should, theoretically, have improved the country's prospects for democratic consolidation.

On the other hand, Congo's petroleum wealth indirectly reinforced many of the most undemocratic aspects of the country's political culture (Clark 2005b). The impact of petroleum income was as much psychological as economic, in that it contributed directly to shaping the political consciousness of all social classes. Because the Congolese knew that the state controlled significant oil wealth, they expected much more from it. Moreover, they grew to envy their leaders, who diverted a large percentage of these revenues to personal possession. Meanwhile, Congo's economy suffered from a case of "Dutch disease," in which all non-oil-related parts of the economy contracted as oil revenues rose.[8] This meant that there were fewer opportunities for ambitious and talented citizens outside the state-controlled sector.

The manner in which the petroleum revenues were deployed by the state, as much as their mere existence, created a dependent population. Oil revenues might have been used by the state to create an independent bourgeoisie, as state-raised income and foreign aid was used in Taiwan and South Korea (Hsiao and Koo 1997; Kohli 2004). Instead, the state simply hired more and more of its citizens to work in the civil service. This pattern reflected both the étatist traditions Congo inherited from the French and the rulers' socialist commitment to full employment for educated cadres. Of course, it was also a simple way to deflect demands for political reform from an educated, but otherwise impoverished, nascent middle class. As a result, the size of the Congolese civil service grew from a mere 3,300 at independence to some 80,000 in 1990, before declining slightly after the start of the democratic experiment (see Table 4.3). Another 20,000 Congolese served in the army and government posts of other categories (Clark 1993: 56). With its small population, Congo had perhaps the largest ratio of civil servants to population anywhere in Africa. Meanwhile, the "people's schools" kept turning out ever more secondary school and university graduates, many trained in administration (Makonda 1988). The only part of the middle class not dominated by the state was the collection of traders, petty vendors, and shopkeepers who worked in Congo's marginal private sector. A majority of these, however, were West African migrants who played no significant role in Congo's domestic politics and were vulnerable to the whims of state agents due to their foreign status (Whitehouse 2007).

A related aspect of government domination of the economy was the nationalization of foreign enterprises or the outright creation of new state-owned enterprises. By the mid-1980s, there were over eighty-five such enterprises employing some 16 percent of those working in the formal economy (Clark 1993: 56). A large majority of these enterprises were unprofitable from the outset or had become so by the late 1980s. Accordingly, under the 1986 structural adjustment programs, these became targets for privatization in order to save the government revenue.[9]

These economic activities of the government bolstered the country's

Table 4.3 Growth of the Congolese Civil Service

Year	Approximate Number of Individuals
1960	3,300
1972	21,000
1979	54,000
1986	73,000
1990	80,000
1993	85,000
1996	70,000

Sources: Figures for 1960–1986, Radu and Somerville (1989: 159); for 1990–1996, Economist Intelligence Unit, *Country Report: Congo* (various years).

managerial class and also created a small proletariat. But these policies were not sustainable over the long term. Once oil prices collapsed in 1985, Congo was soon faced with the need for economic restructuring; the country signed its first structural adjustment program agreement with the World Bank in 1986. Under the conditions of the agreement, it was to reduce the size of its civil service and privatize many of the state-owned enterprises. All of these were heavily overstaffed, and the large majority of them failed to make a profit, relying on government subsidies for their survival. Although the country's independent labor unions had been organized under a state-controlled umbrella in the 1960s (the CSC), this organization did seek to protect workers against cuts in benefits or layoffs following the initial SAP agreement. As a result, the government did not follow through on its commitments.

The reason for Congo's acceptance of the SAP was, of course, that it had accumulated an unserviceable debt. The accumulation of debt in Congo was closely linked to its rising (and later falling) petroleum income. When oil prices were high, international lenders, public as well as private, assumed that Congo would be able to pay off a larger debt, and loaned money freely (Vallée 1988). As a result, debt escalated rapidly from virtually nothing in 1970 to US$1.2 billion in 1980 to some US$4.5 billion in 1990. By 1997, Congo's debt was over US$5 billion, and at that point, the size of its debt relative to its GNP was the single highest in the world with debt equaling 2.47 of GNP (World Bank 2000: 270–271). Of course, by the late 1980s, a large percentage of the country's petroleum income was going to service this debt. Congo's debt service ratio reached 49 percent in 1986 before declining to 18 percent in 1990. During the early 1990s, it fluctuated wildly between 11 and 54 percent as Congo made—and then broke—various restructuring deals with its donors (Economist Intelligence Unit, *Country Report: Congo,* various years). But debt service exercised a constant weight on the burdened economy. Since the citizens did not generally appreciate that much of Congo's oil earnings were going for debt service and investment in the oil infrastructure, they assumed that their politicians were diverting an even larger percentage of revenues than they actually were. These feelings constantly eroded public faith in the government.

Since the government lavished large amounts of oil income on urban services, and invested virtually nothing in agriculture, urbanization accelerated rapidly during the oil boom years (Achikbache and Anglade 1988: 11–14). Government subsidies of imported food further accelerated the trend. Brazzaville, the capital, and Pointe Noire, the center of oil production activities, both grew at astounding rates during the 1970s and 1980s. By 1998, 61 percent of Congo's population lived in urban areas, a percentage surpassed only by Botswana among African states (World Bank 2000: 232–233). People moved from rural to urban areas initially to work in the government or state-owned enterprises, or to provide services to those in the formal economy. With the sudden contraction of government spending in the late 1980s, however, the size of the urban underclass swelled rapidly. Unlike the rural underemployed classes in other African states, Congo's urban lumpenproletariat had firsthand knowledge of the better life that comes with formal urban employment. This class became the willing tool of unscrupulous politicians and later played a direct role in the unraveling of Congo's civil peace.

Finally, the development of Congo's oil resources—ironically given the wealth they represented—made the country more dependent on France than ever. In keeping with their Marxist rhetoric, the Ngouabi regime forged new international partnerships with most of the world's socialist states, including Cuba, China, East Germany, and the Soviet Union. These states provided weapons and military advice, as well as some economic assistance. Surprisingly, however, Congo remained economically dependent on French aid, and even French military assistance, especially at critical moments (Clark 2002a).[10]

Thus, the main trends in Congolese society and politics made the state and population dependent on petroleum income for their future welfare. First, the state remained economically dependent on the capital investment of France (and foreign aid, once the debt crisis arrived). Second, the oil-dominated economy prevented the formation of organic links between the population and the state, one component of Ross's "rentier effect" (2001: 332–333). Third, it was due to Congo's oil income that it was able to accumulate such a large national debt—otherwise donors would have not loaned so much. When oil prices declined, Congo found it hard to service the country's proportionally large debt. In this sense, Congo's petroleum revenues became a millstone that weighed down the country's chances for economic autonomy and liberal political development. Had these revenues been deployed in a different way, however, they might have served to bolster Congo's economy and the development of civil society.

Yet the impact of oil revenues and state policies on Congo's development was not entirely bad for Congo's democratic prospects. Although a true bourgeoisie might have been even more supportive of democracy, Congo's state-generated middle class strongly supported the transition of 1991. In turn, this class favored peaceful democratic development after the transition, serving to support peace initiatives after the 1993 civil war.[11] More generally, Congo's oil revenues did trickle down to the mass of the Congolese people in a variety of ways. The revenues were initially distributed through the progressive expansion of the civil service, parastatal sector, and army. In turn, those with government salaries from such institutions typically supported many members of an extended family. They also purchased the services of domestics and the goods of shopkeepers with their incomes. In this way, the whole society did benefit indirectly from oil revenues. Moreover the government used a portion of the revenues to provide somewhat better educational and health services in the country. This accounts for the relatively higher levels of education and health in Congo compared to most other African states. Together these socioeconomic outcomes should have made Congo somewhat more able to consolidate a democratic system than other African states.

■ The Economic Performance of the Lissouba Regime

If Congo's level of economic development was relatively high compared to other African states, its level of economic performance in the years of the democratic experiment was abysmal. Moreover, this bad economic performance had a palpable impact on the level of social stability in the country. For purposes of this study, two questions about Congo's poor economic performance during 1992–1997 are particularly relevant. First, to what extent was the level of performance related to the structural economic problems faced by Congo's leaders? If the poor economic performance was not caused by such structural forces, then perhaps it owed as much to the selection of bad policies or the inadequate implementation of good policies. Second, what relationship can be traced between the social consequences of the poor economic performance and the actual collapse of the democratic experiment? The first of these questions is addressed here and the second in the final section of this chapter.

Let us begin with the level of GDP growth and inflation during the years of the Congolese democratic experiment. The most relevant years to study are those between 1991 and 1996, inclusive. Economic growth was either negative or very low in every year of the democratic experiment until 1996. The average level of growth for the entire period was 1.2 percent, but most of the growth came in 1996 (6.8 percent for that year) when oil income increased; the average for 1991 through 1995 was a scant .04 percent, or virtually nil.[12] Given that Congo's annual population growth rate has been 2.9 percent over recent years (United Nations Development Programme 1998: 177), average per capita income in the country was actually falling steadily during these years. Accordingly, the UNDP (1998: 141) shows that Congo's per capita income dropped from US$1,066 at PPP in 1990 to US$906 at PPP in 1995 (in constant 1987 dollars).[13] Thus, over the first five years of the democratic experiment, Congo experienced a drop in per capita income of over 15 percent! Yet one should not jump to a conclusion about the impact of these figures, since, as we saw, a huge percentage of GDP is generated by offshore oil production and a large percentage of the revenues goes to repay investment costs and debt. Congo's average inflation rate of 15 percent from 1991 to 1996 also requires some interpretation. The unusually high figure recorded is owed largely to the inflated figure for 1994 (29 percent), caused by the devaluation of the CFA franc. In January of that year, the ratio increased from a rate of 50:1 against the French franc to 100:1 against the franc at a stroke. Congo's typically low rate of inflation compared to non-CFA franc countries is attributable to the stability of that currency due to the guarantee of its conversion into a hard currency at a constant rate.

The practical impact of Congo's awful economic performance between 1991 and 1996 became manifest in the country's annual budget crises. For instance, in 1994 the Assembly created a budget that projected spending of 389 billion CFA francs, but domestic revenues for that year proved to be only 108 billion CFA francs. The budget exercise and deficit for 1995 were equally disastrous (Clark 2002b: B248). Foreign aid only covered a fraction of the deficit. These budget shortfalls were generated by a combination of structural and administrative problems. First, the high price of oil on world markets in 1990 turned out to be a brief phenomenon. Once the Persian Gulf War was concluded, world oil prices soon declined to their lowest real levels since before the oil shock of 1973 (see Table 4.2). As a result, the slight increase in oil revenue that Congo experienced in 1992, due to an increase in production, did not result in higher export revenues.[14] As noted above, much of this income went to pay the dette gagée. Although export revenues initially increased, these fell back over the next two years as oil prices fell on the world market. Export earnings did not recover to their 1990 level again until 1996.

Second, administrative problems related to the change to the multiparty system caused a drop in non-oil revenues in the early years following the transition. For instance, tax receipts fell by over 20 percent in 1992 compared to the previous year (Clark 2000: B228). In subsequent years, the World Bank repeatedly chastised the Lissouba regime for failing to collect customs revenues according to the country's laws. Although some Congolese claim that falling aid also added to the country's woes, the figures do not bear out the claim. Official foreign aid did fall after the unusual year of 1990, in which there was a net transfer of US$191 million, but this was not part of a secular trend.[15]

On the payments side of the ledger, the Congolese government faced a massive salary bill that it was loath to tackle in the early years of the government, despite constant pressure to do so from international financial institutions (IFIs). The size of the Congolese civil service grew unchecked from the onset of the oil boom era (see Table 4.3). By the mid-1980s, the size of the civil service was already out of control; it was nearly as large as that of Côte d'Ivoire, though the latter had a population five times as large (Clark 2000). Two more rounds of hiring occurred subsequently for political reasons. The outgoing Sassou regime engaged in massive hiring (up to

6,000 additional employees) at the time of the 1990 political crisis in a desperate effort to buy political support (Clark 1993: 61; Foreign Broadcast Information Service–Sub-Saharan Africa, "Congo," 10 January 1991). Then the Milongo and Lissouba regimes engaged in further hiring to reward their ethnoregional constituencies for their support during the transition and 1992 election. Not until 1995 did the Lissouba regime begin to make the promised cuts in both numbers of civil service workers and their wages and benefits (Economist Intelligence Unit, *Country Report: Congo,* no. 2, 1996: 5).

During all its time in power, the Lissouba regime failed to pay the salaries of the civil service workers consistently. The results were perpetual strikes among public sector workers, who deeply resented the government's failure to pay their wages. For instance, workers at Hydro-Congo, the state oil products marketing company, struck in April 1992, forcing the removal of the country's director. Likewise workers of the Agence Transcongolaise de Communications (a state-run transportation company) struck the following March when rumors circulated that the company would be privatized (Clark 2000). At the time of the rerun of the legislative elections, salary payments to civil service workers were four months in arrears (*Jeune Afrique,* "La guerre du pétrole est-elle finie?" 9–15 September 1993: 53). A payment of some of these arrears on the eve of the elections helped Lissouba to secure a victory. Yet by February 1995, salaries were again thirteen months in arrears, leading to another two-month strike by all civil service workers. This was briefly settled when the government paid two months' back wages (Clark 2002b: B232). Again, on the eve of the elections that were to take place in July 1997, some public sectors were on strike because the state had failed to pay their wages.[16] Moreover, these workers recalled clearly that their wages were paid more regularly during Sassou's earlier reign. Thus the sociopolitical consequence of these economic failures was that the public grew increasingly dissatisfied with Lissouba's rule. The palpable disaffection with the Lissouba regime evident in the country in 1997 owed particularly to its perceived economic incompetence.

For purposes of this study, however, it is important to estimate to what extent Congo's poor economic performance resulted from structural forces and to what extent from mismanagement by the Lissouba regime. The structural forces did serve to make the task of the Lissouba regime particularly difficult. The long-term mismanagement of Congo's oil wealth during the PCT years (1970–1991) had caused the country to accumulate unsustainable levels of debt. Whether or not Congo accepted a structural adjustment program to deal with this debt is actually beside the point; if Congo had renounced the plan, and defaulted on its debt, it would have thereby foregone any further external financing and faced an even tougher economic challenge.

Alternatively, Congo could have sought to renegotiate a new SAP with the IFIs, which it did finally do in 1994. In either case, the Congolese middle and lower classes would have suffered a sudden contraction of state monies available to them for payment. In the event, Lissouba moved very slowly to implement the structural adjustment program after it was agreed. Like other African states (Van de Walle 2001), Congo agreed to structural adjustment in principle, but only implemented the reforms selectively, in a way that did not threaten the regime in place. Thus, one cannot directly blame the failure of the democratic experiment on structural adjustment per se. Rather, one should point to the debt and general economic mess that Lissouba inherited from his predecessors. Even given the difficult circumstances it faced in 1992, however, the economic performance of the Lissouba regime was dreadful.

■ Comparison and Analysis

The crisis that Congo faced in May 1997 was not necessarily one for Congolese democracy, but it certainly was one for the Lissouba regime. Part of the reason for the crisis of that regime was indeed economic. The economy had stagnated over Lissouba's term in office, for reasons discussed above, and it also experienced relatively high inflation by Congolese historical standards. These problems, along with the general incompetence of the Lissouba administration, meant that the government failed to take in anything like the necessary levels of revenue. As we saw above, the important political aspect of these problems was that Lissouba's government was not able to pay civil service workers their salaries reliably. It is interesting to note that African states that have performed better economically since their democratic transitions have had more success in consolidating democratic regions. Two of the successful cases include Benin and Cape Verde, countries undergoing transitions in 1990 and 1991, respectively. Benin enjoyed average annual economic growth of 4.2 percent and Cape Verde annual growth of 3.7 percent between 1993–1997, and both have experienced alternation of political regimes since their transitions (Clark 2005b).

As is revealed in more detail in the coming chapters, however, the crisis of the Lissouba regime had other causes as well. Specifically, there was a lingering bitterness toward Lissouba associated with his unconstitutional dissolution of Parliament in 1992, and the ethnic fighting that followed it. There was a more general disappointment with Lissouba related to his authoritarian qualities. President Soglo of Benin lost popularity among his countrymen for similar reasons, and his behavior as president has been cited as one reason he lost the 1996 elections in Benin. It is notable that the Beninois electorate did not reelect Soglo despite the reasonably good performance of the economy under his leadership. In Congo, there is no evidence that the country's middle class had given up on Congolese democracy—only on President Lissouba. The economic problems of the Congolese economy might even have represented an opportunity for the Congolese democratic experiment, in that they might have led to the first instance of alternation of the individual holding the presidency. Instead, Lissouba fell into a military confrontation with Sassou that led to a civil war. Although no one can say what exact result the 1997 elections might have brought, it is certain that Lissouba feared very much that he would lose a fair election, just as Soglo had the previous year. Given that the MCDDI-PCT alliance was still loosely intact going into the elections, both the economy and the weight of demographic ethnoregional forces were strongly against Lissouba's reelection.

Let us consider a counterfactual scenario about how the Congolese democratic experiment might have come to an end. One can easily imagine that a long-lasting general strike might have completely paralyzed the Congolese government sometime well before the election. Indeed, a number of short-lived strikes by various parts of the civil service did take place between 1993 and 1997. If such strikes had endured, however, they might have led to workers erecting barricades in the streets or attacking government installations. Under such hypothetical circumstances, Lissouba might at some point have decided to use overwhelming force to crush the unions and disband striking workers. What reaction might this have evoked from the leaders of Congo's ethnopolitical militias? Surely these militia would have gotten involved in the confrontations once Lissouba ordered the army to take down barricades in the parts of towns not dominated by his ethnoregional supporters. At this point, constitutional rule in Congo would have been in grave doubt. The temptation for senior army officers to remove Lissouba from power and take command of the economy would have been tremendously high. Otherwise, the possibility of a civil war between ethnopolitical militia, but stimulated directly by an economic collapse, would also have been likely. In either case the Congolese democratic experiment would have ended—at least temporarily—at that moment. Under such a scenario, few would have hesitated to blame the democratic collapse on economic causes; the only debate would have been whether the economic crisis resulted from poor policies and administration, or from the structural circumstances of the Congolese economy.

Such scenarios are not at all hard to imagine in the contemporary world. During the year 2002, Argentina endured a severe political crisis that was generated by a major economic crisis. In that case, workers and businesspersons alike took to the streets banging on pots and pans to protest the harsh decisions of the government, particularly the freezing of bank deposits. The country saw rapid changes of leadership as regime after regime failed to deal adequately with the crisis. Few would have been surprised to see Argentina's democratic government evaporate under such excruciating economic pressures in the course of 2002.

The utterly dissimilar nature of the collapse of Congolese democracy suggests, on the other hand, that the economic crisis was not the root cause of failure. Had the Congolese economy performed much better in the years 1993 to 1996—let us imagine that Nkossa came on stream in the former year, and not the latter, or that world petroleum prices suddenly shot up due to some Middle Eastern crisis—Lissouba would still have faced a formidable challenge in the 1997 elections. Even had the economy, and thus Lissouba's chances, been somewhat better, the 1997 elections would have marked a critical juncture in the survival of Congolese democracy. Preparations in 1997 were far behind schedule in early June of that year as the elections approached. Large percentages of the opposition feared that Lissouba would try to manipulate the electorate in an unfair manner, as he had done in 1993, or even to engage in outright electoral fraud. Opposition newspapers at that time complained bitterly of the poor preparation of the elections and alleged biases against them. Meanwhile, Sassou was busy preparing his militia for a possible military confrontation, as were those among Lissouba's political advisers who took on such roles.[17]

Another important way to evaluate the impact of the economic crisis on the failure of Congolese democracy is to observe its effect on class relations and class politics. In class terms, the war of 1997 was a war in which the political class splintered in two and each recruited militia from among the lumpenproletariat and, to a much smaller degree, from among the peasantry. The war of 1997 was one in which the two armed camps—each consisting of sections of the political class, partly controlling mobs of poorly trained, undisciplined soldiers—made economic war on the middle class. While the underclass had little to lose through war and something substantial to be gained by looting, the middle class and working classes both did have something to lose: their property. This was systematically looted by the militia soldiers as they occupied various parts of the city. Interestingly, these soldiers sometimes looted from among their own ethnoregional kinsmen, as well as from the ethnic others (see, e.g., Tonda 1998). In this sense the war of 1997 was class war. The middle class and proletariat, then, did serve as a bulwark of democratic government, but they were powerless before the predatory warlord-politicians who did not depend on honest Congolese workers for either political support or as a source of tax revenues.

To explain the civil wars in Congo, it is not enough to point to the mere existence of the large lumpenproletariat, or even to the fact that this class became increasingly desperate after 1991. The work of Banzenguissa-Ganga (1994; 1999) implies as much, though it stops short of saying so outright. While members of this class did fill out most of the ranks of the militia groups and did participate in the looting, they could not have acted alone. They depended on the connivance of the political class to organize them and to allow them to run amuck. While reducing the size of this class by improving the socioeconomic circumstances of its members is a laudable social goal, it will not prevent their participation in future civil wars. Representatives of such social groups are available in practically every society in the world, and certainly every African society. Thugs can always be found to carry out the work of unscrupulous political warlords.

These observations permit some concluding reflections on the impact of the structural features of Congo's economy on the country's democratic experiment. The country's relatively high level of development and relatively large middle class might have served as bulwarks of democracy, as some theories of democratic consolidation suggest. Without that level of development and without the middle class, Congolese democracy might have died even sooner. However, Congo's dependence on oil rents for its economic sustenance served to undermine the democratic experiment. These rents made the political class less dependent on the middle class and more autonomous in their actions vis-à-vis society. In turn, low world oil prices in the middle 1990s contributed to the sharp economic crisis the country suffered in the years leading up to Congo's second multiparty presidential elections. The previous impact of Congo's oil economy had been the accumulation of unsustainable levels of debt. The large sums needed for debt servicing created feelings of betrayal in the population, given that large petroleum revenues were coming in but were then going back out to pay the lenders. Likewise, the short-term performance of the Lissouba administration hurt the chances for the survival of Congolese democracy. As the Benin case shows, short-term performance after a democratic transition may matter more than the underlying economic conditions. That case also reinforces what an analysis of the Congo case by itself would suggest: though difficult structural economic conditions did pose a challenge to democratic consolidation, they did not preclude it. Accordingly, one has to look further to understand fully the collapse of the Congolese democratic experiment.

■ **Notes**

1. Interestingly, these scholars find that higher levels of development, where development has increased the level of "self-expression values," increases the possibility of democratic transition, as well as that of democratic consolidation. See Ingelhart and Welzel (2005: chapter 8).

2. See Przeworski et al. (2000: 79, note 1).

3. Throughout this section, the United Nations Development Programme's Human Development Index (HDI) is used as a shorthand measure of development at the national level. The HDI is a composite of measures of life expectancy, adult

literacy, school enrollment rates, and adjusted per capita income measured by purchasing power parity (PPP) (UN Development Programme 1998: 15). The index is calibrated so that a score of 1 would represent complete human development and 0 would represent complete human deprivation. For 1995, the scores ranged from .960 (for Canada) to .185 (for Sierra Leone). Nineteen of the lowest twenty countries on the 1998 table were in sub-Saharan Africa.

4. Also excluded from this list are a few countries for which there was no data, like Comoros, Namibia, and Swaziland, and the island states (like Mauritius), which have atypical economies for Africa; the comparative analysis in this and the following paragraphs is limited to sub-Saharan Africa.

5. In 1997, Congo had a rate of 372 AIDS cases per 100,000 population, while the average for the African continent was 111 cases per 100,000 population (United Nations Development Programme 1999: 174); only Malawi, Namibia, and Zimbabwe had higher figures, according to this table.

6. The figures from the 1970s, 1983, and 1987 come from *Africa Contemporary Record* (various years); figures are given in million tons per year, and have been converted to thousands of barrels per day at a rate of 1 million tons = 21,000 bpd. Figures for 1989 and after are from the Economist Intelligence Unit, *Country Report: Congo* (various years). A graph showing Congolese production in thousands of bpd for 1980 through 2004 can be found in United States Department of Energy (USDOE) (2005).

7. Elf-Congo was responsible for about 80 percent of Congo's oil production through the early 1990s according to *Jeune Afrique* ("La guerre du pétrole est-elle finie?" 9–15 September 1993: 53). In 1996, the French government partially privatized the parent company, Elf-Aquitaine. The company was acquired by Total-Fina in 2000, at which time the company became known as "TotalFinalElf." In 2003, the company reverted to the simple name "Total."

8. Though not, it must be said, because of the impact on exchange rates; these are controlled by Congo's membership in the so-called Franc zone countries of West and Central Africa.

9. As an intern in the US embassy in Congo in 1990, one of my duties was to prepare a report on the privatization effort for Congo's state-owned enterprises and parastatals. At that time the Congolese government was clearly, though not openly, resisting privatization for the money-losing companies.

10. For more on this topic, see Chapter 7 of this volume.

11. On this topic, see especially Chapter 7 of this volume.

12. These figures calculated from data presented in Economist Intelligence Unit, *Country Report: Congo,* no. 1, 1995: 3; and Economist Intelligence Unit, *Country Report: Congo,* no. 1, 1998: 6. The inflation figure given further on is calculated from the same source.

13. By 1997, when the Nkossa oil field was functioning at its full capacity and oil exports had risen, per capita GDP had rebounded somewhat to $946, using the same measures (United Nations Development Programme 1999: 153). This increase came too late, however, to have any bearing on the survival of the Lissouba regime or on the democratic experiment.

14. The increase owed to the beginning of production on the Zatchi II field controlled by Agip (Clark 2000: B228).

15. For more on French aid to Congo, see Chapter 8 of this volume.

16. This strike was apparently limited to certain categories of state workers. Among them were university professors who had not been paid in several months. When I arrived in Brazzaville in May 1997, several categories of workers, including

professors, were on strike for this reason.

17. A large number of knowledgeable citizens told me bluntly during interviews in 2001 and 2002 that both Lissouba and Sassou "prepared for war, not for elections" in the early part of 1997. In a confidential interview, one insider on the Sassou team admitted to me that Lissouba played into Sassou's hand by provoking a confrontation in June 1997. For more on these events, see Chapter 6 of this volume.

5

The Challenge of Et
Regional Ident

Congo's ethnic and regional cleavages would certainly seem to a historically and analytically naive outside observer to be the most obvious explanation for the collapse of Congo's democratic experiment in 1997. This view is certainly not simpleminded, even if it is mostly a misperception. After all, one cannot deny or disguise the fact that Congo's elected government of 1997 was brought down by a war between two military groups largely formed on the basis of ethnic and regional identities. Thus, the analyst must take seriously the notion that Congo's democratic experiment was doomed from the beginning by the country's ethnic and regional cleavages and by bitter ethnoregional political rivalries.

In keeping with the prima facie role of ethnic and regional contestation in the failure of Congolese democracy, this chapter asks the following questions: Did the experiment fail primarily because of inevitable political confrontation among ethnic and regional identity groups? If not, then why did Congo's politicians find it so easy to mobilize ethnic and regional identity communities both as political constituencies and militia recruits? Relatedly, were there any significant trans-ethnoregional associations in society that might have served to domesticate Congolese politics to a democratic regime? If so, why did these prove to attract less social support than the sectarian militia groups to which the country's disenfranchised youth flocked? And why did transethnic organizations prove so impotent before the malevolent project of Congo's warlord politicians to maintain or seize power through these ethnoregional militia groups?

These queries place Congo's ethnoregional question in the context of the parallel question of civil society in the country. Collectively, they ask: Did Congo's democratic experiment fail because of the weakness of civil society? While most scholars have not treated the problems of ethnic and regional politics as impediments to successful democratization together with that of weak civil society, there is ample reason to do so.[1] Only a few scholars have recognized the advantages of treating the two variables together (e.g., Karlström 1999). Since groups based on ethnic or regional identity compete for loyalty with other groups based on such common bonds as gender, profession, class, and desire for social reform, the broad social categories are locked in constant tension. For example, to the extent that workers from varied ethnic and regional backgrounds come together in labor unions to demand higher wages or better conditions, the bonds that bind the ethnic constituencies within the union are loosened. As Chazan (1994) noted, the cleavages of civil society cut across those created by ethnic and regional identities. This observation is true whether one conceives of civil society merely as the collectivity of civil associations, or as the whole of the population engaged to pressure the state to enact social reforms. The loyalty of individuals to either transethnic organizations in society or to the public mass as a whole complicates and may even transcend the parochial loyalty that the same individuals might have for ethnic kinsmen. Accordingly, these two social variables are considered together in this chapter, though the focus is on the dominant problem of ethnoregionalism.

This chapter begins by asking how the various theoretical approaches to the problem of ethnicity and regionalism may be able to help us understand the problem of ethnoregionalism in Congo. Second, it discusses some of the ethnic and regional lines of conflict that emerged in the late colonial period, and how authorities dealt with these cleavages after the advent of independence. This section discusses the development of civil society in the same period. Third, the chapter reviews the record of ethnic and regional mobilization for political purposes in the period of the democratic experiment. Finally, this record is analyzed, again in comparative perspective, in order to make some judgments about the questions posed above.

■ **Theoretical Approaches to Ethnic and Regional Identities and Democratization**

One great theoretical question of ethnic and regional identity is why individuals maintain political solidarity with those of like ethnic or regional origins when circumscribed in larger political contexts. This question is particularly puzzling to those of a materialist bent since they instinctively expect individuals ultimately to give up such loyalties in favor of the more "rational" attraction of class attachment. Ethnic attachment and political mobilization pose a similar challenge to rational choice. Those of a liberal predilection also find such identities puzzling. In the context of national politics, both ideologies ultimately expect rational individuals to support specific candidates, parties, or platforms on the basis of shared policy views, not on the basis of ethnic or regional parochialism. As progressive ideologies, both modernization theory and Marxism see ethnic and regional fealties as atavisms destined to be obliterated by the transformative effects of economic differentiation and development.

For students—not to mention proponents—of democratization, the lingering ethnic and regional fealties in developing societies pose a particularly urgent problem. The formal, minimalist definition of democracy adopted here entails at least the regular holding of free, fair, and competitive elections. Based on the Western experience with the political parties that arose in Europe and North America in the eighteenth century and on the Latin American experience with parties arising in the nineteenth, most outsiders have assumed that African states would eventually emulate the Western models. Needless to say, they have yet to do so. The political parties that arose during the 1950s as colonial authorities began to allow internal political competition often formed around ethnic or regional constituencies. This was the case in Congo, in a number of other French colonies, and in the Belgian colonies. Where colonial authorities held out more hope for independence in a timely manner, broad, national political fronts, like Ghana's Convention People's Party, often appeared. Neither pattern fit at all the Western example of political parties based on class and/or ideology. Given the political traumas of the postcolonial African state during the course of the 1960s, as reflected in the dysfunctional nature of interpolitical party competition, it is of little surprise that the one-party state emerged as the dominant political form in the 1970s and 1980s.

Nor did the return of widespread multiparty politics during the early 1990s suggest that anything significant had changed in the interregnum: the newly emergent African political parties of the 1990s were as thoroughly dependent on ethnic, regional, and religious constituencies as were those of the late 1960s. In many cases, such political patterns appear to be a root cause of the many failures to consolidate new, democratic institutions in African polities since 1989. Accordingly, political mobilization along ethnic and regional lines in the present climate of experimentation with multiparty political systems in Africa appears to be the single most daunting problem of political reform.

Felicitously, the great theoretical divide on the question of ethnic identity closely parallels the agency-structure dichotomy chosen as the theoretical leitmotif for this study.[2] One of the two most important theoretical positions on the question of ethnic identity, primordialism, employs a basically structural approach to understanding identity. Apparently the first to use the term "primordialism" with reference to ethnic identity was the sociologist Edward Shils (1957), while anthropologist Clifford Geertz did the most to popularize the notion through his well-known essay on "primordial ties" (1973). Meanwhile, one of the most straightforward and comprehensible applications of the concept may be found in the work of the political scientist Harold Isaacs (1975). As used by each of these scholars, the primordialist approach to ethnic identity clearly favors the importance of structure over agency in identity formation. Each of them perceives ethnic structures in society to be virtually immutable, or to change at a glacial pace at best. Further, each expects the identity of individuals in society to be heavily conditioned by these structures, and for their actions to be in accord with group identification.

Primordialists typically begin their analyses by pointing out that individuals have a keen need to belong to groups in society, to feel part of a social network that provides psychological as well as material satisfactions. In turn, the natural groups into which individuals will coalesce are those based on shared language, dialect, religion, physical attribute, custom, and blood kinship. While this phenomenon is universal for most primordialists, it is even more true for the nonindustrialized, or traditional, societies. As Geertz (1973: 109) argues,

> These congruities of blood, speech, custom, and so on, are seen to have an ineffable, and at times overpowering, coercive in and of themselves. One is bound to one's kinsman, one's neighbor, one's fellow believer, ipso facto; as the result not merely of personal affection, practical necessity, common interest, or incurred obligation, but at least in great part by virtue of some unaccountable absolute import attributed to the very tie itself. . . . For virtually every person, in every society, at almost all times, some attachments seem to flow more from a sense of natural—some would say spiritual—affinity than from social interaction.

Also characteristic is the view of Isaacs that, while there may be many layers of identity for an individual, there is a "basic" identity at the core of every person. For Isaacs (1975), one's basic identity is set from birth, and that identity is more fundamental than any secondary identity that one later acquires. This basic identity is grounded in one's kinship with others in a community. Similarly, Horowitz (who cannot be unambiguously labeled a primordialist) also claims that "ethnic identity is generally acquired at birth," though he hastens to add that, "this is a matter of degree" (1975: 113–114). The emphasis on having an identity *at birth*—most assuredly a psychological impossibility—underscores the primordialists' permanent, genetic, and structural conception of ethnic and cultural identities.

Those analyzing ethnic identity from the 1960s to the 1980s did not worry so much about the impact of ethnic diversity—"cultural pluralism," in Young's useful phrase (1976)—on democratization as they did on social cohesion in general. The implications for democratization are the same, however: if cultural pluralism has disturbing implications for national unity and civil peace, its implication for successful democratization is equally dire. After all, democratic transitions rarely take place in the midst of civil war, and democratic consolidation never under such circumstances. Civil peace is a basic prerequisite for successful democratic consolidation. Those with a primordialist view of ethnic communities have been pessimistic about the idea of nation building in developing states; if conceptions and feelings of difference are likely to persist even in the face of rapid modernization and development, how could the inevitable antagonisms of cultural pluralism possibly be contained? The answers for primordialists range from federalism, giving enduring ethnic communities autonomy within explicitly defined regions, to the iron fist of centralized power in an authoritarian state.[3] Multiethnic states like Yugoslavia and the former Soviet Union employed *both* federalist devolution and ironfisted power at the center to contain the centrifugal forces of ethnic differences. Nonetheless, they failed to transform identities at the human level, despite serious efforts to do so. The rapid dissolution of these two states along ethnoregional lines following the collapse of their respective authoritarian governments in the early 1990s served as evidence of support for the primordialist view (though other analysts hastened to provide subtler interpretations). The experience of these two states in particular seem to confirm the implicit primordialist position that liberal government was ill suited for less-than-fully developed societies with unintegrated ethnic communities (see, e.g., Conner 1994).

If the primordialist view puts the analytical emphasis squarely on structure, then the instrumentalist view, or "mobilizationist," approach to ethnic identity puts the emphasis just as squarely on agency. Instrumentalism may have its deepest roots in the rationalist analysis characteristic of Enlightenment thinkers including Jeremy Bentham and the utilitarians. Such analysts expected individuals to reflect rationally on their interests and form into groups for political purposes on the basis of them. In this regard, Marxists are only a subcategory of the rationalists, who believe that, in due course, workers would understand that their real interests lay in class cohesion and political revolution. Accordingly, Marxists have long seen ethnic and religious ties among people as a kind of atavistic false consciousness, destined to be shattered by the crushing forces of capitalist mass impoverishment across sectarian lines. Hence, while primordialists stress the quasi-permanence of specific ethnic identity communities, Marxists and modernization theorists see them as relics that will be transcended by the social and economic changes wrought by industrialization. Other instrumentalists simply reject the necessary and permanent qualities of ethnic identity that they (rightly) associate with the primordial view without offering their own explicit counterviews (e.g., Eller and Coughlan 1996). According to the careful interpretation of Laitin (1986), the work of Cohen (1974) is the single most representative and effective in presenting the instrumentalist position.

Of course, the instrumentalists have to deal with the frequent reality of ethnic and regional conflict in the here and now. To do so, instrumentalists who are also Africanists adopt three particular positions almost universally. First, they begin by emphasizing the artificiality and flexibility of identity communities in African settings. In general, they point out that in precolonial Africa the group identity of individuals changed frequently owing to migration, displacement from the original community by war or slavery, and the expansion and contraction of African empires. An illustration would be the peoples living in the Lunda empire in the century just before European colonization. As the empire expanded its reach and power, the Lunda identity began to slowly displace other identities among tributaries peoples; when the empire began to shrink, peoples who escaped the control of Lunda political authority took on new identities, or reverted to old ones (Bustin 1975). Similar patterns of identity transformation accompanied changing fortunes of the Luba peoples and empire to the north, in the areas of northern Shaba and the Kasai provinces of the Democratic Republic of Congo (Reefe 1981).

Second, Africanist instrumentalists almost universally argue that a major project of European colonialism was to distinguish, identify, and categorize African peoples into various ethnic groups according to language and custom. In so doing, they frequently created new ethnic categories that had not existed in the consciousnesses of the Africans themselves. As frequently, they recombined various ethnic groups into larger or smaller groupings for the sake of analytical clarity that utterly altered the ethnic identities of existing peoples. Legendary among students of central Africa in this regard was the virtual creation of the "Bangala" as a "people," first through a case of mistaken identity, and then through the efforts of Belgian colonial anthropologists (Young 1965: 242–246). Later, the Belgians recognized that no such group had ever existed but, ironically, by that time it had become "a meaningful identity in everyday sociopolitical vocabulary" (Young 1976: 173). Indeed, the major significance of the colonial effort was to render the previously fluid ethnic identity categories relatively static (even if some identity change continued under colonialism). This is most notoriously claimed to be the case in Rwanda, and with disastrous consequences. Lemarchand (1970) was among the first to proffer the idea that Belgian colonialism rigidified the distinction between Hutu and Tutsi (admittedly, not an ethnic one in the normal sense). Newbury (1988), and later Mamdani (2001), progressively made the same case in a less qualified, less ambiguous way. In short, Africanist instrumentalists typically blame Europeans for the existence and nature of ethnic conflict within contemporary African states.

Such analysts still have to account for the persistence of ethnic conflict in a postcolonial history that perpetually gets longer. African populations are well exposed to the notion, most notably by their own leaders, that ethnic difference was created by colonial authorities for narrow purposes of "divide and rule." Given that, how can the instrumentalist scholar account for the persistence of conflict among noneconomic identity groups, particularly ethnic ones? The answer to this question provides the third major argument of the Africanist instrumentalist, and it is here that the mobilizationist applies best. The analysis begins with an acknowledgment of extreme scarcity of resources over which the African state has had a great deal of control. Given such a setting, competition among (some) groups for access to the limited resources is inevitable. In turn, political leaders need to reach public office through whatever means (coup, election, or appointment) in order to get control of these resources for themselves. In search of groups on whose behalf they can mount public campaigns (electoral or otherwise) for office, they naturally turn to the existing ethnic identity groups within society. Such "ethnic entrepreneurs" seek to mobilize their constituencies behind their claims to get access to public offices, and thereby to resources. The constituencies who support such ethnic entrepreneurs in turn expect that some of the fruits of access to public office will be returned to their historical areas and group members.

Thus, far from being natural or inevitable, political conflict among identity communities in the African setting is highly contingent upon the exigencies of the political situation that arise from the need of particular rulers to consolidate their power. On this point instrumentalism provides us with a key insight into identity community politics in Africa: the potential centrifugal forces of identity group difference have often been best contained by effective authoritarian rule. If the process of mastering power in an African state frequently requires a nascent ruler to rely heavily on the support of his own identity community, then the process of maintaining a stable authoritarian regime relies just as heavily on sharing the spoils of power with the leaders of other identity groups. This sharing of power typically also involves sharing the wealth, following a neopatrimonial logic well known to Africanists. Yet the nonmaterial symbolism of honoring the leading figures with titles and offices of state is nearly as important. Some journalists have failed to recognize this reality, arguing that authoritarian rule and conflicts among identity communities go hand in hand (Berkeley 2001). In fact, it is only when authoritarian regimes come under political pressure that they typically turn to the production of ethnoregional violence as a desperate measure to generate support from their core constituencies to keep them in power. Other journalists have understood that authoritarian rulers have a strong interest in enunciating transcommunity (nationalist) ideologies designed to dampen the sense of rivalry among the potential followers of ethnic entrepreneurs. As Braeckman (1992: 191) argued as the anti-Mobutu movement gathered steam in the early 1990s, "When the hour of accounting comes [for] the unity of the country, if it is maintained beyond the change of power, we will perhaps owe the credit to Mobutuism."[4]

This instrumentalist insight has particular import for African states that launch democratic experiments. The original transitions to multiparty rule and the first few elections thereafter are inevitably periods of political uncertainty during which no regime is safely in power. Accordingly, the likelihood of clashes among politically mobilized identity communities is particularly high during such periods. While both schools of thought about ethnic and regional identity understand this, the instrumentalists are particularly alert to ways and means by which such communities can be recreated, animated, mobilized, and deployed for political ends at moments of unsettled national politics.

Despite its insights, instrumentalism has several notable defects as an approach to understanding the reemergence of identity community politics at critical moments in a state's politico-historical trajectory. First, instrumentalists often see identity group politics as simply one among many options for ambitious politicians who seek to mobilize social constituencies in their quest to gain public offices. Yet in the African setting, the mobilization of identity community constituencies is likely to be the *only* viable method to gain political support for public offices. Appeals to class strata of society or the articulation of alternative policy positions on economic issues, for instance, have not proved useful in mobilizing voters to support specific candidates. Identity communities may well be artificial, but they are hardly politically irrelevant; on the contrary, they have consistently proven to be the most relevant cleavage in African societies along which political constituencies can be mobilized. Artificial, or "created," though such communities may be, they still weigh heavily in the political calculus of the here and now of every African polity.[5] The politics of identity need not be violent, it is virtually inevitable in postcolonial African states. Second, instrumentalists have failed to give due recognition to the power and persistence of historical memory among identity communities, regardless of whether the remembered history is real or not. Where there is a history of political violence among identity groups lumped together in a common political space, the probability of the renewal of that violence is quite high. Lemarchand (1994) has shown how the memory of violence itself has become a prime cause of periodic renewals of identity community violence in Burundi. The same observation could be made of many other African states, including Rwanda, Nigeria, Angola, Ethiopia, the DRC, and Congo Republic itself.

The wisest positions on the nature of identity community politics and conflict chart a delicate course between the Scylla of primordialism and Charybdis of instrumentalism, at least in their purer forms. Among the earliest scholarly attempts to begin to stake out this middle ground was the inestimable work of Young. In his celebrated 1976 study of "cultural pluralism" this scholar was at the greatest pains to reject the primordialist approach on the grounds of his miscomprehension of the complexity and contingency of confrontation among identity groups (1976: 34–37). At that moment in the intellectual history of ethnic studies, the community of scholars was certainly in much more need of his corrective argument than anything that might then have been said against instrumentalism. Yet Young did warn against the habit of most Marxist theorists to see ethnic conflict as "false consciousness," and thereby to deny the "objective" qualities of identity and identity politics (39–41). In his later work with Turner (Young and Turner 1985), Young again implicitly takes a middle-ground position in this great debate in his analysis of identity politics in Zaire.

Laitin sagely found his way between the two positions by identifying what he called "the two faces of culture" (1986: 11–16). The first face of culture is revealed by the recognition "that *shared cultural identities facilitate collective action,* for people who share a culture can communicate with each other more easily" (11, emphasis in original). For Laitin, the most notable analysts of this face of culture were Weber and (later) Geertz, seeing culture as an independent variable that helped determine people's economic and social behavior. The second face of culture helps us understand that "individuals are [also] utility maximizers and will therefore manipulate their cultural identities in order to enhance their power and wealth" (12). Laitin associated this emphasis with Bentham, among the earliest rational choice theorists, and with the anthropologist Abner Cohen. The purpose of Laitin's study was to demonstrate that the behavior of the Yoruba people and politicians could not be understood without reference to both faces of culture. This study is an invaluable reference as a synthesis of the two competing paradigms of identity among ethnic, regional, and religious groups within plural societies, and the position it represents has recently become more common.

By the second half of the 1990s, Robertson was able to claim that, "a scholarly consensus is emerging that ethnic groups and national are *constructed,* as is nationalism, ethnic conflict, and its accommodation" (1997: 265, emphasis added). For Robertson, constructivism provided a superior, synthetic paradigm that superseded the old debate between "primordial and instrumental perspectives." Robertson draws on cases of nationalism and ethnic identification across several world regions to show that "the origins and consequences of ethnic groups, national, nationalism, and ethnic conflict in world politics are contextual and interactive," rather than being either artificial (as instrumentalism has it) or real and inevitable (as primordialism has it) (266). He is on solid ground in deploying the language of constructivism for his synthesis, since this approach refuses to privilege either agents or structures in social analysis.[6] Robertson concludes that, "Constructivism makes it possible to assess ethnopolitics as both real and imagined, and allows us to better understand the world of our making" (280). Indeed, the ethnopolitical groups that appear on the stage of various

African postauthoritarian political dramas result from a dialectical process in which ethnic entrepreneurs seek to build constituencies from the mosaic of existing identity structures that they find in place, artificial though they may be. In such circumstances, to paraphrase Marx, politicians build their own ethnic and regional political constituencies, but they do not build them just as they wish. Whether such a process leads to ethnic violence and the collapse of fragile, new regimes depends on the contingencies of local circumstance and history, as well as the motives and behavior of those who seek power.

If one takes the primordialist position on ethnic identity, then the facts of the case of Congo speak for themselves: the democratic experiment in the country was doomed from the start by implacably hostile ethnic communities, the roots of whose conflict lie deep in history. On the other hand, if one takes a staunchly instrumentalist view, there is historical work to be done. One must show that ethnoregional constituencies that emerged in 1991 were artificial and resulted from the mobilizing work of power-hungry politicians. This can be done relatively easily, but it leads to an equally misleading result. Such a research agenda assumes that the artificiality of ethnoregional identity groups made them superficial and that the politicians in questions had abundant options in their respective quests for political office. Neither is the case. If, however, one takes such a constructivist position on the problem of ethnic and regional identity in Congo, one is confronted with a more complicated kind of research. In that case, the challenge is to achieve some awareness of the nature of the lines of ethnic and regional cleavage that have emerged in the past and to understand the depth of social feeling that may accompany them. A second challenge is to understand the kinds of choices that the politicians faced with regard to ethnic and regional politics and how each choice affected their possibilities for attaining office. In short, one has to reach an understanding of the ethnoregional context for political action and the range of choices available to the politicians, given both demography and historical feeling. Following this model, the next section inquires into the development of ethnoregional identities in Congo in the late colonial and postindependence periods until 1991.

■ The Emergence and Domestication of Congo's Ethnic and Regional Identities

The study of the onset of national politics in Congo in the 1950s makes it clear that Congo's ethnoregional identity groups have emerged out of an interaction of actors and structures. On the one hand, there was nothing inevitable about the emergence of particular ethnoregional identity groups as political constituencies; the same parts of some constituencies that have worked together toward a political end might just as likely have become rivals for political power. It was the great fluidity of Congo's ethnic "structures" that allowed the country's political figures to reconfigure the country's ethnoregional landscape to suit their needs. On the other hand, the politicians who have mobilized ethnoregional groups, forging and crystallizing their identities for political ends, had to work with the identity structures that they found. These structures had issued forth from the confrontation of colonial practices with the preferences of local authorities who had represented the array of Congo's precolonial ethnic peoples. Yet it is striking how the advent of genuinely competitive politics in the 1950s, and again in 1990–1991, allowed Congo's ethnic entrepreneurs to refashion identity groups into new political constituencies.

To understand how fluid and uncertain the ethnic identities of the Congolese are it is only necessary to review some of the various taxonomies of the country's ethnic groups. All of these taxonomies acknowledge that ethnic identity in the country is "nested," with each large ethnic formation having subgroups, and many of the subgroups having further divisions. Yet it is revealing to see how little agreement there was among colonial-era social observers on the proper categorization of the Congolese on an ethnic basis. Not only do various observers construct different sets of large ethnic categories, but they place specific subgroups into different categories. This reveals that ethnic identities quite frequently overlap, especially in territories where large ethnic formations meet. Congo's regional identities are likewise surprisingly mutable and indeterminate. Although a great rift between northerners and southerners has long divided the country, Congo certainly has no equivalent of the Mason-Dixon Line. Ethnic groups on the border between north and south have frequently sought to identify themselves with one or the other regional group on a largely situational basis.

To illustrate the myriad ways Congo's peoples have been categorized, it is useful to review some ethnic schemas developed by a sampling of observers over time. It is also important to note the areas of relative consistency for the major groups in the various schemas. Table 5.1 summarizes the ethnic taxonomies of four different scholars, including the number of subgroups for each group, and the percentage of the population represented where given. As this table suggests, the Kongo, Téké, and Mbochi groups are consistently listed as major Congolese ethnic groups, and the three groups maintain their identities up until today. Beyond that basic observation, however, there is a great deal of murkiness about the social cohesion, classification, and demographic weight of Congo's ethnicities. Not only do these four authors list different subgroups, but they sometimes list them under different major group headings. This is not surprising since some subgroups (consider the Téké-Lari) represent a blending of older ethnic groups and share cultural habits across the lines of the major groups. Complicating the picture further is the problem that some subgroups bear the same name as the parent grouping: among Kongo's many subgroups, one is called Bakongo; Mbochi and Téké are also ethnic subgroups of larger clusters bearing the same names. Some of Kounzilat's ethnic groups are considered subgroups of other ethnic clusters by other authors (Kounzilat

Table 5.1 Major Ethnic Categories by Region According to Four Observers

Region	Bruel (1935)	Wagret (1963)	Woungly-Massaga (1974)	Kounzilat (1993)
South	Les Mba (Kongo) (8 subgroups)	The Kongo (46%) (10 subgroups)	Kongo (53%) (11 subgroups)	Kongo (41%) (12 subgroups)
Center (Plateaux)	Batéké (5 subgroups)	Batéké (10%) (7 subgroups)	Téké (13%) (8 subgroups)	Téké (8%) (12 subgroups)
North[a]	Boubangui (7 subgroups, including Babochi)	Mbochi-Kouyou (13%) (8 subgroups)	Mbochi (12%) (6 subgroups)	Mbochi (7%) (10 subgroups)
			Boubangui (4%) (7 subgroups)	Oubanguein (2%) (3 subgroups)
	Populations of Moyenne Sanga and Haute Likouala Essoubi (13 subgroups, including some non-Congo)	Oubanguien (6 subgroups)	Maka (4%) (5 subgroups)	Maka (2%) (5 subgroups)
				Baya (2 subgroups)
				Sangha (3%) (13 subgroups)
Western border areas[b]	Bakota (13 subgroups)	Pahouin (4 subgroups, including Mbeti)	Kota (10%) (5 subgroups)	Kota (3% for Kota, Punu, Duma)
	Populations of the Ogooué loop (6 subgroups, including Mbété and Bandzabi)		Mbeti (3%) (no subgroups)	Punu (5 subgroups)
				Punu (3 subgroups)
				Duma (2 subgroups)
				Mbere (2 subgroups)
				Kélé (2 subgroups)

Notes: Percentages indicate percentage of population.
a. Bruel includes non-Congo subgroups.
b. Bruel includes Gabonese subgroups.

1993). Further complicating the picture, the demarcations on the maps of these scholars and others do not coincide at all; the territories that Congo's ethnicities inhabit are apparently somewhat fluid, as are the identity categories themselves.[7]

The more the great variety of classification schemes are studied, including all of their various subgroups, and sub-subgroups, the more vexation is felt with the positivist scholar who wants to know, "How many ethnic groups does Congo have?" Clearly, it depends on how one counts them. By the 1960s, French scholars like Sautter (1966: 168–174) had begun to recognize the futility of accurately or definitively categorizing Congo's ethnic peoples and the impossibility of associating them with specific geographical spaces (185–188). It is somewhat surprising that scholars working later (see, e.g., Kounzilat 1993) have been willing to try again to accomplish these tasks.

The Emergence of Ethnic and Regional Identities in Congo

Given the flexibility and contingency of ethnic identity, it is necessary to chart the succession of political figures and forces that have mobilized ethnic and regional identities over time. Each of these efforts has left a legacy with which subsequent generations of Congolese have had to grapple. While none has created permanent ethnic or regional identity groups, each effort has imprinted the country's ethnopolitical map with lingering divisions that remain relevant for subsequent rounds of competitive politics. It is only at moments of political maneuver, such as when the political space is opened by competition, that one witnesses major new efforts to reforge ethnic and political identities. In the interim periods, politics tends to revolve around competition from *within* the dominant ethnic (e.g., Mbochi versus Kouyou or Lari versus Bakongo) or regional groups in power. To understand fully the configurations of ethnoregional politics that emerged at the beginning of the democratic experiment, one must be aware of the earlier lines of cleavages that marked—and scarred—the country.

Meanwhile, a range of civil society groups have been created over time that promised to cut across the ethnic and regional lines of cleavage and thus to change fundamentally the country's politics. To date, the alternatives represented by nonethnic, nonregional civil groups have failed to capture the imagination of the Congolese in political terms; every moment of political maneuver has been dominated by the politics of ethnicity and region. Yet advocates of nonethnic politics in Congo perpetually try to reorient the country's politics along some other lines, as others do throughout Africa.

The role of colonial rule in generating ethnoregional politics in Congo was critical yet largely inadvertent. Although colonial agents certainly had stereotypes about the personal qualities of individuals representing various ethnicities, they were not consciously trying to divide and rule Congo. Rather, it was in the very act of circumscribing a political space where a variety of ethnic peoples lived that they (eventually) spawned identity group politics (rather than a politics of class or policy issues). The quotidian activities of colonial state building—and the local reaction to them—did refashion, mold, and sometimes rigidify the existing identities, however. Most notably, in the early years of the development of Brazzaville, the colonial authorities created two African villages adjacent to the city center: Bacongo to the southwest in 1909 and Poto-Poto to the northeast in 1911 (Martin 1995: 33). In the succeeding decades, these authorities channeled migrant workers from the south into Bacongo and those from the north into Poto-Poto according to their "race" (40). The identities marked out by this geographical separation were greatly solidified by the differential use of language in the two quarters by church officials over subsequent decades. Over the years 1910 to 1913 the colony's head religious authority, Monsignor Prosper Augouard, decided that the vehicular language of Kituba, along with Kikongo, would be used for religious education in Bacongo, while the vehicular language of Lingala would be used in Poto-Poto (42). These policies created a fundamental identity difference that had not previously existed and gave birth to the country's most basic political division, south versus north, which exists to this day.

Different ethnic groups benefited or suffered from European contacts over time in a way that accentuated identity differences and conflicts. The earliest economic beneficiaries of contact with European traders were the rulers of the Loango kingdom, as noted in Chapter 3. The preeminent ethnic group to emerge from this kingdom was a people whom French colonialists called the "Vili," universally considered a Kongo subgroup, but one with a distinctive and independent history.[8] Since the French brought their institutions to the Kouilou region on the coast very early in the colonial enterprise, the Vili were "the first to benefit from the contributions of Western civilization," namely, a missionary education (Gauze 1973: 3; see also Moukoko 1999: 365). Indeed, the Vili produced an impressive succession of Francophone literary figures throughout the twentieth century. Surprisingly, the northern Mbochi also were early beneficiaries of their association with colonial authorities. According to Gauze (1973: 1), they were "the first tribe in Moyen-Congo to become politically prominent," owing largely to the mission station in M'Boundji in the Cuvette region, though Gauze goes on to say that they "lost ground during the period between the two world wars to other tribes" (2). Those to benefit at the expense of the Mbochi in this period were apparently the Bakongo groups of southern Congo, and particularly the Lari subgroup, prominent in Brazzaville. According to Martin (1995: 42–43, 67–68) the Bakongo and Lari benefited from better education, access to paid employment in factories, and managerial experience in the burgeoning capital city as early as 1916, while the Poto-Poto groups were much disfavored because "their socialization and acculturation to the colonial order was weaker than that of populations who lived on the Bacongo side of town" (43). The one major group that is never said to have benefited from preferential colonial treatment is the Téké, whose representatives have indeed failed to play key roles in postcolonial Congolese politics.

Reinforcing the emergence of distinctive identity groups in the colonial period was the nature of civil society of that period. Catholicism, with its universalist Christian message, might have served to unite and transcend these identities, but it did not in the colonial practice. Instead, mission stations scattered throughout the country, educating local cadres in local languages, mostly produced competing ethnopolitical elites. Perhaps the most important sort of civil society organization to emerge in the colonial period was the *amicale,* or self-help society, but these organizations tended only to draw members of given ethnicity more closely together. The most momentous of these was André Matsoua's Association des Originaires de l'A.E.F. formed in Paris in 1926 (see Chapter 3). Despite its reference to the whole of French West Africa, this organization gained its main influence among the Bakongo people, especially the Lari subgroup, of Moyen-Congo. Much less well known, but also characteristic of colonial civil society, was a similar organization formed by Mbochi civil servants in 1938. This organization was the political training arena for the country's first important Mbochi politicians (Gauze 1973: 2). At a more quotidian level, the football teams, drinking societies, and social clubs that sprang up in Brazzaville during the colonial period almost universally drew upon participants coming from either Bacongo or Poto-Poto, but almost never from both populations (Martin 1995).

Indigenous religious movements were another form of parochial group in society that reinforced local differences. The two most important of these, the cult of Matsouanism and of the N'Zambie Bougie, are discussed in Chapter 3. Contemporary Matsouanists long for the day when a resurrected Matsoua will reappear on Congolese territory to liberate them from oppression. As we saw above, the N'Zambie Bougie cult was first associated with the Vili, and then with a larger ethnoregional grouping (Bernault 1996: 273–276). The cult spread throughout the Kouilou region and deep into the bordering Grand Niari region that existed during the early 1950s. The church gained some 50,000 adherents in that era (Moukoko 1999: 185). Thus, while Christian sects served to cut across, and thus undermine, ethnoregional affiliations in other areas, the local cults of Congo reinforced ethnic and regional differences. Only the Catholic and other Christian churches promised to help transcend ethnic and regional differences, but the influences of these churches did not penetrate deeply enough into the consciousness of Congolese citizens to unite them.

The fundamentally ethnic and regional bases for Congolese politics became evident soon after the opening of the political space after World War II. Many of the patterns established in that period have proved durable. As we saw in Chapter 3, there were two rounds of political competition in Congo during the waning years of French colonialism. The first pitted Tchicaya (the southern Vili) against Opangault (the northern Mbochi). The major political issue of the early and mid-1950s was over the abolition of the so-called dual college system, under which French colonists and black Africans voted in separate ballots for representatives from each group (Bernault 1996: 129–130). More generally, the African delegates, including Tchicaya in the French Assembly and Opangault in the territorial assembly (where he won office after being defeated by Tchicaya for the more important post) fought for an expansion of civil and political rights for African residents. Thus, on the key policy issue of the day, there was no substantive difference between the two main political actors. Tchicaya consistently won elections because of his more robust ethnic and regional base; he enjoyed the support of not only the southern Congolese stretching far beyond the Vili people but also that of a majority of the Téké in the middle regions of Congo. Opangault could count only on the numerically inferior Mbochi and associated northern groups for support, while most Lari and non-Lari Matsouanists were essentially boycotting politics in protest over French treatment of Matsoua.

Tchicaya's fading political grip over Congolese politics in 1956 was not due to any policy issue, but to the full entry of the Lari (and Matsouanists) under the leadership of Fulbert Youlou in 1956. Several aspects of Youlou's rapid mobilization of his ethnoregional constituency among the Lari, other Kongo subgroups, and many non-Kongo groups in the Pool area are striking and characteristic of Congo's politics. First, Youlou's authentic ties with either the Lari or the Matsouanists were dubious, and yet this proved an advantage when the hour of mobilization came. Youlou's native village in Pool had actually had a Téké population before relatively recent (twentieth century) migrations of Lari and Bakongo into the area. Moreover, he was sent away to the seminary at the age of eleven, first to Brazzaville and then out of the country, and he only returned at the age of twenty-nine, in 1946 (Bernault 1996: 244). During his years in seminary he was obviously taught that Matsouanism was an abomination to the true Catholic faith, a faith that he represented as a priest as of 1946. Upon Youlou's return to Brazzaville, he found that the Lari elders and chiefs were divided among those who chose to continue boycotting politics and those who wanted to join the political fray. Further, the Lari youth were alienated from both sets of leaders. The genius of Youlou was to appeal to all of these groups and forge them into a solid electoral constituency. For instance, in 1950 Youlou led a group of Matsouanist pilgrims to Rome and let them believe that he personally spoke with the ghosts of Matsoua and Kimbangu (246). Meanwhile, he appealed to the youth, mostly on account of his own youth and education, and some thought him to be the reincarnation of Matsoua (Gauze 1973: 22). Youlou's leap into formal politics came quite suddenly when he announced his candidacy against both Tchicaya and Opangault shortly before the January 1956 elections. The closeness of the elections in which Tchicaya gained 29.8 percent, Opangault 28.5 percent, and Youlou 26.6 percent (Gauze 1973: 21) ensured that Congo's politics would remain highly charged. The results also reflected a solidification of each ethnoregional constituency.

Events in the rest of 1956 demonstrated that Tchicaya's popularity was waning fast and that Youlou's star was rising. By the time Youlou was over-whelmingly elected mayor of Brazzaville in November 1956, the UDDIA had established a presence in Pointe Noire and in Tchicaya's former south-western fiefs. Meanwhile, Tchicaya's Vili rival, Tchitchellé, abandoned the PPC in Kouilou and made an alliance with Youlou. Although the core of Youlou's support was among the Lari of Pool, his rhetoric was one of terri-torial unity, and his practical political activity one of implanting the UDDIA wherever he could. He appointed Téké and Mbochi political fig-ures to important party positions (Gauze 1973: 30–31).

With the eclipse of Tchicaya, Opangault and Youlou soon squared off as political rivals, and renewed violence between Youlou's Kongo support-ers and Opangault's Mbochi backers soon erupted. Youlou's UDDIA party replaced the PPC as the local affiliate of the territory-wide RDA party, while Opangault's MSA remained aligned with the French socialist party, the French Section of the Workers' International (SFIO). The important thing to recognize about Congo's political parties at this time, though, is that neither had a distinct, clear ideology nor political program. While some thought of the UDDIA as a conservative party because it temporarily made an alliance with a party representing whites in 1956, Youlou frequently crit-icized the colonial administration in harsh terms in his speeches (Bazenguissa-Ganga 1997: 59–64). The MSA was certainly not consistent-ly more radical on other issues of the day. Although the MSA's external affiliate was putatively socialist, this had no bearing on its internal policies. Likewise, the RDA had gradually transformed itself from a quite radical party in the early 1950s to a Gaullist and pro-French Union party by 1958. By that year the "great" issue in Congo's politics, like that of other French territories, was that of the proposed new French constitution. On this fun-damental issue, the UDDIA and the MSA were in agreement in favor of accepting the new constitution and joining the French Community (Bernault 1996: 280).

Congo's politics underwent constant twists and turns over the next four years as Youlou and his UDDIA sought to consolidate their power. As

Youlou proceeded in his quest, he increasingly deemphasized his political base among the Lari and tried to present himself as a figure of unity. As previously noted, he first persecuted Opangault, jailing him in 1959, and then rehabilitated him, making him vice president in 1961. In this way, Youlou sought to co-opt the ethnic constituencies of other political figures; he first sought to defeat and demoralize rival political parties, also representing ethnic or regional constituencies, and then offered their leaders positions in his own administration.

The ethnoregional patterns of Congolese politics that emerged in 1956 and continued well into the Youlou administration were persistent and distinct. First, parties were clearly associated with personalities and not with policies or ideologies, as most (but not all) other African settings. Second, the basis of political mobilization for a given leader was always initially an ethnoregional constituency. After securing support in a home region or among an ethnicity, the next step for any leader was to attempt to encroach on the ethnic or regional territory of his rivals. Third, the particular ethnic or regional political blocks that emerged over time were not entirely predictable. For instance, the political leaders of the Lari and Vili subgroups of the larger Bakongo identity group have started with their subgroup as their initial basis of support, and none has ever fully unified the Kongo behind a specific party. Likewise and interestingly, no towering Téké political leader has yet to appear on the Congolese scene, but, during the first political opening, Vili (Tchicaya), Lari (Youlou), and Mbochi (Opangault) political figures all scrambled for additional support among the Téké, with the Lari and Mbochi having the advantage of proximity. Fourth, alliances among the blocs represented by ethnoregional constituencies are not based on the fealty of related identity groups but are purely strategic, that is, for the purpose of gaining power. And, as the about-face of Tchitchellé in 1956 shows, important ethnopolitical entrepreneurs can rapidly switch sides as the political winds change direction.

Despite these patterns, both the manner of Youlou's overthrow and the politics of the subsequent years show clearly that Congo's politics was not only about the mobilization of ethnoregional constituencies. After all, it was not a coalition of ethnopolitical forces that confronted Youlou in 1963, but a coalition of labor unions and youth (Bazenguissa-Ganga 1997: 71–73). And every historian of the period emphasizes the galvanizing effects of the visit of Sekou Touré to the Congolese capital, during which the Guinean president condemned "imperialism and its lackeys" and called upon the people to overthrow "regimes that exploit the masses" (cited in Bazenguissa-Ganga 1997: 71). When the first of the three "glorious days" of the revolution began, the poor of Bacongo as well as the poor of Poto-Poto massed to confront the embattled Youlou (Gauze 1973: 152). Congo's two leading army officers of the day, one Mukongo and one Lari, actually convinced Youlou that he must resign (Bazenguissa-Ganga 1997: 153; Bernault 1996: 18). For one brief moment, the cleavages of class and generation trumped those of ethnicity and region.[9]

The Domestication of Ethnic and Regional Loyalties

Despite how Youlou's regime ended, it is striking that more than two decades of fervent antitribalist rhetoric did not at all extinguish the ties of language, place, and ethnicity that bound people together and allowed them later to be mobilized by ethnic entrepreneurs. Youlou himself certainly realized the danger that such ties posed to his regime, as his attempt to create a sole legal national political party in 1962 suggests. His successors, who created in turn the Mouvement National de la Révolution (MNR) and the PCT, even more fully realized the threat that ethnoregional political forces posed to their rule and sought to avert them through the single-party route. The ideologists of these regimes bluntly referred to any kind of ethnoregional politics as tribalism and associated the phenomenon with imperialism and neocolonialism. They argued forthrightly that "tribalism" had been consciously created in Congo by the French as a strategy of divide and rule (Mampouya 1983: 56). The apologists for the PCT regimes ridiculed Alphonse Massamba-Débat not only for his halfhearted devotion to socialism but, even more viciously, for "getting rid of all of the Marxists in order to hide himself in the tribal shell" (67).

The apparent, but not real, "domestication" of ethnoregional identities began under Massamba. Contrary to the criticism leveled against him by later PCT apologists, Massamba was arguably the least tribalist ruler Congo has yet seen. As a political expediency in the 1950s, he did "try to present himself as one of the legitimate representatives of Matsoua," but this was not because of ethnic affiliation; rather, as a fellow anticolonialist, he had "simply eased [Matsoua's] pain a little bit" during a chance encounter in Fort-Lamy where Massamba met Matsoua on his way to exile (Bazenguissa-Ganga 1997: 87). History shows that Matsoua's own self-image was that of a figure of national liberation, not a leader of an ethnic bloc; it was only after his death that Matsoua's image was appropriated in this way. Massamba was born a Mukongo (of the larger Kongo ethnic group) in the Pool town of Nkolo (or Kolo). He had a secular education and outlook on politics, and he was put in power by a group of (mostly young) labor leaders who organized themselves into the Conseil National de la Révolution (CNR) immediately after Youlou's ouster. Massamba's ideology was one of African socialism, not unlike that of Julius Nyerere or Kenneth Kaunda. Whatever his shortcomings, Massamba supported the formation of the MNR with the idea of creating a political movement that transcended ethnoregional politics. Unlike his predecessor, Massamba did not launch his political career on the backs of an ethnic constituency; unlike his successors, he did not seize power in a coup d'état backed by his coethnics in the army. Rather, Massamba was *asked* to take power by the leaders who overthrew Youlou (86–87). In his non-ethnoregional approach to politics, the Congolese politician who most resembles him is his fellow Mukongo André Milongo (see Chapter 7).

Meanwhile, the main purpose of the mass organizations created by the MNC and adapted by the PCT is clear: to attempt to forge a new, national Congolese identity and to create other cleavages (of generation, gender, and class) that cut across the cleavages of region and ethnicity. Besides the MNR itself, the three key organizations created under Massamba included the Jeunesse de la MNR (JMNR), the Union Révolutionnaire des Femmes du Congo (URFC), and the Confédération des Syndicats Congolais (CSC). Had these institutions succeeded, a new civil society would have emerged in Congo, one made up of associations representing these groups and standing between individual citizens and the state.

The rapidity with which these state-sponsored organizations evaporated in 1990–1991 revealed the shallowness of their roots in society. During the 1970s and 1980s, the Congolese population constantly sought to create alternative social groups, mostly local, in which they participated with passion. These groups included women's mutual aid societies, funeral organization committees, farming cooperatives, and so on (Kabongo-Mbaya 2000: 120); virtually all of these civil society groups were local and composed exclusively of one ethnicity.[10] Ironically, given the PCT's ideology, the groups that flourished most abundantly were religious groups (Kabongo-Mbaya 2000: 121; Martin, forthcoming). The state officially recognized seven different churches as "religious associations" under its 1984 constitution, but the secretariat general of the administration in Brazzaville recognized the existence of another ninety-five "cults" in the late 1980s (see Tonda 1988: 74, n. 1). As discussed previously in Chapter 3, traditional cults believing in magical powers and the influence of supernatural forces on earth (like ndjobi) were powerful throughout Congo. Such groups represented the *real* civil society of Congo under the one-party state.

Moreover, despite the rhetoric of the new regimes, it is undeniable that the regimes of Ngouabi, Yhombi, and Sassou (I) were all dominated by northerners. Each of these rulers sought to disguise this reality by staffing their cabinets, the PCT's central committee, the rubber stamp Parliament (the Assemblé Nationale Populaire), and other organizations with representatives from all of Congo's regions.[11] Many other African dictators, including Mobutu, have used the same strategy (Clark 1995b: 362–363). Yet if one looks at the institutions and individuals who were key to the president's security, they were almost entirely from loyal northern ethnicities. Just as Mobutu had his infamous Division Spéciale Presidentielle, Sassou had his "specially trained, well-armed and well-paid elite Presidential Guard (the

Red Berets) . . . composed of hand-picked northerners, bolstered by Cuban advisors and operational personnel" (Decalo 1996: 36). Even the army was dominated by northerners and generally had a loyal, northern Chief of Staff, such as Jean-Marie Michel Mokoko, who occupied the post after 1987. Sassou relied on key Mbochi/northern personnel for politico-ideological guidance (Théophile Obenga, Joseph Elenga-Ngaporo, Camille Bongou), economic support (Otto Mbongo), diplomatic guidance (Jean-Marie Elengué, Rodolphe Adada), administrative expertise (Justin Lékoundzou), as well as military security (Mokoko, Pierre Oba, Pierre Aboya).

The most important *real* politics of the 1970–1990 period continued to be ethnic, namely, the intra-Mbochi rivalry between the Kouyou and Mbochi subgroups within the army.[12] Given that the Mbochi (even in the large sense) were a minority in the country, both groups went to great pains to conceal the true nature of the power struggle. As a result, their struggles took place behind the façades of national unity and putative internal battles over ideological interpretation. Some scholars took the apparent debates over appropriate interpretations of Marxism-Leninism in a developing state setting at face value (e.g., Radu and Somerville 1989), while others saw through the illusion (e.g., Decalo 1990). The most evident manifestations of this rivalry were the assassination of Ngouabi in 1977 and the putsch orchestrated by Sassou in 1979. Although the first event remains shrouded in controversy, most knowledgeable Congolese believe the assassination was organized by power-hungry Mbochi officers seeking to remove their Kouyou rivals. Likewise, most Congolese believe that Sassou's seizure of power was the final realization of this goal, displacing as it did Yhombi, another Kouyou. At the time of Sassou's coup, however, these events were interpreted as a struggle between committed Marxist-Leninists (Sassou's faction) against pro-Western pseudosocialists (Yhombi's faction). Many of the other dramatic political events that were discussed in the press as pro-Chinese versus pro-Soviet conflicts, such as the coup attempts of 1972 and 1987, were actually struggles among military factions based largely on intra-Mbochi identities (Decalo 1996: 83). Just as Stalin used the fiction of ideological deviation to eliminate many of his enemies, rival military commanders were frequently removed on such fraudulent grounds. By such Machiavellian maneuvers as these, ethnic politics continued under the nominally Marxist regimes dominated by northerners.

■ **The Reemergence of Ethnoregional Politics During the Democratic Experiment**

It is undeniable that the primary basis for political competition in Congo after the democratic opening was ethnoregional in character. Some scholars are uncomfortable with this fact, and have tried to explain it away as a kind of epiphenomenon of an underlying class conflict.[13] Consistent patterns in Congo's ethnoregional politics have been identified by European and Congolese observers alike (Weissman 1993; Frank 1997: 5–6; Dimoneka 1997: 28–30). In every case, political movements began with a politically renowned personality. Such personalities always started by mobilizing their own ethnic or regional base, even as they preached a message of national unity. The primary question to consider, however, is not whether ethnoregional politics was "natural," or inevitable, but whether it doomed the democratic experiment from the beginning.

During the national conference of 1991, there was an illusion that Congo had transcended its political past of ethnoregional contestation. The delegates to the conference represented a range of civil society groups, labor unions, religious confessions, scientific groups, and national institutions, as well as a plethora of new political parties (Bazenguissa-Ganga 1997: 375–376). In principle, none of the nonparty groups should have had an ethnic or regional basis, even if few had deep roots in society. A casual observer might have thought that transethnic civil society groups had won the day in Congo. Moreover, the debates at the conference did not take the form of interethnic conflict, though there was criticism of the PCT regime for its Mbochi favoritism. The fact that the conference was chaired by Catholic Monsignor Ernest Kombo also boded well for interethnic understanding, insofar as the Catholic religion stretched across all ethnoregional sectors of society. One nonethnic line of cleavage at the conference was between generations, pitting the barons of the old regime against new aspirants for power (381–383); the older generation prevailed, as discussed in Chapter 3. Even less promising was the fact that the conferees spent the bulk of their time examining the real and alleged crimes of the PCT regimes, rather than debating the country's future.

In the absence of any real debates on policy direction or what form Congolese democracy might take, however, ethnoregional coalition making was tacitly dominating the genuine politics of the conference. With the numerically inferior northerners marginalized, the struggle for leadership of the transitional government eventually came down to a contest between two southern technocrats: André Milongo, a Mukongo from Pool, and Pascal Lissouba, an Nzabi from Niari. After four ballots, Milongo emerged the winner by a narrow margin.

The specific ethnoregional coalitions that emerged during the electoral campaigns of 1992 reveal both the structural aspects of Congolese ethnoregionalism and the fluidity of identity possibilities that politicians used to their advantage. That Sassou would continue to be a major political figure, and that he would emerge as the champion of the north was no surprise. Sassou had shown statesmanship at the conference by confessing the sins of the PCT past, and he maintained considerable political capital, including support in the army. Clearly he represented the best hope for northerners to maintain influence in the new state. Even more revealing of the structural roots of ethnic politics in Congo was Milongo's gradual displacement from political influence by Bernard Kolélas. Milongo was a well-educated technocrat with strong external connections, having worked in the World Bank and IMF. Meanwhile Kolélas's primary appeal was to the traditionalist Lari of Brazzaville and Pool, despite the support of some exiled intellectuals in France (Babu-Zalé et al. 1996: 60–75). Kolélas's consistent and unflinching anticommunism, as well as his closeness to the Lari masses, gave him a strong appeal among the remnants of the Matsouanist movement, a base of support that Kolélas did not deny himself. That Sassou and Kolélas would emerge at the head of two ethnically based parties was altogether predictable.

Entirely less predictable was the regional coalition of forces that Lissouba forged to support his political reemergence, and its appearance speaks to the contingency and flexibility of the ethnic and regional constituencies that can emerge at moments of political movement. Lissouba had cultivated the idea of a distinctive regional identity among a group of southern intellectuals, excluding any Lari, under the label of "Grand Niari" from the time of his political marginalization in 1968 (Bazenguissa-Ganga 1997: 124; Moukoko 1999: 141). This term has its origins in physical geography, but it was also the name of one of seven administrative regions into which the colonial authorities divided Congo from 1950 to 1960 (see map in Sautter 1966: 182). As Gray (2002) has demonstrated, the demarcation of regional boundaries within states can have a crystallizing effect on the identities of the inhabitants circumscribed together, no matter how weak the prior identification. Yet it must be emphasized that identification with Grand Niari as a regional bloc had not been politically significant in Congolese history for many decades. It was there that a regional alliance of conferees from the regions of Niari, Bouenza, and Lékoumou (Nibolek) emerged (Bazenguissa-Ganga 1997: 394). Although most Congolese analysts barely mention the coalescence of this regional group at the conference, it was surely one of the most momentous of political developments there. Further, the particular configuration of Nibolek as a politico-regional force was entirely circumstantial. With the MCDDI demonstrating itself to be a major political force in Pool, and with the PCT temporarily eclipsed by its recent misdeeds, the country's non-Pool BaKongo sought a prominent political southerner from outside Pool around whom they could rally. Lissouba, with his political experience, "scientific" standing, and international credibility fit the bill perfectly. His origins as an Nzabi (of the larger Duma group) further redounded to his credibility as a nonethnic leader.[14] As Bernault noted (1996: 363), "Nibolek" came to be used as a "virtual ethnonym," which "underlines the modern nature of ethnicity, an identity fundamentally political, temporary, and reversible."

Intriguingly, many observers of ethnopolitics in Congo have historically connected the Nzabi with the much larger Téké ethnic cluster. Indeed, the two Duma subgroups do live in geographical proximity to each other in a southwestern part of Congo along the Gabonese border. The main political significance of this connection is that Gabonese president Omar Bongo is of Téké ethnicity and hails from a region of Gabon adjacent to Lissouba's home district in Congo. Bongo apparently intervened on Lissouba's behalf, when the latter was imprisoned in 1977 and nearly given a death sentence for allegedly plotting against Ngouabi (Lissouba 1997: 120–121). The two were said to be close on ethnic grounds. Some media sources have even mistakenly identified Lissouba as a Téké himself. Yet Lissouba did not enjoy significant support in Congo's Plateaux region, dominated by the Téké, despite his active patronage of such Téké political figures as Raymond-Damase Ngollo, Clement Mierassa, and David Charles Ganao. Lissouba won only 10 percent of the vote in Plateaux in the first round of the 1992 presidential elections, while Sassou carried 57.6 percent of the voters there (Weissman 1993: 72). Sassou's support in Plateaux was thus even greater than in his native Cuvette region, where he competed with Yhombi.

Nonetheless, the ethnoregional nature of the support for the major candidates was confirmed in the local elections of May 1992, the legislative elections of June and July 1992, and the presidential elections in August 1992. In the local elections, the MCDDI won narrowly in Brazzaville while it dominated Pool, and, as expected, Lissouba's UPADS prevailed in the three Nibolek regions. Jean-Pierre Thystère-Tchicaya's Rassemblement pour la Démocratie et le Progrès Social (RDPS) carried the day in Pointe Noire, while Yhombi's RDD party narrowly beat the PCT in Cuvette (Economist Intelligence Unit, *Country Report: Congo*, no. 3, 1992: 10–11). Similar patterns characterized the legislative elections during the following two months, in which UPADS won the most seats (thirty-nine), followed by the MCDDI (twenty-nine). In the first round of the presidential elections, Lissouba carried the three Nibolek regions by a margin of at least 80 percent, and he was also the first place finisher in Kouilou. Kolélas won only the Pool region and a narrow plurality in ethnically diverse Brazzaville. Sassou prevailed over his rival Yhombi in Cuvette and also carried the northern regions of Likouala and Sangha. More interesting, Sassou soundly beat the veteran Téké politician David Charles Ganao in the Plateaux region by a margin of 58 to 15 percent (Weissman 1993: 71–73). Finishing third overall, Sassou threw his support behind Lissouba in the second round of the presidential elections, allowing the former prime minister to prevail over Kolélas by a margin of 61 to 39 percent. In the second round, Lissouba won at least 89 percent in each of the four northern regions.

Nearly as soon as Lissouba was in office, ethnoregionally based factions *within* his camp began maneuvering for influence over control of the government. The dominant faction throughout his term was a group of Bembé ministers from Bouenza region. Intriguingly, one of those apparently most influential with the president was his chief of staff and alleged mistress, Claudine Munari. As chief of staff throughout his reign, Munari exercised considerable control over access to Lissouba. Munari was supported by a "gang of four" other Bembé, all ministers or UPADS operatives: Martin Mberi, Christophe Moukouéké, Nguila Moungounga Nkombo, and Victor Tamba-Tamba (Kouvibidila 2000: 221). These loyalists stayed with Lissouba until the end, and all went into exile in 1997 except Mberi, who rallied to Sassou on the eve of his military victory. Two other groups of lesser regime loyalists, respectively from Niari and Lékoumou, battled this dominant group for influence (*Africa Confidential,* "Congo: The Barons Mind the Shop," 22 January 1993: 6). Once these contests had subsided, other competitions among ethnoregional blocs within the regime emerged. This intrabloc struggle strongly recalled the infighting between the Mbochi and Kouyou factions during the single-party era.

While ethnic factions fought for influence inside the presidential camp, Lissouba himself patronized other ethnoregional barons in hopes of bringing their constituencies into his camp, or at least reducing their hostility to his regime. The pattern was most notable in Lissouba's selection of three northern prime ministers: Stéphane Bongho-Nouarra, from Ouesso, whose government lasted only a few weeks in 1992; Yhombi, a Kouyou from Owando, chosen as prime minister in the wake of the highly contested 1993 legislative elections; and Charles Ganao, perhaps the country's leading Téké politician of the time, named prime minister in August 1996 in the cabinet reshuffle as Lissouba prepared for the 1997 elections. Lissouba also sought to let the losers of the 1992 to 1994 battles—both political and physical—find meaningful roles in his regimes. In the mayoral elections of 1994, Kolélas became mayor of Brazzaville and Thystère-Tchicaya mayor of Pointe Noire. In his cabinet reshuffle of January 1995, Lissouba named Philippe Bikinkita, a cousin of Kolélas, to be his minister of interior (Clark 1997b: 75).

Although the classic patterns of ethnic infighting and ethnic balancing emerged during Lissouba's term, it was not these patterns themselves that were the instruments of the destruction of Congolese democracy: this dishonor falls to the political militia, or "private militia," of the three main political actors. In this chapter, the question to be asked about the militia is: To what extent did the militia appear "spontaneously" and to what extent were they consciously organized?[15] The answer is that the appearance of the militia depended very much on the agency of the main political actors, even if "the diffusion of violence cannot be reduced solely to their manipulative capacity" (Quantin 1997: 174). Certainly, the composition of the militia reflected the contingent ethnoregional structures of Congolese society. But they only emerged through the active efforts of the ethnopolitical leaders.

A great majority of the educated citizens of Congo's urban centers concur with the view that ethnicity has been created by politicians for political ends. In dozens of interviews held in Brazzaville and Pointe Noire in 2001 and 2002,[16] not a single respondent was prepared to agree that ethnic conflict was natural or historically rooted in precolonial antagonism. Rather, they emphasized the extent of intermarriage and other forms of ethnic mixing in cities before the onset of the first civil war in 1993. Thoughtful citizens are completely aware that Congo's politicians have manipulated ethnoregional identities for political ends.

Yet the same respondents all have tales of horrific mistreatment of themselves, family members, or friends during Congo's first two civil wars. Indeed, the ethnic cleansing of Brazzaville's partly segregated neighborhoods was a signal feature of the first civil war (Sundberg 2000). During that war, virtually all Lari were driven out of the Mfilou and Diata neighborhoods, dominated by residents coming from the Nibolek regions, and, likewise, those from Nibolek were driven out of Bacongo and Makékélélé. Those owning property in one of the "alien" districts typically lost it to members of the rival groups.[17] A great many were physically assaulted in these purges, and many women sexually assaulted. Houses on the borders of the various neighborhoods were frequently looted.

If the purpose of the militia was essentially political, then how is such horrific violence against ordinary citizens explained? In his works, Bazenguissa-Ganga (1994, 1999) has emphasized that most of the militia fighters were young (fourteen to thirty in age), badly educated, and unemployed. Many partook freely of drugs and took advantage of the opportunity to enrich themselves and satisfy their violent urges. Although some of my respondents in Brazzaville painted a different picture of those who joined the militia,[18] they fully agreed that the politicians who created the militia groups hardly controlled their activities at all. In fact, they emphasized that the various militia groups often committed acts of violence or thefts against those from their own ethnic communities. Bazenguissa-Ganga notes the same phenomenon and also describes how militia fighters turned on their own political leaders when they were dissatisfied (1999: 48–49). My respondents also pointed out that the militia groups were to some extent ethnically diverse, in that some Kouyou supporters of Yhombi joined the Zoulous, while northerners of many ethnicities joined the Cobras.[19] Thus, the violence of the militia groups was as much common criminality committed against fellow citizens as it was an expression of ethnic hatred.

Following the end of the one-party era, it was nearly inevitable that Congo's politics would have been played out on an ethnoregional basis, given the country's past. When ethnic or regional politics has been played out once, it is likely to return in the future. Yet, as we saw, there was great flexibility in the kinds of constituencies that could be constructed, and that built by Lissouba was novel and unpredictable. Moreover, ethnoregional political contestation did not necessarily have to lead to ethnoregional violence—this was a product of the political will of desperate politicians and not at all a natural expression of interethnic animosity in Congo. The question that remains is whether ethnoregional politics was compatible with the continuation and evolution of the democratic experiment in Congo. Some light can be shed on this question by comparing Congo's experience with that of other African states that launched their own democratic experiments in the same era.

■ Ethnoregional Politics in Comparative Perspective

The experience of most other African states that began experimenting with democracy in the 1991 to 1994 period shows that ethnic and/or regional politics usually dominated the electoral landscape, though there was considerable variation in the form. Writing of Benin, Decalo (1997: 56) claimed that "the ethnic basis of all politics remained alive and well in Benin and, indeed, continues to play a role in all contests." Mehler (2005: 130), commenting on the 1993 elections in the CAR observed that "voting behavior showed a clearly regionalist pattern, suggesting the emergence of ethnic politics as a significant feature of the political landscape." There were clear regional voting patterns in most of the other new democracies as well, including states as diverse as Malawi (VonDoepp 2005: 179), Niger (Villalón and Idrissa 2005b: 36), and Madagascar (Marcus 2005: 159). In only a few states, like Mali (Villalón and Idrissa 2005b) and Mozambique (Manning 2005), was ethnic and regional politics subdued from the beginning of the democratic experiment.

Despite this common pattern, however, ethnoregional electoral contestation does not necessarily doom a democratic experiment. The best known success stories include Mali and Benin, but the experiments are also continuing in Malawi, Zambia, and Niger—all cases where ethnic or regional politics is prominent on the political landscape. Although ethnic or regional contestation might not be the best form for politics to take in transitional democracies, the fact of ethnoregional politics does not seal the fate of a democratic experiment.

Even more importantly, there is some evidence that ethnic and regional politics can fade in importance over time. In Niger, for instance, the minority Djerma dominated during the period of the one-party state, until 1991, when the larger Hausa group took control of the country's national conference (Gervais 1997: 94). As Villalón and Idrissa interpreted the events leading up to the 1993 elections, however, the advent of openly ethnic politics "should be seen not so much as an ethnicization of politics as a breaking of an ethnic domination, and the creation of a multiplicity of regional power bases, aligned with different group interests" (2005a: 35–36). In keeping with that interpretation, Niger's first freely elected president, Mahamane Ousmane was of a minor ethnic group that was linked with the Hausa (35). Ousmane's successor, Tandja Mamadou, elected in 1999, was Niger's first president to be clearly of neither Djerma nor Hausa ethnicity, reportedly being half Peul and half Kanuri. This development suggests that the significance of ethnicity may be receding in the politics of Niger.

Benin, where the democratic experiment has been less troubled, appears to have undergone a similar evolution. In 1991, there was great resentment in the south of the country against the perception of northern domination, personified by the long-serving President Mathieu Kérékou. Accordingly, Nicephore Soglo represented a southern alternative and received 82 percent of the vote in the southern regions in the 1991 elections, while Kérékou continued to dominate the north, winning 94–98 percent of the votes in the northern provinces (Decalo 1997: 57). Yet, remarkably, Soglo squandered all of his regional advantages, and Kérékou returned to power in a free election in 1996 and was again reelected in 2001. Somewhat similarly, Madagascar's Ratsiraka enjoyed a political renaissance after losing the 1992 elections, and returned to office through another election in 1996. In both cases, disappointment with the first presidents produced by the democratic experiments was more important than the huge popularity of the former dictators. Both cases also show that ethnoregional patterns of voting are far from permanent as democratic experiments evolve.

The distinguishing feature of sociopolitical development in Congo was not ethnoregional politics, but rather the organization of ethnoregional militia groups. One of the few other African states experimenting with democracy that saw the same phenomenon was the CAR. After rebels in the army, including the former president's son, revolted and demanded President Patassé's resignation, Patassé himself created his own party militia from ethnic loyalists (Mehler 2005: 137). This militarization of ethnoregional politics ultimately led to an insurgency that overthrew the elected regime. There was no similar pattern of the newly elected presidents creating private militias in Benin or Mali, states that have had more success with democratic consolidation, nor in Malawi or Zambia, where the results are more ambiguous. Hence, the private militias were not a necessary outcome of a change from one ethnicity in power to another, but rather an instrument for power consolidation fabricated by elected politicians.

Had the political sphere not become militarized in Congo, is it possible that ethnicity and regionalism would have receded in importance during subsequent electoral cycles? One test of the idea is to ask whether an ethnically minority president (like Lissouba) might have come to power with broad support outside his home region(s). This line of inquiry brings us to the specific question that has preoccupied thousands of Congolese since 1997: Could Sassou or Kolélas have come to power peacefully in the elections that had been scheduled for that year had there been a free and fair vote?

There is considerable reason to think so. First, disaffection with Lissouba was palpable in Brazzaville on the eve of the 1997 elections. A great many people blamed Lissouba for the violent confrontations of the 1992–1994 period, and there was great bitterness toward him by the Lari who had suffered the most in that war.[20] Nearly all of those from outside his own regions believed that Lissouba had not respected the rule of law, and that he had failed to deliver on their economic aspirations. Moreover, there was a strong sense in the city that the elections had not been properly prepared. Only weeks before the elections were to take place, thousands of citizens were still lining up outside government centers to get their voting cards. Most ominously of all, Lissouba's prime minister, Charles Ganao, had rejected the idea of an independent electoral commission like the one Congo had had in 1992.

Meanwhile, Sassou had undergone a remarkable political renaissance during his years out of power. Like Kérékou in Benin, Sassou was able to put his reputation as a Marxist squarely behind him. When he felt threatened by Lissouba's government, he traveled abroad to Gabon and to France. While in France, he demonstrated unequivocally that he retained positive ties with members of the Chirac government. Meanwhile, on the domestic scene, he mended fences with an important number of his erstwhile opponents from outside the north. Allegedly some of these new partisans, like Jean-Charles Tchicaya from Pointe Noire, strongly encouraged him to run for office again in 1997 (*Jeune Afrique,* "Denis Sassou-Nguesso," 15–21 January 1997: 24). Sassou had gained at least some credit with ordinary Congolese by avoiding direct participation in the war of 1993–1994. Civil servants recalled with nostalgia that the payment of their salaries had been relatively regular under the Sassou regime, compared with that of Lissouba.[21] When Sassou returned to Congo in January 1997 after over a year in France, he was greeted by a giant mob of supporters at the airport, much to Lissouba chagrin (*African Research Bulletin,* "Congo: Ex-President's Triumphalism," January 1997: 12531). Sassou's supporters claimed, citing Africa Radio No. 1, that between 100,000 and 150,000 supporters had been on hand at the airport for his return (Pigasse 1998: 51) on 26 January. According to one poll published by the Institut INAFRES in April 1997, three months before the scheduled elections, Sassou would have finished first in the presidential contest with 33 percent of the vote, to 24 percent for Lissouba and 17 percent for Kolélas; the poll showed Sassou besting Lissouba in the second round by 63 percent to 37 percent.[22] Although Kolélas unequivocally saw himself as the leader of the alliance with the PCT dating to 1993 (*Jeune Afrique*, "Bernard Kolélas," 26 March–1 April 1997: 23), it is quite conceivable that he would have supported Sassou in the second round of the elections, given the bitterness he felt toward Lissouba at the time. It is not inconceivable that Sassou would have won a free election in 1997 and thereby upended the ethnoregional calculus of politics that had prevailed up until that time.

■ Conclusion

The specific configuration of ethnoregional politics that emerged in 1997 reflected neither a natural expression of the country's cultural pluralism nor a wholesale fabrication of new identities cut of whole cloth. Rather, the ethnoregional constituencies emerged from the desire of ethnopolitical entrepreneurs to assemble constituencies that could elect them and the receptiveness of the people to whom they appealed. Yet three realities made *some* kind of ethnoregional politics after 1991 inevitable. First, Congo had a bitter history of ethnoregional contestation during its first period of political openness in the late 1950s. This history motivated politicians and citizens alike to seek redress for the perceived injustices exacted against various ethnicities in the past. Second, the civil society that was created during the one-party period did not resonate with the population and had exceedingly shallow roots in society. Thus the ties that might have cut across those of ethnicity and region were weak and could not unite a significant percentage of people across ethnoregional lines. Third, the politicians were not prepared for a serious debate on policy issues (like structural adjustment), and it is unlikely that the citizens would have responded to such a debate on policy grounds.

Nonetheless, the fact of ethnoregional politics in 1992 did not necessarily doom the Congolese democratic experiment. Rather, it was the militarization of politics by the political class that condemned Congo both to civil war and an end to the democratic experiment. It is altogether conceivable both that ethnoregional coalitions would have continued to morph in subsequent election cycles and that policy issues might eventually have come to the fore. Had the democratic experiment continued only one or two more election cycles, the transethnic civil society groups that gained more strength within the population might have taken hold. In that case, Congolese citizens might have found themselves voting against the politicians posing as representatives of their identity communities on grounds having nothing to do with ethnicity or region.

■ Notes

1. For instance, the collection of ten essays on civil society and political imagination edited by Comaroff and Comaroff (1999) contains exactly one reference to the question of ethnicity (in chapter 4, by Karlstrom [1999]). Conversely, none of the thirteen essays in the edited volume of Harbeson, Rothchild, and Chazan (1994) on civil society and the state treat the question of ethnic or regional identity in any serious detail.

2. The related question of regional identity is temporarily bracketed for the moment here while we pursue the question of ethnic identity. I return to the question of regionalism further on.

3. Certainly, Huntington's (1968) implicit preference for strong-willed, capable governments for the unindustrialized and newly industrializing states that populated the world in the 1960s betrays a belief that premodern social conflicts stemming from ethnic difference could only be contained through this method.

4. Young and Turner (1985: 153) noted in their important work that "Mobutu . . . never openly celebrated the ethnic virtues of the Ngbandi [his own ethnic group]." Indeed, to have done so would have undermined the nationalist ideology that Mobutu publicly promoted in the 1970s and 1980s.

5. On this paradox in Rwanda, see Clark (2006).

6. It is a pity that Daniel Green's excellent collection of essays (2002) on constructivism and comparative politics had virtually nothing to say about the question of ethnic identity and ethnic politics for comparative politics.

7. Of these four observers, only Wagret (1957: 124) and Kounzilat (1993: 22) have ethnic maps. Others can be found in Decalo, Adloff, and Thompson (1996: xxv), Bernault (1996: 2), and Frank (1997: 4). Bernault's map is a reproduction of a map by the French scholar Marcel Soret, who produced the map around 1960.

8. On the colonial origins of this ethnonym, and the identity of the people it labels, see Bernault (1996: 133, note 45) and Moukoko (1999: 364).

9. A hard core of Lari supporters of Youlou continued to "fan the flames of Lari discontent" against the new regime, both through public demonstrations and agitation from outside the country (Gauze 1973: 155).

10. Accordingly, to the extent that they created what we now call "social capital," it was of the "bonding" rather than "bridging" variety (see Inglehart and Welzel 2005: 248). One important exception are the female Catholic "fraternities" discussed in Martin (forthcoming).

11. See, for instance, the listing of cabinet officers in the first cabinets of Ngouabi (1970), Yhombi (1977), and Sassou (1979) in Baniafouna (1995b: 263–267).

12. "Mbochi" refers both to a large ethnic category of many subgroups, as suggested in Table 5.1, and to a subgroup with the same ethnic category.

13. For example, Sundberg (2000: 95) where she says, "Class is the crucial feature of Congolese society even if it is hidden by ethnicity and diffused by clientelism." Despite this contradictory assertion, this article has many keen insights into Congo's ethnoregional politics.

14. Lissouba is also sometimes referred to as a Téké (e.g., Frank 1997: 9) but the geographical area from which he hails does not confirm this judgment. Lissouba himself refers to his grandfather as belonging to the Dzabi group (Lissouba 1997: 18). This group is not normally considered a Téké subgroup, but, as noted above, there is plenty of room for controversy on such issues.

15. In Chapter 6, I explore the origins of the militia as well as their relationship with the regular army.

16. The interviews were conducted in Brazzaville and Pointe Noire in March 2001 and in Brazzaville during May and June 2002. The majority of the respondents were well educated but even poorer, though employed, citizens agreed that ethnic conflict in Congo did not have deep roots.

17. One Lari acquaintance of mine owned a house in Diata, which he leased out to tenants before 1993; at the time of the conflict, the tenants, from a southern region, essentially took over the house and stopped paying any rent.

18. For instance, in an interview in Brazzaville on 30 May 2002, two leaders of a human rights group told me that among those who joined the militia were "functionaries, taximen, journalists, police officers, and professional soldiers." They claimed that people of "all social functions" can be found in the militia. Likewise, Sundberg (2000: 98) indicates that one of her respondents who had joined the Zouluo was a doctoral candidate in economics.

19. On this point, see also Bazenguissa-Ganga (1999: 45).

20. I was staying in the home of a Lari friend in Makékélélé during the weeks before the outbreak of the war that began on 5 June 1997. Although some of my friend's neighbors were afraid to speak openly, those who did were caustic in their assessment of Lissouba's record.

21. According to interviews with some ten public employees working in various ministries in Brazzaville in late May and early June 1997.

22. INAFRES is the acronym for the Institut Africain de Futurologie et de Recherche Économique et Sociale, based in Gabon. Although its Gabonese home base does make the poll suspect, in light of Sassou's relationship as the father-in-law of Omar Bongo, the same poll revealed in July 1998 that Bongo had little support in the country compared to Paul Mba Abessole. See Soni-Benga (1998: 270).

6

The Army and Militias: Forces in Conflict

Because the army's role in Congo's democratic experiment was indirect, any hypothesis that the "army problem" was behind the failure of democracy requires some explanation. In typical cases of coup d'état, army personnel seize control of the state from an existing civilian or military government. The first round of military takeovers in Africa took place in the 1960s when military officers wrested control of the state from the civilian governments that had been set up at the hour of independence. The most typical pretexts for military coups included the corruption or incompetence of civilian authorities, a breakdown of civilian political institutions, or the adoption of radical ideological positions by civilian leaders. This phenomenon gave rise to a sophisticated literature on the incidence of coups d'état that appeared in the 1970s and 1980s (e.g., Horowitz 1980); some scholars continue to study African coups as a generic phenomenon (e.g., McGowan 2003). In Latin American studies, analyses of the same period focused on class relations and policy choices, as militaries in such countries as Argentina, Brazil, and Chile seized power from populist or leftist governments.

Military intervention has not always taken the form of coup d'état, however. Military authorities have sometimes intervened to force a settlement on groups of civilian politicians who reach an impasse in the exercise of their authority. These cases often arise when constitutions are ambiguous about the respective prerogatives of office holders, or when civilian politicians simply ignore the rule of law.[1] Yet another form of military intervention is rebellion by specific units where the goal is not the seizure of state power. In Africa, such interventions usually take place when elements of the armed forces become disgruntled about their conditions of service or the nonpayment of salaries. Among many other instances, the CAR witnessed such interventions as these in the late 1990s (Mehler 2005).

Following the sudden appearance of many new democracies around the world with the end of the Cold War, a new literature emerged, which sought to understand the circumstances under which militaries acted against elected, civilian governments in the contemporary context. As we shall see in

143

the final section, African military figures and organizations frequently became embroiled in the affairs of governments elected under multiparty constitutions. Indeed, military interventions against democratically chosen governments in Africa were more common than in other world regions. One recent study has investigated the incidence of military intervention against liberalizing regimes, finding that the regimes' trajectory toward or away from democratic legitimacy is a major determinant (Clark 2007).

Most of this literature is not strictly relevant to the Congo case, however, because it was not the army *directly* that ended the democratic experiment in 1997. There is some uncertainly about the identity of the first units that Lissouba dispatched to Mpila on the fateful morning of 5 June 1997. Most authors have simply said that he sent "army forces" or military units to Sassou's residence, though one author has specified that the forces were elements of Lissouba's militia, and not the army (Sundberg 2000: 90). Sundberg's observation is revealing and reinforces the notion that only part of the regular army was ever loyal to Lissouba during his presidency. Even some of the army personnel not actively opposed to him would have balked at the specific mission of assaulting Sassou's residence. In any case, the Congolese democratic experiment was *not* ended by a classic coup d'état.

There was an important context for the events of June 1997 that bears recalling. Going back to 1991, there had been a series of confrontations between Milongo's transitional government and the Congolese army during this government's short tenure. Other confrontations between the army and the Lissouba regime followed during subsequent years. At the time of the 1993–1994 civil war, the army was thoroughly divided, with many units refusing to carry out their orders and many individual officers deserting their posts.[2] Lissouba had good reasons for distrusting the loyalty of the army once he came to power. The recollection of these circumstances raises the following vital question: Was Lissouba *forced* to create his own militia to protect his civilian regime against the army and to protect a republican government?

The hypothesis examined by this chapter is that Lissouba was forced to act as he did in creating his own militia because of challenges from the army and its disloyalty to his regime. In turn, the argument goes, Kolélas was forced to follow suit, and then Sassou also felt compelled to reinforce the presidential guard that eventually became his private militia. Finally, it is important to note the absence of an army loyal to the republican constitution that could suppress the activities of the various private militias that confronted each other. In this way, the blame for the failure of Congo's democratic experiment could be assigned *indirectly* to the country's lack of a republican army.

The question asked about the militias in this chapter is different from that asked in the last. In the context of Congo's ethnoregional tensions, the question was whether the militias arose spontaneously, from the grassroots, to protect the interests of the country's ethnic groups or, on the contrary, whether they were created by the country's "ethnic entrepreneurs" seeking power. The analysis there makes it clear their existence owed to the active will of politicians. Here the question is whether or not the structure and behavior of the army forced Lissouba and Kolélas to create an alternative means of enforcing the decisions of the civilian regime, leading to a cycle of violence that soon spun out of control.

■ Congo's Army Problems in 1991

Congo's transitional government in 1991 and the newly elected government in 1992 faced not one problem with the army, but actually three. Each of these problems is linked to the three problems explored in the last three chapters: an undemocratic political culture, ethnoregional contestation, and insufficient resources to meet social demands. The political culture problem for the new, civilian governments was that military officers had come to expect to play a leading role in politics over the years between 1968 and 1991; although the key officers had allowed the national conference to proceed, they were still loath to cede all authority to elected, civilian officials. The second challenge posed by the army was its strongly ethnoregional composition. Specifically, the ranks of the army were overly filled with representatives from the north and Mbochi officers in particular. Finally, the economic problem posed by the bloated armed forces was that they consumed too much of the economy's limited resources. Both the Milongo and Lissouba regimes soon discovered that negotiations with the armed forces would be obligatory if their civilian regimes were to survive.

The challenge of army domination can best be understood as an aspect of political culture by recalling that the regimes of Ngouabi, Yhombi-Opango, and Sassou I (1979–1991) were all, in addition to everything else, military regimes. The common perception that these regimes were ideologically driven Marxist regimes is almost entirely wrong. Aside from the close relations that these regimes had with the Soviet Union, China, and Cuba, there was very little Marxist substance to any of them. For Ngouabi himself, the self-designated founder of the Congolese revolution, Marxist ideology was mostly a convenience, as Decalo makes abundantly clear (1990: 67–69). It was, in fact, civilian ideologues and unhappy youth who attacked the Massamba-Débat government for its lack of socialist conviction. It was the Massamba government's inability to control these social forces, and particularly its inability to prevent a confrontation between the (Bakongo-dominated) Civil Defense corps constituted by JMNR elements and the army that led to its demise. The JMNR's paramilitary units soon began to receive sophisticated military equipment from foreign powers, much to the alarm of the regular Forces Armées Congolaises (FAC) (Bazenguissa-Ganga 1997: 128). The Civil Defense militia of the JMNR, though led by southerners,[3] had no direct connection with the purely ethnoregional militias that would appear thirty years later.

In April 1966 Massamba made a concession to the leftist forces supporting his regime by appointing Ambroise Noumazalaye as his new prime minister, replacing Lissouba. Noumazalaye, who had just returned from a Soviet party congress, was then considered to be more reliably Marxist than Lissouba. Only two months after taking office, Noumazalaye's government adopted a law changing the name of the FAC to the Armée Nationale Populaire (ANP). More significantly, the government moved to put in place a Collegial High Command directed by a political commission to bring the army firmly under civilian control (Bazenguissa-Ganga 1997: 129; Decalo 1990: 62). When Ngouabi sharply criticized these moves, Massamba demoted him to the rank of an ordinary soldier and ordered him reassigned to Pointe Noire. This move led to military mutinies by Ngouabi's supporters in Brazzaville during which they occupied government buildings and arrested several regime officials, even chasing the ministers from their offices. Order was only restored when Ngouabi's demotion was rescinded and a new chief of staff appointed (Decalo 1990: 63). Thus, far from being the leader of the Congolese revolution, Ngouabi was the army officer who stopped it from proceeding along a leftward trajectory at a key moment. As Decalo argued, "Ngouabi's rise to power had little to do with a desire to further either Marxism or the Congolese revolution" (67). As for the formal declaration of a People's Republic in 1969, "it was quite literally the only wild card left within the context of a highly volatile Brazzaville replete with a variety of power-aspirants each mobilizing youth, unionists, and the urban unemployed by radical rhetoric and the espousal of millennial dreams" (68).

In the contest between the PCT and the army, it was always the army that came out on top. Over the twenty years of the Marxist experiment in Congo, the country's military rulers constantly purged the party of those who putatively lacked sufficient revolutionary fervor. At one low point in 1972, the PCT was purged of its cadres to the point that the entire membership amounted to fewer than 160 members (Decalo 1990: 71). Moreover, in all of those many party purges, it was "always the military head of state who . . . purged the Politburo, Central Committee, and party of those deemed unreliable from his personal vantage point" (68). Le Vine (1987: 125) concurs with this view, arguing, "Though Ngouabi had created the Congolese Labor Party (PCT) in December 1969 to give his Council for the Revolution both popular legitimacy and mass support, it was Ngouabi's (and Yhombi's) Military Committee of the Party that in fact ran the country, with the PCT itself remaining semicomatose and without an effective national role to play." No one could have made a serious case that Congo had anything other than a military regime during Yhombi's two-year stint in power, given the officer's known lack of ideological enthusiasm. A case could be made, on the other hand, that the regime of Sassou I was becoming less and less military. Le Vine (1987: 126) has argued that Sassou favored technocrats in important government posts in order to bolster the government's economic and administrative performance. Even those who came from the military had formal university training in specific fields, including engineering and economics. He points out that the cabinet named in August 1984 had only three military personnel among its twenty-eight ministers (126). He also notes that Sassou abolished the provisional Military Committee of the Party in 1979, under which the military had exercised direct rule, and revitalized the party's central committee and Politburo at the 1984 Party Congress (128). Yet, at the end of the day, this same analyst concedes that "the Sassou-Nguesso regime [was] still a military regime; the trappings [were] still very much in place and no one doubt[ed] that Sassou and his army colleagues remain[ed] Congo's ultimate political arbiters" (129). Sassou was willing to let the influence of the army recede into the background as long as his power was not opposed, but, until 1990, the army was always ready to put down any challenges.

One important early project of Ngouabi had been to establish the dominance of the ANP over other security forces within Congo. Indeed, he only definitively established himself as the undisputed ruler of Congo by confronting the JMNR's Civil Defense corps, then led by André Hombessa, in late August 1968. When these paramilitary forces refused to submit to command by the army, Ngouabi's forces engaged them in a battle in which over one hundred were killed and their power was broken (Decalo 1990: 66). Once Ngouabi was secure in power, he reorganized the gendarmerie, putting it, also, under the direct command of the army. Finally, the national police were similarly reorganized to become, effectively, an arm of the ANP (72). In 1970, following a coup attempt mounted from Zaire and allegedly involving the gendarmerie, this organization was completely disbanded and replaced by a "people's militia from its more militant and loyal elements" (73). With the dominance of the army established, all other security bodies in the country remained under control for the rest of the PCT period. It was even two senior military officers, Prime Minister (and General) Louis-Sylvain Goma and Interior Minister (and Colonel) Célestin Goma-Foutou who presided over the meetings that planned the national conference (Bazenguissa-Ganga 1997: 375).[4] Once the conference was under way, chief of staff (General) Jean-Marie Michel Mokoko warned the conferees against their criticisms of the army, suggesting that they would have to curtail their criticisms if they found themselves in power (Economist Intelligence Unit, *Country Report: Congo,* no. 2, 1992: 10).

The second army problem for the civilian regimes that later came to power was the army's domination by the large Mbochi ethnic category, including both the Mbochi and Kouyou subgroups. As elsewhere in Francophone Africa, the Congolese army began its existence as a local force commanded by French officers. In keeping with French perceptions of the inherent abilities of various ethnicities, the tiny officer corps was mostly Bakongo or Lari and the ranks were mostly northerners, especially Mbochi, including the Kouyou subgroup (Decalo 1990: 59–60).[5] At that time the Kongo officers could scarcely imagine the less highly trained northerners taking power, but a remarkable confidence and unity was taking root among the Mbochi-Kouyou paratroop forces (Bazenguissa-Ganga 1997: 127). At the time of the 1963 coup, the highest ranking officers were two Bakongo captains, David Mountsaka and Félix Mouzabakani. These two officers earned fame at the time of the Trois Glorieuses by obtaining the resignation of Youlou. Upon taking power Massamba promoted all key officers by one rank and named Mountsaka army commander, with Mouzabakani continuing as his chief of staff.

The gradual domination of all of Congo's security services by Mbochi officers proceeded slowly over many years. The senior southern officers all lost their posts for political reasons or alleged financial improprieties. Mouzabakani and several other officers were expelled from the army for their involvement in an alleged pro-Youlou coup in 1964 Mountsaka was implicated in the effort to help Youlou escape the country and later relieved of command; and Norbert Tsika was arrested in 1966 for fraud and again in 1969 for involvement in a pro-Kolélas coup attempt (Bazenguissa-Ganga 1997: 128; Moukoko 1999: 241). The first explicit northern (Kouyou) assertion of power came when Massamba attempted to arrest Ngouabi in 1966. At that moment, Ngouabi's loyal Kouyou troops actually detained their chief of staff (Mountsaka) and other senior officers. Bowing to the influence of Ngouabi's loyalists, Massamba replaced Mountsaka with another southern chief of staff (Luc Kimbouala-Nkaya, a Bembé) and made Ngouabi commander of the elite paracommando battalion (Decalo 1990: 63). This largely Mbochi-Kouyou unit was by far the most militarily capable and politically influential in Congo over the next several years.

Once Ngouabi came to power in 1968, a steady elimination of the most prominent southern officers occurred. Mountsaka never returned to a significant military role, was subsequently sentenced to twenty years in prison for alleged involvement in the Ngouabi assassination, and went into exile in 1980 upon his early release (Moukoko 1999: 241). By 1968, Mouzabakani had already been purged for plotting to bring Youlou back to power and helping him escape to Leopoldville. He was subsequently implicated in several other alleged coup plots, imprisoned from 1969 to 1973, and later implicated in Ngouabi's assassination, forcing him into exile

(245). Kimbouala-Nkaya was relieved of his command in 1971 for allegedly conspiring to undermine the government with his fellow Bembé, Martin
Mberi; he was briefly imprisoned in 1972 and then assassinated hours after
the murder of Ngouabi in 1977. Likewise, Alfred Raoul, an officer of
mixed ethnicity from Pointe Noire and part of the famed group of officers
trained at the St. Cyr military academy in France, was implicated in the
same coup attempt of 1972 and lost all influence in the army. Lieutenant
Augustin Poignet, born in Sibiti (Lékoumou) of a French father and
Congolese mother, actually briefly served as president upon the resignation
of Massamba in 1968. This southern officer was then implicated in a coup
in 1970 and forced into exile where he remained until 1991. Most other
non-northern officers met similar fates in the course of the 1970s, whereas
northern officers including Yhombi and Sassou proceeded steadily up
through the ranks.

The subordination of the other security services mentioned above was
also a method by which northerners gained definitive control of the means
of armed violence in Congo. The Civil Defense corps, which had grown to
the threatening size of 2,000 when it was crushed in 1968, was staffed
almost entirely by Lari and other Kongo militants, and it was headed by the
Lari revolutionary, André Hombessa (Decalo 1990: 62, 66). Likewise, the
police and the gendarmerie, the other two security forces brought under
army control, had been dominated by Kongo cadres before their subordination to the northern army. Thus, in subordinating these institutions to the
army, Ngouabi was bringing them under northern, as well as army, control.
To his credit Ngouabi did leave some prominent southerners in the army,
especially Louis-Sylvain Goma, who was chief of staff of the army in 1968
and again, after an interim, in 1975. Nonetheless, the army became progressively more northern-dominated under Yhombi and Sassou's first regime.
All of the chiefs of staff under these northern presidents were also northerners of either Téké or Mbochi ethnicity.

How did Congo's three northern presidents achieve such a domination
of the army without evoking more effective reactions against their ethnic
favoritism? Part of the answer lies in the fact that Congo's presidents were
careful to maintain a regional balance in the cabinet. Southern figures such
as Jean-Pierre Thystère-Tchicaya and Ange-Édouard Poungui among many
others, played major ideological and administrative roles in the Sassou
administration. During the 1980s, under the Marxist administration, it was
impolitic at the very least to discuss ethnic domination in any institution,
let alone the army. Within the army itself, there *were* a significant number
of southern, including Lari, officers. According to one of these officers,
moreover, there was respect for the various chiefs of staff who held the top-
most army post due to their excellent training. This same source emphasized that the southern officers generally held administration jobs not

involving command authority or access to arms. Even under the tense environment of the Sassou II administration, however, he was willing to acknowledge that there was a "certain predominance" of northern officers in the army.[6]

The ethnic composition of the army posed a problem for any civilian regime for an obvious reason: any freely elected civilian regime was likely to be dominated by southerners, given the ethnoregional character of the parties that emerged. In turn, a civilian regime animated by a southern-based party could not avoid having doubts about the loyalty of an army dominated by personnel from the north.

The third army problem for Congo in 1991 was its excessive size and cost. The army had grown on pace with the Congolese civil service, mushrooming to a size much larger than the country needed. At Congo's independence, the Congolese armed forces were a scant 700 soldiers, and by the time of Ngouabi's coup had grown only to 1,800, whereas the gendarmerie then numbered some 1,400 (Decalo 1990: 59; Bazenguissa-Ganga 1997: 126). Over the next two decades, the army had swollen to some 10,000, with another 10,000 or so in paramilitary units and the (reformed) gendarmerie.[7] Moreover, according to one source, a stunning 67 percent of the army was comprised of commissioned and noncommissioned officers, and 40 percent were senior officers. At that time, army colonels were earning almost US$2,000 per month and generals some US$4,000 per month (Economist Intelligence Unit, *Country Report: Congo,* no. 3, 1992: 13). Like other bureaucracies of the public service, the size and the pay of the army needed to be cut. Yet any politician who did so clearly risked stimulating military intervention. It was doubtless for this reason that the army was spared the salary reductions imposed on the civil service in 1988 (Decalo 1996: 37).

■ **Military-Civilian Contestation
Under the Transitional Regime**
The leadership of the Congolese army played a surprisingly helpful and mature role in the tense transition process that Congo underwent between July 1990 and June 1991. On 4 July 1990 the central committee of the PCT finished a weeklong meeting on the future of the party, and for the first time it acknowledged that the question of democracy in Congo was broader than a mere reform of PCT structures. On the same day, President Sassou appeared on television to announce the freeing of all of the country's political prisoners. These events stimulated an explosion of political organizing activity and rising public demand for a national conference. The first organization to take the lead in confronting Sassou's government was the CSC, the union confederation. By September, the unrelenting attacks on the gov-

ernment of the CSC's secretary-general, Jean-Michel Bokamba-Yangouma, had created a crisis that threatened to initiate violence between workers and government forces. Into this setting entered the longtime defense minister General Raymond-Damas Ngollo, Chief of Staff Mokoko, and Prime Minister Pierre Moussa. These three northern figures soon worked out a compromise between the PCT and the CSC that defused the crisis and allowed the transition to proceed peacefully (Mokoko 1995: 28–29).

By most accounts, the behavior of Ngollo and Mokoko, the country's two senior military figures, was exemplary over the next several months. In November 1990 the PCT announced at a party conference that the military would be officially "depoliticized," and Mokoko testified that the army would not interfere with civilian political reform processes. The Sassou administration did not move quickly enough for the opposition, however, and by the following January the frustration of the opposition had risen to the boiling point. At this critical juncture, Mokoko emphasized once more that the army would not intervene to save the government, and Sassou was compelled to move up the scheduled opening of the national conference to the following month. Had Mokoko acted otherwise, it is far from inconceivable that either Sassou or several of his senior military officers might have made an effort to suppress the civilian forces then campaigning for democracy; it is also conceivable that they might have succeeded.

The twenty most senior military officers in the country, including Ngollo and Mokoko, attended the national conference (Mokoko 1995: 33). The first and most important question that the conference faced was whether or not it would be "sovereign," or have the right to install a new government. In Congo, as in many other African states, this was a crucial moment. Although Mathieu Kérékou of Benin had been the path breaker in allowing the first sovereign national conference, several other African leaders staged conferences that did *not* possess sovereign powers, and did not lead to political transitions (Clark 1998c). In Congo, Sassou's PCT supporters were a minority in the conference, and neither the military nor the president himself was willing to intervene.

From the beginning of the conference, Mokoko found himself defending the honor and prerogatives of the armed forces. Besides the political attraction of the conference, all of the delegates enjoyed a special per diem provided by the state. Ngollo and Mokoko argued that not only those actually providing security, but also "the rest of the garrison" should receive a per diem as well (Mokoko 1995: 35). They founded their view on the "indispensable" need for cohesion in the military, and on the idea that those few given the opportunity to provide security would appear to be a kind of mercenary force (35). Among the most important activities of the conference was a thorough review of political assassinations in the country, especially those of three high officials killed in 1965 and of several important figures killed in the wake of Ngouabi's assassination in 1977. In all of these cases, Mokoko vigorously defended the honor and professionalism of the armed forces. A more recent case of assassination, that of Captain Pierre Anga, had occurred in 1988 after Mokoko had become the chief of staff. He was particularly outraged at the charges that soldiers had mutilated Anga's body for purposes of gaining magical powers and denied the charge categorically (38–40). Thus Mokoko showed himself to be both a republican, a citizen desirous to have the will of the people expressed and misdeeds exposed, but also a partisan of the rights of the military.

Ngollo and Mokoko played a dual restraining role during the national conference and afterward. When addressing the often-vengeful and angry politicians then opposing Sassou, Congo's senior officers urged them not to pick fights with the disempowered president. In the manner of the conference's leader, Ernest Kombo, they urged the civilian politicians to forgive the misdeeds of the past and acknowledge that the responsibility was often shared. When addressing their fellow military officers and troops, they warned them against any intervention in the process of political reformulation then under way. These senior officers "put on the coat of the diplomat more often that the helmets of soldiers" (Mokoko 1995: 41). Indeed, Ngollo and Mokoko mediated between the supporters of Sassou and the opposition at the beginning of the conference, allowing the opposition to take control. At that point two blocs gradually emerged, one group (mostly Lari and Bakongo) supporting Milongo for the premiership and another (including many former MNR and PCT cadres, and especially those from Nibolek) supporting Lissouba. Between these two groups, too, Ngollo and Mokoko served as mediators, allowing the reform processes to unfold peacefully.

In his autobiography covering the period of the transition, Mokoko reveals respect for the principle that elected leaders, civilian or military, should have final authority, but also a strong sense that the civilians should not interfere with the army. Once Milongo was elected prime minister and had assumed his duties, Mokoko agreed to continue as military chief of staff given the "profound changes" that the military would soon experience (Mokoko 1995: 46). His attitude toward Milongo's lack of knowledge of the military was rather patronizing in that he claims that he took it upon himself to explain to the new prime minister how the military functioned. When Milongo proposed to name an active duty colonel (i.e., lower ranking than Mokoko) as minister of defense in June 1991, however, Mokoko immediately threatened to resign; he suggested that Milongo name a colonel chief of staff, indicating that it was inconceivable for any general (like himself) to take orders from an officer of an inferior rank (47–48). To resolve the matter, Milongo decided to take the defense portfolio for himself. Mokoko refrained from direct criticism of Milongo, and merely observed that he was "badly counseled." Over the ensuing months, Mokoko publicly disagreed with some of Milongo's proposed new appointments to the military and complained bitterly about the perceived "will to control the FAC that infected the entourage of the Prime Minister" (51).

Tensions between Milongo and Mokoko remained high for the remainder of the year. Milongo's preoccupation during this time was to reduce the size of Sassou's presidential guard. On 30 September, in closed session, the Conseil Supérieur de la République (CSR—the transitional legislature) passed a law reducing the presidential guard from 900 to 300 soldiers, with only 163 attached directly to and chosen by the president (Kouvibidila 2000: 42). The remaining 600 were to be reattached to the special Groupement Aéroporté (GAP) that Sassou had created. Meanwhile, Mokoko's preoccupation was to hold the "estates general of the army" that the national conference had envisioned for late 1991. On 14 October 1991, however, several officers close to Milongo wrote to tell him that the real purpose of the estates general was to "reverse the situation created before and during the sovereign national conference," that is, the situation of military subordination to civilian authority (43). These officers also suggested that Mokoko and his colleagues from "the North and from Nibolek" would succeed because of their numerical superiority, especially at the rank of general. Accordingly, they called for six colonels from the south (Pool) to be promoted to the rank of general (43). By the time of Milongo's visit to Paris in November, rumors of a coup were circulating throughout Brazzaville, and Milongo returned home. The CSR then set up a nine-member commission of Milongo supporters to investigate the alleged coup plot (*Africa Confidential,* "Congo: Characteristic Ambiguity," 6 March 1992: 6). Meanwhile, the government was due to begin recruiting a new 2,000-strong gendarmerie, with French support, in February (Economist Intelligence Unit, *Country Report: Congo,* no. 1, 1992: 14).

The final showdown between the army and the Milongo government came in January 1992 following a cabinet reshuffle announced on 30 December 1991. In a final revision of his cabinet made on January 2, Milongo named a Téké, Colonel Michel Gangouo, as the new secretary of state for defense. Gangouo had been sacked, imprisoned, and allegedly tortured under the Sassou regime (*Africa Confidential,* "Congo: Characteristic Ambiguity," 6 March 1992: 6). Then, on 14 January, Gangouo announced the appointment of seven new officers, all colonels, to the military high command, and the dismissal of some Mbochi officers close to Sassou, including former chief of staff Colonel Emmanuel Elenga.[8] According to Mokoko (55), the appointments were "visibly partisan," and ignored the "regulations and administrative practices in force in the ministry of defense." While perhaps true, this observation ignored the fact that appointments to the Congolese armed forces had been "visibly partisan" over the preceding twenty years.

On the day following Gangouo's announcement, 15 January, troops of the GAP and the marines surrounded the headquarters of the military high command and the radio station. They demanded Gangouo's immediate dismissal, the reinstatement of the officers dismissed in the defense minister's announcement, the rescinding of the orders naming new officers to several command posts, and the opening of the army estates general within ten days (Kouvibidila 2000: 44). Another communiqué from one military unit taking part in the rebellion demanded a new military law and an augmentation of salaries (45). It appeared from the beginning that the rebellion was spontaneous and not orchestrated by Mokoko.

With the situation still unresolved, the airborne troops prevented Milongo from boarding a flight to Pointe Noire on 18 January.[9] Later the same day, Milongo and Mokoko met to discuss the situation but neither backed down, and the standoff continued. Milongo appeared on television the following day to repeat his refusal to dismiss Colonel Gangouo from his post. In response, Colonel Guy Mabiala, the commander of an infantry brigade, announced by radio on 20 January that Prime Minister Milongo had been removed from his post. The announcement provoked the raising of barricades in Bacongo, and then a crackdown by the military, leading to three deaths and many more injuries. The bureau of the CSR and Kombo tried to arrange a meeting between Mokoko and Milongo for 21 January at the general staff headquarters, but Milongo refused to attend. Instead, on 22 January, Milongo led a boisterous procession of his supporters to the Palais des Congrès, defying the military vehicles along the route.

The next day the CSR commission of inquiry dealt the Milongo regime a severe blow when it released its report on the allegations of a coup attempt that had circulated at the end of the previous year. The report was a bombshell: it concluded that there had never been an army coup plot, but rather a plot by several of Milongo's ministers to discredit Mokoko and bring the army under control by spreading rumors of a forthcoming coup.[10] Most directly implicated were Interior Minister Alexis Gabou—later accused of fixing the local elections—Justice Minister Jean-Martin Mbemba, and Police Director General Étienne Goma. According to the report, these ministers had conspired with other regime officials, two army colonels, and Thystère-Tchicaya to use the pretext of an alleged coup plot to bring the army firmly under the control of the Milongo regime. After three more tense days during which the army controlled the country's strategic institutions, Milongo backed down. On 26 January, Milongo announced the composition of a new cabinet excluding Gangouo, and actually naming Ngollo again as minister of defense. All of the recent military appointments were rescinded. As one disappointed critic put it, the crisis was resolved only by "putting the constitution in the closet and treading on the principles of democracy underfoot" (Kouvibidila 2000: 49).

Meanwhile, Sassou had gained political capital by refusing to back the rebels, and Milongo narrowly avoided a vote of censure in the CSR.

Lissouba, who returned from a foreign journey in February 1992, cannot have failed to absorb the lesson of the January standoff between the Milongo regime and the army. Given his alliance with the PCT at that time, Lissouba then had less to fear from the army than did Milongo or Kolélas. Yet he certainly understood that the army would not be intrinsically loyal to a regime he headed, even if it came to power through free elections.

Following its failed confrontation with the army, the Milongo regime never regained its political momentum. In May 1992, another crisis shook the regime over the botched municipal elections. Nearly everyone, including Milongo himself, blamed the badly—and fraudulently—executed elections on Interior Minister Gabou (*Africa Confidential*, "Congo: Testing the Waters of Democracy," 19 June 1992: 7). The accusations led several "rebel ministers," including Gabou, to call upon the public to engage in "resistance" in favor of the government and against the opposition coalition known as the Alliance Nationale pour la Démocratie (AND). The CSR then called for the rebel ministers to be sacked, and Milongo was forced to oblige with a cabinet reshuffle announced on 21 May 1992; only two ministers, including Ngollo, survived the shakeup. At the end of the crisis, the CSR set up an independent electoral committee to supervise the forthcoming legislative and presidential elections. The committee successfully organized fair elections later in the year, ensuring the defeat of Milongo, Kolélas, and the MCDDI at the polls. The army was not directly involved in politics again until after the elections and the first crisis of the Lissouba regime.

■ **Civil-Military Relations Under the Lissouba Regime**
The Congolese army continued in its mediating role during the first two crises of the Lissouba regime. The first of these involved the breakout of the UPADS-PCT coalition immediately after the elections, and Lissouba's subsequent dissolution of Parliament. The second involved the contestations over the elections of May–June 1993, and then the rerun of the elections in October 1993.

The Army in the Crisis of 1992
In the political crisis that wracked Congo immediately following the 1992 elections, the army chiefs stayed neutral and uninvolved. Lissouba had barely been sworn in on 31 August 1992 before his administration faced daunting political negotiations with his new PCT partners in the AND coalition. The PCT had formalized its partnership with Lissouba on 13 August, three days before the second round of presidential elections, by

publicly calling on its constituency to vote for Lissouba in the forthcoming polls. Sassou himself endorsed the coalition, indicating that it had been a political decision "negotiated on a clear basis that was written and signed" (Kouvibidila 2000: 159). Yet fraught negotiations between UPADS and PCT loyalists followed the nomination of Stéphane Bongho-Nouarra (from northern Sangha region) on 1 September. When the cabinet was announced on 8 September without accord between the partners, the PCT only got three minor cabinet posts, the ministries of agriculture, education, and commerce. The minister named to the last position refused to take up his post (187).

More intense negotiations among all three major political forces followed during the month of September. In the National Assembly, the MCDDI had been joined by six other political parties, including Thystère-Tchicaya's Rassemblement pour la Démocratie et le Progrès Social (RDPS), to form the URD (Union pour le Renouveau Démocratique) bloc. Meanwhile, the AND was renamed the Mouvance présidentielle (presidential domain). On 24 September it became clear that the URD and PCT were cooperating when the Assembly elected its new officers: the president of the Assembly was André Mouelé of the PCT whereas four of the other six officers were from the URD or PCT. On 30 September the URD and PCT signed official documents sealing the alliance that had been negotiated earlier (Kouvibidila 2000: 186, 192). Over the next month still more political wrangling ensued, with each side wondering whether a coalition of such unlikely partners as the MCDDI and PCT could remain intact.[11] Instead, the new alliance became more firm and began to call upon Lissouba to appoint a new prime minister issuing from the new parliamentary majority.[12] Lissouba's hardline supporters convinced him not to do so, however. In frustration, the URD-PCT coalition organized a vote of no-confidence in the Bongho-Nouarra government on 31 October, and the measure passed with sixty-six votes in favor. Deputies of the Mouvance présidentielle then walked out of the Assembly. Four days later the new majority adopted the minutes of the 31 October meeting, making the dissolution of the previous government official (200–201).

During November the crisis grew hotter still, and yet the military still did not intervene. A number of observers perceived that Lissouba himself did not grasp the seriousness of the crisis (e.g., Kouvibidila 2000: 221). Nearly from the beginning of his term, Lissouba was under the powerful influence of a group of Bembé zealots, the "gang of four."[13] These partisans seem to have manipulated the president and fed his ego to the extent that he failed to recognize the necessity of dealing directly with his parliamentary foes. Bongho-Nouarra recognized the reality of his new situation before Lissouba, finally agreeing to resign the prime ministry on 13 November. Four days later, however, Lissouba announced the dissolution of the National Assembly and the organization of new elections by the end of the year. Rejecting Lissouba's move as unconstitutional, the URD-PCT political forces called for a general strike the next day. The coalition's partisans in Brazzaville then quickly erected barricades in the parts of the city they controlled. On 26 November, the opposition group announced that they would boycott any fresh elections, and, two days later, they announced that they were organizing a major march to the presidency on 30 November.

During these first three months of his presidency, Lissouba made no move to confront the power of the army directly. His appointment of Ngollo as defense chief was no doubt an overture designed to reassure the army. The reassignment of Mokoko at this early stage would have been disastrous, possibly inviting a coup d'état. Meanwhile, however, Lissouba gave Interior Minister Martin Mberi the task of "ethnically restructuring the police and non-army security services" (Decalo 1996: 37). This restructuring involved three different security services: the political police, the (rural) *gendarmerie nationale,* and the presidential guard. All three of these services were reassigned to Bembé senior officers close to, and, in case of the police, one *related* to Mberi. These commanders in turn recruited fresh personnel from Nibolek into the various services. A Téké general, Emmanuel Ngouelondele, became Lissouba's new military aide-de-camp (37).

The opposition march on the presidency on 30 November proved to be an early critical juncture for the Lissouba regime. The march was elaborately organized, with the PCT supporters gathering at the *rond point* (roundabout) of Moungali, and those supporting the MCDDI and URD at the Marché Total in Bacongo. From there, the two streams would march to the French Cultural Center, where they would join together for a final march to the presidential palace (Kouvibidila 2000: 226). Lissouba hardliners in the presidency warned that security forces would fire on the political leaders if they were found among the marchers. The warning chastened Sassou and Thystère-Tchicaya, who refrained from marching, but only steeled the resolve of Kolélas to participate (227). For Congolese of both political orientations, the nature of the march evoked the trois glorieueses of 1963, as the signs reading "Lissouba demission" (Lissouba resign) attested.

Without the equanimity of the army's two senior leaders, this march could have ended in either great bloodshed or a civilian overthrow of the newly elected regime. In the event, Mokoko and Ngollo took careful steps to restrain each side, neither of which trusted the actions of the army. Mokoko arranged to have his troops overseeing the demonstration to carry arms without ammunition; some just outside the presidency wielded weapons loaded with blanks (Mokoko 1995: 61; Kouvibidila 2000: 299). Tensions rose dramatically after the presidential guard opened fire on the demonstrators at two different places, killing three and wounding several more.[14] Mokoko and Ngollo met the leaders of the demonstration at the presidency and reached an accord with them under which they could enter the presidency peacefully and with their security guaranteed by the regular army.

Having played the role of peacekeepers in a volatile situation, Mokoko and Ngollo next took on the role of mediators and peacemakers. First Ngollo and then Mokoko took to the radio to call insistently upon the country's major political figures to participate in a meeting "under the aegis of the military high command" (Mokoko 1995: 61). On 3 December the two sides agreed to the principle of a national unity government with a neutral prime minister to rule until the legislative elections would be rerun; the composition of the government would be 60 percent URD-PCT and 40 percent AND (Mouvance). Mokoko was made president of the follow-up committee to oversee the implementation of the accord. On 6 December Lissouba named Claude Dacosta, a Cabindan of mixed parentage but also an old friend, to be the interim prime minister. Once the peak of the crisis had passed, however, Lissouba's team was loath to live up to its agreements and dragged its feet in the implementation. Accordingly, Mokoko had to keep the pressure on both sides over the subsequent weeks. In the end a last minute intervention by Gabonese president Omar Bongo with all the parties was required on the night of 22–23 December to get a final agreement on the new cabinet (Kouvibidila 2000: 247).[15] The new cabinet was announced on 25 December. It not only retained Ngollo as minister of state in charge of defense, but also named another neutral army figure, Colonel François Ayayen, as minister of interior. In keeping with the 3 December accord, it featured twelve URD-PCT figures and nine ministers from the Mouvance filling the other posts. Thus, it is clear that the regular army played a positive role in the political dispute that wracked Congo in late 1992.

The Advent of the Militias
and the Army's Role in Congo's First Civil War
Alas, despite the neutral, positive role of the regular army—and, in fact, partly because of it—each of Congo's major ethnopolitical groupings soon afterward sought to create its own political militia. Each of the three original militia groups had a distinctive origin, arising out of the dynamics of the political and security situation. The first two militia groups had their origins as the bodyguards of two of the presidential candidates, Sassou and Kolélas (Quantin 1997: 182). In Sassou's case, he remained president of the republic until Lissouba's investiture, and, in that capacity, he maintained his 500-strong presidential guard, mostly composed of Mbochi loyalists. Kolélas publicly maintained a small bodyguard, but he also began discretely training a larger force of fighters loyal to his party in the Pool region even before the elections. *Africa Confidential* ("Congo: Testing the Waters

of Democracy," 19 June 1992: 7) reported the existence of three specific camps in the outlying areas around Brazzaville training Lari fighters and staffed by Israeli trainers in mid-1992, before the presidential elections. Thus, according to Quantin (1997: 182), "These two groups, around the PCT and the MCDDI, formed the oldest organizations on the paramilitary scene." Although Quantin maintains that Milongo "did not develop his own militia," the prime minister must certainly have known of the existence of the illegal camps.

Also according to Quantin (1997: 183), Lissouba only began to train his own militia after his rupture with Sassou at the end of 1992. This militia, however, was not composed of Lissouba's ethnic kinsmen, but of Bembé youth, trained in the Bouenza town of Aubeville under the direction of Interior Minister Martin Mberi.[16] This militia, the Aubevillois, was trained by Israeli instructors who were recruited to Congo specifically for that purpose. Meanwhile, the president's supporters began arming other groups of youths in the Brazzaville neighbors of Mfilou and Diata to defend (and ethnically cleanse) their neighborhoods. This latter group became known as the Zoulous. With the confrontations that began in late 1992, Kolélas's armed supporters began to organize more systematically, and became known as the Ninjas. Sassou's Cobra militia was fortified by officers who defected from the regular army to train the idle youth in Brazzaville's Talangai and Mpila neighborhoods and other Mbochi areas. Unlike the civil defense units formed in the 1960s, these groups were explicitly ethnopolitical, rather than ideological, in orientation.

Given that Lissouba was forced to install a unity government in December 1992, how did his regime manage to continue the buildup of the militia groups during the early months of 1993? The answer is that Lissouba quickly set up a panel of advisers to monitor the activities of several ministries upon the installation of the unity government (Economist Intelligence Unit, *Country Report: Congo,* no. 1, 1993: 14; also, Mokoko 1995: 64). According to Mokoko (64), this advisory team included "the quasi-totality of the ministers departing from [Lissouba's] censured government." Most notably, Mberi was given the job of watching over security developments, and he continued to bolster the pro-regime militias from outside the government.

During the first four months of 1993, the focus of political activity in the country was the newly constituted Commission Nationale d'Organisation et de Supervision des Élections Législatives Anticipées (CONOSELA) (Kouvibidila 2000: 255–282). The Mouvance and the URD-PCT bickered endlessly over seemingly every detail of the CONOSELA organization, staffing, and functioning. At the same time, both sides were eager to involve senior military figures in the CONOSELA's efforts, and these officers proved to be practically the only voices of reason in the fraught discussions. In the initial negotiations over CONOSELA, Interior Minister Colonel Ayayen was one of six government representatives, and the Force Publique (Armed Forces) was represented by three other colonels (261–262). Ngollo was later chosen to serve as a neutral arbiter between the two sides in CONOSELA, whereas Ayayen was unanimously elected to coordinate the technical meetings on national and local commissions for election organization (264). Later, in March, a coordination committee for CONOSELA was selected, and this body featured Ngollo and Colonel Gilbert Mokoki as "observers." Mokoko was also involved in the body's proceedings in a variety of informal ways, and took on the role of president of the followup committee (Comité de Suivi) (274 and 278). Throughout the tendentious discussions, neither side accused any of the army representatives of partisanship. Meanwhile, outside the CONOSELA meetings, representatives of the AND and URD-PCT hurled vicious accusations back and forth.

The first round of the legislative elections was rerun on 2 May 1993 peacefully and, initially, without much complaint from either side. Nonetheless, the postelectoral maneuvering had already begun. On 6 May, as the coordinating committee of CONOSELA examined the elections results, the rapporteur for the committee published a communiqué authorizing local electoral committees to publish results from their circumscriptions. The same day, however, the president of the committee, Jean-Martin Mbemba of the URD, sent his own communiqué to journalists indicating that only CONOSELA could publish the electoral results and that it would only do so once they were completely compiled (Kouvibidila 2000: 309–310). By that time, most of the Congolese media, international elections observers, and the diplomatic community had all decided that the contests had been reasonably free and fair (Kouvibidila 2000: 311; Economist Intelligence Unit, *Country Report: Congo,* no. 3, 1993: 13). Nonetheless, three days later, Kolélas made a stunning speech denouncing the results, claiming that there had been massive fraud, and demanding a revote in all of the specified circumscriptions. When all of the URD-PCT loyalists on CONOSELA rallied to this view, the body reached a deadlock that neither Mokoko nor anyone else could break. Mbemba refused to sign off on any results, and, in frustration, the interior minister finally published the "raw" results from each constituency without CONOSELA having completed its compilation (Kouvibidila 2000: 316; Mokoko 1995: 66). The government announced that the second round of elections would be held on 6 June, while the opposition continued to reject the results of the first round and called for a boycott of the second round.

For the remainder of May, an uneasy peace held while arms continued to proliferate among the partisans of Congo's politicians. Sassou's residence in Mpila was surrounded by "a veritable army (several hundred soldiers), far exceeding the 15 men to which he was entitled" (*Jeune Afrique,* "Démocratie Armée," 17–23 June 1993: 23). On the day of the second-round voting, opposition supporters and militiamen used arms to intimidate would-be voters and even shot up the residence of Commerce Minister Gabriel Bokilo. Militiamen were distributing arms from army camps to unemployed youths and drug addicts in the popular quarters. When it was announced that the Mouvance had captured all of the eleven remaining seats, full-scale rioting began in Bacongo, controlled by MCDDI partisans, and in Talangai, controlled by PCT forces. Parts of the city occupied by the opposition were barricaded so that official security forces could not enter. Behind the barricades violence and disorder reigned for the next four weeks. Tens of thousands of persons were displaced when they were driven from their homes, and several dozen were killed (Economist Intelligence Unit, *Country Report: Congo,* no. 3, 1993: 14). Meanwhile, Lissouba again asked Mokoko to negotiate a temporary agreement between his "presidential domain" and the opposition in mid-June. These negotiations failed, however, when the opposition refused to dismantle their barricades as a precondition on the grounds that the barricades protected them from the presidential guard (Mokoko 1995: 67). Mokoko subsequently asked Lissouba to limit the activity of this guard to protecting the presidential residence.

On 23 June Lissouba sought to push ahead with the organization of a new government by naming a new prime minister, former president Yombi-Opango. The new government, announced at the end of June, retained Ngollo as minister of defense, and also included Lissouba's first two prime ministers, Bongho-Nouarra and da Costa. As the crisis dragged on into the middle of July, Lissouba finally took more decisive action. On 16 July 1993 the president called Mokoko to the presidency and fired him in the presence of the minister of defense (Mokoko 1995: 72).[17] Lissouba dismissed Mokoko on the grounds that he had failed to raise the barricades and disarm the opposition militias as ordered. In his account, Mokoko claims that he had lost respect for the Lissouba government because it failed to obey the decisions of the Supreme Court and that he had refused to obey orders to avoid unnecessary bloodshed (70–71). Put otherwise, he justified his nearly open insubordination on the grounds that a commander dedicated to respect for the law and republican values could not follow the orders he had been given. Lissouba appointed another Téké colonel, Claude Emmanuel Eta-Onka, to replace the fired general.

According to Mokoko, Lissouba had made "various promises" to "certain of my military comrades" in the days before his dismissal, implying that other officers had pledged their loyalty to the president in return for political or economic favors (Mokoko 1995: 71). He goes on to add that Lissouba had "succeeded in breaking the unity of the Comité de suivi and Military High Command" as a result. One prominent journalist, on the other hand, was quick to repeat the rumors that Mokoko had "vague putschist impulses," and argued that Mokoko's "repeated interventions in the political debate" had caused suspicions against him to rise; Mokoko, the journalist claimed, "left the impression that the Congolese ship of state had two commanders," the president and the army chief of staff.[18] In fact, one can understand the position of both Mokoko and Lissouba in the standoff: Lissouba was right to believe that the army commander should obey the orders of an elected president and that the army had a responsibility to ensure public order, and Mokoko was right to believe that the army should stay out of partisan political fights and avoid civilian bloodshed if possible.

With the firing of Mokoko, the army began to lose its ability to act as a unifying force for the country, and the influence of Ngollo gradually waned over the coming months. Ngollo did act as a successful mediator between the leaders of the Mouvance and the URD-PCT coalition in the negotiations that ended the June–July 1993 fighting. Ngollo arranged for a cease-fire between the armed groups on July 26 and went on to play a role in the organization of an international mediation effort (Zartman and Vogeli 2000: 275–276). But it was the external figures that played the key roles in the accords reached in Libreville on August 4;[19] these included, in particular, Gabonese president Omar Bongo (again) and former OAU deputy secretary-general Mohammed Sahnoun. Other OAU officials and several foreign ambassadors to Congo played a supporting role.

Lissouba subsequently charged Ngollo with overseeing the implementation of the Libreville Accord, but Ngollo did not enjoy success. Tensions escalated sharply after the rerun of the second round of elections on 3 October, in which the Mouvance won two seats whereas the opposition won nine, confirming the narrow majority of the Mouvance in the Assembly. Low level violence between the various militia groups ensued throughout the rest of October without the army being able to control the situation (Economist Intelligence Unit, *Country Report: Congo*, no. 4, 1993: 13). When members of the government—probably Prime Minister (and General) Yhombi—ordered units of the regular army to bombard Bacongo in November 1993, Ngollo did nothing or could do nothing to intervene. As the war was winding down, the peacemaking initiative was taken up by some fifty deputies in Parliament from both Nibolek and Pool, and not by Ngollo, leading to an agreement 30 January 1994.[20] Ngollo's last significant act of mediation came in April 1994 when clashes erupted in Mpila between Sassou's Cobra militia fighters and elements of the "ministerial reserve" (Economist Intelligence Unit, *Country Report: Congo*, no. 3, 1994: 12). In the interim, neither Eta-Onka nor any other military figure ever gained a fraction of the influence of Ngollo or Mokoko. When

Lissouba charged Yhombi with forming a new, slimmer government in January 1995, the two leaders finally eliminated Ngollo from the cabinet and replaced him with the far more partisan Bongho-Nouarra. Worse still, the unity and command integrity of the army disintegrated completely during the war that lasted from November 1993 into February 1994. When government officials ordered army units to dismantle barricades or undertake punitive missions into Bacongo, members of those units from Nibolek and Pool would temporarily desert their units.[21] Some of those who deserted at this time joined the militias and did not return to the service of the national army until after Sassou's return to power in 1997. The orders from the government to use heavy artillery against Bacongo further eroded the cohesion of the army. At first the government targeted political sites, such as the opposition radio (Alliance Radio) and the building housing the MCDDI headquarters. After a strong response from the Ninja militia, however, the government ordered the army to shell the population of Bacongo itself. Under such orders, many gunners fired their shells so that they landed in the Congo River rather than on the homes of innocent civilians (Kounzilat 1998: 25, 26). Under these circumstances, this war turned into a horrific round of ethnic cleansing in which houses were looted and burned, and innocent civilians were assaulted and killed by drugged militiamen (Friedman and Sundberg 1994). The death toll, usually estimated to be between two thousand and five thousand, was far higher than in the previous round of fighting.[22]

During 1994 a gradual political reconciliation between the Mouvance présidentielle and the URD permitted a truce between the Ninjas and Lissouba's various public security elements and militias. As early as February, army officers from Pool and Nibolek had drawn up a plan to create and deploy a 400-person peacekeeping force for troubled areas of Brazzaville. Amazingly, the command was given to Colonel Philippe Bikinkita, a relative of Kolélas's who had formerly commanded the Ninjas, and the second in command was Colonel Jean-Marie N'Guembo, commander of the Ministerial Reserve (Economist Intelligence Unit, *Country Report: Congo*, no. 2, 1994: 14). After Kolélas's election to mayor of Brazzaville in July 1994, the rapprochement between the Mouvance and the URD became more solid. In August, Kolélas publicly embraced UPADS secretary-general Christophe Moukouéké. Following up on this momentum, Lissouba staged a "National Forum on the Culture of Peace" under the auspices of UNESCO in December. In a short communiqué at the end, all sides, including Sassou, pledged to reorganize the security services and to facilitate the collection of arms.[23] In January 1995, the representatives of the MCDDI and UPADS agreed in principle to disarm civilians and to integrate most militia members into the regular army.[24] Having made peace with the URD, however, Lissouba's government lacked the incentive to disarm the Ninjas. Far from it, Lissouba named Bikinkita to be his new minister of interior, replacing Mberi.

Meanwhile, there was growing tension between the security forces of Sassou and the Lissouba government as the latter sought to bring all of the security agencies firmly under its control. Fresh Israeli military advisers arrived as early as February 1994 to train Lissouba's Presidential Guard, headed by Colonel Ferdinand Mbahou from Bouenza, only days after the accord of 30 January. Mberi maintained direct control over the Israeli-trained Réserve ministerielle and this force operated with impunity in Brazzaville, alienating both the army and the population. In December 1994 Mberi dismissed the director-general of Congo's police force for voicing public criticisms of the unit's behavior and appointed a more pliable chief (Economist Intelligence Unit, *Country Report: Congo,* no. 1, 1995: 7). During the same year, Sassou's loyalists in the army passed pilfered arms to his militia forces. In one dramatic episode in May 1994, unknown thieves stole a large cache of arms and ammunition from a military training school in Gambona (Plateaux), not far from Sassou's hometown of Oyo in southern Cuvette. Although government figures were certain that the stolen hardware went to Sassou's militia, they lacked the confidence in their own forces to achieve a defeat or disarmament of Sassou's militia (Economist Intelligence Unit, *Country Report: Congo,* no. 4, 1994: 12).

During 1995 and 1996 the Lissouba government accelerated its efforts to achieve an ethnic balance in—and control over—the security forces. In the cabinet reshuffle of January 1995, Lissouba replaced Eta-Onka with General Daniel Mabika, a loyalist from Lissouba's own Niari region. In November of that year, he dismissed seventy-seven other senior military and police officers he thought close to Sassou and replaced them, also, largely with southerners.[25] In March 1996 he put François Ayayen, a northern general (from Likouala) who had supported him vigorously since 1993, in charge of his personal staff, replacing Nouélondélé. By early 1997, of fourteen colonels and generals on the general staff, only two were from the north, and each held insignificant posts: Colonel Fulgor Ongobo (Cuvette), the navy commander, and Colonel Bienvenu Maleka (Likouala), the inspector general of the air force. The remainder were from Bouenza (five), Pool (three), Kouilou (three), and Niari (one). Ongobo was then suspended in April 1997.[26] At the same time, Lissouba's government sought to realign the security forces "from below." An agreement signed 24 December 1995 by Kolélas and by senior representatives of Sassou and Lissouba provided that eight hundred fighters from each leader's militias would be recruited into the police, gendarmerie, or army.[27] In the event, Lissouba's government recruited more than its quota whereas Sassou refused to let his Cobra fighters join the security forces in protest (Economist Intelligence Unit, *Country Report: Congo,* no. 3, 1996: 7). One source indicated that some

2,200 of the Aubevillois were recruited into the three security services between June 1995 and February 1996 alone (*La Lettre du Continent,* "Une Armée de Miliciens?" 29 February 1996).

Interestingly, mutinies or revolts by the troops of the regular army during the entire period were small scale and not generally reported in the press. After the war of 1993–1994, the militia fighters recruited by the government sometimes turned on their own sponsors when they failed to receive their pay; even the home of Mberi himself was once the target of disgruntled fighters (*Jeune Afrique,* "Martin le Terrible contre les 'rapaces,'" 17–23 November 1994: 30). Once recruitment into the regular security services was a possibility, the young, usually destitute fighters, demanded rapid incorporation and regular pay. As for those fortunate enough to be recruited, they frequently revolted for faster promotion, higher pay, and better conditions. At least three significant revolts by former fighters of Nibolek origins occurred between early 1995 and early 1997 (Economist Intelligence Unit, *Country Report: Congo,* no. 2, 1997: 10).

Throughout the entire interwar period, between 1994 and 1997, the integrity and influence of the army was perpetually eroded because of the private militias. One source estimated the numbers for the militias at about 1,200 for the Cobras, 1,500 for the Ninjas, and 2,000 for the Zoulous in early 1994, and the army had suffered many defections and losses of arms (Economist Intelligence Unit, *Country Report: Congo,* no. 2, 1994: 13–14). When the bipartisan peacekeeping force collected some weapons in the southern districts of Brazzaville in April 1994, they found that the weapons held by militia fighters were more sophisticated that those used by the army (Economist Intelligence Unit, *Country Report: Congo,* no. 3, 1994: 13). The regular army was starved for new equipment and maintenance funds and rarely engaged in training or maneuvers in the years before the 1997 war (*La Lettre du Continent,* "Armée Nue et Milices Equipées," 23 January 1997).

On the other hand, training and reinforcement of the militias continued at several locations outside the capital after the wars of 1993–1994, while untrained youths volunteered for self-defense groups within the capital. By early 1997, the Cobras had grown to some 2,000 to 3,000, and Sassou still retained the support of many regular army officers and troops. The Ministerial Reserve was renamed the Cocoyes after Mberi's replacement, and this force was expanded to some 4,000. Although many Ninjas had laid down their arms, or even defected to Sassou, in 1994, Bikinkita began training new recruits in 1995 and 1996; they numbered about 1,500 by late 1996.[28] Even as the war of 1997 began, Lissouba's supporters were busy recruiting and hastily training yet another militia, the Mambas, to protect the Nibolek neighborhoods of Brazzaville. According to the best informed source, the total number of militia fighters then was between 7,500 and

10,000 (Bazenguissa-Ganga 1999: 43). By this time, few officers in the army retained a greater loyalty to the nominally republican army than to the outside militia groups that they had trained, paid, inspired, and commanded.

Given the state of the Congolese army in 1997, it would be most interesting to know exactly which armed government units assaulted Sassou's residence on the fateful morning of 5 June 1997. Although there are many accounts, none are definitive on this important detail. Some exiled partisans of Lissouba, such as Martial de-Paul Ikounga (2000), simply avoid any discussion of the issue; others say that agents of the "judicial police," accompanied by several regular troops in six armored cars approached Sassou's residence.[29] Sassou opponents claim that he was not even in the residence at the time of the confrontation, having sought refuge in the French Embassy (Koula 1999: 59). As noted by Sassou's supporters, Lissouba's government advanced three different justifications for their assaults on Sassou's residence: that they were seeking to disarm illegal militia groups, that they were attempting to arrest criminals responsible for murder in the Oyo incident a few days earlier, and that they were trying to forestall a planned coup d'état by Sassou's forces (Pigasse 1998: 95–117). When alluding to the second justification, Lissouba's officials called the action a "simple operation of the police."

Meanwhile, the supporters of Sassou who have published accounts in France are inconsistent in their own accounts. For example, in the blow-by-blow account of the war of 1997 by Jean-Paul Pigasse (1998: 126–128), the author at one point summarizes a captured document allegedly written by the "Commander of the North Operational Group-Mpila, with the approval of the General commanding the land army," dated 28 May 1997. The document describes in detail exactly what army units and weapons will be used to secure exactly what strategic points leading to the residence of Sassou. The author apparently includes the document to demonstrate that Lissouba had ordered his army commanders to prepare their assault on Sassou soon after Congo's political principals had pledged to compete peacefully in the election contest. The same author subsequently reports that, in the early morning of 5 June, the residence of Sassou was surrounded by a dozen armored vehicles (138). Another Sassou loyalist indicates that the operation was executed by "les Forces Armées Congolaises" (Soni-Benga 1998: 101, 103) and "la Force Publique" sprayed a fusillade of bullets into Sassou's home (112). These references are intended to reveal the violence of the assault against Sassou and the bravery of his own forces in resisting it.

Yet when Sassou's partisans wish to convey the impression that the army refused to follow Lissouba's orders on the grounds that they were illegal, they claim that the attack against Sassou was conducted by Lissouba's militia forces. In a press conference given on 11 June in Paris, Sassou's then-spokesperson Rodolphe Adada said, "One can solemnly confirm today that the army no longer obeys the orders of Pascal Lissouba. The attacks against Denis Sassou Nguesso have been carried out by tribal militias, coming from Pascal Lissouba's province, armed and trained by him in the camps of Obeville [sic] and Loudima." Soni-Benga (1998: 108) contradicts his other accounts at one point, saying that the conflict initially involved a fight between the Zoulous of Lissouba and the Cobras of Sassou, before the army divided into three parts, one supporting each of Congo's major political figures. One neutral analyst also insists that it was the Aubevilleois, and not the army, that surrounded Sassou's headquarters in Mpila. She indicates that Lissouba simply could not trust the army because the "FAC consisted of too many soldiers and especially officers who in a conflict would rather be loyal to Sassou Nguesso" (Sundberg 2000: 90). If Sundberg is correct, then Lissouba's militia would have to have taken possession of the armored cars that were witnessed at the scene before the operation began.

Despite the uncertainty of this significant point, the overall picture of Congo's army problems is clear enough for us to make some solid evaluations on the internal evidence. On the question of the army's political culture, it is true that the army's senior officers felt, in 1991 and after, that they enjoyed the prerogative of participating in political affairs, including holding cabinet positions. They also felt that civilian authorities had no right to arbitrarily reorganize the army, promote or demote officers, or alter the army's existing internal rules. Yet in their actual behavior, the army's senior officers generally were either neutral or helpful in their political roles. Both Ngollo and Mokoko tried repeatedly to mediate between Congo's squabbling politicians to preserve social and political order in the country. In this and other ways, these two key figures showed loyalty to the idea of a republican army that would obey legitimate civilian authorities. Neither attempted to mount a coup d'état, though there was ample pretext for them to have done so. That both Ngollo and Mokoko accepted their respective dismissals from government service without public complaint attests to their loyalty to civilian authority. Only when officers were unfairly maligned by civilian politicians, as in January 1992, did some threaten to seize power, but the army's leaders did not encourage or support such threats. Thus, the militias and their leaders were far less committed to obeying civilian authorities than were the officers of Congo's regular army.

On the question of the unbalanced ethnoregional composition of the army, it was true that the army was disproportionately staffed by Mbochi and other northern officers in 1991. Yet neither Ngollo nor Mokoko was Mbochi, and neither was intrinsically loyal to Sassou. As noted, both showed impressive loyalty to the idea of a republican army in the service of legitimate, elected authorities. It is true that elements of the army refused to carry out their orders in 1993 and 1994 when they were ordered to disarm the militant supporters of Kolélas and bombard Bacongo. But this is hardly evidence that the army would only obey the orders of a northern president: under similar circumstances honorable soldiers anywhere might have behaved similarly. Further, when Lissouba sought to rebalance the army in terms of its regional composition, he did not stimulate a coup from within army ranks. Indeed, Lissouba had taken this process quite far by the start of the 1997 war without provoking a coup, and despite the hardship he imposed on those deprived of their army salaries. The widespread perception that Lissouba wished to create an army loyal to him and his *own* ethnoregional supporters, however, eroded support within the army for the principle of republican loyalty.

Finally, on the question of the army as an economic problem, it was not the case that army units rebelled or threatened civilian authorities for higher salary payments or expensive improvements in their conditions. In fact, hundreds of officers and soldiers lost their pay after being excluded from the army without resorting to coups. Yet the only groups of soldiers to stage mutinies against their officers for better conditions were those newly recruited from the ranks of the militias. It *is* true that massive unemployment among Congo's youth, males in particular, made it easier for the politicians to recruit soldiers for their militias. Had they not been recruited and paid, however, by politicians, these unhappy youths would have had to accept their lot in life or find other sources of income and diversion. The fact that fighters in all of the political militias often preyed upon members of the very ethnic and regional groups that they were nominally recruited to protect, and that they often threatened their own leaders, does not invalidate the point: without the active connivance of Congo's political principals, these youths would never have become so heavily armed and dangerous. The fact that Milongo never created his own militia and lamented that others had done so is evidence that better behavior was possible.[30]

In sum, Congo's army did pose real challenges for any civilian government. The army inherited by the new government in 1991 was too large and costly, too heavily staffed with northern officers, and too imbued with a sense of entitlement. Yet none of these challenges justified the organization of parallel personal militias. A capable and fair political administration could have conceivably carried out army reform without provoking civil war. Neither Sassou nor Kolélas was justified in the creation of militias during 1991 and 1992. Both had begun to transform their bodyguards into larger armed groups even before Lissouba's dissolution of Parliament in November 1992. Likewise, Lissouba failed to restrain his presidential guard from the first use of violence against civilians in democratic Congo, even as the regular army protected his residence. He went on to allow the training of militias for use against the civilian populations that the regular army was loath to attack at a time when the army was still willing to follow legitimate orders.

■ Comparative Perspectives on the Military in Democratic Consolidation Efforts

As the foregoing analysis shows, the evidence from inside Congo does not strongly support the hypothesis that Lissouba was forced to organize private militias in 1993 in order to deal with the country's army problems. Nor was he forced to try to disarm Sassou's militias in 1997. Here we examine the evidence represented by the experience of other African states undergoing democratic experiments after 1990. If that evidence shows that other African leaders faced similar military challenges to those of Lissouba, and that their inability to deal with them led to the collapse of democratic experiments, then perhaps one would second guess this initial conclusion. This final section thus evaluates the question of whether structural problems with national security forces inherited by Africa's post-1990 democratic leaders *forced* them to take steps that derailed their own democratic experiments.

The case that seems to best support the structural military thesis is that of the CAR. President Ange-Félix Patassé, elected in September 1993, confronted an army that had been dominated for twelve years by his military predecessor, General André Kolingba. During his years in office Kolingba had shown favoritism to members of his own Yakoma ethnic group and other southerners in his army recruitment; Patassé, meanwhile, was from a northern group, the Kaba, part of the larger Sara ethnic cluster. Also like Congo, the CAR had a profoundly nondemocratic political culture, including in the army, and severe financial problems when the democratic experiment began. And Patassé's history with his own military was even more fraught than that of Lissouba. Patassé's government suffered three increasingly powerful mutinies in Bangui during 1996, in April, May, and November, respectively. The second of these was bloodily put down with the intervention of the French (Mehler 2005: 136–137). Like Lissouba, Patassé created a private militia group, between the May and November revolts, to help secure him in power. Moreover, Patassé won a second term as president in an election judged free and fair by outside observers in 1999 (143). Subsequently, in May 2001, he faced a major coup attempt in which his chief of staff was killed. He only managed to overcome the coup attempt with the help of Libyan and Congolese fighters (145). Then, in December 2001, Patassé's decision to sack his chief of staff, General François Bozizé, led to another round of fighting as Bozizé fled the country. Finally, Bozizé organized an army in Chad, returned to the CAR, and finally toppled the Patassé government in March 2003 (147–148).

Despite this prima facie evidence for the structural military thesis to explain the failure of the CAR's democratic experiment, a deeper analysis shows Patassé's own *uncoerced* behavior had a great deal more to do with his demise. Throughout his years in power, Patassé showed himself to be exceedingly corrupt, incompetent, repressive, and disrespectful of the rule of law. The first revolt against Patassé was due to military salary arrears, and the second was for the same reason, as well as the reassignment of some Yakoma-dominated units to locations outside the capital. The third revolt of 1996 echoed these concerns, but also called for Patassé's resignation (Mehler 2005: 136–137). Not only did Patassé deal poorly with these revolts, but he allowed—or directed—his militia to engage in ethnic cleansing in Bangui afterward. After his reelection in 1999, Patassé was more violently repressive of the press and of opposition figures than before. His human rights record was abysmal, attracting universal condemnation. Many of his political opponents, including a parliamentary deputy, were simply murdered by his henchmen after the 2001 coup attempt. Some five hundred people were killed and some 80,000 people forced to flee their homes in the repression that followed (145). Patassé's behavior was repellent to most of the political class and many other Central Africans not from the president's own densely populated area of the northwest. Thus Patassé had given the army many legitimate reasons to act, and many were relieved when Bozizé overthrew the old regime.

Two elected rulers of Guinea-Bissau met the same fate as Patassé largely for the same reasons. The first was President João Vieira, the country's military dictator from 1980 to 1994 who won a tolerably fair election—albeit with only 52 percent support—at the polls in July 1994. Unlike Lissouba and Patassé, Vieira had had plenty of time to put his own loyal supporters in key army posts well before he became an elected president. Nonetheless, his political behavior differed little from that of the two central African rulers. By 1998 his popularity had waned in all quarters, including the army. When Vieira tried to replace his more popular army chief of staff, the majority of the army revolted. In the short civil war that followed, the rebels led by chief of staff Ansumane Mané defeated not only Vieira's army loyalists, but an expeditionary force of Senegalese, as well (Forrest 2005: 255–257). Mané took power after the rebel victory, but he soon made strongly democratic stands when he first promised timely new presidential elections and then announced that he would not be a candidate.

Vieira's opponent from 1994, Kumba Yala, won the presidency in the second round of elections in January 2000. Unfortunately for Guinea-Bissau, his political style was not very different from that of Vieira. After a feud with Mané in late 2000, Yala had loyal army troops hunt down the army chief and murder him. Yala persecuted minority Muslim religious groups, demonstrated blatant ethnic favoritism toward his own Balanta co-ethnics, and harassed or jailed opposition political figures. By 2001 he had alienated most leading figures in his own administration. Forrest (2005: 262) attributed Yala's behavior chiefly to the antidemocratic values that still prevailed among the political class in an era of political reform. Later Yala began to show a complete disregard for the autonomy of other branches of government. In late 2001 he had three Supreme Court justices dismissed and later jailed on dubious charges of corruption. Reacting to an economic crisis in November 2002, Yala proceeded to dissolve Parliament and call for new elections, elections that should have taken place within three months under the constitution. After some nine months had dragged by without the organization of new elections, the army undertook a bloodless coup against Yala in September 2003. Elected, civilian government was restored within two years. Remarking on the behavior of the military during the 1998 war and after, Guinea-Bissau's leading analyst detected "the emergence in the heart of the military leadership of proto-democratic values, including respect for constitutional rules, neutrality, a commitment to electoral procedures, and political tolerance. It further highlights the fact that, despite the civil war of 1998, the military in Guinea-Bissau served as a 'republican' barrier to democratic breakdown" (Forrest 2005: 263). In this case, as in Congo, the army acted to throttle elected but undemocratic political figures who themselves threatened democracy.

Niger's story of democratic experimentation seems at first to implicate the military in the collapse of a democratization effort, but the larger story shows the military in a much better light. Like Guinea-Bissau, Niger had been in the grip of military rule for some twenty years when serious reform efforts began in the early 1990s. Following a successful and invigorating national conference in 1991 (Robinson 1994b), Niger had free elections in 1993, electing Mahmane Ousmane president. Alas, the great challenge for Niger proved to be making government work with a Parliament dominated by an opposition coalition of a different tendency than the president.[31] A political impasse eventually emerged by late 1995 under which the president and prime minister sought to dismiss each other and, in these circumstances, the military stepped in with Colonel Ibrahim Baré Maïnassara taking power. Unlike his counterpart in Guinea-Bissau, however, Baré *did* stand in the presidential elections staged in August 1996. Further, when the preliminary results were clearly against him, Baré stopped the voting midway through and dissolved the national election commission (Villalón and Idrissa 2005a: 40). He was later declared president by a new, handpicked commission.

At this point in the story, one could only conclude that the military had halted the democratic experiment, taking advantage of a difficult moment in the process of working out institutional relations. Subsequent events, however, are highly redemptive of the republican credentials of the Nigerian military. After two and a half years of illegitimate, highly contested, and ineffectual rule, Baré was assassinated by members of his own presidential guard in April 1999. The guard's head, Major Daouda Mallam Wanké, then briefly took power and announced a nine-month period of transition (Villalón and Idrissa 2005a: 41). Staying true to his word, Major

Wanké proceeded to organize presidential and legislative elections for October and November 1999. Wanké was not a candidate, and the presidency was won by the veteran politician Tanja Mamadou, who was subsequently reelected president in November 2004.[32] Thus, the army had an important role in restoring democratic institutions, as well as disrupting them, in Niger.

Only one other African state launching a democratic experiment after 1991, Madagascar, has experienced significant military intervention so far. Military intervention in Madagascar came in the context of the disputed presidential elections of December 2001. The postelectoral conflict between President Didier Ratsiraka and Marc Ravalomanana was over the question of whether Ravalomanana had won more than 50 percent in the first round or not. Although two competing electoral commissions agreed that Ravalomanana had bested Ratsiraka in the contest, they differed over the 50 percent question and thus whether a second round was required. The country's Supreme Court later sided with Ravalomanana, though not without controversy (Marcus 2005: 169–170). The army, with which Ratsiraka had intimate ties as a former navy admiral and one-party dictator, split between the two rivals, and a contest for physical control over the regions ensued during the first half of 2002. In the end, Ravalomanana's supporters (including many hundreds of army deserters) finally took control of the entire country, forcing Ratsiraka into exile. In this case, then, elements of the army helped install an apparently fairly elected president, and the army as an institution refrained from supporting one of its own in an unconstitutional way.

Finally, we turn to the case with which Congo deserves the most systematic comparison, that of Benin. At the transition in 1990, Benin's new government faced all three of the army problems that Congo had faced in 1991. In the course of numerous coups d'état between 1960 and 1974, the Beninois army had abandoned the ideal of being a "silent apolitical prop of legitimate authority," and had transformed the ideal "into the concept of the military as arbiters of political power and, later still, as the source of political legitimacy" (Decalo 1990: 100). Also as in Congo, the military in Benin was absorbing an abnormally large share of the government's budget, even in the 1960s. Officers were then receiving the same pay scale as French officers, costing the state millions (100). The cost had grown steadily over the years as the total size of the army, gendarmerie, and specialized militias had grown from about 4,000 in the 1960s to some 8,350 on the eve of the national conference (Decalo 1990: 100; Derrick 1995: B6). With the northern president Mathieu Kérékou in power for fourteen years, the army was also generally dominated by his fellow northerners (Decalo 1990: 101). Thus President Nicéphore Soglo faced many of the same problems as President Lissouba did upon coming to power.

Neither President Soglo nor former president Kérékou behaved anything like their Congolese counterparts, however. Soglo behaved more similarly to Milongo than Lissouba in his governing style. Soglo did not permit his entourage of supporters to control him, or the security forces of the country to pursue or harass his political opponents. The behavior of Kérékou made it easy for him to behave in this fashion: unlike Sassou, Kérékou kept a low profile during Soglo's term and certainly created no militia group to back him or his party. When it came time for a new presidential election, both parties competed peacefully, and the results restored Kérékou to office. Although two informed observers did report some "low-level military discontents" during Soglo's term, these did not seriously threaten the public order (Magnusson and Clark 2005). As the second term of Kérékou neared its end, a leading student of Benin wrote that "as of yet, no real institutional military challenge has threatened the new democratic regime" (Magnusson 2005: 77). Had the behavior of Congo's leading politicians been better, perhaps the same could have been said of Congo.

The other African cases show clearly that newly elected leaders faced similar challenges from the military, as did Milongo and then Lissouba in Congo. Yet one does not find the institutional militaries intervening for the reasons one might expect. It is not apparent in any case that a regime was overturned either because the army sought greater material benefits or because an ethnoregional rebalancing was taking place within the army. Only in Niger does one find a senior officer taking power (in 1996) on the ground that civilian politicians could not properly run the government. In that case, the army later redeemed itself, restoring an elected, civilian government to power. In the cases of Guinea-Bissau and the CAR, military leaders took power because elected regimes had become so corrupt, ineffective, and repressive that they themselves threatened democracy, despite having been elected. In Guinea-Bissau military authorities returned civilian rulers to power after the crisis had passed. Both in Congo and elsewhere, the institutional military actually acted to nurture or preserve democratic experiments. In no case did the military intervene in politics out of the blue, or in the absence of a serious political crisis. As in Congo, military structures may have made the challenge of democratic consolidation marginally more difficult, but in no place did the political culture, ethnic composition, or political economy of the army, by itself, clearly cause the end of a democratic experiment.

■ Notes

1. One early instance of this phenomenon was Mobutu's intervention in the standoff between Joseph Kasavubu and Patrice Lumumba in 1960; the military of Congo-Kinshasa subsequently returned to the barracks for five years before reentering the political scene in 1965. Much more recently, in Mali, Lt. Colonel Amadou

Toumani Touré played the hero's role when he and a group of other officers ended the dictatorship of General Moussa Traoré in March 1991. Touré then took charge of a transition committee that organized a national conference, allowed a referendum on a new multiparty constitution, and oversaw legislative and presidential elections, all in little over one year's time (Villalón and Idrissa 2005b: 55–60).

2. This was confirmed for me by a former US military official posted to central Africa during these years.

3. Chief of this unit was Ange Diwara from Sibiti (Lékoumou), who would later mount a coup against Ngouabi in 1972 and be killed by the army in 1973.

4. It is interesting to note that these two officers were of Vili ethnicity.

5. One prominent exception to this pattern was Joachim Yhombi-Opango, a conservative Kouyou, who graduated as a lieutenant from the prestigious Saint-Cyr military academy in France just before the start of the Congolese "revolution."

6. Interview with a Lari Army Colonel, Brazzaville, 4 June 2002.

7. The figures on the size of the army in 1990 do not exactly agree, and the precise size of the army at that time is uncertain. Decalo (1996: 37) put the size of the armed forces at 8,700, the gendarmerie at 2,500, and an "augmented militia" at 5,000 in 1994; according to him, the total numbers "briefly topped 20,000 in 1990 but they slowly declined as some paramilitary units were disbanded." The Economist Intelligence Unit put the figures for the army at 11,000 for early 1992 (*Country Report: Congo,* no. 3, 1992: 13), while Moukoko (1999: 125) put the figure at 10,000 in 1994, noting that the army had been "completely weakened due to the multiple desertions of the southern soldiers."

8. See, for example, Economist Intelligence Unit, *Country Report: Congo,* no. 1, 1992: 14; and Kouvibidila (2000: 44). Interestingly, of the seven new colonels named to the High Command, three were actually from the north, though not protégés of either Sassou or Mokoko.

9. The course of events in the remainder of this paragraph is compiled from reports given in Economist Intelligence Unit, *Country Report: Congo,* no. 1, 1992: 14–15; *Africa Confidential,* "Characteristic Ambiguity," 6 March 1992: 5–7; and Kouvibidila (2000: 45–48).

10. Kouvibidila (2000: 52–53) and *Africa Confidential,* "Characteristic Ambiguity," 6 March 1992: 5.

11. The new alliance was deemed "against nature" by the foreign press because Kolélas had long enunciated a promarket, politico-economic ideology during his long years in the political wilderness (*Jeune Afrique,* "Le Lion et l'Agneau," 20–26 May 1993: 22–24). In reality, the new alliance only underscored the irrelevance of Western ideologies to Congolese politics.

12. The legal, constitutional aspects of this standoff are examined in Chapter 7 of this volume.

13. On this group, see Chapter 5 of this volume.

14. There was controversy at the time over the numbers killed and wounded, and this controversy was never resolved. For two accounts, see Mokoko (1995: 61) and Kouvibidila (2000: 229–231).

15. Bongo was a well-suited mediator in particular because of his credibility with Lissouba and Sassou. As noted in Chapter 5, Bongo allegedly has ethnic ties with Lissouba and had previously intervened on his behalf. Meanwhile, Bongo had married Sassou's daughter in 1990. Accordingly, Bongo reportedly supported Lissouba and Sassou against Kolélas in the 1992 elections (*Africa Confidential,* "Congo: Testing the Waters of Democracy," 19 June 1992: 7).

16. This group was also known as the Réserve ministérielle, and they were later

called the Cocoye. See Bazenguissa-Ganga (1999: 41).

17. Interestingly, the subheading for the section is entitled "Reasons for My *Resignation*" (Mokoko 1995: 70). According to Mokoko (72), that morning he had issued an ultimatum to the presidential guard to "dismantle the mechanisms of terror put in place in the city" by 3:00 PM, the time at which he was called to the presidency.

18. The journalist is Francis Kpatindé in *Jeune Afrique,* "Que va faire l'armée?" 24–30 June 1993: 16. Mokoko later ably defended himself in a reply published in *Jeune Afrique,* "Droit de Réponse au . . . Général Jean-Marie Michel Mokoko," 15–21 July 1993: 20.

19. The Libreville Accord provided for a rerun of the boycotted second round of parliamentary elections under international supervision and for the formation of an international jury to review the contested results from the first round of voting (Zartman and Vogeli 2000: 276).

20. The text of this accord, the "Communiqué inter-régional Pool-Pays du Niari," can be found in Baniafouna (1995b: 243–247); there is some analysis in Zartman and Vogeli (2000: 278).

21. Confidential interview in Washington, DC, with former US military official stationed in Brazzaville, 15 July 1998. Also see Economist Intelligence Unit, *Country Report: Congo,* no. 1, 1994: 14, where it states that "army units were reported to be disobeying orders and switching loyalties according to the regional bias in their ranks."

22. As noted by Zartman and Vogeli (2000: 401, note 1), there is absolutely no consensus on the number killed in the wars of 1993–1994, but the figures range from 2,000 to 10,000. Bembet (1997: 53), a fierce Lissouba critic, gives the typical range of 3,000 to 5,000.

23. The closing speeches of UNESCO director-general Federico Mayor and Monsignor Kombo can be found in Baniafouna (1995b: 250–252); the short communiqué on security signed by, inter alia, Mberi, Ngollo, Sassou, Kolélas, and Thystère-Tchicaya is on p. 253.

24. On the actual agreement see *Marchés Tropicaux et Méditerréens,* "Congo," 13 January 1995: 95; for more of the context and chronology, see Clark (1997b: 75).

25. Reported in chronological notes by country under "Congo," *Afrique Contemporaine* 177 (1st trimester 1996): 78.

26. This information gathered from *La Lettre du Continent,* "Congo: Général François Ayayen," 14 March 1996; Economist Intelligence Unit, *Country Report: Congo,* no. 3, 1996: 8; Economist Intelligence Unit, *Country Report: Congo,* no. 4, 1995: 7; Soni-Benga (1998: 90–91); and Bazenguissa-Ganga (1999: 42). Data on the general staff is from *La Lettre du Continent,* "Armée Nue et Milices Equipées," 23 January 1997. Ongobo's suspension is reported in Economist Intelligence Unit, *Country Report: Congo,* no. 3, 1997: 9.

27. See *Jeune Afrique,* "La Paix des Braves," 11–17 January 1996: 10; Economist Intelligence Unit, *Country Report: Congo,* no. 3, 1996: 7; and *Marchés Tropicaux et Méditerréens,* "Une Pacte de Paix Enfin Signé," 29 December 1995: 2880; each of these sources gives different details on the agreement.

28. The figures are taken from Bazenguissa-Ganga (1999: 40–42) and *La Lettre du Continent,* "Armée Nue et Milices Equipées," 23 January 1997.

29. See the accounts in Fédération Internationale des Ligues des Droits de l'Homme (1998) and in Koula (1999: 59).

30. On this subject, see the interview with Milongo conducted on 5 June 1997 included as annex 16 in Soni-Benga (1998: 233–234).

31. On this issue in Congo, and more generally in democratizing Africa, see Chapter 8 of this volume.

32. Tanja is the family name of Niger's president, but most press sources cite it first, as is the style in Francophone Africa.

7

The Constitution and
Political Institutions

This chapter examines the hypothesis that Congo's democratic experiment may have failed because of poor or inappropriate constitutional design, electoral laws, or national-local division of powers. Can either the events leading up to democratic failure or the moment of democratic failure itself be traced to a badly designed organization of constitutional powers in the country? As in the previous chapters, some important counterfactual questions are raised: Would Congo's democratic experiment have fared better if it had adopted a different sort of constitution in 1992? Would the Congolese have managed to consolidate their new democratic regime if the Assembly had adopted a different set of electoral laws? Or would some different combination of constitutional and legal arrangements have led to a better outcome?

Before examining these questions, it could legitimately be asked, "Is there sufficient evidence that institutional design may have mattered enough to even justify the inquiry?" Even those who have devoted much study to the impact of institutional design seem to have their doubts. One such scholar, Juan Linz (1994: 70), opines at the end of an exhaustive study of presidential versus parliamentary democracy, "There can be no question that neither parliamentarism nor presidentialism, nor a mixed system, is able to handle successfully intractable problems such as those faced today by Lebanon, Cyprus, and probably societies involved in civil war or in the problems of some African countries." Another senior comparativist starts his study by conceding that "institutional arrangements derive their importance from the influence they exercise on the context within which conflicts are resolved. They do not guarantee the resolution of conflicts. If ethnic or religious conflicts are especially acute, no institutional form of democratic governance may be capable of resolving them peacefully" (Suleiman 1994: 137). At least one important empirical study of fifty-six democratic experiments between 1930 and 1995 reinforces the doubts of these seasoned scholars (Power and Gasiorowski 1997). Specifically, the study found that the choice between presidential or parliamentary constitutional types did not influence the ability of newly democratizing states to consolidate their regimes.

177

Nonetheless, a great many other scholars studying even the difficult cases of Latin America and Africa continue to believe that "some political institutions are more likely than others to successfully facilitate conflict management in divided societies" (Belmont, Mainwaring, and Reynolds 2002: 3).[1] The management of conflict in divided societies, in turn, is a critical element of democratic consolidation. Many of those studying either individual cases or subgroups of the entire population of states experimenting with democracy find evidence that the configuration of executive, electoral, and other sorts of institutions matter in conflict management and ultimately democratic consolidation.[2] One recent edited volume studying all of the cases of democratic experiments in Africa since 1992 (Villalón and VonDoepp 2005) was premised on the idea that institutions may matter, and several of the authors clearly concluded that institutions were important for the countries they studied.

Many scholars who believe that institutions matter insist that institutional design must be studied in its particular context and in relationship to numerous other social variables, rather than merely "seeking to establish a correlation between institutions and outcomes" (Frye 2002: 102). As Magnusson (2005: 82) noted with reference to an African example, "the Benin case helps to illustrate the utility of analyzing electoral systems as *one element* within larger webs of institutions, rather than as an isolated unit of analysis" (emphasis added). This study is premised on the same idea, namely, that the impact of any one variable, such as institutional design, is understood within the context of all of the others. If institutional design matters in some of these other cases, it might matter, to some degree, in the Congo case.

There is also room to debate Linz's view that institutional design has the least potential impact for "divided societies." Indeed, one could easily argue precisely the opposite: in societies with a well-established political culture of democracy and a high standard of living, a democratic system of any sort of design might easily be consolidated. Perhaps institutional design matters even more for the societies prone to identity group conflict than others. Moreover, although Congolese society may have been divided in a number of ways, it was not so clear in 1991 which social cleavages would prove to be the dominant ones. The first major challenges that Sassou faced in late 1990 were not from other ethnoregional leaders, but from the country's religious establishment (Okoko-Esseau 1995) and the country's umbrella labor union, led by Sassou's fellow Mbochi, Jean-Michel Bokamba-Yangouma (Clark 1993).

Finally, the chronology of events themselves strongly suggests a major role for the country's institutional arrangements in the democratic failure. As we saw previously, the first crisis that the new Lissouba regime faced was provoked by the president's sudden and unexpected loss of his parliamentary majority in November 1992. This crisis led to the first politically related deaths in Congo and to a far larger crisis over the new legislative elections the following year. In turn, one can attribute the rapid buildup and arming—if not the very existence—of the country's personal militias to the tragic events of 1993. These militias, as we saw, were never disbanded and later became the most important social actors in the war of 1997. To understand fully Congo's democratic collapse, one has to be aware of the institutional arrangements that framed the conflicts of 1992–1993 and 1997, and also to consider whether some other institutional arrangements might have led to a different and better outcome.

The remainder of this chapter undertakes the following tasks. First, it identifies four different issues of institutional design that are relevant to the Congo case and discusses each briefly. Second, it discusses how the various elements of Congo's institutional design became relevant parts of the political context for the political crises that wracked the country in 1992–1993 and 1997. Third, it examines several other African cases that confronted similar problems to those of Congo under institutionally similar and different conditions.

■ Relevant Issues of Institutional Design

Based on a review of the chronology of events in Congo, four issues of constitutional and institutional design have relevance to the country's democratic experiment. Likewise, at least one of these four issues appears to have affected the trajectory of the other democratic experiments in Africa then unfolding during the 1990s (Villalón and VonDoepp 2005). These issues include the nature of the powers of a state's chief executive(s), the electoral formula for the selection of the legislature, the degree of centralization of authority at the state level, and the existence and role of supreme judicial bodies charged with constitutional interpretation. The first two of these issues have been extensively studied, while the third has been studied rather less, and the last issue has garnered relatively little scholarly attention.

The most studied issue of institutional design is the nature of the relationship between a state's chief executive(s) and the legislature. The three basic models are the presidential model, the semi-presidential model, and the prime ministerial or simply "parliamentary" model. The semi-presidential model entails dual executives, with a prime minister serving as head of government and a president acting as head of state. Each of the three models has a great many variations, most usually categorized by the relative powers of the executive(s) vis-à-vis the legislature. In the case of the semi-presidential model, the constitutional relationship between the two executives is obviously of critical importance. The first and longest-lived example of a semi-presidential system is that of the French Fifth Republic, issuing from the French constitutional crisis generated by the Algerian liberation war of 1954 to 1962. During the recent wave of democratic experimentation in the world, this model has been widely adopted by many of the new, transitional democracies. It has special relevance to Africa because the widespread adoption of constitutions mimicking that of the French Fifth Republic is an important legacy of French colonialism on the continent. Congo was among the large number of former French colonies that adopted a semi-presidential model at the outset of its democratic experiment in the early 1990s.

Since the authors of the Congolese constitution and those of most other African constitutions chose semi-presidentialism as their preferred form of executive leadership, it is appropriate that we concentrate our analysis here. As with most of the constructed concepts of social science, the concept of a semi-presidential system has not gained a universally accepted definition. Apparently all who have studied the concept concur that such a regime must feature an elected president who is head of state and a prime minister responsible to a parliament. The major debates on whether a regime is semi-presidential or not hinge on whether the president must be *directly* elected, what level of authority a president wields (e.g., must a president have more than ceremonial powers), and whether the prime minister must be "parliament dependent" (Elgie 1999: 2–6). Even the scholar who has devoted the most sustained attention to the concept has changed his mind on the most appropriate definition: in his earlier work Elgie (1999: 13) requires only that the president be "popularly elected," so as to include regimes where the president is chosen indirectly, usually by a legislative assembly; more recently (2005: 100), he requires that the president be "directly elected" for a regime to qualify as semi-presidential.

Elgie (2005: 102–109) has usefully divided semi-presidential regimes into three types, based on the relative power of the president: those that are "highly presidentialized," those with ceremonial presidents, and those in which there is a "balance of presidential and prime-ministerial powers." The distinction is critical because different varieties of semi-presidential regimes suffer from varying sorts of potential problems. Congo's 1992 constitution gave the president considerable legal powers from the beginning, and, as we saw above, Lissouba sought tirelessly to expand those powers through both legal reinterpretation and political fiat. Nevertheless, the problems of both the highly presidentialized and balanced models are relevant to Congo.

For semi-presidential regimes in which the powers of the two executives are constitutionally balanced, the dangers are fairly obvious. It is quite easy to imagine that there might be deadlock between the two executives, clashes over the appropriate policies to follow, and conflict over the fine points of the legal powers of each executive (Linz 1994: 19, 36–37; Elgie 2005: 107). The highest profile examples of this problem have been the various "cohabitation" regimes that have come to power in France over the last twenty years, beginning with that of 1986–1988 (Suleiman 1994:

150–151). For unconsolidated democratic regimes, one can well imagine that the necessity of cohabitation might lead to a regime crisis or even democratic breakdown. Yet another danger for new, potentially consolidating democracies is that the presidents in such regimes will gradually accrue more and more power in their office at the expense of the legislature. Colton and Skach have attributed precisely this problem to semi-presidential Russia and have advocated movement toward parliamentarism for all the semi-presidential states of Eastern Europe (2005: 123–124). They insist that the model works only for states with strong parties, something the states of Eastern Europe lack.

As for the "highly presidentialized" type, one must agree with Elgie (2005: 102) that "these regimes often suffer the same problems as their purely presidential counterparts." In turn, presidentialist regimes have severe and unrelenting critics. Virtually all of the most visible scholars intensively studying institutional design have concluded that presidentialism is a bad system both for consolidating nascent democracies and for ensuring popular representation in established democracies. Sartori (1994: 107) criticizes "pure presidentialism" for its instability, noting that the United States is the sole exception to the intermittent quality of all other presidential regimes. He goes on to argue that the US system works in spite of, and not because of, its divided, presidentialist system (109). Lijphart (1999: 128) agrees that presidentialist systems are unstable, but criticizes them even more strongly for being a "majoritarian" (as opposed to consensus) model of democracy (110–111, 159). Prominent scholarly analysts of many Latin American states, including Arturo Valenzuela (1994, on Chile), Cynthia McClintock (1994, on Peru), Michael Coppedge (1994, on Venezuela), and Mark Jones (1997, on Argentina) have all concluded that excessive presidentialism is a major ailment of the countries they study, even if it resonates well with local political cultures.

Perhaps the most comprehensive catalog of faults with presidentialist systems has been compiled by Juan Linz (1994: 6–46). He has cataloged a list of no less than seventeen deficiencies in such systems.[3] Fortunately, only six of these have relevance to Congo, after collapsing five of the criticisms into two.[4] These criticisms, briefly condensed, are as follows: presidential regimes have a problem of "dual legitimacy" in that both presidents and legislatures can claim final sovereignty (6–7); they are "rigid" in that presidential terms are fixed (8–10) and, as a result, they prove to be plebiscitary in character (29–30) and presidents have fraught relations with their militaries if they lose legitimacy before the end of their terms (46); presidential regimes lack accountability because voters cannot easily discern whether legislatures or executives are responsible for policy failure (10–14); such regimes create zero-sum contests in which losers are totally excluded (18–21), and they are particularly bad in multiethnic societies without a dominant group for this reason (42–44); they produce highly unstable cabinets staffed by amateur politicians (30–32); and presidential regimes only work well, because of "antiparty" presidential tactics, with a two-party electoral pattern, but they are unlikely to produce such patterns (34–36). Although Congo's system is correctly called semi-presidential, these criticisms of presidentialism are relevant, as we shall see below.

Despite the apparent faults of semi-presidentialism in its various forms, the model does have some stout defenders. Most notably, Sartori (1994: 107, 109, and 114) rejects "pure presidentialism," citing the instability of Latin America's many presidential regimes, the over concentration of power in the presidency, and the tendency of presidents to be uninitiated outsiders. On the other hand, Sartori also rejects a "pure parliamentary" model on the ground the prime minister lacks sufficient power to govern. As he argues, "A prime minister who cannot control his ministers (because he cannot fire them), and who does not even have a free hand in choosing them, cannot be expected to be really in charge" (110). He therefore concludes that "semipresidentialism can improve presidentialism, and, similarly, that semiparliamentary systems . . . are better than plain parliamentary ones" (110).[5] In his subsequent discussion, however, he specifies that *no* variety of parliamentary system works well unless its parties have "parliamentary fit" (Sartori 1994: 112, emphasis added). By this he means "parties that have been socialized (by failure, duration, and appropriate incentives) into being relatively cohesive or disciplined, into behaving, in opposition, as responsible oppositions and into playing, to some extent, a rule-oriented fair game" (112). Thus, in Sartori's view, the (usually developing) states that lack disciplined parties are left with semi-presidentialism as their best possibility, though it is far from ideal (115).

The other elements of institutional design may be discussed more briefly. With regard to electoral systems, the most fundamental choice is one between proportional representation (PR) systems, in which the voter chooses a list of candidates representing a party for the entire country, and the district system, in which the voter chooses among individual candidates competing to represent a specific district. As with the question of executive leadership, many kinds of intermediate formulas are possible. These include complex formulas under which voters may choose representatives for both a district and the state as a whole (as in Italy and Germany), or multimember district systems in which multiple legislators represent a single district (as in Ireland). Winners may be selected by plurality, or a runoff between the highest finishers may apply.

In general, and other things being equal, the district system has the advantage that it tends to reduce the number of parties that are elected to the legislature, as in Britain and the United States where two parties dominate. This result is particularly strong when the advocates of a minority view are dispersed across a state's territory. The disadvantage of this type of system is that it tends to prevent minority parties—and their constituents—from achieving representation in the legislature. Because the district system tends to magnify the gains of plurality winners and proportionally disadvantage minority parties, advocates of "consensual" democracy such as Lijphart (1999: 14–16) strongly dislike this type of system. Lijphart (25–27) much prefers proportional representation for these reasons. Sartori also much prefers proportional representation "when a polity is polarized or characterized by a heterogeneous political culture" (1994: 111). Another general advantage of proportional representation is that such systems generally produce more disciplined parties, though this is far from always being the case, as such states as Brazil show. The system's great disadvantage is that it can create a fragmentation of the electorate that returns a wide range of parties, including those representing political extremes, as in Italy.

The relative value of competing electoral systems is quite often discussed in the context of executive leadership design. That is, certain types of electoral systems are thought to be more appropriate for presidential, semi-presidential, or parliamentary executive systems. For instance, the executive type may dictate the degree of party dominance required in the legislature to make governments both effective and representative. In highly presidentialized systems, like those of Latin America, scholars have had two opposite concerns about legislatures when it comes to balancing executive powers. On the one hand, they worry that an electoral system may allow one party associated with the president to dominate the legislature, stifling the voice of the opposition, as in Mexico under the PRI (Weldon 1997: 244–245); on the other, they also worry that an electoral system will lead to such total fragmentation of the legislature that presidents can easily manipulate the weak parties represented there (Mainwaring 1997: 68–82). In parliamentary systems, by contrast, any chance of effective government may depend on the dominance of one party or coalition in the legislature. Finding the right combination of executive leadership and electoral system design to produce government that is both representative and effective is tricky indeed but also critical to successful democratic consolidation.

Also related to executive power is the question of presidential elections systems. In general, if presidents are to be directly elected, one either has to allow them to be elected with a plurality of votes or provide for a two-round voting system. In some cases, when no candidate achieves a majority, the legislature or some other body is called on to choose among the top finishers. For countries just beginning to experiment with democracy, the possibility of a plurality president seems destabilizing indeed, though second-round elections that produce very close results are also problematic.

The question of the centralization of authority poses the same fundamental question as that of electoral and executive design: what distribution of powers across different levels of the political system can produce government that is both effective and representative?[6] Political systems that accord significant powers to regional and local governments, or systems generally called "federal," may offer significant advantages in the process of democratic consolidation. In principle, regional and local governments should be more attuned to local concerns, more responsive to their constituencies, and more knowledgeable about local impediments to reform. Further, they also promise to encourage greater citizen participation in democratic institutions for the same reasons. For those who fear overconcentration of governmental authority at the national level, such as Elazar (1997), Linz (1994: 43), and Lijphart (1999: 185–199), there is a clear preference for decentralization of power to local and regional authorities. Others conclude that decentralization of powers can strengthen political parties by facilitating integration between party leaders and the grassroots (Mainwaring and Shugart 1997b: 417).

Federal systems have a special appeal for societies composed of highly distinctive identity groups, especially when they are concentrated in specific regions. Federalism potentially allows such groups local autonomy and dampens their enthusiasm for secession. It permits minority groups to participate meaningfully in a larger democratic system in which the majority ultimately rules. States such as Cyprus, India, Fiji, and Bosnia-Herzegovina could scarcely hang together without such arrangements (Ghai 2002: 141–153; Lijphart 2002: 51–53). Also, and less noticed by most non-Africanists, federal arrangements with important local offices may provide meaningful political roles for the representatives of minority groups who fail to attain national office. If such leaders are deprived of such roles, they are much more prone to contest the legitimacy of the central state in disruptive or violent ways.

Other scholars have been more acutely attuned to the challenges and risks of decentralization and federalism. Although federalism has often been debated as a possible solution for conflicts in multiethnic societies, Ghai (2002: 170) has concluded that "constitutional recognition of cultures tends to sharpen differences between communities." Moreover, the diffusion of power to local authorities can enervate central administrations to such an extent that they are unable to carry out major development and state-building projects, as a number of scholars have recognized (e.g., Solnick 2002). In Nigeria, the regional governments have been even more corrupt and incompetent than the national government.

Because of the enormous gap between state elites and ordinary citizens in African countries, decentralization of state authority became a major preoccupation of governments, scholars, and international aid officials in Africa beginning in the late 1980s (see, e.g., Vengroff and Johnston 1989; Boko 2002; Ndegwa 2002; and Olowu and Wunsch 2003). The need for decentralization appeared to be particularly acute in the former French colonies, all of which had maintained the French legacy of centralized states. To the extent that decentralization of power to regions is part of a country's constitution, it can be considered part of its institutional design. Finally, the issue of judicial review in two different areas is highly relevant to the Congo case. Ordinarily, judicial review refers to the right of judicial bodies to decide whether laws are in conformity with the constitution (Lijphart 1999: 223). The highest judicial bodies may also pass judgment on the constitutionality of executive actions, as well, however. As Lijphart (225–228) argues, the power of judicial review can range from quite strong to lacking altogether. As his analysis implies, the strength of judicial review may result from either constitutional provision or from custom and practice. Only the former can be considered an issue of institutional design, while the latter source is a matter of political culture. Lijphart (224–225) distinguishes between those states that formally put special "constitutional courts" into their fundamental laws and those that do not. He identifies those states with constitutional courts as having a "centralized system" of judicial review and indicates that they "tend to have stronger judicial review than countries with decentralized systems" (228).

The form of electoral oversight is another judicial arrangement relevant to the Congo case. Specific forms of electoral oversight may be a constitutional requirement or the result of other forms of law. In a great many cases, in the era of democratization, special electoral commissions or councils were set up to oversee the organization of elections and to review complaints by dissatisfied parties when these arose. Before the 1990s, most African countries did not have such bodies, and elections were usually run by government administrations themselves. In the French tradition, it was usually the ministries of interior that oversaw elections and published their results. Many scholars have concluded that independent electoral commissions are extremely valuable in situations where social trust is low and postelectoral strife likely.

■ The Impact of Congo's Institutional Design

Here we examine how Congo's institutional design in each of these four areas affected its democratic experiment. As we saw in the previous chapters, the crisis of late 1992 that grew into the war of 1993–1994 began with a standoff between the majority in Parliament and the president. This crisis and the ensuing war, in turn, appear to be the events that launched Congo down the path of mistrust, militarized politics, and, ultimately, war and democratic collapse.

Executive-Legislative Relations

Congo's 1992 constitution provided for a semi-presidential form of government, but it was clearly a "highly presidentialized" type. Under the constitution the president served as the commander in chief of the armed forces

(Article 84), he appointed the prime minister (Article 75), and he presided over the council of ministers (Article 76).[7] In case of "public calamity or national disaster" the president was empowered to declare a state of emergency (if only for fifteen days without parliamentary approval) (Article 109). By contrast, the prime minister's main responsibilities were to arrange for *(dispose de)* administration and the security forces, for which he was "responsible before the president of the republic and the National Assembly" (Article 89).

Nonetheless, the president was charged under the constitution to choose a prime minister coming from the parliamentary majority. The first sentence of Article 75 makes this clear: "Le president de la République nomme le Premier minister issu de la majorité parlementaire à l'Assemblée nationale" (The president of the Republic names the prime minister coming from the parliamentary majority in the National Assembly). A second major article dealt with the president's dissolution of the Assembly under specific circumstances. In its entirety, the critical Article 80 reads as follows:

> When the equilibrium of the public institutions is broken, notably in case of a persistent and sharp crisis between the executive power and the Parliament, or if the National Assembly overturns the government two times in the period of one year, the president of the Republic may, after consulting the prime minister and the president of the National Assembly, decide to dissolve the National Assembly.

One further article is relevant to the crisis of late 1992 and the analysis below. Article 123 specifies that "when the National Assembly adopts a motion of censure or when it disapproves the program or a general policy declaration of the government, the prime minister must submit the resignation of the government to the president of the Republic." These articles provide the legal context of the devastating impasse that wracked Congo at the birth of its democratic experiment.

If these articles are considered collectively, and in order of their appearance in the constitution, it is clear that Lissouba acted outside the spirit of the law when he announced the dissolution of Parliament on 17 November 1992. The order of the articles makes it clear that the constitution envisioned the possibility of "cohabitation," as in Fifth Republic France. The opposition in Parliament had made a formal alliance, the URD-PCT, in September and announced the existence of this alliance to the nation.[8] There can be no doubt that that political bloc constituted the parliamentary majority, though Lissouba's camp simply claimed that there was no majority in Parliament and noted that his bloc was a plurality. Nonetheless, the opposition bloc organized a vote of no-confidence in the Bongho-Nouarra government on 31 October demonstrating their majority status and cohesion. According to the constitution, Bongho-Nouarra should have submitted the resignation of his government shortly after the minutes of the no-confidence vote were accepted on 4 November. At that point, Lissouba should clearly have accepted the resignation and named a prime minister "coming from the parliamentary majority." Thus, it is not that cohabitation failed in Congo, but that *it was never tried.*

Although a cohabitation in the Congolese government might well have been difficult politically, there is not much evidence that it would have reduced the government's efficacy. First, the effectiveness of the Lissouba government hardly set a high standard to surpass insofar as it perpetually avoided much-needed reforms. Further, there was very little—virtually nothing, in fact—dividing Congo's political formation along ideological lines. All parties in the political game, including the formerly Marxist PCT, recognized the inevitability of undertaking structural economic reform, while formally under structural adjustment or not. Congo faced the choice of either cutting the number of public employees or simply not paying those who remained nominally on the public payroll. No greater challenge than economic reform faced Congo—the only potential area of ideological conflict—but the parties had few if any ideological differences on this or other issues. In fact, a government of cohabitation would have allowed all the political formations to blame the pain of structural economic reform on their rivals.

Legally President Lissouba could hide behind Article 80 of the constitution, which did allow the president to dissolve Parliament. And indeed, there was a "sharp crisis" between the executive and legislature in November 1992, though it had not persisted for very long. Lissouba might more easily have resolved the crisis by naming an opposition prime minister. Instead, he used the constitution in a fashion that its authors did not anticipate, as the "father" of the Congolese constitution attested to me in person.[9] One reason that Lissouba succeeded in his dissolution of Parliament, it must be acknowledged, was the ambiguity and imprecision of the 1992 constitution. Any president could claim that there was a "sharp and persisting crisis" between Parliament and the executive at any time that an opposition majority in Parliament emerged, and such a claim could not be judged objectively. In large part Lissouba created the crisis of 1992 by defying the parliamentary majority. Without a clearer statement in Article 80 of when the president was entitled to dissolve Parliament, Articles 75 and 80 produced a legal contradiction in the duties and rights of the executive. Thus, the most obvious problem with the 1992 constitution was not the configuration of executive-legislative relations for which it provided, but its ambiguity on this issue.

Would the Congolese democratic experiment have fared better had the constitution provided either for a purely parliamentary system or a purely presidential system? It does not seem likely at all. As for the parliamentary option, this system was abandoned by virtually all African states in their first decade of independence, and currently only Ethiopia is led by a prime minister. In the African cultures that value the standing, power, and prestige of a presidential leader, the "first among equals" status of a prime minister falls short.[10] It is hard indeed to imagine the fractious Congolese reaching peaceful decisions in the absence of strong, if legitimate, leadership.

That being the case, would a presidential system not have worked better? While a purely presidential system would have avoided the crisis of October–November 1992, it would have created other problems like those identified in the first part of this chapter. Lissouba showed a great many signs of dictatorial tendencies from his first days in office, among them the dissolution of Parliament itself. A large number of Lissouba's Congolese critics had already concluded that the elected president was acting as a dictator within months of taking office (e.g., Nsafou 1996; Babu-Zalé et al. 1996; Bembet 1997, among others). By demanding a rerun of the legislative elections in 1993, Lissouba achieved virtually all of the powers in practice that a purely presidentialist constitution might have provided. Thus, any counterfactual democratic outcome would have depended upon the avoidance of the 1992–1993 civil war. Had it not been for that war, the militias built up during that time might not have existed in 1997. But it seems clear that Lissouba feared to face Sassou more in an electoral contest in 1997 than he did to face his militia and armed supporters in a military confrontation; had Lissouba been confident in his popularity, it is logical that he would simply have protected himself against the possibility of coup d'état, as he had done since 1992 and let the elections run their course. Meanwhile, had Sassou been successfully arrested (or killed) on the eve of the 1997 elections, most observers would have pronounced the democratic experiment dead at that juncture. These reflections lead us toward the tentative conclusion that, to paraphrase Churchill, perhaps the semi-presidential system was the worst possible one for Congo, except for all of the others.

Congo's Electoral Systems

Following the French electoral model, the Congolese presidential electoral law requires the winning candidate to gain an absolute majority of votes in either a first or second round of polling. If no candidate gains a majority in the first round, only the top two finishers proceed to the second round. This provision was important enough to have been specified in the constitution itself (Article 69). This presidential electoral system had the advantage of allowing the winning candidate to forge a coalition in the electoral period, in turn providing the new president a majority in the Parliament. Indeed, the electoral rules worked in precisely this way. In the first round Lissouba won 36 percent of the votes, Kolélas won 20 percent, Sassou won 17 percent, and Milongo won 10 percent. Six days after the first round of voting,

Sassou publicly endorsed Lissouba, and the two camps let it be known that they had an agreement for cooperation after the elections. In the second round of the voting, Lissouba prevailed by a margin of 61 percent to 39 percent for Kolélas, with Lissouba winning a large majority in the north of the country as well as in his Nibolek homeland.

Congo's legislative electoral system featured direct elections in single-member districts for the National Assembly and indirect elections by elected local authorities, forming electoral colleges at the regional level, for the Senate.[11] The system used the country's existing division into nine regions and separate communes for six cities.[12] Each region had been previously organized into a varying number of districts, with the cities separated out into *arrondissements* (municipal subdivisions). Districts with less than a population of 15,000 received one seat in the Assembly, while larger districts were divided up into as many as five seats, based on increments of 15,000 constituents. The divisions within the cities and of the larger districts were known as *circonscriptions électorales* (electoral circumscriptions) (Loi électorale: Articles 22, 27, and 28). This system created a National Assembly of 125 members, though one that was not limited in size by statute. The Senate was composed of sixty members, ten coming from each district and the Brazzaville region. The district and regional councilors (for the regions) and the communal and arrondissement councilors (for the urban areas) comprised the electorate for the Senate (Article 35). Under the constitution, and again mimicking the French system, the Senate had relatively much less power than the Assembly.

As for presidential aspirants, candidates for the Assembly were required to gain a majority of votes to win their seats. Circumscriptions in which no candidate won a majority thus had to hold a second round of voting between the top two candidates. The two rounds of legislative voting in 1992 were conducted on 24 June and 19 July, respectively. These two rounds of voting produced thirty-nine seats for the UPADS, twenty-nine for the MCDDI, eighteen for the PCT, and nine for Thystère-Tchicaya's RDPS (International Foundation for Election Systems 1992: 9). Yhombi's party, the Rassemblement pour la Démocratie et le Développement won five seats. The remaining twenty-five seats were held by parties represented by one or two deputies and eight independents. With the AND-PCT alliance intact at the moment of the elections, Lissouba could initially have counted on majority support in Parliament. In the indirect elections for the Senate, UPADS won twenty-three seats and the MCDDI fourteen.

In both elections, the voting patterns were distinctly ethnoregional. In the first round of the presidential elections, Lissouba carried each of the three Nibolek regions with more than 80 percent and gained a strong plurality in Kouikou; Kolélas carried only the Pool region, but also won a narrow plurality (30 percent) in divided Brazzaville; Sassou easily won the northern regions of Plateaux and Likouala, and finished with strong pluralities in Cuvette and Sangha. Similar patterns prevailed for the main candidate's party in the legislative elections (Weissman 1993: 69–98).

Contrary to the expectations of most analysts, who focus mostly on the developed world, the single-member district system did not lead to the domination of two parties. The top two parties together only won 54 percent (sixty-eight seats) in the legislature. A host of smaller parties (fifteen) were represented in the Assembly, whereas the PCT and RDPS qualified as medium-sized parties. These parties were, of course, primarily vehicles for the election of local political personalities rather than the expression of minority views on issues. Since the emergence of two dominant parties might have immediately polarized Congo into two camps, for example south versus north, an outside observer might have been pleased with the final results in July 1992. The representation of the major parties in the Assembly roughly coincided with the weight of the regional populations that supported each. As long as AND, dominated by UPADS, and URD, dominated by the MCDDI, remained at odds with one another, however, the situation gave Sassou and his PCT the ability to make or break any coalition.

Further, it does *not* appear that a proportional representation system would have produced a different result. If one assumes that those voters supporting a given presidential candidate would also have supported his party—a reasonable assumption—then a PR system would have produced a very similar result. There was a surprising correspondence between the percentage of the votes that each of the main candidates received in the first round of the presidential elections and the percentage of seats that each of their parties won in the legislative voting, as revealed in Table 7.1.

Only one other party won multiple seats (two), the Union pour le Progrès Social et la Démocratie led by Ange-Édouard Poungui and Jean-Michel Bokamba-Yangouma. Twelve other parties held one seat, while the

Table 7.1   **Presidential Votes by Candidate vs. National Assembly Seats Won by Presidential Candidates' Parties, 1992**

Candidate	Percentage of Presidential Vote	Party	Percentage of Party Seats
Lissouba	36.0	UPADS	31.2
Kolélas	20.3	MCDDI	23.2
Sassou-Nguesso	16.9	PCT	14.4
Milongo	10.1	Independent	n.a.
Thystère-Tchicaya	5.8	RDPS	7.2
Yhombi-Opango	3.5	RDD	4.0
Ganao	2.9	UFD	2.4

Source: Calculated from tables in Clark (1997b): 71, 73.
Note: n.a. indicates not applicable.

remaining three were held by independents.[13] Thus, there is no reason to believe that Congo was not well represented by the Assembly elected in 1992 if it is recognized that personalities and ethnoregional allegiance were the dominant forces in the country's politics. The Assembly reflected the country reasonably well in ethnoregional terms. Correspondingly, there is no compelling reason to think that an alternative PR electoral system would have changed the fate of the democratic experiment.

Would some other kind of system have produced an array of parties that could have worked in the semi-presidential executive system? For instance, what might have been the result of a PR system with a threshold of 5 percent of the vote for party representation, as is common in Europe? Such a system would likely have eliminated all of the parties except for the top four (see Table 7.1), and it would have increased by about 25 percentage points the seats that each held. In that case, UPADS would have won 49 seats, the MCDDI 36, the PCT 23, and the RDPS 11. At the end of 1992, however, the URD coalition included both the MCDDI and the RDPS. With the addition of the opposition PCT in the sudden alliance of the URD-PCT signed in late September, the opposition would still have had a majority in Parliament. The practical result, presumably, would thus have been the same, with the PCT holding the balance.

Decentralization in Congo

With regard to the powers of regional and local bodies, the constitution of 1992 mentions these almost as an afterthought in three short articles toward the end of the document. The articles (169–171) only indicate that local "collectivities" have a "legal personality" and that they enjoy administrative, financial, economic, cultural, and social autonomy. The final of the three articles indicates that "the law determines the juridical status, the powers, the attributions, and the functioning of the local collectivities and their relations with the central power [government]."[14] The electoral law of January 1992 provides some of the specifics for the local legislative bodies. Chapter V, Section 2, of the law (in Baniafouna 1995b: 119) provides for regional- and district-level councils and for communal councils for the six cities designated as "communes." Each of these communes is subdivided into a varying numbers of arrondissements with their own councils, as follows: Brazzaville (7), Pointe Noire (4), Loubomo (2), NKayi (2), Mossendjo (2), and Ouesso (2).[15]

Although the 1992 constitution definitely did not provide for a federal system, the influence of French centralism remaining strong, the new system did allow a modest amount of decentralization. As the representatives to all of these councils were elected by direct universal suffrage under the electoral law, these bodies were far more representative than they had been under the *parti unique* (single party). The 1992 electoral law did not specify anything about the election of mayors or regional prefects.

From the beginning of his presidency, Lissouba professed a passion for decentralization, perhaps stemming from his UNESCO work in this area. His cabinet formed in December 1992 featured a minister of "interior, security, and decentralization" (François Ayayen) and his cabinet of January 1995 a minister of "economic and administrative decentralization" (Martin Mbéri). Unfortunately, the chaos of his administration's first eighteen months delayed any concrete action on this front until after the war of 1993–1994 wound down. After a thorough debate, Parliament passed a major law on decentralization on 28 May 1994. According to one reading (*Marchés Tropicaux et Méditerréens,* "Congo," 3 June 1994: 1136), the law "foresees a total autonomy of management for the communes and the regions and a limited autonomy for collectivities such as the districts [and] arrondissements."[16] Many other public institutions, including some faculties of Marien Ngouabi University, were slated to be decentralized to locations outside of Brazzaville.

The most politically significant effect of the law, however, was its provision that the commune (city) mayors would be elected directly by the communal assemblies. This provision allowed Kolélas to be elected mayor of Brazzaville and Thystère-Tchicaya to be elected mayor of Pointe Noire in July 1994, both with the acknowledged support of President Lissouba.[17] When the May law was passed, Lissouba announced plans for a revision of the constitution that would make the decentralization of powers more formal and lasting (Economist Intelligence Unit, *Country Report: Congo,* no. 4, 1994: 13). It must be acknowledged that these new roles for two of Congo's most important leaders quieted considerably their opposition for the rest of Lissouba's term. Both were ministers in Lissouba's last, brief government.

In a number of other ways, however, the legacy of French centralism lived on in post-1992 Congo. Despite Lissouba's rhetorical support for decentralization, Brazzaville remained the hub of political, intellectual, and social life in the country. Most NGOs maintained their headquarters there, and most had no regional offices. Even more importantly, the pattern of having the national president appoint regional prefects, rather than having them elected by regional councils, remained in effect.[18] As a result, regional prefects had little autonomy and their offices were not an outlet for opposition figures.

Would a system either more centralized or more truly federalized have made a difference in Congo's democratic experiment? According to many Congolese, the highly centralized system of the single-party period did serve the purpose of building a sense of national identity. For instance, during the 1970s and 1980s, government employees were frequently sent to perform public service work (such as teaching) in regions other than those in which they were born.[19] Despite this advantage, however, most Congolese had come to favor greater decentralization by the 1990s; the corruption of the centralized state in the 1980s and 1990s made them distrustful of the entire political class located in Brazzaville. Conversely, the Congolese appear to have no more politico-cultural affinity for federalism than they do for pure parliamentarism. During the Lissouba years, only a tiny percentage of public revenues were shared with local and regional governments, which gained little influence as a result. Further, full-scale federalism might well have accentuated the feelings of ethnoregional identity difference among the Congolese, making national politics more difficult than ever.

The High Courts and Electoral Oversight Mechanisms

Congo's 1992 constitution provided for a wealth—perhaps a surfeit—of high judicial bodies. The first, the High Court of Justice, was empowered to judge the president, members of the government, members of Parliament, magistrates, and "chiefs of court" for any crimes or misdemeanors that they might commit (Article 138). Under Title IX of the constitution, "Du Pouvoir Judiciare" (Judicial Powers), two further courts were mentioned: a Supreme Court and a High Council of the Magistracy. The function of the Supreme Court was completely unspecified in the constitution, though the fundamental law stipulated that "the law establishes the organization, composition, and functioning of the Supreme Court" (Article 129). The High Council of the Magistracy was charged with proposing judges and prosecutors to the president for appointment and setting their rules of conduct (Article 135). A final body, the Constitutional Council "assure[d] the constitutionality of the laws, treaties, and international accords," and it was to be the "principal regulator of the activities of the public authorities" (Article 142). Finally, the Council was charged to "ensure the fairness of the election of the President of the Republic[,] to examine any complaints, and to proclaim the results of the poll" (Article 143). Likewise, the Council was to "rule in case of contestation of the fairness of the legislative and local elections" (Article 144).

Despite this excess of judicial institutions specified in the constitution, there was nothing inappropriate about these institutions in the main. They only failed because Congo's politicians failed to resort to them in a timely manner, in a spirit of fairness, and with respect for their judgment. Although Lissouba did not constitute the Constitutional Council in 1992 or 1993, as he was urged to do by his own supporters,[20] the Supreme Court acted in a judicious and nonpartisan manner during the crises of 1992 and 1993. Interestingly, however, the Electoral Law of January 1992, preceding the constitution itself, had specified under Chapter IX that the Supreme Court had the responsibility to judge electoral disputes.

In mid-March 1993, the Supreme Court received a petition from the second vice president of the senate, an opposition MCDDI supporter, asking for an interpretation of the meaning of Article 75 of the constitution, "notably on the concept of a parliamentary majority in the National Assembly."[21] In its opinion, the court identified a "parliamentary majority" as a group or coalition of groups that had the enduring ability to introduce and pass legislation by a majority vote. Second, citing Article 100 of the constitution, the court noted that the parliamentary majority could change while the Assembly was in session, and new Assembly officers could be elected. These two findings very clearly identified the URD-PCT as the parliamentary majority. Finally, the court gave the obvious interpretation of the president's duties and responsibilities, noting that his power to name the prime minister "was conditioned by the political context, especially the obligation that he name a prime minister *coming from the parliamentary majority in the National Assembly.*"[22] The opinion made it clear that the court had found against the president and indicated that he should have named a prime minister from the opposition. By then, however, a settlement had been reached—after bitter contestation—to form the unity government of 25 December 1992.

The next issue to come before the Supreme Court concerned the election results of the May 1993 elections and their publication. Before the 1992 elections, the transitional government had put in place first a commission to oversee the local elections in March (the COLOSSEL), and, second, another commission to oversee the legislative and presidential elections in May (the CONOSEL).[23] These bodies had functioned to general satisfaction, despite the protests about the irregularities in the local elections. On 3 January 1993, following the bitter clashes that ensued after the dissolution of Parliament, Lissouba decreed the creation of yet another body, CONOSELA. Bitter disputes over the composition followed, and only on 20 February was the Coordination Committee of fourteen members and three observers (including General Ngollo) announced. Including roughly equal numbers of Mouvance and opposition supporters, this commission proceeded to bicker over nearly every conceivable aspect of its operations (Kouvibidila 2000: 273–282).

The legal dimension of the disputed 1993 elections concerned the publication of the results by CONOSELA. Despite the confirmation of many international observers that the elections had been generally free and fair (Kouvibidila 2000: 311; Economist Intelligence Unit, *Country Report: Congo,* no. 3, 1993: 13), and despite the full participation of opposition observers in the process, Kolélas bitterly denounced the results—but only four days after the vote. The rest of the opposition was soon in full throat, echoing his claims. Within CONOSELA, the coordinating committee announced that it was ready to transmit partial results in 106 undisputed circumscriptions to the interior minister for publication. The president of CONOSELA, MCDDI member Jean-Martin Mbemba, however, insisted that no partial results could be announced under the electoral law and that the elections would have to be rerun in all the disputed circumscriptions before any results could be legally announced (Kouvibidila 2000: 309, 314). Finally, on 20 May, the interior minister published the partial results based on a report of CONOSELA's follow-up committee, with the notation that the contested seats could be challenged in the Supreme Court.

Instead of turning to the Supreme Court for justice, the opposition turned to barricades and militias. The government went ahead with the second round of elections on 6 June, with the opposition boycotting. Three days later, Lissouba wrote to the Supreme Court, asking if the interior minister was authorized to publish the results of the second round. The following day, the court gave its opinion, indicating that (1) it did not have the power to authorize the interior minister to publish the results, and (2) electoral disputes could only be brought before the court *after* they had been published.[24] The latter finding recognized the dilemma of the government and implicitly sanctioned its actions.

On 28 June, the court issued two further opinions, one in response to queries from an opposition cabinet member (Clément Mierassa) submitted on 10 June, and another in response to queries from Lissouba submitted on 11 June. In response to Mierassa's questions, the court ruled that the results of the first round *had not* been published in conformity with the presidential decrees, and that the organization of the second round of elections "did not conform with the [legal] texts in effect."[25] But the court's answer to Lissouba's queries was far more powerful. In effect, the court again implicitly sanctioned Lissouba's publication of the electoral results by noting that an appeal could take place only after the proclamation of the results. Second, the court found that the National Assembly could be seated and begin activity while it awaited a decision of the court on any disputed elections results. Instead of waiting for these results, the opposition had announced the formation of its own "alternative government," headed by Thystère-Tchicaya on the day before the decisions were issued (Foreign Broadcast Information Service, Congo, 28 June 1993: 6).

As for the Constitutional Council, this body made a very tardy and ignominious appearance on the Congolese political scene. In February 1997 eighteen opposition parties wrote a memorandum to President Lissouba demanding that he put in place the institutions called for in the constitution, especially the Constitutional Council, as well as an independent electoral commission (Soni-Benga 1998: 142). Only on 30 May, however, were the first six (of nine) members elected by the high council of the magistrature, the university's faculty of law, and the national attorney's guild (148). The other three were chosen, respectively, by the president of the senate, the president of the National Assembly, and President Lissouba. Finally, on 23 June, with the country at war, Lissouba called on Parliament to swear in the new council at the Palais du Parlement. On 19 July, the council rendered its one and only decision: to extend the mandate of President Lissouba beyond the end of August on the grounds that the elections scheduled for 27 July would not be able to take place, given the war then in full force. Critical observers later heaped ridicule on the Lissouba government for the timing of the council's investiture, the manner of its composition, and the partisanship of its members (140–158). By the beginning of the 1997 war, Lissouba's government had refused to put in place the independent electoral commission that the opposition had demanded.

In sum, then, there was nothing obviously defective about Congo's democratic institutions. A large percentage of Congolese of all classes appear *not* to believe that democratic failure in the country was based on bad institutional design.[26] Although the semi-presidential system posed some challenges, either of the other alternatives would likely have been even more problematic and would have posed equally daunting challenges of leadership. As for the single-member district electoral system, it does not seem to have produced a result that would have been different from a PR system. Such a system would not likely have prevented the claims of fraud that the opposition made in 1993, especially since the charges were not substantiated by international observers.[27] It was the closeness of the outcome that stimulated the protests, and the outcome would have been equally close under a PR system. Decentralization of power in Congo played a helpful role, especially in the mayoral roles gained by Kolélas and Thystère-Tchicaya, but it is not clear that more decentralization would have been more beneficial. It is unlikely that Sassou, given his past and personality, would have been satisfied with any other role than the presidency. Finally, with regard to the high courts with powers of constitutional review and electoral commissions, these institutions were available, but they were rarely turned to in good faith by the politicians with political grievances. Nor were the politicians willing to await judicial decisions before acting.

■ **Comparative Perspectives on
Congo's Political Institutions**

Here we ask whether institutional design appeared to be a key element in the success or failure of other democratic experiments in Africa during the same period. This comparative analysis will give us a better perspective on the Congolese experience, and perhaps set it in a different light. The analysis above shows that institutional design did not seem to be the key element in the failure of the Congolese experiment, nor is it obvious at all that other institutional designs would have made the experiment a success. Evidence from other cases, however, can either strengthen this tentative conclusion or bring it into question. This evidence can also help us to perceive which elements of institutional design have the most widespread effects on democratic experiments in Africa.

With regard to executive authority, two cases seem to support the observation that semi-presidentialism is a dangerous configuration for new democracies. Niger adopted a semi-presidential model at the outset of its own democratic experiment and subsequently followed an early political course not dissimilar from that of Congo. President Mahamane Ousmane of Niger began his term in office in March 1993 backed by a supportive coalition of parties in Parliament. In September 1994, however, one of the partners defected to the opposition, leaving him without majority support. Rather than name an opposition prime minister, Ousmane used this constitutional power to dissolve Parliament. The government then organized new legislative elections in January 1995. Unfortunately, though, the new elections produced a new Parliament with roughly the same division of party strength as before, forcing Ousmane finally to name an opposition prime minister. Institutional paralysis set in soon afterward, with no cooperation between the executive and the legislature, ending with a complete breakdown of communication. With Niger's political institutions in crisis, the military finally stepped in to dismiss the president, dissolve Parliament, and begin a new set of consultations among members of the political class (Villalón and Idrissa 2005a: 36–39). The Niger case represents the most compelling confirmation that cohabitation is difficult or impossible in the African context.

The next chapter in the Niger story raises questions about this tentative conclusion, however. Niger soon adopted another semi-presidential constitution, but one that gave virtually all of the political cards to the president. At the next elections, the military figure who had organized the January coup, Ibrahim Baré Maïnassara, presented himself for the presidency and then blatantly "stole" the election when it was apparent that he was losing (Villalón and Idrissa 2005a: 39–40). In that context, the new constitution soon "raised fears over permitting the concentration of power" (41). As a result, following Baré's assassination in 1999, Niger reverted to the type of semi-presidentialist constitution that it had initially adopted in 1993. According to Villalón and Idrissa (43) in their conclusion, "This striking continuity in the face of the earlier difficulties was justified by the dominant argument within both the political class and public opinion: the failure of [Niger's] Third Republic was explained not primarily as a failure of institutions, but rather as a failure linked to the behavior of politicians, *la classe politique*."

The Congolese political class and public reached the same conclusion about their 1992 constitution and the democratic experiment that followed. The constitution of 2002 has a different design, not because of Congo's earlier experience but because Sassou has sought to consolidate his power unfettered by a potentially independent prime minister.[28]

Madagascar's early experience with a semi-presidential constitution also raises doubts about whether the model is the best for new African democracies, but also about the dangers of over-concentrated powers. After Madagascar's founding elections in 1993, the newly installed president, Albert Zafy, soon found himself confronted with a powerful and determined prime minister, François Ravony. Ravony represented a party in the presidential coalition, but not Zafy's own party. Under Ravony, Parliament supported an independent judiciary, tried to keep track of presidential spending, challenged Zafy's cabinet appointments, and ultimately introduced a motion of impeachment (Marcus 2005: 158). Unable to tolerate the constitutional independence of the prime minister, Zafy organized a referendum on a constitutional revision concentrating more power in the presidency, which he won in September 1999 (158). After these revisions, both Zafy and his successors, Didier Ratsiraka and Marc Ravalomanana, used these constitutional revisions and subsequent ones to extend presidential powers as far as possible (160–173).

Benin, the country apparently most successful in its democratic experiment, was the only former French colony *not* to adopt a semi-presidential system. The decision was quite conscious on the part of the Beninois political class (Magnusson 2005: 82). While this arrangement appears to be one of the secrets of Benin's success, it depends acutely on the probity of the individual holding the presidency. The system clearly permits the president to accrue extensive power in his office and leaves him relatively unrestrained by any other public figure or body. Moreover, the system has not prevented serious conflicts between the executive and legislative branches, some of which have had to be settled in the constitutional court (85). In periods when the president has been able to dominate the legislature, as under Kérékou, corruption levels have risen quickly. Thus, Benin has not been spared the dilemmas of the semi-presidential system, but it has been able to manage them better. The presidentialist systems in Malawi and Zambia, meanwhile, have produced presidents who have been more able to consolidate executive power rapidly and to use that power for personal and political advantage. Magnusson argues that the Beninois system only works because it couples its presidentialist system with a legislative system that makes it "almost impossible . . . for the president's political party to control the assembly" (85).

As for the electoral systems of the African states experimenting with democracy, they have not produced the kinds of results that those who theorize based on European and Latin American cases expect. In particular, as Tables 7.2 and 7.3 suggest, the number of parties making it into the legislature depends as much on local context as on the electoral system. The PR system in ethnoregionally polarized Mozambique produced only three parties in the legislature. The PR systems in the other African states produced more parties representing minority ethnoregional constituencies, but not minority political views. As a group, these systems generated barely more party representation than the single-member district (SMD) systems. The five SMD systems produced majority parties in only two cases, the same number as the five PR systems produced. Fragmented Congo and the CAR produced more than ten parties each. In general, the problem of effective governance has been far worse than the problem of fair representation in these cases, and none of the countries in question has developed disciplined parties loyal to the political ideals of party leaders. It does not appear that

Table 7.2 Results in First Legislative Elections After Transitions in Countries with Proportional Representation Systems

Country	Year	Number of Parties	Percentage for Leading Party	Executive-Legislative Relationship
Benin	1991	12	19	President forges unsteady coalition of parties
Guinea-Bissau	1994	5	62	President's party dominates
Madagascar	1993	25	35	President forges unsteady coalition of parties
Mozambique	1994	3	52	President's party narrowly controls Parliament
Niger	1993	12	35	Initial pro-presidential coalition breaks up; failed cohabitation
Averages		11.4	40.6	

Source: African Elections Database, http://africanelections.tripod.com/index.html.

Table 7.3 Results in First Legislative Elections After Transitions in Countries with Single-Member District Systems

Country	Year	Number of Parties	Percentage for Leading Party	Executive-Legislative Relationship
CAR	1993	12	40	President forges steady coalition of parties
Congo	1992	19	31	Initial propresidential coalition breaks up; Parliament is dissolved
Malawi	1994	3	48	Opposition bloc initially controls Assembly
Mali	1992	11	64	President's party controls Parliament
Zambia	1991	2	83	President's party controls Parliament
Averages		9.4	53.2	

Source: African Elections Database, http://africanelections.tripod.com/index.html.

either system has produced better results in terms of democratic consolidation than the other.

Virtually all students of democratization in Africa agree that decentralization of authority to local and regional governments has had a positive impact on democratic consolidation. Magnusson (2005: 87–89) judges that devolution of power to local bodies has been one of several keys to Benin's success. Analysts hail the effects of decentralization for many reasons, but one of the most common is for its impact on the gradual transformation of political culture at the local level. As Magnusson notes (89), "People are able to see the effects of local voting in these areas, and accountability at the local level is increasing as a result." Similarly, VonDoepp (2005: 191, 193) recognizes the central Malawian government's effort to reclaim authority previously ceded under the Local Government Act of 1998 as part of its overall effort to reestablish the dominance enjoyed by the country's former dictator.[29] Only in rare and specific circumstances, as in Madagascar under Didier Ratsiraka, have elected rulers actually used devolution of authority to expand the scope of their authority. The strategy only worked in Madagascar because the local authorities remained dependent on the central government for their revenues, and this has been the pattern nearly everywhere. Although the limited decentralization that Congo experienced was welcome, the process did not go nearly far enough to have a significant impact on the country's fundamental political dynamics.

Turning finally to the issue of constitutional courts and electoral oversight mechanisms, a survey of other democratizing African states shows how utterly ubiquitous such institutions have become. Students of Benin (Magnusson 2005: 77, 85), Madagascar (Marcus 2005: 159), Malawi (VonDoepp 2005: 185–187, 192–193), and Mali (Villalón and Idrissa 2005b: 65) have argued that newly empowered constitutional courts or supreme courts have played an important role in defining executive-legislative relationship or arbitrating the legal aspects of political disputes, thereby facilitating progress toward democratic consolidation. All of the states listed in Tables 7.2 and 7.3 except Guinea-Bissau have (or had) either constitutional courts or supreme courts endowed with the power of constitutional review.[30] Similarly, all of the same states except for the CAR had national electoral commissions, under some name or other, during the 1990s. The question about these institutions was not whether they existed, but whether and how they were *used* by the political parties in question. In Madagascar, for instance, President Ratsiraka altered the composition of the country's High Constitutional Court on the eve of the 2001 presidential elections, knowing that it oversaw and judged the actions of the country's National Electoral Commission (NEC) (Marcus 2005: 169–170). His electoral opponent, though, refused to accept the count of the NEC. Many other African states experimenting with democracy experienced similar attempts at manipulation, including Congo. Thus, democratic consolidation depends as much on a respect for the legal role of such institutions as it does on their mere existence.

The record of institutional performance in other countries tends to confirm the conclusion reached by analyzing Congo alone: appropriate political institutions may be necessary for democratic consolidation, but they are far from sufficient. Appropriate institutions may be critical "at the margins," and when the important parties have good will. But they cannot save a situation when the key political leaders are set on the concentration of power at all costs, or when the opposition is ready to resort to war, rather than legal recourse, to resolve disputes. As Mehler (2005: 135) observed of the CAR, "It quickly became evident that institutions played only a limited role in the fundamental political dynamic of the country. Elites interacted with one another and jockeyed for power and position, but the constitutional framework was less important in this process than more purely political factors." Virtually the same thing could be said of Congo, and one cannot help but notice the similarities of political culture in the two states. Nonetheless, the negative role played by the lack of clarity on the critical question of the president's prerogatives vis-à-vis Parliament in the Congolese constitution cannot be completely dismissed. This, more than the division of governmental powers, inadvertently provided the legal issue over which power-hungry politicians carried out a military struggle that poisoned Congo's experiment from the beginning.

■ Notes

1. Indeed, all of the contributors to Reynolds's (2002) edited collection believe that institutional design has some influence on the ability of divided societies both to manage conflict and possibly consolidate democratic regimes.

2. The cases studied in Reynolds (2002) include six individual cases (among them, Eritrea and Nigeria), as well as postcommunist and postcolonial groups of states.

3. One pair of scholars, Mainwaring and Shugart (1997a), have helpfully consolidated the list to a mere five.

4. Two of the critiques are actually defenses of parliamentarism, rather than criticisms of presidentialism; two others actually pertain to *semi*-presidential regimes. Those that have been collapsed can be identified by separated page references. Among the criticisms that are not relevant to Congo is the troublesome role of the vice president, an office for which Congo's 1992 constitution does not provide.

5. By *semi-parliamentary,* Sartori means a parliamentary system with a strong, independent prime minister (or chancellor) as in Britain and Germany.

6. For a brief but illuminating overview of federalism and decentralization, see Lijphart (1999: 186–99); for a slightly longer but also very valuable overview, see Elazar (1997).

7. For the French text of the constitution, see "La constitution de la République du Congo" (1992). The translations are mine.

8. The first two documents formally recording the URD-PCT alliance were signed on 30 September 1992 and 4 October 1992. Both were signed by Kolélas and Thystère-Tchicaya, president and vice president of the URD and by Sassou and Ambroise Nounazalaye, president and secretary-general of the PCT. They are reproduced in Baniafouna (1995b: 185–187).

9. The impressive jurist in question was Nestor Makoundzi-Wolo, who was trained in Bordeaux and presided over the national commission charged with drawing up the constitution in 1991. Since Makoundzi-Wolo was a partisan of Lissouba, his testimony is all the more impressive. The interview took place on 1 June 2002 in Brazzaville. Makoundzi-Wolo was jailed by the regime of Sassou II in late 1998 but later released. He died, apparently of natural causes, in 2004. For biographical information, see Moukoko (1999: 209).

10. See Chapter 3 of this volume on this issue in particular.

11. The Congolese electoral law of 21 January 1992, signed by "Général d'Armée Denis Sassou-Nguesso," is reproduced in Baniafouna (1995b: 112–138). Interestingly, this law was in effect before the constitution itself because of an earlier postponement of the referendum that took place on 15 March.

12. In August 1994, the Congolese Parliament passed a law creating a new region, the West Cuvette Region (Cuvette Ouest). This step was not a matter of great political controversy for the informants with whom I spoke in Brazzaville in 2001 and 2002. The initiative for the new division apparently came from political figures for the region itself. They cited the region's socioethnic and linguistic homogeneity; with only some 38,000 residents at the time, however, it was by far the country's smallest. See Foreign Broadcast Information Service–Sub-Saharan Africa, "Parliament Passes Bill Creating West Cuvette Region," 29 August 1994: 2–3.

13. No Western primary source ever reported the *complete* results, accounting for every seat, of the legislative elections, but they are recorded in Kouvibidila (2000: 129).

14. My translation.

15. The number of *arrondissements* is not specified in the electoral law, but the districts of the ten regions and the arrondissement divisions for the six communes can be found on the Congo page of www.geohive.com, accessed 6 December 2005.

16. My translation. Also see the coverage of this development in *Marchés Tropicaux et Méditerréens,* "Congo," 10 June 1994: 1185; and Economist Intelligence Unit, *Country Report: Congo,* no. 4, 1994: 13.

17. See both *Marchés Tropicaux et Méditerréens,* "M. Kolelas, maire de Brazzaville," 22 July 1994: 1559; and Economist Intelligence Unit, *Country Report: Congo,* no. 4, 1994: 14.

18. Exceedingly little has been published in the media or in scholarly publications about the role, activities, and influence of the regional prefects. I'm grateful to Brice Massengo, Didier Gondola, and Rémy Bazenguissa-Ganga for providing me some information on their limited role, particularly their loyalty to the central government.

19. This was related to me by a number of public service workers in Brazzaville, Pointe Noire, and Loubomo in interviews in 2001 and 2002.

20. One of those who urged Lissouba to constitute the Constitutional Court was the constitution's main drafter, Makoundzi-Wolo, who confirmed this to me during an interview in Brazzaville. Also see Moukoko (1999: 209).

21. The opinion is reprinted in Baniafouna (1995b: 192–195). My translation.

22. Cited in Baniafouna (1995b: 193). Emphasis added.

23. Respectively, these were the Commission Spéciale de Supervision des Élections and the Commission Nationale d'Organisation de Supervision des Élections. See Kouvibidila (2000: 86, 120).

24. The letter and opinion can be found in Baniafouna (1995b: 224–226). Emphasis added.

25. The opinion, no. 8 of the Supreme Court, can be found in Baniafouna (1995b: 227–231). The quotation is from p. 230. Opinion no. 9, the response to Lissouba's question, is on pp. 232–234.

26. During a trip to Congo in March 2001, as a part of an International Foundation for Elections Systems (IFES) mission, I attended three sessions of regional meetings euphemistically called the Dialogue Nationale Sans Exclusive. The point of these meetings was to discuss the (then) draft constitution for Congo that was subsequently adopted early the following year. Although most of the participants were Sassou supporters, most did not blame the conflicts of 1993 and 1997 on the former Congolese constitution, but rather on the behavior of Lissouba. Among the countless opponents of Sassou whom I interviewed in 2001 and 2002, not a single one thought that the failure of Congolese democracy in 1997 could be attributed to Congo's semi-presidential constitution.

27. The international jury set up after the Libreville agreement of August 1993 did eventually invalidate the results in nine constituencies, but only three of these were in constituencies where supporters of the presidential domain had been seated. See Foreign Broadcast Information Service–Sub-Saharan Africa, "Minister Sets Peace as Precondition for By-Elections," 9 February 1994: 1.

28. For more on the origins and effects of the 2002 constitution, see Chapter 10 of this volume.

29. For information on Malawi's Local Government Act see www.clgf.org.uk/2005updates/Malawi.pdf, accessed 15 December 2005.

30. I thank Joshua Forrest for familiarizing me with the former system of legislative review in Guinea-Bissau.

8

The Complex Impact of French Policy

Due to France's intensive relationship with Congo, which dates from the colonial period, France's foreign and economic policies toward Congo are of prime concern in the explanation of Congo's failed democratic experiment. France (by which I mean French business interests in Congo as well as the French state) has been by far Congo's largest source of investment and development aid and the country's chief trading partner. Accordingly, it is suspected that the French role was critical in the trajectory of the democratic experiment. Did the Congolese democratic experiment fail because of the behavior of France and/or French interests? Or, might the Congolese experiment have survived for some time longer had French policies and actions been different?

An important question to ask about this topic is whether the inquiry ought to be somewhat broader. That is, should Congolese relations with other foreign "partners," including multinational actors like the EU, international financial institutions (IFIs), or other individual countries also be studied? The economic impact of IFI policies were already reviewed in Chapter 4. Some scholars have argued, though, that the *regional* context for democratization is also quite important (Magnusson 2005: 89–92). That would seem to be the case for Congo, too, since some of its regional neighbors played important roles in the 1997 war that ended the democratic experiment. Specifically, the government of Gabon allowed its territory to serve as a conduit for the flow of arms into Congo during the war, and the Angolan regime undertook the decisive intervention that ended the war in Sassou's favor (Clark 1998b). The CAR was also involved in the war, albeit in a much less important way. For a variety of reasons, however, these interventions need not be studied separately. As for the role of Gabon and the CAR, the actions of these states can be usefully subsumed under the more general rubric of French policies and actions in the region. As for the role of Angola, as dramatic and decisive for the war as its actions were, its intervention was *not* decisive for the fate of democracy in Congo. By the time of Angola's intervention in September 1997, the fate of the democratic experiment that had begun in 1991 was already sealed—it is virtually inconceivable that Congo could have resumed the experiment without a major interregnum at that point in its history. Accordingly, it is well justified to confine the focus to Franco-Congolese relations in this chapter, bearing in mind that the policies of other actors, including the United States, sometimes bore on the fundamental Franco-Congolese relationship.

The remainder of this chapter is organized according to the following format. The first part puts the role of France in the Congolese democratic experiment in historical and theoretical context. France has been intensively involved in the affairs of its former African colonies, but there are debates, mostly implicit, about the consistency of French policies, the motivations for French involvement, and the priorities that France has had for Francophone Africa. With the uncertainties revealed by these debates in mind, we can attempt a reasonable assessment of the impact of French policies and actions. A second section reviews the record of French relations with Congo from independence through the single-party period, and then in the period of the transition. Franco-Congolese relations in these periods provide a sort of baseline against which subsequent French actions should be evaluated. A third section traces the trajectory of Franco-Congolese relations during the Lissouba period and then analyzes the impact of French actions on the course of the democratic experiment. The final section puts France's record in Congo in comparative perspective with its relations with other Francophone African states in the era of renewed democratic experimentation. As ever, this perspective helps to confirm or disconfirm the tentative conclusions that we reached based on the case analysis.

■ The Nature and Reach of French Influence in Francophone Africa

The starting point for the analysis of French influence over democratization in Francophone Africa is to recognize the considerable potential of French policies and actions to determine the course of events. Although this fact is well-recognized by students of Francophone Africa, it is less well appreciated by many students of non-Francophone Africa and Africa neophytes. Particularly during the Cold War, scholars often studied the international relations of all of sub-Saharan Africa without paying sufficient attention to the weighty role of France.

France's postcolonial practices in Francophone Africa have covered the gamut of possible external avenues of influence (Gardinier 1997b; Manning 1988: 180–181, 195–198; Martin 1995). French influence is strongly in evidence not only in the former French colonies but in the former Belgian colonies of central Africa as well. At the diplomatic level, France maintains well-staffed and active foreign missions in all seventeen sub-Saharan states that use French as an official language. The political classes and publics of most Francophone African countries continue to see France as a "great power," capable of determining the outcome of local political events far from France's own borders. Whatever the realities of French influence, France's psychological grip on the inhabitants of Francophone Africa remains surprisingly strong.

Well into the 1990s, France maintained military bases in five different Francophone African states and in the French overseas département of Réunion; and it maintained security agreements with eight former colonies that permitted French intervention in case of security threats (Gardinier 1997b: 14). France demonstrated its continuing power by militarily supporting Mobutu Sese Seko of Zaire against invading rebels in the 1970s and Hissène Habré of Chad against Libya during the 1980s (Turner 1997: 251; Lanne 1997: 271). At the time of the 1994 Rwandan genocide, when no other foreign state or the United Nations collectively would intervene, France mounted Opération Turquoise, with its well known double effect.[1] In 1996, France deployed its forces in the CAR to put down an army mutiny against the elected regimes of Ange-Félix Patassé (Mehler 2005: 136–137), an action that probably helped the CAR's democratic experiment endure for longer than it otherwise would have. French forces subsequently engaged in a major peacekeeping mission in Côte d'Ivoire, providing a separation between rebel and government forces in that troubled state (Glaser and Smith 2005: 11–24). Thus, the French governments of both the left and right have shown the will and capacity to intervene in Africa.

No less impressive has been France's economic influence with the states of Francophone Africa. The most visible aspect of French economic weight is the widespread use of the Communauté Financière Africaine (CFA) franc as a national currency (Chipman 1989: 186–226; Gardinier 1997b: 15–16). Until the introduction of the euro in Europe, the CFA franc was tied to the French franc (FF) at a fixed rate (50 CFA francs per FF until January 1994, and 100 CFA francs per FF until 2001). This unique currency arrangement helped keep France as the first ranking source of imports for virtually all of its former colonies; France has been a major export destination for the Francophone African states, as well. When the CFA franc was belatedly devalued in 1994, many Francophone Africans took the financial news as an insult to the special Franco-African relationship, one referring to it as a "brutal decision" (Nsafou 1996: 214). French investment in both natural resources and light manufacturing, almost always leading all foreign investors, provided additional influence in the former French and Belgian colonies. The investments of the (formerly state-controlled) French oil firm Elf-Aquitaine in the Francophone African petroleum-producing states of Cameroon and Gabon, as well as Congo, are enormous, and most outside analysts (e.g., Yates 1996) have concluded that these investments essentially "buy" internal political control.

Yet another pillar of French economic leverage is development aid, dispensed through France's "Ministry of Cooperation." During the Cold War and since, France has usually been the largest bilateral aid donor in Africa. Until recent years, most French aid was channeled through state accounts, typically serving to cover the deficits caused by the gap between budgeted expenditures and revenues. Aid of this kind provides a particularly powerful lever with which to move recalcitrant African governments.

The third leg of French influence in Africa has been French language and culture. This dimension of French influence may be more subtle, but it is no less effective in securing French interests. In fact, culture and language define and embody French interests in a way that is hard for most Americans to understand. In promoting the French language in Africa, France both exercises and, temporarily, preserves its influence against the inevitable tide of English transmitted through the airwaves and over the Internet. Illustrative of France's preoccupation with maintaining the place of the French language in Africa was France's reaction to Paul Kagame's new policies upon seizing power in Rwanda in 1994. When Kagame announced that English would be used alongside French as a language of education and government business, the French government quickly announced the grant of French language textbooks for the Rwandan school system.[2] France provides a wide array of cultural programs in Francophone Africa, and it has hosted many tens of thousands of African students in France (Gardinier 1997b: 13). A great variety of nonstate groups in France, ranging from Freemasons and the Catholic hierarchy to various relief and development-oriented NGOS, constantly reinforces the ties of the community known as "Françafrique" (Gaulme 1994). According to Le Vine (2004: 341), some six hundred cultural and social NGOs based in France operated in Africa during the late 1990s.

On these general dimensions of French influence in Francophone Africa there is little debate, even if French influence is underestimated in the United States. On the finer points of French influence in Africa, however, there has been considerable variation of opinion, though the debates have often been implicit. One of these questions existed before the end of the Cold War and persisted into the new era: How much power does France actually have over the states of Francophone Africa? Some Francophone African scholars (Toulabor 1995; Martin 1995), as well as some Western scholars (Yates 1996), have often portrayed French power as if it were near absolute. Of course, French military power is visible and has obvious effects, but France has been increasingly reluctant to use military force without a mandate from the international community, such as those it received before its interventions in Rwanda (1994) and the Democratic Republic of Congo (2003). The number of French troops stationed in Africa has declined rapidly since the mid-1990s (Le Vine 2004: 344). Thus the question is really over how much leverage France wields through the use of campaign financing, assistance in elections rigging, and the threat of economic punishment.[3] Others have seen the Franco-African relationship more as a kind of international patron-client one (Clark 2002a; Le Vine 2004). Under the implicit bargain between France and the leaders of an African state, France gets privileged access to the local market, a relatively free hand to propagate its cultural values directly in the local society, and sometimes the right to have military bases, or at least the right of passage for military forces. Yet the African rulers also enjoy benefits of the relationship, including France's political support for a given regime, a steady flow of French aid, and the encouragement of French business investments. Although those controlling the African states may form something of a comprador class, they are not powerless; they are free to renegotiate the terms of the deal when they see fit, though of course they will not always emerge with better terms. Ultimately Francophone African rulers always have the option of going the route of Sekou Touré. The costs may be high, but most Francophone African rulers enjoy considerable flexibility in how they deal with France and the nature of the "deals" they get.

Since France did not intervene militarily in Congo during the democratic experiment—except to evacuate non-Congolese citizens at the onset of the 1997 war—the issue of overt intervention is not relevant to the case. But were there subtler means of French influence in Congo sufficient to undermine the country's democracy? Could French money and political influence, especially with the opposition, have served to cripple, then destroy, Congo's democracy?

Another issue of the French presence in Africa since the end of the Cold War in 1989 concerns the most fundamental motivation of the French political establishment. The debate generally comes down to whether France's primary motivation for its neocolonial presence in Africa has been economic or politico-psychological. Of course it is perfectly coherent to believe that France is pursuing both economic gain and the glory of the cultural community of "Francophonie" in Africa. Yet most authors tend to put their emphasis on one side or another. Andereggen (1994: 135), for instance, clearly puts the emphasis on the political:

> France's decision to retain its influence in Africa after independence is mostly due to its desire to continue its status as a world power, albeit inferior to the United States and the former USSR. In addition the French had a keen desire to continue the strong sentimental ties that bound them to their former African empire. France's dominating position at the center of a group of sovereign, but dependent, countries gives it a privileged position among its Western allies.

French officials, such as former prime minister Édouard Balladur, have often been equally direct in their claims that France remains a great power and that Africa is its "main field of action."[4] However, scholars devoted to the dependency tradition typically put the emphasis squarely on France's economic motivations (Massengo 2000: 163–179; Yates 1996). These scholars follow clearly in the historical tradition of Coquery-Vidrovitch (1972) and the theoretical tradition of Samir Amin. Parallel to this debate is one over which French institutions, public or private (commercial), take the leading role in shaping French policies. This difference in perspective is relevant to Congo because French economic interests appear to have been threatened there, if only briefly, while French cultural and political interests were not.

Another long-term debate over French policies addresses the issue of consistency. Does French policy reflect a master plan for maintaining a neocolonial empire in Africa? Or is French behavior mostly reactive, responding to unexpected crises that arise and threaten French interests? On this issue most analysts agree that French policy is becoming less coherent, though some French critics (e.g., Verschave 1998; Verschave 2000) maintain that France has not changed its view of its interests in Africa, and that it pursues its perceived interests systematically.

For the past fifteen years the most vital debate over France's role in Africa has concerned the question of continuity versus change in French behavior. The debate was sparked by President François Mitterrand's famous pronouncement at the June 1990 La Baule Franco-African summit that French aid would thereafter be tied to democratic progress. The initial skepticism that France could or would change substantially its African policies was subsequently reinforced by Mitterrand's backtracking at the 1991 Francophone summit at Chaillot (Gaulme 1994: 46–47; Clark 1997a: 2–3). As Le Vine (2004: 248) economically noted, "As it turned out, the La Baule message, however encouraging, was neither clear nor unambiguous." After La Baule, French officials quickly changed the emphasis to French support for *economic* reform, rather than political reform, and changed the aid requirement from one of democratic progress to one of respect for the rule of law (Le Vine 2004: 249; Gaulme 1994: 47). Enthusiasts noted that France did not stop democratic transitions in Benin, Congo, Niger, and Mali, and that it even gave rhetorical support to opposition movements. Careful analysts were able to identify real, if somewhat ambiguous, changes in the flow of French aid based on political reform (Cumming 1995: 397–398). Skeptics (e.g., Martin 1995; Toulabor 1995: 113–114), meanwhile, saw the changes as being mostly cosmetic.

Yet France's policies were changing, and not only for idealistic reasons. A variety of forces pushed the new regime of Jacques Chirac toward a continuation of reforms after his rise to the French presidency in 1995. Tighter budget constraints, deeper integration into the European Union, and the disastrous results of French actions in Rwanda (1994) and Zaire (1997), all reinforced the need for a French retrenchment in Africa (Le Vine 2004:

344). The reduction of French (and Foreign Legion) troops in Africa continued in the late 1990s and into the early 2000s. On the eve of the introduction of the euro within the EU, the need for fiscal discipline over the French budget kept the pressure on for aid "rationalization" for Francophone Africa. As for French backtracking on its aid/political-reform linkage, this trend has characterized all foreign donors. France was far from the only foreign donor to recognize quickly after 1990 that political reform often brought with it instability and violence that threatened values even more fundamental than democracy.

For those who believe that France's policies in Africa do remain coherent, and that continuity rather than change better characterizes French policy, many see the emergence of a new Franco-US rivalry in Africa as the reason. It is quite clear that there were substantial French and American policy differences over the political crisis, then genocide, that savaged Rwanda in 1993–1994 (Clark 1995b). It is also true that Franco-US tensions over economic resources and investment possibilities grew much sharper during the 1990s (Schraeder 2000). At the end of the day, however, the United States simply has insufficient interest in Francophone Africa to sustain a robust and coherent reaction to French influence. Whereas France once resisted the policy prescriptions of the IFIs with the goal of ingratiating itself with Africa's reluctant reformers, it now mostly goes along with the (US-dominated) IFI policies.

An awareness of these trends in France's broader policies and debates over their interpretation is critical to a deep understanding of the French role in Congo between 1992 and 1997. A number of senior Congolese political figures, including former president Lissouba himself, have specifically charged that the French destroyed the nascent democracy by supporting a coup against his elected regime. Moreover, a great many ordinary Congolese believe—or at least contend to foreign researchers—that France is largely to blame for the civil war of 1997 and, by extension, the near-term extinguishing of the democratic experiment.[5] The debates about overall French policy in Africa help sharpen the questions to be asked about France's role in Congo after 1992. Did the decline in French aid to Congo after 1992 reflect France's dissatisfaction with Lissouba's growing authoritarianism, and his disastrous management of the economy, or his overtures to possible "Anglophone" (i.e., US, South African, and British) partners? Was French policy at the time of outbreak of the 1997 war a continuation of an ongoing effort or the reaction to an unexpected crisis? If the French did somehow orchestrate Sassou's return to power, was the motive economic or political or both? And what effect did France's rhetorical policies have on the course of the democratic experiment? Do the Congolese remain so much in the psychological grip of French social and political forces that the mere expression of French preferences can profoundly alter the course of local events? To reach a deep appreciation for the complexity of the answers to these questions, still more context is needed, namely the context provided by an overview of France's interactions with Congo leading up to the era of the democratic experiment.

■ Franco-Congolese Relations from Independence to 1992

This section is divided into two parts. The first outlines in brief the nature of French-Congolese relations from independence through the end of the 1980s. This sketch serves as a baseline against which subsequent French behavior can be analyzed and accessed. In keeping with the view of France as a neocolonial power in Francophone Africa after 1960, France has maintained close relations with Congo under all of the regimes in power there since independence. The second section discusses French relations with the transitional regime of Milongo. French behavior during this period also reveals France's ambivalent attitude toward the Congolese democratic experiment and its subsequent, inconsistent policies. It is also clearer in the latter period that the various social and political forces within France were increasingly acting at cross purposes within the former French colony.

Franco-Congolese Relations from Youlou Through Sassou I

For the first few years of Congo's independence, relations between the metropole and former colony were untroubled. The Youlou regime in Congo had a favorable line toward an independent Katanga in Congo-Kinshasa and was hostile to Patrice Lumumba, mirroring the foreign policy preferences of France. During these years, France maintained the sort of warm relations that it did with most of its other colonies, excepting Guinea, which had famously defied DeGaulle. The fact that France subsequently maintained relations nearly as cordial with "revolutionary" Congo, on the other hand, is somewhat surprising. As we saw above, Congo's politics became progressively radicalized from the mid-1960s through the mid-1970s. Formal diplomatic relations with the United States were severed under the Massemba-Débat regime in 1965 following the mistreatment of US diplomats in Brazzaville. Meanwhile, Congo developed friendly relations with China, the Soviet Union, and Cuba in the mid-1960s and benefited from the aid of these socialist states into the early 1990s.

Yet interestingly, the close relationship between Paris and Brazzaville was only temporarily soured between 1965 and 1972 (Decalo 1996: 111). Despite some harsh anti-Western, and even anti-French rhetoric, and the nationalization of some French enterprises, Congolese leaders did not follow in the footsteps of Sékou Touré. Ironically, Elf-Congo, the local affiliate of Elf-Aquitaine, was created in 1970, the same year as the official launch of Congo's putative Marxist-Leninist experiment. Elf-Congo went on to become the dominant petroleum producer in Congo, accounting for over three-quarters of the country's production in the 1990s.

Despite their divergent ideologies, the persistence of friendly relations between France and Congo is easily explained by economic interests and cultural ties. Urban, educated Congolese continued to identify with France more than they with did any East bloc partner throughout the nominally Marxist period. Moreover, France remained a more important trading partner and source of technical and financial aid than any communist country.[6] For their part, the French were equanimitous about Congo's putative Marxism, as they were about that of other African and European partners. As Cumming (1995: 385) has argued, "The French saw American aid [in Africa] as more of a problem than Soviet assistance," and, indeed, Congolese and French anti-Americanism were complementary during the 1970s and 1980s.

Whatever remaining tensions lingered in Franco-Congolese relations during the Ngouabi years were relieved during the short presidency of the pragmatic Yhombi-Opango. These warm relations continued to blossom during the presidency of Sassou-Nguesso, in spite of the latter's initial reputation as a serious Marxist. France continued to be Congo's main sources of both foreign aid and imports, and Elf-Congo profitably capitalized on the oil boom beginning in 1979. During the oil boom years, Sassou invited French capitalists to participate, and they did so with gusto. For instance, French investors opened new supermarkets in Brazzaville and Pointe Noire, constructed one major new hotel in Brazzaville (the Meridien), and took over another built by the Soviets (the Cosmos) (Le Vine 1987: 137). Meanwhile, the French were giving substantial aid in the fields of communication, agro-industry, mining, health, and education and supporting some 450 *coopérants* (aid workers) in Congo (Decalo 1996: 111).[7] When Jacques Chirac, then the mayor of Paris, visited Brazzaville for the country's centenary in 1980, he was "the most popular guest by far" (Radu and Somerville 1989: 225), despite the presence of many East bloc representatives.

During the second half of the 1980s, as Congo's Marxist pretenses began to evaporate, the country was actually becoming more dependent on France. The collapse of world oil prices in 1985 left Congo exposed to strong debt pressures following its spree of early 1980s borrowing (Vallée 1988). As East bloc aid declined, France stepped in to fill the assistance void, helping Sassou survive the subsequent socioeconomic crisis. Congo's debt escalated from US$1.4 billion in 1980 to US$4.8 billion in 1990, and the country was forced to accept a structural adjustment program in 1986. France was responsible for more than half of all Congolese debt and had supported Congo's cause in the IMF and World Bank, which owned most of the remainder. Meanwhile, Sassou developed warm personal relations with many members of François Mitterrand's "Africa team," especially the former president's son, Jean-Christophe, and with the head of Elf-Aquitaine, Loïk Le Floch-Prigent (*Africa Confidential,* "Congo: Characteristic Ambiguity," 6 March 1992: 6).

Indeed, the French government and Sassou were very good to one another during the second half of the 1980s. France consistently kept Congo in good standing with the IFIs by providing debt concessions as necessary. In 1990, the last year before the transition, France transferred some FF705 million (US$140 million) to Congo in aid. Meanwhile, Sassou had begun to mortgage Congo's future by borrowing against the state's share of anticipated petroleum earnings, to be repaid directly in oil. According to one source, the "dette gagée" had reached some US$180 million by 1990 (Baniafouna 1995a: 73–74).

For its part, Elf-Congo enjoyed an extremely favorable contract with the Congolese state that dated back to 1968. Under the contract, Elf-Congo only paid a small licensing fee and a tax of its profits earned after recouping investment costs. Under this system, and given Congo's debts, the Congolese state gained virtually no petroleum revenues after 1986, according to one source (*Jeune Afrique,* "Rente: La Nouvelle Donne," 27 July–2 August 1995: 38). Instead, state revenues went directly to pay off prior debts. Elf's contract was overly generous to the producer compared to those of other African oil-exporting countries (Economist Intelligence Unit, *Country Report: Congo,* no. 2, 1996: 11). Virtually all observers also believe that Sassou skimmed a portion of Congo's petroleum revenues for himself.

Despite Mitterrand's call for reform at La Baule, France did nothing concrete to undermine the regime of Sassou during its final months. Indeed, the French government was arranging arms deals with Sassou even as the campaign for democracy in Congo unfolded, and it also helped him arm his personal militia (Baniafouna, 1995a: 211; Krop 1994: 49–57). Meanwhile, there was no overt sign of encouragement to the opposition from the French government. As noted above, Mitterrand had already virtually retracted his call for democracy by the time the transition in Congo occurred, leading some interpreters to argue that the statement at La Baule was merely a tactical maneuver, forced on France by world events. Subsequent events seem to support this view.

Franco-Congolese Relations During the Transition

Given that most Congolese identified Sassou with French interests, it is not surprising that the Congolese eschewed any major role for France in the transition. As a consequence, France's relations with the transitional regime of André Milongo were never good. By contrast, US relations with Congo blossomed during the period of the transition. France's poor relations with Congo during the transition set the stage for the subsequent mistrust and allegations of a French hand in stimulating the war of 1997.

According to Congolese observers, there were several interrelated reasons for this development. First, there is the simple fact that France had virtually no control over events that led to the national conference in 1991 or over the conference itself (Menga 1993: 59–60). Inasmuch as France perceived itself to be the major arbiter in Francophone Africa, this was a blow to the country's pride. Since the first transition in Francophone Africa, that in Benin, had taken place *before* any French officials began speaking of the need for political reform, the French were already on the defensive. The case of Congo's conference, then, again raised the specter of a rapid deterioration of the French position in Francophone Africa.

Second, as the Congolese conference unfolded, one of France's worst fears came to pass when the conferees delved deeply into the relationship with Elf-Congo. The conferees soon called for an audit of Elf-Congo's financial dealings and an examination of contracts between Elf-Congo and the government. Significantly, a US accounting firm was charged with this task (Baniafouna 1995a: 74). Many delegates suspected that Elf-Congo had overstated its operating and investment costs in Congo, expenses that could be deducted from the taxes that Elf-Congo had to pay (Economist Intelligence Unit, *Country Report: Congo,* no. 2, 1993: 18). Secondly, the conference established exact—and far less generous—guidelines for the sharing of petroleum revenues that the Congolese state was to use in future negotiations with its petroleum partners.[8] In due course, Milongo would respect these sentiments by seeking both to renegotiate contracts with Elf-Congo and to diversify Congo's petroleum partners.

For their part, the Congolese were very sensitive to French interference during this time. When the French journal *Libération* reported that French mercenaries were in Congo in April 1991, the French ambassador was summoned and bluntly informed that the Congolese army would deal with any threats to state security in short order (Foreign Broadcast Information Service–Sub-Saharan Africa, "Congo," 11 April 1991). The fears of Congolese reformers were further exacerbated by Sassou's trip to France in August, where he was received cordially. At that time, Sassou was still under investigation on corruption charges by committees created by the conference, and some Congolese feared that he might be conspiring with French security agents on ways of aborting the transition.

Also troubling to French officials was the warmness with which the United States perceived the transition in Congo. Although US relations with Sassou had in fact been relatively good since 1988,[9] the United States could still scarcely resist celebrating the fall of yet another Marxist-Leninist regime in 1991 (Economist Intelligence Unit, *Country Report: Congo,* no. 2, 1993: 12). In December 1991, Milongo made a triumphant trip to Washington, where he was received at the White House by President George H. W. Bush. Bush promised Milongo his support for Congolese democracy while the US ambassador in Congo also saluted the new Congolese government (Menga 1993: 133).

Perhaps to signal their displeasure with the new Congolese regime, or even to punish it, France reduced its aid for 1991 over the previous year (Baniafouna 1995a: 73).[10] Moreover, when Milongo went to Paris in the immediate aftermath of the conference in July 1991, he was snubbed by the French government. Given his perception, shared by most Congolese, that the French had promised a "democracy bonus," this "bitter experience" left the transitional prime minister in shock and sadness.[11] Instead of increasing aid to this fledgling new democracy, France demanded immediate fiscal reforms of the transitional regime. The French government complained that Milongo had no plan to return Congo to solvency, rationalizing its sudden stinginess. The French government, hardly having been the strongest advocate of structural adjustment in Africa before, now demanded strict budget control, reductions of civil service personnel, and privatization (Economist Intelligence Unit, *Country Report: Congo,* no. 3, 1992: 15; Menga 1993: 15).

Congo's financial situation was dire at that moment due to the profligacy of the Sassou regime in its final months. In a desperate effort to generate public support, Sassou had increased the pay scale for public employees in 1990 and again in January 1991. During the same months he recruited some 12,000 new state functionaries, bringing the total to some 80,000. These steps raised the state's annual salary costs from 78 billion to 120 billion CFA francs in 1990, and to 135 billion CFA francs in 1991.[12] These costs caused Congo to accrue new arrears on its debts and thus to fall out of compliance with Paris Club and World Bank repayment requirements. Milongo's government could neither simply fire these new employees—at least, not without provoking severe public disorder—nor could it pay them. Milongo's only recourse was to borrow another US$230 million from Elf-Congo and Agip against future oil earnings, increasing further the dette gagée (Mokoko 1995: 79).

By the first months of 1992, Franco-Congolese relations had reached a low point. Many Congolese saw France's hand behind the alleged coup d'état plots of December 1991 and January 1992 (see Chapter 6), though the French journal *Le Point* reported that French security forces had actually helped abort the coup (Foreign Broadcast Information Service–Sub-Saharan Africa, "Congo," 30 December 1991). Having failed to elicit French financial support, Milongo published a direct appeal to Mitterrand in *Le Figaro* in January, pleading for French noninterference and political support, regretting that the latter had theretofore been in "short supply" (Foreign Broadcast Information Service–Sub-Saharan Africa, "Prime Minister Appeals," 31 January 1992). The following month, responding to a question at a news conference, Milongo complained that Elf was interfering in Congo. Also in February, a Brazzaville monthly called *La Rumeur,* which was reportedly owned by "a close relation" of Milongo, published an article calling for the "massacre of French nationals" (Foreign Broadcast Information Service–Sub-Saharan Africa, "French Embassy Said to Protest," 14 February 1992). The French ambassador in Congo protested the publication of this article, and Franco-Congolese relations remained poor until Milongo's departure from office. Milongo's final trip to France as prime minister in April 1992 generated only a paltry US$2 million in additional French aid for specific projects (Economist Intelligence Unit, *Country Report: Congo,* no. 3, 1992: 15).

■ Franco-Congolese Relations, 1992–1997: The Evidence of Interference

Those who condemn French policies and actions for having destroyed Congolese democracy also point to the poor relations between the Lissouba regime and the French administrations of Mitterrand and Chirac. Since Lissouba had gained office through free and fair elections, so the argument went, his regime deserved the unqualified support of France. In the event, however, the record of French support was decidedly mixed. Likewise, the evolution of Franco-Congolese relations between 1992 and 1997 is more complex than some critics have acknowledged.

The Record of Franco-Congolese Relations, 1992–1997

The first stage in French relations with Congo after Lissouba's election was a honeymoon period, albeit one that lasted only a few months. Just after Lissouba's election, the French cooperation minister, Marcel Debarge, visited Brazzaville and pledged a large grant of some US$110 million designed to support Congo's structural adjustment plan and to help Congo clear its arrears with France's development fund, the Caisse Française de Développement (CFD) (Economist Intelligence Unit, *Country Report: Congo,* no. 4, 1992: 13). In December 1992, Lissouba visited Paris, where the aid pledge was confirmed and still more promised. This visit went well, though Lissouba "failed to elicit a clarion call of public support from President Mitterrand" (Economist Intelligence Unit, *Country Report: Congo,* no. 1, 1993: 15). Moreover, relations between Elf's Le Floch-Prigent and Lissouba were initially much better than they had been between Milongo and the Elf chief (21). There was also renewed military and security cooperation during this period. In January 1993, French general Jean Varey visited Congo and expressed satisfaction with growing Franco-Congolese military cooperation; later the same month a contingent of French troops arrived, reportedly to safeguard French nationals who might be fleeing Zaire.[13]

Relations between the new Lissouba government and Elf-Aquitaine quickly turned sour, however, eventually leading to a general deterioration in Franco-Congolese relations. Lissouba decided to pursue the National

Conference's project of diversifying Congo's oil partners, inviting in Amoco, Chevron, British Petroleum, and Conoco for talks (Economist Intelligence Unit, *Country Report: Congo,* no. 2, 1993: 18). These were disrupted, however, by the collapse of Lissouba's first government. In the context of the rerunning of the legislative elections, Lissouba was desperate to gain fresh funding to pay Congo's numerous civil servants, whose salaries were then in arrears. Like Sassou before him, he turned to Elf-Congo for aid, asking for US$300 million in February 1993. Elf's president, Le Floch-Prigent, personally blocked the deal (Economist Intelligence Unit, *Country Report: Congo,* no. 1, 1994: 18). Lissouba took this refusal as a sign that Elf executives still favored Sassou, whom he believed they wished to return to power. Indeed, both the Kolélas and Sassou wings of the opposition perceived Elf's snubbing of Lissouba as tacit support for their own causes.

Meanwhile, the French government and even French civic organizations regarded Lissouba's dissolution of Parliament with suspicion and felt exasperated with the new Congolese government. Distracted by France's parliamentary elections in March 1993, Mitterrand put Congo on the back burner. France pledged a scant US$140,000 for the rerun of the Congolese elections in 1993, only 1.5 percent of their estimated cost (Economist Intelligence Unit, *Country Report: Congo,* no. 2, 1993: 12). In the French elections, the Gaullists prevailed, and Balladur was installed as prime minister. The regime in Paris took a tough line on the slow pace of reforms in Congo. Meanwhile, Sassou's long stays in France, and his frequent, if informal, contacts with French officials nurtured the impression of French support in the minds of Lissouba officials.

It was in this context of declining relations that the "Oxy affair" burst onto the Congolese scene.[14] Having been spurned by Elf, Lissouba had undertaken secret negotiations with officials of the US company Occidental Petroleum in April, and a loan of US$150 million was arranged to be paid on 1 May 1993. This debt was to be repaid directly from the government's share of production and at only 10 percent of the world price. When the loan money arrived, it was disbursed immediately, only hours ahead of the first round of the parliamentary elections. These payments apparently made a substantial difference in Lissouba's narrow victory in the elections. Nonetheless, Lissouba now harbored tremendous bitterness toward Elf and the French government, while the latter grew panicky at the idea of encroachment in what had been France's private hunting reserve *(chasse gardée).* Bitter recriminations flew back and forth, and Lissouba even suggested that the French ambassador should leave Congo for interfering in its affairs *(Jeune Afrique,* "Le mal du Congo s'appelle Sassou," 15–21 July 1993: 68).

During the ensuing civil violence, Lissouba's camp certainly felt that the French had indirectly encouraged the fighting by tacitly supporting the opposition. In November, a reporter for Radio France International was expelled from Congo for "lack of objectivity" in his coverage of the ethnic violence (Babu-Zalé et al. 1996: 170). In December, French cooperation minister Michel Roussin privately raised doubts about Lissouba's abilities as a leader and his potential for resolving Congo's difficulties with "the chief of state of a neighboring country." This lack of confidence further irritated Lissouba and his team (Baniafouna 1995a: 213; Foreign Broadcast Information Service–Sub-Saharan Africa, "Congo," 3 January 1993).

The French also witnessed with alarm Lissouba's complete failure to carry through his promised economic reforms and the growing corruption in his government. Despite substantial French aid, Congo had not cleared its arrears with the CFD by the end of 1993 (Foreign Broadcast Information Service–Sub-Saharan Africa, "France Pledges Support," 10 December 1993). There was one reform, however, that the French could make themselves: the devaluation of the CFA franc. This reform of course affected all of the franc zone and not just Congo. This monumental step was finally undertaken in January 1994, following the death of Côte d'Ivoire's long-serving president, Félix Houphouet-Boigny. The devaluation of the CFA franc (see Chapter 4) evoked immediate inflation throughout the franc zone, but the rate was highest in Congo. Although inflation was officially about 60 percent for 1994, Congolese observers claimed that the prices for staples like bread, manioc, and rice increased between 100 and 200 percent (Baniafouna 1995a: 197–198; Nsafou 1996: 214–215). Both ordinary and intellectual Congolese felt that it was *their* value, as human beings, that had been devalued by the Balladur administration in Paris.

Lissouba's supporters chiefly claimed that France turned against the Congolese president because he had permitted non-French companies to operate in Congo alongside their French competitors. Indeed, Lissouba used the necessity of privatization to further diversify Congo's trading partners. For instance, a US firm, Atlantic Tele-Network outbid France Télécom for Congo's privatizing telephone network in late 1996 (*Marchés Tropicaux et Méditerréens,* "Congo: Privatisations," 13 December 1996: 2633). Meanwhile, South Africa was showing a strong interest in the Congolese hydroelectric power sector and in commercial farming. More important by far, however, was the greater presence of non-French firms that Lissouba allowed into the petroleum sector. Chevron was given a 30 percent stake in Elf's new Moho field, while Chevron and Exxon each gained 30 percent to Elf's 40 percent on the Mer Profonde Sud permit. Moreover, Exxon received its first permit in 1996 to prospect in an offshore oil field, portending a greater diversity of oil partners for Congo's future (Economist Intelligence Unit, *Country Report: Congo,* no. 2, 1996: 12; *Country Report: Congo,* no. 4, 1996: 15).

The bitterest recriminations against France, however, were reserved for its behavior during the 1997 civil war. France essentially declared itself neutral at the beginning of the war and maintained this position to the end. For Lissouba, such a position was unconscionable. In his view, it was the duty of France to back him on the grounds that he represented the legitimate authority of the state, while Sassou was a rebel, seeking to seize power by force of arms (*Jeune Afrique,* "L'Amertume de Lissouba," 9–15 July 1997: 7). His legitimacy was bolstered by the fact that he had been freely elected and had defeated Sassou in the process. At most, Lissouba had hoped that France would come to the aid of his regime, as it had come to the aid of the regime of Patassé the previous year (as discussed in Chapter 6). At least, he hoped that France would back him rhetorically. When neither happened, Lissouba called in the French ambassador and dressed him down; later, Lissouba's presidential guard roughed up the ambassador's bodyguards. In retaliation, the French placed an embargo on Congolese applications for visas to visit France, except in "humanitarian cases" (6).

During the course of the war, supporters of Lissouba repeatedly charged that the French presidency and Elf both favored the return of Sassou and that they provided him with arms to make his triumph possible. One specific charge made at the war's outset was that the French troops that evacuated foreigners from the airport turned over valuable military equipment to Sassou's forces as they left the country (*Jeune Afrique,* "L'Amertume de Lissouba," 9–15 July 1997: 7). Lissouba's supporters also claimed the French mercenaries were helping Sassou's forces. As the war raged, Lissouba's supporters complained more and more frequently of external interference. By September, Lissouba was specifically condemning Chirac via Congolese National Radio for supporting a "coup d'état," while the National Assembly named agents of Elf-Aquitaine as important suppliers of arms to Sassou (Foreign Broadcast Information Service–Sub-Saharan Africa, "Congo—Lissouba Accuses France," 11 September 1997). The arms were alleged to have entered Congo chiefly via Gabon, ruled by the openly pro-French Omar Bongo. After the end of the war, a great many reports confirmed that arms had indeed flowed to Sassou via Gabon, and Sassou's own commanders even acknowledged receiving aid from Gabon (Verschave 1998: 309–315; Foreign Broadcast Information Service–Sub-Saharan Africa, "RDR Joins Sassou," 21 October 1997). The evidence strongly suggested that they were authorized by the French presidency and not simply by Elf.

Although these arms were not the deciding factor in the military contest, it could be claimed that they had two very important consequences. First, they helped Sassou's forces survive and to gradually seize control over the northern reaches of the country during the summer of 1997. This in turn put Sassou in a position to seize control in Brazzaville later in the year. Second, and more important, France's behavior sent an important signal to others that France would not be chagrined to see the Lissouba regime collapse and Sassou return to power. In essence, French nonsupport for Lissouba gave the green light to Angola to take the leading role in resolving the conflict in one corner of France's *chasse gardée*.

While the war raged, French officials treated Lissouba and Sassou as political equals. Since a number of Sassou's representatives had remained in France before the war began, they were able to make their case heard with French officials, while those of Lissouba suffered under the visa boycott. Chirac repeatedly told Lissouba that he should settle his differences with Sassou via mediation. The person chosen to oversee the mediation effort, in turn, was Omar Bongo, a close friend of Chirac and the son-in-law of Sassou. When Lissouba himself visited France in early September, both Chirac and the new Prime Minister Lionel Jospin refused to meet him on the grounds that his term as president had officially expired on 31 August (*Marchés Tropicaux et Méditerréens,* "La Situation au Congo-Brazzaville," 24 October 1997: 2329). By this point, Lissouba had lost all faith in Bongo's neutrality as a mediator and refused to attend the major summit organized in Libreville in September.

These events and alleged actions are the basis for the claim that France essentially strangled Congolese democracy in the cradle. This recounting makes it clear that France sought to exercise its influence over events in Congo. Moreover, French officials sought to punish first Milongo and then Lissouba for diversifying Congo's trading partners and sources of investment. Finally, Chirac, who gained power in 1995, made no secret of his support for Sassou and ultimately provided him with some of the means to retake power. When Elf chairperson Philippe Jaffré visited Sassou on the very next day after his swearing-in, the perception that France had sponsored Sassou and thereby destroyed Congolese democracy seemed to be confirmed (Economist Intelligence Unit, *Country Report: Congo,* no. 1, 1998: 14). Likewise, those who perceived France to have reinstalled Sassou in power were surely not surprised when the new Congolese president, at that point mostly unrecognized abroad, received a warm welcome from Chirac when he visited Paris in December 1997, or when he was fully endorsed as president by Paris in 1998 (*African Research Bulletin,* "Congo: Paris Lends Support," 16 April–15 May 1998: 13428).

French Actions During the Democratic Experiment
Despite the strength and credibility of such views, the question of the effect of French policy and action in Congo has not been fully explored. A deep analysis of events suggests that French influence-seeking and interference was *not* directly responsible for the collapse of Congolese democracy, though it may have narrowed the possibilities for consolidation. This is certainly not to claim that France did not act in a self-interested way, or even

neocolonial fashion. But many Congolese, in putting too much blame on France, have allowed their own political class to escape responsibility for their role in Congo's failed democratic experiment. Even had France acted differently, there is sufficient reason to doubt that the results for the democratic experiment would have been much better.

Let us turn to the argument that France does not bear primary responsibility for the failure of democracy in Congo. First, there is some reason to believe that democracy was already critically ill in Congo, if not dead, before the tragic events of 5 June 1997, as the previous chapters have suggested. As we saw, Lissouba committed more than one act of dubious constitutionality during his first term and then unfairly manipulated the electoral processes during the rerun of the 1993 legislative elections. Although the vote may have been technically fair, his dispersal of overdue payments to the functionaries only days before the vote helped ensure his narrow victory. Between 1993 and 1997, the Lissouba regime compiled a terrible record of respect for human rights and certainly tried to intimidate the political opposition.[15] Finally, there is grave reason to doubt that the polling in 1997 would have been fair. Lissouba himself had cast doubt on the idea that "imported" democracy was right for Africa in early 1996 (*Jeune Afrique,* "Je suis contre la démocratie importée!" 28 February–5 March 1996: 28–33). In May 1997, the Congolese government was months behind schedule in making the preparations for the elections, and many Congolese anticipated a postponement. Long lines of citizens were then forming outside government buildings to receive voting cards, which were not being issued on time. Many doubted the likely fairness of the upcoming elections. For these reasons, Marc-Éric Gruénais (1997) wrote of the "end of a pseudo-democracy" in referring to the 1997 civil war. French interference after the 1997 war had begun could hardly have changed this situation.

Second, there is evidence that both French officialdom and Elf would likely have acquiesced in a Lissouba victory, even if it had been tainted. Both parties regularly supported their friendly Francophone African presidents under such circumstances and, by 1997, that is exactly what Lissouba had become. Despite Lissouba's bitterness over the Oxy affair, and Balladur's vexation with the Lissouba government, a new modus vivendi had been reached in 1994, and this had survived Chirac's rise to power in 1995. The new relationship between Paris and Brazzaville was certainly marked by more realism and caution on both sides, but Lissouba and Chirac seemed to have come to terms.

Most importantly, Elf-Congo remained the dominant petroleum partner in Congo, even if it had more serious competitors than before. In fact, the diversification of oil partners was a trend common throughout Francophone Africa, including in Gabon and Cameroon. Essentially, Lissouba had acquiesced to a continuing dominant role for Elf in return for the company's support. Le Floch-Prigent was sacked as head of Elf in October 1993, partly because of the Oxy fiasco, and was even subsequently jailed on corruption charges. The new head of Elf, Philippe Jaffré, then moved quickly to establish close ties to Lissouba. The new understanding was sealed when a law was approved in the National Assembly in December 1993 authorizing Elf to take the leading role in developing the fabulously rich Nkossa field and to explore in the new Haute Mer field.[16] Had Lissouba won the 1997 elections, his critics would likely have been calling him a puppet of French interests within a few years.

After relations between Congo and Elf improved further in 1994, the Congolese state agreed to sell its 20 percent stake in Elf-Congo to the French parent company in April 1995. This move simplified Elf-Congo's operations, pleased World Bank privatization advocates, and gave Lissouba's regime a short-term cash bonus. It even opened Lissouba to the charge that he had grown too close to Congo's main petroleum partner, though he was still pressing ahead on the renegotiation of oil contracts that had been in place since 1968. Under the new agreements, implemented during 1996, the Congolese state's share increased to at least 30 percent of all oil revenues, regardless of the companies' investment.[17] Congo's oil partners were also obligated to render their accounts transparent under the new agreement, which pleased those who had suspected Elf of cheating. Also reflecting the "new realism" of the Congo regime was the fact that Elf-Congo has only a 51 percent stake in the Nkossa field, the other half being divided among Chevron (30 percent), Hydro-Congo (15 percent), and Engen of South Africa (4 percent) (Economist Intelligence Unit, *Country Report: Congo,* no. 2, 1996: 11). Hence, by the end of 1995, Elf and Lissouba had reached a new understanding, under which Elf's position in Congo was assured, and the Congolese state would receive a larger share of the profits.

Meanwhile, on the diplomatic front, Franco-Congolese relations had also improved. France clearly did not relish the idea of seeing Congo consumed by chaos, and French officials from the cooperation ministry played a very supportive role in the many sets of mediations that contained the virtual civil war that erupted in June 1993 (Zartman and Vogeli 2000: 275). Lissouba's trip to Paris in March 1994 helped smooth over the lingering bitterness from the previous year. In order to ease the pain of the CFA franc devaluation, France granted Congo a major writeoff of public debt, amounting to nearly US$1 billion, or half of the total held by France, according to one source (Economist Intelligence Unit, *Country Report: Congo,* no. 1, 1994: 20). France agreed around the same time to help Congo restore order to its military (Economist Intelligence Unit, *Country Report: Congo,* no. 3, 1994: 11, 14).

The passing from power of François Mitterrand did not have an enormous impact on Franco-Congolese relations, perhaps because the conservative (Balladur) government remained in place in Paris. Lissouba indicated that he found Chirac warm and helpful, though also a man of toughness and conviction (*Jeune Afrique,* "Je suis contre la démocratie importée!" 28 February–5 March 1996: 33). France strongly supported Congo in its round of negotiations with the IMF, which led to an agreement in June 1996. Likewise, France supported Congo in its negotiations with the Paris Club, which agreed to grant Congo debt concessions the following month. In July 1996, Chirac visited Brazzaville, where he was warmly received, and where he emphasized the importance of democracy in Africa, an implicit endorsement of Lissouba.[18] Later in the year, Lissouba undertook trips to visit French clients in Gabon and Togo, while he dispatched Prime Minister Charles David Ganao to Morocco and Paris. In Lissouba's autobiography, released in early 1997, the Congolese president included an embarrassingly saccharine homage to France and French culture and language (Lissouba 1997: 219–228).[19] Thus, it appears that Chirac and Lissouba developed at least correct relations by the end of 1996. At this point in time, France would surely have preferred stability and Lissouba's loyalty in Congo to a risky war to try to return Sassou to power.

Third, to understand the motives and impact of French action, it is important to look more closely into the French role in the final act of the Lissouba regime. Specifically, how is France's initial inaction when the democratically elected Lissouba regime fell into conflict in 1997 to be explained or understood? To begin this analysis, recall that Lissouba struck the first blow in the conflict. Certainly Sassou's maintenance of a militia was provocative and an affront to state authority, but it was not more so in June 1997 than it had been in June 1995 or June 1996. Yet Lissouba did not move against Sassou then. More to the point, the timing of Lissouba's move against Sassou's forces was critical. Perhaps Sassou's associates were guilty of provoking ethnopolitical violence in Cuvette the previous month (though no more so than Yhombi's partisans). More importantly, however, this dispute had been successfully mediated by UNESCO's Federico Mayor at the end of May. After this incident, Congo's three main political rivals shook hands in Brazzaville and agreed to engage in a peaceful electoral competition.[20] Although the subsequent killings near Oyo gave Lissouba a pretext for action, his dispatch of troops to Sassou's compound was not justified by those killings. In this context, socialist French premier Jospin's initial worry was that France might come immediately to the assistance of Lissouba, and he insisted on neutrality (Economist Intelligence Unit, *Country Report: Congo,* no. 3, 1997: 12–14). Indeed, for France to have supported an undemocratic client like Lissouba would have been more characteristic of France's behavior in Africa. And in fact, when the war began, Lissouba indicated that he believed that France should intervene—on his behalf. Had France taken this course, it inevitably would have been accused of helping Lissouba to establish a dictatorship in the country.

Another answer is that France was not inactive. As in 1993–1994, the French were genuinely supportive behind the scenes of Bongo's mediation effort. Both Chirac, the president, and Jospin, the prime minister, would certainly have liked to see these efforts succeed. French diplomats played an active role, along with the US ambassador in Congo and the Special Representative of the UN and the Organization of African Unity (OAU), Mohammed Sahnoun, to promote a cease-fire and then a political modus vivendi (Zartman and Vogeli 2000: 281–286). In 1997, the French government actually supported a multinational peacekeeping force for Congo, although the United States did not, to the frustration of some French policymakers.[21] Had a peacekeeping mission been attempted, it would have immediately confronted the task of helping to organize the very elections that were delayed by the events of 5 June. There is evidence that France would have wished the negotiations to succeed, but it was Lissouba who repeatedly blocked progress in the negotiations.

Some have suggested that France was trying to turn over a new leaf in its Africa policies; if so, though, why did Chirac move to assist Central African president Patassé the previous year? At least two things differentiate the two cases. First, at that time France still had a mutual defense treaty with the CAR that allowed it to protect the Central African government in case of attack, but France had no such treaty with Congo. In Niger, where France also lacked such a treaty, it also refrained from intervention during the various political upheavals of the 1990s. Second, in the case of the CAR, troops had mutinied against the Patassé government essentially to achieve better pay and conditions, whereas in Congo Lissouba ordered the attack on Sassou's militia for the putative purpose of neutralizing them ahead of the elections.

This brings us to the question of French behavior during the war itself: What is one to make of the apparent support for Sassou? First, it should be noted that official support for the aid to Sassou came only some time after the war had begun, as Chirac's frustration with Lissouba grew. At the war's outset, there was a lack of unity among the French networks interested in Africa, but Chirac himself seems to have been neutral in deed, if not in sentiment. If Chirac turned decisively against Lissouba in the course of the war, it was because Lissouba's unwillingness to negotiate with Sassou's representatives seemed unduly obstinate to him. Second, it should be noted that resources flowed from France to *both* sides during the war. A group of enterprising French journalists uncovered, for instance, how a French bank jointly controlled by Elf and Gabonese president Bongo made huge loans to Lissouba's officials during the war, with which they purchased weapons.[22]

This, too, reminds us of the lack of unity among the many French networks interested in Africa. Even official French behavior toward the Lissouba administration was more ambiguous than it has often been portrayed. In the middle of the war, Lissouba's finance minister negotiated a major privatization deal with Elf and Shell, providing for the sale of downstream petroleum businesses in Congo. The finance minister went to Paris in August 1997 to finalize this deal himself (*Jeune Afrique*, "Le Seuls Interlocuteurs du FMI," 27 August–2 September 1997: 36–37). Third, at the outset of the war, Sassou, too, had his complaints against the French, arguing that the French had allowed Lissouba to fly in supporters when they briefly controlled the airport in June (*Jeune Afrique*, "L'Amertume de Lissouba," 9–15 July 1997: 7).

The final thing to be said on this question is that a military victory for one side or the other would not have likely led to a restoration of democratic rule in Congo. In the event, the Sassou victory has led to an essentially "electoral authoritarian" regime. Had Lissouba won, though, there would have been little reason to expect a better outcome. Only a negotiated settlement, like those that had ended the previous Congolese disputes of the 1990s, might have led to a restoration of democratic practices.

Finally, let us examine the geostrategic logic of official French action at the time that the war broke out. Is it possible that French intelligence services were whispering in Sassou's ear, encouraging him to provoke a confrontation with Lissouba?[23] It seems most doubtful, given the then prevailing strategic situation. The fall from power of Mobutu Sese Seko in Zaire, which had taken place in May 1997, had provoked French fears about the loss of its clients in Francophone Africa. Recall that the French decided to support Mobutu right to the bitter end, while the United States had turned against him and tacitly supported the Rwanda-Uganda–backed Alliance of Democratic Forces for the Liberation of Congo.[24] In these "Anglophile versus Francophile" alignments, Lissouba had decided to throw his support to the Francophile side, maintaining friendly relations with Mobutu till the end; Sassou in turn had good relations with Laurent Kabila (*Africa Confidential*, "And Across the River," 20 June 1997: 4). In fact, this may have been part of Lissouba's contemporary effort to reassure Paris of his diplomatic reliability. At the same time, the French viewed the apparently imperial aspirations of the (Anglophile) regimes of Yoweri Museveni (Uganda) and Paul Kagame (Rwanda) with great alarm. Since Angola was then aligned with the other "Anglophile" powers, it does not seem likely that France would have initially sanctioned the aid that Angola was giving to Sassou even before the conflict erupted.

In the case of Congo, both French officials and other networks made vigorous efforts to maintain their influence in Congo and shape the behavior of the posttransition regimes there, continuing the well-established patterns of the earlier era. With regard to Congo's democratic experiment, however, the authoritarian impulses of the political class are much more to blame for its failure than France's policies or the behavior of Elf-Aquitaine. France did little to support the elected regimes, but it did not directly orchestrate the fall of Lissouba. As we saw, the Chirac administration had come to terms with Lissouba, if only because he had become a virtual client. The policy of the French state and the behavior of Elf did, however, create a difficult environment for the consolidation of Congolese democracy. Sassou was surely encouraged in his ambitions, if only tacitly, by the promise of French aid should war erupt. Meanwhile, Lissouba may well have been harboring the wrong-headed illusion that the French presidency would have sided with *him* in the event of war. As we saw, resources from Elf and its associated banks apparently went to both sides during the war, a situation that one or both camps must have foreseen. Thus, the behaviors of the French state and other French interests highly conditioned the circumstances in which the Congolese leaders made their calculations.

■ France's Role in Congo in Comparative Perspective

Another way to assess the role of France in Congo is to examine France's apparent influence in the experiments of other Francophone African countries since 1990. In assessing France's more general influence, the conclusions on a number of other questions are relevant: Was France hostile to the spread of democracy in general? Did France take any actions to prevent transitions to multiparty political systems in its areas of influence of Africa in the 1990s? Once transitions had occurred, did France take economic, political, or military actions to undermine them? Or, to the contrary, did France take actions to actually support the sustaining of democratic systems in some African cases? To the extent that one can establish a general pattern of French behavior toward would-be democratizers in Africa, a framework can be created in which the evidence presented above can be more fairly evaluated.

Much of the doubt about France's support for democratic political reform stems from the changing and ambiguous rhetoric that the country's leaders used at the beginning of the era of political reform. Up until 1990, of course, French policy in Africa had virtually nothing to do with promoting democracy, though the French had long supported respect for the rule of law in the former French colonies. According to Le Vine (2004: 247), French president Mitterrand began making significant changes in French policy in early 1990, ordering French ministries to favor those African states "introducing reforms," political as well as economic. "Henceforth [financial] support would go to those with good human rights records and visible movement toward democratic reform" (247). At virtually the same moment, however, then-mayor (of Paris) Jacques Chirac was in Abidjan delivering a very different message. Speaking there in an official statement, Chirac asserted that "multipartyism" was "a kind of luxury that developing countries, who had to concentrate their efforts on economic expansion, did not have the means to offer." He went on to say that a single-party constitution did not preclude democracy, and that democracy "was not respected" in some multiparty states.[25]

These mixed signals preceded by several months Mitterrand's dramatic statement at the June 1990 Franco-African summit at La Baule where he clearly indicated that French aid would thereafter be conditioned on political reform.[26] By this time, the transition in Benin was already well under way, the national conference there having taken place in February 1990. Nonetheless, the La Baule pronouncement captured the attention of Francophone African rulers—and publics—in a way that earlier policy changes had not, and it clearly stimulated further reform.

Yet the La Baule statement hardly marked a clear and definitive rhetorical commitment by France to political reform in Africa. Official French rhetoric in support of political reform subsequently became more nuanced and conditional. For instance, the final statement at the end of the fourth conference of the heads of Francophone states held at the Chaillot Palace outside Paris was far more ambiguous. The document did declare continuing support for human rights and the deepening of democratic processes. Yet it also specified that each African country would have to set its own, individual pace for political reforms and that each would have to determine its own procedures for change (*African Research Bulletin,* "Congo," 16 November–15 December 1991: 10610). In June 1993, Cooperation Minister Michel Roussin reiterated this position with regard to Gabon, indicating that reform would have to proceed at a pace appropriate to the circumstances.[27] Over the subsequent years, French rhetoric became even more ambivalent about supporting democratic reform, especially in response to the unrest experienced in reforming countries, including the CAR, Chad, Niger, and Rwanda, as well as Congo. In particular, many French leaders placed the Rwandan genocide of 1994 in the context of Rwanda's political reform movement that had begun in 1990. As a result, at the Franco-African summit at Biarritz, France, in November 1994, Mitterrand sought to justify France's earlier intervention in Rwanda in Opération Turquoise, but quietly emphasized the need for stability over the need for political change (e.g., Glaser and Smith 2005: 170–174).

Official French behavior toward reform movements in various Francophone African countries proved equally ambiguous and was progressively less supportive of democratic reform from mid-1990 onward. For instance, while France had supported moderate democratic reforms in Gabon in 1990, by the time of the presidential elections in December 1993,

France went so far as to assist President Bongo in the falsification of the elections results (Gardinier 1997a: 153, 156). Similarly, in Chad, France did nothing to stop the overthrow of Hissène Habré in December 1990 and may have even aided Idriss Déby in taking power by force (Lanne 1997: 274; Le Vine 2004: 249, 380). France subsequently did little to pressure Déby to institute the political reforms he had promised. French policy was similarly ambiguous in Cameroon. According to one country specialist (Takougang 1997: 168), France "is believed to have placed additional pressure on President Biya to institute [political reforms]. At the same time, however, France still saw Biya's administration as the pillar of political stability in Cameroon. In other words, any reform had to be under Biya's leadership." Later, in the October 1992 presidential elections, France made its preference for Biya explicit (169). According to one student of Burkina Faso (Boudon 1997: 139), France's support for Burkinabè president Blaise Compaoré was consistent, and this action helped preclude a real change of regimes in the country. Finally, and most importantly, France stuck by Côte d'Ivoire's Houphouët-Boigny until his death in December 1993. France was equally devoted to his successor Henri Konan Bédié in ways that stifled the possibility of a political change there. France provided ample financial support to Bédié in the months before the October 2005 presidential elections and stood by him during the subsequent electoral disputes (Mundt 1997: 195–196).

On the other hand, several political transitions did occur in Francophone Africa in the early post–Cold War period, and France did not stop these. Besides that in Congo, real transitions to multiparty systems took place in Benin, the CAR, Niger, and Mali. One might be tempted to hypothesize that France took steps to keep its clients in power in more developed (Côte d'Ivoire) or oil-rich (Cameroon, Gabon) states, while it took a more laissez faire attitude toward the impoverished states of the Sahel. Congo itself, however, undermines the hypothesis.

Following the transitions to multipartyism in several African states, France was not obviously hostile to the democratic experiments and apparently did nothing to undermine the democratic regimes in these. France may well have been more generous with some of them than others (Gazibo 2005), but it did not noticeably reduce aid to these transitional regimes compared to the old holdovers from the one-party era. Besides Congo, the CAR suffered the most definitive collapse of its new, multiparty regime. Yet there is no particular evidence that France had a hand in this outcome. Indeed, France intervened to support the new regime of Félix Patassé against military mutinies in 1996 and 1997, as noted above. France did not act to save the Patassé regime from a military rebellion/invasion lead by François Bozizé in 2002, but, by that time, Patassé has lost most of his credentials as a democrat. It is true that Bozizé's forces invaded from Chad, whose own government had strong French support, but there is no evidence that France was behind the action, or even that it ended a democratic experiment. In Mali, France did nothing to stop the military coup that overthrew the dictator Moussa Traoré in 1991, and it has subsequently been supportive of the new regime and two different elected presidents (Villalón and Idrissa 2005b). In the far more troubling case of Niger, where democratic experimentation has been an off and on affair, there is no indication that French actions have been the source of the problem (Villalón and Idrissa 2005a).

This comparative analysis leads us to ask: What general patterns can be discerned in French intervention and nonintervention, and do these patterns take into account at all the democratic legitimacy of the regimes that French behavior affects? Le Vine (2004: 343) concludes that there are "thematic strands" that "run through" the various French decisions to intervene or not. "These strands consist in part of French strategic interests, in part of reflexive support and habitual loyalty to a policy line established in the 1940s by de Gaulle, in part of the genuine personal commitment of French presidents to African members of the 'family,' and in part of the durable and self-reinforcing clientelistic networks of economic and political reciprocities that gave substance to much of the Franco-African relationship." This is a useful summary of the logic of French decisionmaking, but democratic legitimacy did become another conditioning element in French decisions after 1990. After 1990, France did not intervene overtly to save dictatorial regimes, though it provided financial and rhetorical support to openly nondemocratic regimes in such countries as Cameroon, Gabon, and Togo. French "client" regimes in Benin, Congo-Brazzaville, Mali, Niger, and Rwanda all *did* lose power when France chose not to interfere, though it did intervene in the CAR.

This brings us back to the fact that, in the case of Congo, it was not rogue elements of the army or a private militia that started the war; rather, it was President Lissouba's own troops, following his orders. Since Lissouba had by then sacrificed much of his democratic legitimacy through violations of the rule of law and the use of force to impose his will, the French were not violating the principle of respecting electoral legitimacy by refusing to come to his aid. Some Lissouba supporters have charged that the French were backing Sassou's return to power by any means, electoral or military.[28] This position, however, will forever remain hypothetical since Lissouba did not allow the elections to proceed. Had he done so, and had it been clear that he had prevailed in the poll, it seems doubtful in the extreme that the French would have then backed a military effort by Sassou to retake power, however much they might have favored his return. As noted above, Lissouba may well have been emboldened in his attempt to throttle Sassou's forces in 1997 by the vain hope that he could count on French support.

In short, then, French behavior toward other democratic experiments in Francophone Africa does not support the notion that Congo's democratic experiment ended because of a direct French determination to return a favored dictator to power through force of arms. French behavior toward other former colonies experimenting with democracy was as complex and ambiguous as it was toward Congo. Congolese politicians were fully informed of French behavior elsewhere in Africa, moreover, and this information became an important part of the context of their own decisionmaking. Thus, Congo's democratic experiment took place in a neocolonial context, created both by French behavior toward Congo *and* toward other former French colonies. This context does not explain the failure of the Congolese democracy experiment, but it did create politico-psychological conditions that must be taken into account to understand that failure.

■ Notes

An earlier version of a portion of this chapter was previously published in Clark (2002a).

1. The double effect was to allow the rump of the Rwandan national army and the Interahamwe to escape Rwanda, as well as to help bring an end to the internal fighting.

2. Economist Intelligence Unit, *Country Report: Rwanda*, no. 2, 1995: 26.

3. On the role of French election rigging in Gabon, see Gardinier (1997a: 160, n. 26).

4. Quoted in Marlise Simons, "France's Rwanda Connection," *New York Times*, 3 July 1994, 6.

5. See, for example, Foreign Broadcast Information Service, "Congo—Lissouba Accuses France of Backing Sassou," 11 September 1997. The assertion that the Congolese blame French interests is based on interviews conducted in Brazzaville, Loubomo, and Pointe Noire in 2001 and 2002. Although most Congolese have limited access to international media, the content of political coverage reported in such publications as *Jeune Afrique* and *Le Monde Diplomatique* is widely known.

6. Indeed, Guy Menga (1993: 13) disparaged French contributions to Congo compared to the impressive Palais du Congrès, built by the Chinese. But this observation overlooks the more sizable and steady aid of France to Congo.

7. Only in the military field were Congo's East bloc (and Chinese) partners more prominent than the French, but Congo was still sending significant numbers of officers and noncommissioned officers for training in France as well as in the East bloc.

8. Articles 5.1 and 5.2 of the final act of the conference, reported in Baniafouna (1995a: 215–216).

9. The good relations owed primarily to the fact that Sassou had served as a mediator for the 1988 Angola-Namibia Peace Accords, and Brazzaville had been the venue for the talks.

10. Unfortunately, I have not found a complete accounting of French aid to Congo before, during, and after the democratic transition.

11. Menga (1993: 59–60). See also Nsafou (1996: 213). Apparently, Milongo was only able to get some very minor grants for specific projects, amounting to only

about US$2 million. See Economist Intelligence Unit, *Country Report: Congo,* no. 2, 1992: 15.

12. Baniafouna (1995a: 75). According to Menga (1993: 61), France specifically required that the new employees be fired immediately.

13. Foreign Broadcast Information Service–Sub-Saharan Africa, "Minister, French Official Discuss Defense Topics," 19 January 1993: 2; and "French Defense Ministry Sends Troops to Brazzaville," 29 January 1993: 1. In fact, Franco-Congolese military cooperation had begun the previous year when the two countries held joint military exercises in April. See *Marchés Tropicaux et Méditerréens,* "Congo," 24 April 1992: 1054.

14. The information in this paragraph is taken from the following *Jeune Afrique* articles: "La guerre du pétrole," 27 May–2 June 1993: 14; "Le mal du Congo s'appelle Sassou," 15–21 July 1993: 68; and "La guerre du pétrole: est-elle finie?" 9–15 September 1993: 54.

15. The episodes of arbitrary detention, extra-judicial murders, extortion of members of the Aubevillois and Zoulou militias, torture of detainees, and other such crimes are documented in the trimestrial newsletter *Lumière,* published by the Organisation Congolaise de Droits de l'Homme (OCDH).

16. *Le Nouvel Afrique-Asia,* no. 52, January 1994: 35.

17. *Jeune Afrique,* "Rente: La nouvelle donne," 27 July–2 August 1995: 38–39. Under the old system, the Congolese state got a smaller percentage, plus some taxes on the profits of the oil companies.

18. For an analysis of Chirac's speech, see *Marchés Tropicaux et Méditerréens,* 26 July 1996: 1637; for extracts of the speech itself, see 1639–1640.

19. Certainly music to official French ears, he even mocked the courage of the supposedly hearty Americans while extolling the moral courage of French intellectuals (Lissouba 1997: 226–227).

20. On the Owando affair of May 1997 and its resolution, see Pourtier (1997: 18–19), Sundberg (2000: 88), and Zartman and Vogeli (2000: 280). For a view of these events sympathetic to Sassou, see Pigasse (1998: 109–116, 125–133). According to Pigasse's version, Lissouba was readying the military commander for an attack on Sassou's Mpila residence even as the negotiations for a reconciliation of the Owando affair were ongoing.

21. See, for instance, the article by former prime minister Michel Rocard in *Le Monde,* 14 August 1997.

22. Antoine Glaser, Stephen Smith, and Maris Malagardis, "Un rôle intermédiaire dans le conflit congolais," *Libération,* February 4, 1998.

23. Several different knowledgeable Congolese claim to believe that Sassou somehow tricked Lissouba into striking the first blow in the war. These well-informed observers claim that secret Sassou supporters in Lissouba's camp, including Martin Mberi, who later joined Sassou's postwar cabinet, goaded Lissouba into attacking Sassou's compound in June 1997. Some of these sources are well known figures, but they asked for anonymity in giving their comments.

24. On the Franco-American competition in Africa at this time, see Peter J. Schraeder (2000).

25. Cited in Glaser and Smith (2005: 126); my translation.

26. For one particularly important commentary on the La Baule summit, see Fottorino (1990), cited in Le Vine (2004: 247).

27. *Afrique-Express,* no. 5, 24 June 1993: 23, cited in Gardinier (1997a: 155).

28. A number of ordinary Congolese expressed this opinion to me during interviews in Brazzaville in 2001 and 2002.

9

Understanding the
Failed Experiment in Congo

This chapter reviews and summarizes the findings of the previous six chapters dealing with the two main questions. First, why did the democratic experiment fail in 1997, and, second, what kind of answer can one reasonably give? Most of our attention to the epistemological question has been implicit, embedded in the structure of the query, rather than explicit. Nonetheless, the nature and certainty of the substantive conclusion depends on the prior conclusion on the epistemological question. Accordingly, it is appropriate to begin with some reflections on the epistemological question before turning our attention to the substantive issue of democracy in Congo.

■ **Epistemological Findings**

What can we say, in the end, about the possibility of giving a definitive answer to the question of why democracy failed in Congo? First, it does not appear that any of the hypotheses explored in each of the six preceding chapter holds *the* explanation for its failure. Only if we began from a strongly ideological perspective, would it be possible to make a case that any one of the six variables discussed previously fully explains the failure of Congolese democracy. If we decided in advance that some feature of the Congolese polity, society, or economy was central to an explanation, the other elements could reasonably be subsumed under the master variable. For the analyst who chose one of the "deep" and "fundamental" causes, such as political culture, identity community diversity, or class structure, the other elements of the Congolese situation could easily be described as merely "intervening variables," whose presence was a by-product of the forces that destroyed Congo's democratic experiment. One could easily view the nature of the Congolese army or the country's choice of institutional design as products of these deeper causes that possess the real explanatory power. It would be easy for an analyst to devote an entire study to this one fundamental cause and mention other, more proximate, causes of the collapse of the Congolese experiment only in a peripheral way. The decisions made by the most important political actors in Congo could be presented as the inevitable choices of a politician from a given class, of an actor imbued with certain political values, or of a person of a given ethnic identity in an artificial polity created by alien outsiders.

On the other hand, a scholar with a lifelong devotion to the study of, say, military rule or institutional design, might focus on these more proximate causes as the key to explanation. Such a scholar would note, as did Magnusson and Clark (2005), that Congo shared many of its societal structural characteristics with other African states whose democratic experiments had a rather different outcome. A case could then be made that the *other* proximate variables, those not deemed key, have little to tell us about Congo's situation through some selective comparisons, or these other variables might simply be ignored altogether. In this way, a person studying Congo as a case could reasonably present impressive circumstantial evidence for any one of our more proximate explanations explored in this volume. It would not be surprising if such a claim for one of the more proximate variables was more an insinuation than a careful argument, more implication than logical exposition. For instance, we know that Lissouba had a dispute with Elf in 1993 over the former president's desire for a pre-electoral loan; we know that there was lingering bitterness on both sides after the affair; and we know that French political authorities were worried about the possible loss of economic influence in Congo. Based on these facts of the case, it is tempting to conclude that French policies, and those of French economic interests, are responsible for the war of 1997 and the collapse of Congolese democracy. As in Chapter 8, however, I have attempted to present a more complex and subtle picture.

In keeping with this finding, it is important not to fall victim to what Morgenthau (1974), writing about theories of historical evolution, once called the "myth of the single cause." In trying to understand either patterns of political practice and change over substantial stretches of time and space, or in trying to understand specific events as we have done here, Morgenthau warned against the selection of a single variable and parallel subordination of competing explanations to explain historical events. Yet Morgenthau himself soon afterward fell under the seductive spell of writing general theory himself. In fact few serious observers of the sociopolitical world can long resist the Siren song of making generalizations about the substance of the social world, even if a few—mostly poststructuralists—manage to dwell entirely in a world of epistemological reflection. The greater the pull of theoretical generalization, the greater the temptation to identify the singular cause of social practice and change. In the end, Morgenthau could not resist this temptation, either, and political power became the central explanatory variable in his grand generalizations about the social world.[1] Ironically, in light of his earlier work in *Scientific Man*

Versus Power Politics (1974), Morgenthau became a kind of personification of positivist theorizing in international relations and, as such, the target of countless constructivist and poststructuralist critiques.

Yet Morgenthau's original point about single causes applies well to the case of the Congolese democratic experiment. The case appears to be much like the traffic accident in which an intoxicated and distracted driver, operating a vehicle with faulty brakes, strikes an illegally parked car. Perhaps the streetlight meant to illuminate the street has burned out and the pavement is wet with rain.[2] A social observer is left to wonder: What *really* caused the accident. Was it the intoxication of the driver? The faulty brakes? The poor lighting conditions or the wet pavement? The immediate answers to those questions certainly reveal more about the prejudices, interests, and experiences of the observer than they do the facts of the situation. Brake mechanics are sure to focus on the car's mechanical condition and call for tougher inspection laws; advocates for better public services would point to the burned out streetlight first; and the police would certainly emphasize the intoxicated condition of the driver.

At this point, we should recall the task King, Keohane, and Verba (1994) assigned to the students of cases in their epistemological scheme. These authors specified that progress toward reliable generalizations depended on the students of cases finding *the* causes of events in the cases they tackled. Their aspiration is for the case studies to contribute to generalization through the accumulation of the lessons of such cases together in general models. An examination of a succession of specific single causes in the Congo case, however, does not reveal that any single cause can be identified as *the* source of the failure of the country's democratic experiment. To understand the case, it is essential to be aware of all of the structural givens that provided the context in which specific decisions were taken. As a result, our understanding of the Congo case, though valuable in itself, may not, regrettably, contribute much to the task of finding general explanations for the failure of democratic consolidation. It may, on the other hand, help us to understand other, similar cases where the structural circumstances are comparable.

The logical response to this epistemological dilemma is to study many cases together, and this is what most political scientists, including King, Keohane, and Verba (1994) both do and advocate. If one studied the reports of one thousand car accidents, in how many cases—or better, in what *percentage* of them—would one find mention of faulty brakes, driver intoxication, or poor driving conditions? The typical way of proceeding is, then, probabilistically. And in fact many students of democratization have proceeded in this manner and with generally good effect; they have alerted us to the most likely social conditions with which we might expect either successful or unsuccessful democratic consolidation.

Yet two observations might be made about this social science approach. First, this sort of method can give us clues about what to look for in studying a specific case, but it cannot tell us the answer either before or after the case is studied in detail (even if a single answer could eventually be identified). Because alcohol may be related to more car accidents than either illegally parked cars, faulty brakes, or bad driving conditions, and because alcohol was a factor in the case studied, does not mean that alcohol was *the* cause of the accident in question. In the case in question, let us specify that the intoxication of the driver was mild, or borderline, from a legal standpoint. If we are trying to assign causation, we are more likely to take all of the other circumstances into account and come to a multicausal conclusion; if we are trying to assess guilt, we may be more likely to absolve the driver of responsibility. Likewise, in the case of the Congolese democratic experiment, all of the general theoretical research is important in making us aware of the possibly relevant contexts and structural conditions in which the experiment took place. But none of it *explains* the Congolese case.

A second important observation is that the type of research that attempts to find generalizations across multiple cases through systematic methods (rather than the targeted comparisons used above) generally privileges structures. That is, we look for structural similarities across large numbers of cases. In what percentage of cases did the states experimenting with democratic systems adopt semi-presidential systems? In what percentage of cases in which there was economic growth did democratic experiments continue versus the percentage for those in which there was no growth? Social scientists generally begin by looking for associations between structural circumstances and outcomes before proceeding to control for the other variables that might be responsible for the causal outcomes.

One important epistemological lesson that one learns by studying any case closely, including the present one, however, is that *agency matters.* None of the structural circumstances of the case forced the actors to behave as they actually did. The recent work of Samuels (2003) and Hermann et al. (2001) reasserts the view that strong and decisive leaders have sometimes been able to reshape the politics of their countries despite the odds posed by the structural circumstances. According to most accounts, however, Lissouba was not a strong or decisive leader, despite his tendency to stubbornness. In fact, he was often a "victim of groupthink," to quote the widely used phrase of Janis (1972).[3] Specifically, a number of Congolese thought President Lissouba to be a virtual prisoner of Martin Mberi and the "gang of four," who provided him only with the information and perspectives that reinforced the president's own prejudices and misperceptions.

Much of the work done by political psychologists is squarely in the positivist tradition that King, Keohane, and Verba (1994) seek to defend. One can study dozens of political decisions in the aggregate or attempt to quantify personality traits in a great variety of ways. And categories can be created for political personalities or for leadership style, as Jackson and Rosberg (1982) did so successfully in attempting to understand the impact of rulers' personalities on the political trajectories of African states. Some classic works on agency, however, seek to understand the individual personality traits or fundamental values ("operational code" in the famous phrase of Leites [1951]) of the leaders in question as the sources of behavior. Even when important things about a leader's values, personality, and leadership style are understood, however, his or her behavior is never entirely predictable, for the choices to be made can never be completely foreseen.

One of the most intriguing studies of personality and leadership has explored how the interaction of decisionmaking style with the structural contexts of action has led to various kinds of government failure (Kowert 2002). This study shows that outcomes depend on neither leadership style nor on structural circumstance alone but, rather, on the interaction of the two. A close study of the Congo case also suggests that its democratic failure cannot be understood without attention both to structural circumstance and to the choices of the political principals.

Returning to the analogy of the car accident, note that some of the causes of the accident relate to agency and others to the structure of the situation. But the dialectic of agent and structure makes the situation far more complicated. The driver of the vehicle made the choice to take the wheel while he was intoxicated—although the consciousness of such a choice is not entirely obvious. With regard to the condition of the brakes, the operator made certainly choices about the maintenance of his vehicle, but it is possible that he might not have known about his brakes. If he suspected that they were faulty, he would not likely admit it. On the other hand, the surface condition of the street and the lighting would appear to be structural features of the situation. Yet, it could also be asked: Did some aspects of these structural features of the situation depend on the choices and decisions that came before? Did the city council decide to prioritize other expenditures over the maintenance of street lighting, and did this decision lead to the visibility conditions that were particularly dangerous on the night of the accident? Likewise, the presence of an illegally parked car on the street at the time of the accident was a structural condition for purposes of analyzing the subsequent accident. But this structural given resulted even more immediately from a choice—that of the other driver to park illegally—than did the poor lighting conditions. The more the entire situation is studied, the more one realizes all of the structural conditions have resulted from more or less proximate choices, and that the structural circumstances have conditioned the relevant choices. This fundamental realization is what led Giddens (1984) to his structuration theory of social explanation, and also what has led constructivists to refuse to privilege either agency or structure in their social analyses.

Reflection on the apparently multiple contexts of the democratic failure in Congo appears to confirm this neutral position on the agent-structure problem. The Congolese democratic experiment suffered several blows to its viability before 1997, and then a definitive, crushing blow in June 1997, in the decisions made by President Lissouba and a handful of other major political figures. These actions destroyed Congolese democracy for the time being. Each decision served to alter the sociopolitical context—the social structure—for each subsequent decision. Much earlier political choices of both external and internal agents created more fundamental contexts. Those made at the Berlin Conference in 1884–1885 preceding the partition of Africa are among those whose reverberations can still be discerned in the nature of contemporary Congolese politics. Decisions made by influential French individuals more proximately also served to create a context for action in Congo. The more closely such decisions are considered, the more one recognizes the dialectical relationship of agents' actions and structures.

The choices and decisions of agents in Congo (and elsewhere) have such effects because of the fluidity of the structures we imagine to be permanent and fixed. The many structural features of Congolese society and politics with relevance to the democratic experiment are structures of the mind, not natural, permanent, or inevitable structures. Whether it was southerners, Niboleks, or Bembé politicians who dominated Congolese politics under Lissouba depends—if one is Congolese—on whether one is a northerner, a Vili citizen of Pointe Noire, or one of Lissouba's Nzabi kinsmen. The other structures of Congolese society, including political culture, class, or military, are also part of a collective intellectual consciousness. They have accrued over time as a result of their reinforcement through repeated individual actions that tend to reconfirm their importance. As we know well, however, revolutions of the consciousness are possible, and structures that we unconsciously come to perceive as permanent can melt away with surprising rapidity. Among these was the concept of the legitimacy of the one-party state, a political given that dominated the landscape of Africa for twenty-five years.

In short, then, this study confirms the position that attention to both structures and agents is critical to a deep understanding of outcomes in specific cases. Further, the structures that we examine in search of the context for action are only more or less stable. Although they may persist for decades, they are not permanent fixtures of societies. One must be aware of how social structures in a given society have arisen in the past and how actors are attempting constantly to change the nature of the political game. In a context of relatively fluid structures, agency matters.

One other epistemological finding of this study was less anticipated, but is no less evident at the end. Namely, that the array of social structures that could be examined to understand an episode like Congo's democratic experiment overlap to a surprising degree. This is particularly apparent with regard to the more proximate structural contexts of the experiment. Take, for example, Congo's "army problem." As we saw in Chapter 6, there was not a single problem with the army inherited by Lissouba in 1992 but, in fact, a series of intermeshed problems created by the country's economy, its political culture, and its history of ethnoregional politics. What leads a soldier to fail to do his duty to his state, to support a private militia or an opposition politician, rather than obey the orders of his commanding officer? Any number of things may induce such uncivil behavior, including low or infrequent pay; a distrust of the senior staff due to the perception that his commanding officers favor an ethnoregional group that has either suffered discrimination or enjoyed exceptional privileges in the past; or a belief that the army has a right to intervene in civilian politics because he has seen such behavior so often in the past. Congo's army problem was and remains, then, an aspect of the country's economic weakness, its ethnoregional tensions, and its politico-cultural authoritarianism. Similarly, we can easily understand how the choice of a semi-presidential institutional design is a reflection of Congo's legacy of dependence on France as a source of political inspiration.

Two structural features of all societies at first seem to be fundamental and irreducible one to the other: economic underdevelopment and political culture. Observers of many other societies have either concluded or started from the premise that these two structures are primary. In general, those of a more Marxian analytical bent have privileged the former, and those who have studied the development of political values in the West the latter. Either of these two fundamental structural features of Congolese society might seem to be a good starting point, a foundational base upon which to build a solid analysis of the country's politics and likely evolution.

Alas, reflection on the material presented in the preceding chapters suggests that even these apparently foundational structures of society are deeply bound up in each other. To a considerable extent, each is a cause of the other, and neither can fairly be considered a "first cause." Congo has remained impoverished in the postcolonial era for a host of reasons, but the internal structures of society are at least as important as the country's structural position in the world economy. In fact, Congo's oil wealth has meant that it has gained a great deal economically from international trade. With the revenues raised through oil sales, the country might have imported hundreds of millions of dollars worth of capital goods with which to stimulate industrialization and development. But most of this money has been squandered on political patronage, misguided investments, excessive public hiring, theft, and luxuries for the political elite. All of these politico-economic patterns reflect the country's political culture, itself a reflection of the country's authoritarian and economically illiberal history.

On the other hand, the country's poverty has constantly reinforced its profoundly nondemocratic political culture. The country's poverty has prevented the emergence of the "self-expression values" that Inglehart and Welzel (2005) have found essential to successful democratization. The enduring poverty and lack of economic growth in Congo, despite its oil wealth, has precluded the appearance of a bourgeoisie or independent business class; indeed, oil wealth ensured that the middle class that did appear has been dependent on state patronage for its material well-being. Meanwhile, the country is burdened with a distressingly large reservoir of undereducated and desperate youth. In a situation of such scarcity, few think about changing the rules of the game. Rather, nearly everyone thinks about daily economic survival, which entails accepting the rules of the game and getting what one can. A market economy that allows opportunities for enrichment through hard work, accumulation of savings, and hope for higher living standards for subsequent generations breeds a culture of economic fair play, honesty, and the rule of law; an economy based on a diminishing natural resource whose price fluctuates wildly breeds a culture of desperation and short-term profiteering.

Let us stop here to summarize some of the apparent difficulties of reaching one single explanation for the failure of the Congolese democratic experiment. The cultural structures of the society are deeply complex, reflecting layers of political practice that have accrued in the political culture since precolonial times; almost all of the patterns from all the periods of Congo's history have been deeply authoritarian. The ethnoregional identities in the country serve as the main basis for political mobilization, yet, paradoxically, they are also surprisingly fluid, having changed rather frequently as various ethnoregional political entrepreneurs forge and reforge identities. The economy of the country has produced considerable wealth, mainly through petroleum revenues, but these have not been invested or deployed in such a way as to stimulate self-sustaining economic growth. These politico-cultural and politico-economic realities seem to have emerged out of an interaction of agents and existing structures over many decades of political memory. One cannot discern with any precision which of these structures are primary or have "caused" the others to emerge as they have. Meanwhile, a host of more proximate problems (like the nature of the Congolese army) and choices (like the country's institutional design) also seem to have shaped the country's prospects for successful democratic consolidation. One can only try to imagine how better policies designed to deal with these problems, or different choices at key moments, might have influenced the democratic outcome.

These reflections condition strongly the kind of conclusions to be reached about why the Congolese democratic experiment failed. First, the conclusions should demonstrate awareness of the agent-structure dialectic; they should at once admit the autonomy of decisionmakers and try to judge the impact of their choices, while being cognizant of the structural context. Second, the conclusions about structures should demonstrate cognizance of the interlinkages among the country's various sociopolitical structures and their fluidity. The only basis for these conclusions is an understanding of the dynamics that took hold in the interaction of agents and structures in the years following the transition to a multiparty system.

■ Substantive Conclusions

In keeping with these findings, let us begin with some of the key choices or decisions of the important actors that seem to have doomed Congo's democratic experiment. On the presidential side of the equation, two specific acts can be identified as having an unequalled impact on the course of events during Congo's short democratic experiment. The first was Lissouba's decision to dissolve Parliament and call for fresh elections on 17 November 1992; this was followed two weeks later by the use of armed force to stop protestors who were then demonstrating in parts of Brazzaville. The second was Lissouba's decision to send troops to Sassou's compound on 5 June 1997 in an effort to arrest him, disarm his militia, and/or arrest several of his associates implicated in the Oyo murders—the real intention remaining controversial. A case can be made for several other choices or decisions that were also of significance: Lissouba's decision not to offer the PCT more and better cabinet posts in September 1992, his choice to allow Martin Mberi to begin forming a militia in late 1992, his decision to make the nefarious deal with Occidental Petroleum in order to pay the functionaries in May 1993, or his decision to attack Bacongo with heavy weapons later in the year and thus resolve the first round of fighting in Congo by force, among others. But each of these was dependent upon his earlier, more fateful choices.

On the side of the opposition, Sassou's decision to abandon his coalition with Lissouba in September and to enter into a new coalition with Kolélas was also of great importance. This decision was certainly legal, though, and possibly a legitimate response to the composition of the cabinet that Lissouba proposed the same month. In this sense, the decision ended up having bad consequences for Congo, but it was not apparently intended to end the democratic experiment at that time. The decisions of both Sassou and Kolélas to form militia groups, though, around the same time were clearly designed to keep open the possibilities of resolving political disputes through force of arms. Kolélas's rejection of the disputed election results and subsequent decision to use his militia to prevent government forces from entering his fiefs following the disputed elections of May 1993 were even more momentous. The choices of both opposition leaders to maintain their militia groups after the peace accords, which were worked out over the next several months, should count as separate and discreet decisions that affected the political environment for the remaining years of the experiment.

In reviewing any set of acts that have a momentous social outcome, one is inevitably led to ask about the sequence of the ill-intentioned acts committed. Essentially, who struck the first blow? Every major crisis between the two superpowers during the Cold War has become the object of scholarly analysis of this sort. In the case of Congo's nascent democratic experiment, clearly Lissouba committed the first illegal act for political advantage. Recall that the presidential elections of August 1992 had unfolded peacefully, despite the political traumas of the transitional period. Trying though those times had been, Lissouba's investiture as president essentially marked the beginning of a new era and a clean slate. At the time that he dissolved Parliament under conditions not specified by the constitution, neither Sassou nor Kolélas had committed illegal acts under the new regime. Although Sassou had certainly committed crimes during his first presidency, these had been acknowledged and forgiven at the national conference. Even if both opposition leaders had bodyguards that could be counted as the core of their future militia groups, neither had at that point threatened to undermine the rule of law of the new order through force.

Although the acts of the key political players always matter in determining the outcome of events, the structures in which the actors are imbedded impose more or less onerous constraints on the autonomy of their actions. This raises the question: Was Lissouba compelled in any way to act as he did? Was he responding to structural pressures that made whatever choice he made detrimental to the consolidation of democracy? In the main, the answer is "no." Lissouba had only very recently taken office, and he then possessed a substantial stock of public good will. Although he later faced serious economic pressures, these were not foremost in anyone's mind at that moment. Nor was the army threatening to intervene in the political arena at that moment, as it later did under similar circumstances in Niger; indeed, the army's senior leaders were seeking to resolve the crisis.

An apologist for Lissouba might claim that the structural constraints of the 1992 constitution forced him to act as he did, and there is an argument here, but it does not stand up under sustained scrutiny. If Lissouba had accepted the antipresidential coalition and its prime ministerial designate in late 1992, he would have found it difficult to put through a coherent program of economic and social reforms. There would likely have been recurrent conflicts between the president and prime minister. And, it might be argued, these would have threatened Congo's future stability. There is a rather devastating rebuttal to this point of view, however: once Lissouba did control Parliament, by the end of 1993, he subsequent failed to put through any coherent reform program for the rest of his presidency. Rather, the reforms that Parliament enacted were halfhearted (like decentralization) or self-serving to the presidency (like the sale of shares in Elf-Congo to the parent company). Further, none of my respondents in Brazzaville thought that Lissouba had dissolved Parliament mainly for the reason of ensuring good policy coordination between the legislature and Parliament. Not even the former president's supporters described his action in that way.[4] His opponents, however, did have a cogent explanation for why Lissouba could not accept the URD-PCT coalition formed in 1992: it would have represented too much of a challenge to his personal power from the beginning of his term in office.

Since Lissouba did have a great deal of freedom of action in late 1992, one must conclude that this (unforced) decision was crucial in Congo's political evolution. Lissouba made a decision at that time that he need not have, and nearly everything else in Congo's medium-term future followed from it. We do not know, of course, how much longer the democratic experiment in Congo might have survived had Lissouba acted differently. It is possible that the country would have experienced the kind of political gyrations that Niger experienced throughout the 1990s as it cast off the French Fifth Republic model constitution and tried new ones (Villalón and Idrissa 2005a). One can easily imagine Congo's main military leaders, Ngollo and Mokoko, taking power temporarily under such circumstances, but also restoring power to civilian leaders. Or some other crisis might have ended the experiment more definitively and brought some other dictator to power.

Lissouba's decision of November 1992 had a disproportionately bad impact on Congo's political experiment because it came so early. The Congo case certainly shows that leadership matters, and that the structural features of a country do not necessarily determine its political destiny. In addition, it also confirms what other cases of democratic experimentation suggest, namely that leadership matters most at the beginning. This explains why so many Americans idolize George Washington: he had the forbearance as the first US president to tolerate intensive criticism and to forego the easy opportunity to accumulate power for himself and keep it. Each passing month and year that a democratic system survives increases its chances of surviving into the future. Every peaceful transition from one chief executive to the next inculcates that value more deeply into the political class. Eventually, over a long period of time, the values are so fully absorbed into the political consciousness of leaders that they can be taken for granted, and violence ceases to become "thinkable" as a political means. Had Lissouba shown more patience, more forbearance, and more statesmanship in the early days of Congo's experiment, it might have persisted for many more years than it actually did. His good example—had there been one—might have created a positive political trajectory along which Congo could have traveled for some time.

What of the subsequent actions of Kolélas and Sassou, those that created an environment of disorder, undermined respect for the institutions of the state, and inflamed the ethnoregional passions of angry young Congolese? Were they compelled to take such actions in the interest of fairness? They justified their actions on the grounds that Lissouba had politicized the state's republican institutions and that he had attempted to concentrate all power in his office. But did the structural features of the Congolese society *compel* them to act as they did? Would the alternative have been political oblivion?

The answer to the last question is "quite possibly." Given the authoritarian and extralegal political tendencies that Lissouba demonstrated, one can easily imagine him manipulating politics to stay in power in beyond the legal limits of the 1992 constitution. Nonetheless, if Sassou and Kolélas had wished to act in the interest of continuing the democratic experiment, they would have met Lissouba's acts with rhetorical protest and peaceful demonstrations, not violent confrontation. Either could have gained political capital outside his own ethnoregional constituency by acting in this way. But would either have sacrificed support from within his own constituency in responding to Lissouba in a nonviolent manner? There is good reason to think not. Certainly hotheads among both the Lari and Mbochi youth responded readily to the call to arms, but others—the mature, the loving parents, the peaceful, the entrepreneurial—all would also have responded well to calls for nonviolent resistance. In short, no structural forces compelled either Kolélas or Sassou to act as they did at these early stages. Although we will never know, Congo had an outside chance of continuing its democratic experiment beyond the Lissouba era had both of these key figures acted differently.

The epistemological section above warns against identifying any structural feature of a society as *the* controlling force over its destiny. Nonetheless, it is surprising how often one is drawn back to political culture as a master key to understanding Congolese politics, including that during the democratic experiment. First, consider the specific political acts just discussed in terms of political culture. Congo's political traditions— precolonial, colonial, and postcolonial—were ones in which violence often decided, strength was revered, ties of kinship were most politically reliable, and, in the latter two periods, ones in which the rhetoric and realities of politics were radically at odds. In short, "Why did Lissouba, and his opponents act as they did at critical moments?" The simplest answer is that they acted in accord with their own political values, in terms of process. Whatever their long-term ends, all had been conditioned by Congo's political experiences to seek or maintain power by demonstrating their strength and toughness, by cynically manipulating ethnoregional constituencies, by vilifying political opponents, and by skirting the rule of law as necessary. Perhaps one or all of Congo's uninspiring politicians possessed such values by tragic genetic accident or family experience, but all came of age in a political environment that reinforced these values. None of Congo's other structural circumstances better contextualizes the actions of each.

Second, as we saw in previous chapters, the impact of various sociopolitical structures in Congo's democratic experiment can usually be presented or understood best in terms of political culture. The violent nature of ethnoregional politics in Congo is not a result of ethnic diversity, or cultural pluralism, itself, but of the *practice* of ethnoregional mobilization for political ends. The experiences of Tanzania, Zambia, Malawi, and other African states suggest that it could be otherwise. By extension, the main challenge of army reform in Congo is also a problem of political culture: the de-politicization and de-ethnicization of the army are primarily problems of changing the values of Congolese citizens. As for institutional design, a variety of institutional designs could work in Congo if people's political values accepted them as legitimate and inviolable first, and if the entire political class were devoted to the rule of law. Whereas some designs may reinforce a virtuous cycle of inculcating these values better than others, no constitutional design, no matter how carefully crafted, can survive the profoundly nondemocratic manipulations of a political clique determined to maintain power, either inside or outside the law. As for the impact of French policies in Congo, this also depends largely on how they are perceived and received by the Congolese public. "Dependency" for the Congolese is as much a state of mind as it is an objective economic condition. Breaking free from the politically stultifying, if deep and widespread, belief that French interests control everything in Congo will do as much to brighten the country's political prospects as diversifying its trade and investment partners. In short, the Congolese have been manipulated, but partly because they have allowed it.

It bears reemphasizing at this point that Congo's political culture did *not* make the failure of the democratic experiment inevitable. If so, then political culture perhaps could be identified as the cause of failure. The values of individuals as well as those of societies can change, as argued in Chapter 3, and the political opening of 1991 was a moment when prior values were cast into doubt. Had the individual elected to office in 1992 been more committed to democratic modes of governance, then perhaps those values would have been more fundamentally and enduringly reshaped at that time.

The one structural feature of the society that cannot be directly tied, and certainly not reduced, to political culture is the economy, including the basic poverty, the lack of a bourgeoisie, and rentier effects of petroleum production and sales. Even had Congolese democracy survived its launching, and even its second set of constitutional elections, it would have faced daunting economic challenges along the way. Like the Russians in the 1990s, the Congolese were growing increasingly restless and frustrated with the lack of economic progress under the new political dispensation by 1997. A post-Lissouba authoritarian political actor might easily have been able to blame this lack of progress on the experimental political system and use this pretext to take or retain power extra-constitutionally. Eventually, street protests and strikes, frequent occurrences in Congo from 1992 to 1997, might have provided a different context for a return to military rule.

This situation raises the question whether political culture could possibly be reduced to a function of the country's economic well-being. This, of course, was the more or less explicit conclusion of the modernization theorists of the 1950s and particularly of the 1960s, including those of the left (e.g., Moore 1966) and the right (e.g., Huntington 1968). This point of view suggests that social and political values follow logically and inevitably from the economic well-being and confidence of individuals. While this point of view went out of fashion for some time, it was still implicit in much development planning throughout the 1970s and 1980s. Moreover, it has recently been updated to be rather less mechanical and now has undaunted new defenders, including, notably, Inglehart and Welzel (2005). These authors argue confidently that changes in sociopolitical values "are roughly predictable, for they are closely linked with socioeconomic development." They go on to claim that "socioeconomic development brings roughly predictable cultural changes—and beyond a certain point, these changes make democracy increasingly likely to emerge where it does not yet exist, and to become stronger and more direct where it already exists" (15). Although these authors revise early modernization theories by arguing that cultural values have some autonomy and can be resistant to change by economic progress (18–22), the title of their study announces their more fundamental position: that there is a *sequence* of social change that begins with improving economic conditions. These improving conditions lead to a gradual change of values from "survival" to "self-expression," which in turn lays the social foundation for political liberalization and ultimately stable democracy. The experiences of East Asia's "tigers" of the 1980s and 1990s seem to be the paradigm cases of this phenomenon.

Although the question of the general truth of such claims is far beyond the scope of this book, its application to Congo is not. The claims suggest that even if one could demonstrate definitively that authoritarian and other nondemocratic values were most responsible for the failure of Congo's democratic experiment in the 1990s, this is not the end of the discussion. The work of Inglehart and Welzel, among others, suggests that these values are closely connected with, if not produced by, the country's state of impoverishment. The root cause of the democratic experiment's failure is economic underdevelopment, and Congo had no hope of consolidating a democratic system without prior economic progress. This point of view essentially identifies Congolese political values as an intervening variable in a sequence of causation that begins with economic development. Since Inglehart and Welzel have impressive data to support their claims, this argument deserves to be taken seriously.

While the general relationships identified by these authors—and many others before—seem to be correct, this does not mean that the Congolese experiment was absolutely doomed from the start. Certainly, the odds were against Congo, as they were against other African states that began experiments at the same time. Yet the case of India, at least, suggests that the sequential relationship of economic development and democracy may not be inevitable. Famously, India began its own democratic experiment more than fifty years ago, and that experiment survived a fifteen-year period of slow growth, and then another subsequent fifteen-year period of even slower growth, before a period of impressive economic development began (Kohli 2004: 259–277). It may well be the case that India's democracy will deepen if it continues to enjoy the impressive economic growth of the past ten years, but most agree that India's pre-1980 system did deserve the name "democracy." Among other reasons, it meets the criteria to be classified as a democracy according to the operational definition of Przeworski et al. (2000), used in Chapter 1. Benin also now meets those conditions, having experienced its fourth peaceful, multiparty election in 2006. Like Congo, Benin did not have the odds in its favor, but its democratic experiment has now survived for over fifteen years. Like India, Benin has recently seen years of economic growth that may allow its democracy to survive and the values of the post-1990 period to become more firmly rooted in the consciousness of its people.

Congo may well have other social needs that are greater than the need for open, multiparty politics. The experiences of India and Benin suggest, however, that a return to democratic experimentation would not preclude a subsequent improvement of economic conditions for the people. They also suggest that another democratic experiment need not necessarily await a sustained period of economic growth first. If indeed political values are the key to the sustaining of democratic experiments, there is hope for democracy in Congo. The country's political culture remains thoroughly undemocratic but is not a permanent feature of the society. For the time being, as Chapter 10 of this study shows, authoritarian values have the upper hand. At the grassroots, though, some social organizations are functioning in a democratic way, and these may provide valuable experience for a future generation of Congolese politicians. Even at the level of formal political institutions, the space for opposition political activity has not been completely closed. The ruthlessness of the Sassou II regime has done little to nurture a culture of tolerance for a loyal opposition in Congo, but the democratic experiment of the 1990s is far from forgotten. Although the experience was bitter, the ideal of peaceful political competition among parties has not been renounced by anyone in principle, unlike in the 1970s and 1980s. Accordingly, the next opening in Congolese political space may meet with better results if the hard lessons of the 1990s have been absorbed into the Congolese political consciousness.

■ Notes

1. See, in particular, Morgenthau's insistence that one must "abstract out" the political side of the human personality and set aside the other dimensions in order to theorize about the political world (Morgenthau and Thompson 1985: 16).

2. This analogy is borrowed, in adapted form, from Stretton (1969: 71–72).

3. Notably, this view was presented to me by Jean-Pierre Thystère-Tchicaya during an interview in Miami on 21 September 2006, though I had heard similar analysis several times before.

4. President Lissouba's supporters generally spoke about the "betrayal" of Sassou and the PCT at this critical moment and the president's need to take action to maintain his authority.

10

After the Experiment: Electoral Authoritarianism Since 1997

Following the May–October 1997 war, Congo entered into an inevitable period of transition. No relaunching of a democratic experiment was immediately possible after such a traumatic event. Although most of the war damage occurred in Brazzaville, the capital contained nearly one-third of the country's population. Aside from the approximately ten thousand civilians killed in the war, hundreds of thousands of people were displaced from their homes, and tens of thousands of homes were destroyed in the war. Several tens of thousands of refugees fled the country altogether, mainly to the Democratic Republic of Congo. The main hospital in Brazzaville was heavily damaged in the fighting, and a cholera epidemic broke out in refugee-swelled Pointe Noire in early 1998 (Economist Intelligence Unit, *Country Report: Congo,* no. 1, 1998: 12). As the government gradually sought to restore some basic services, and individual citizens tried to repair their broken lives, the remnants of all the militia groups, now operating essentially as criminal gangs, continued preying on the civilian population.

Within a few months, however, Sassou faced an existential choice about his own future as a ruler and about that of his country. He could either relaunch the democratic experiment that had begun in 1991, or he could simply work to consolidate his own rule, averting any real competition for power. In terms of legitimacy and his security in power, there would have been advantages to participating in and winning competitive, fair elections. Although a rapid return to competitive multiparty politics would have been difficult in the aftermath of war, it had been done elsewhere, as in Sierra Leone and Liberia. Moreover, besides conferring him with international legitimacy, this course would have almost certainly made the danger of coup less likely, since liberalizing regimes in Africa have proved less vulnerable to military intervention (Clark 2007). But this course carried the obvious danger that he might have lost the election. Sassou's choice shows that he lacked confidence that he would prevail in such free, competitive elections: he decided instead to perpetuate fear in the population, undermine the unity of the political opposition, and finally manipulate the electoral rules in order to perpetuate himself in power. This strategy led to yet another round of civil war—the deadliest and most vicious of all—before he could consolidate his power.

Despite his choice, Sassou could scarcely resort to the kind of one-party, let alone Marxist-Leninist, ideology that had characterized his first regime. Neither the international community nor the newly altered political culture would permit such an anachronistic ideological cover for dictatorship. Instead, Sassou had to "play the game" of democracy, even if he played it unfairly. Sassou therefore began taking steps soon after seizing power to set up what is most accurately called an "electoral authoritarian" regime.[1] In the wide spectrum of regimes between liberal democracies and forthrightly authoritarian regimes, that of Sassou is far toward the authoritarian end of the range. Opposition parties are allowed to exist, but their operations are hampered by the government. As discussed below, the elections of 2002 were not only unfair and uncompetitive, but also the sociopolitical environment was one that precluded free political competition.

As Table 10.1 shows, Congo's Freedom House scores for political rights and civil liberties have fluctuated within a narrow range since Sassou's seizure of power in 1997.[2] These fluctuations reflect external perceptions of the country as much as the internal realities. It is true that Sassou has been willing to loosen authoritarian controls on the population somewhat when he has felt more secure in power. For instance, when the war of 1998–1999 ended, some civil liberties, such as freedom of speech and the press, improved marginally, as reflected in Congo's 2000 score for civil liberties. The decrease in the same score in 2006, however, resulted from the failure of Congolese courts in 2005 to sanction military officers for massacres committed in 1999.[3] This ruling reflected no real change in the realities of the rule of law in Congo, but only outside perceptions of it. Since 1998, opposition newspapers have been able to function, albeit with some harassment from

Table 10.1 Congo's Freedom House Scores Since the Civil War of 1997

	1998	1999	2000	2001	2002
Political rights	7	6	6	5	6
Civil liberties	5	5	4	4	4

	2003	2004	2005	2006
Political rights	5	5	5	5
Civil liberties	4	4	4	5

Source: www.freedomhouse.org.
Note: 1 = best; 7 = worst.

the government. The electronic media is controlled and/or censored by the government, and foreign media correspondents have been harrassed. The mild fluctuations in the Freedom House scores, including the fall of the Political Rights score from seven to five, do not obviate the fact that Congo has been thoroughly dominated by Sassou and his coterie of followers since 1997.[4]

Following the war of 1997, Congo's political culture was in a state of flux, again at a critical juncture.[5] The recent experience with multiparty politics had been bitter, but people did not necessarily want to return to dictatorship either. Although most citizens craved a return to peace and order, many also understood that a viable, enduring order depended on political legitimacy. In the contemporary African context, in turn, political legitimacy depends on free elections. Sassou's choices in 1998 and thereafter to prevent the resumption of the democratic experiment therefore had a crucial impact on the evolution of the country's elite political culture. His actions served to reinforce the authoritarian and paternalistic politico-cultural norms that had held sway in Congo before 1991. They also served to reinforce the ethnoregional nature of Congolese politics, as Sassou relied so heavily on his fellow northerners to maintain his power. Had his choices been different, Congolese political culture might have undergone changes that would have favored sustained and peaceful multiparty competition.

Historically, the antidemocratic norms of the political elite have been reinforced by his behavior.[6] Sassou's second reign of power has represented a reinforcement of the values of "father, family, and food" identified and described so well by Schatzberg (2001) in the politics of "middle Africa." Both the period of the one-party, Marxist experiment and the period of the democratic experiment were efforts, even if mostly rhetorical, to move away from these traditional norms of politics. The current regime has no ideology of development and no ideal of democratic participation to begin the process of changing these antidemocratic norms. More than in his first political incarnation, and more than Lissouba preceding his second, Sassou now postures to present himself as the "father" of his country. He is a stern and traditional father, offering protection to those who bend to his will but unrelenting punishment to those who oppose him. Meanwhile family is a doubly useful metaphor in the postplural Congolese polity: Sassou depends on his own "family" (writ large) to rule the country, whereas ordinary citizens must depend on their own families for virtually all social needs as the functions of the state go unfulfilled. Finally, food, understood as the patronage of the state required for survival, has never loomed larger as a political instrument of control. If the state sector of the economy briefly withered, the private sector has scarcely blossomed—or been *allowed* to blossom—to meet people's everyday needs. The rule of law and protection of private property in Congo are far too fragile for private enterprise to flourish, and thus access to the state's oil revenues is a bigger obsession than ever under Sassou II.

The first three sections below outline Sassou's use of these antidemocratic and characteristically postcolonial politico-cultural tools in his rule over Congo in the aftermath of the democratic experiment. These sections cover the period from 1997, when Sassou retook power, to the elections of 2002. With these elections, Sassou provided himself with the fig leaf of "legitimacy" that would allow him to rule without a major political challenge until the next presidential elections, scheduled for 2009. The final section below discusses the stagnant politics of the period between 2002 and 2006, leading up to the 2007 legislative elections.

■ Sassou the "Father"

Following his return to power in 1997, Sassou reasserted his role as a traditional father of his people. A traditional father can tolerate no challenges to his right to lay down the rules for the "family." Two of Sassou's most important goals as father coincided closely with those that any sovereign government would pursue: physical control over the entire national territory and international recognition of the government's legitimate authority to exercise such control. In achieving the first goal, however, Sassou proceeded in a particularly paternalistic manner. Rather than negotiate with those who would challenge him, he opted to master and intimidate them militarily.

It was in the adoption and pursuit of a third goal that Sassou showed himself most clearly to be acting in the traditionally paternalistic way that Schatzberg (2001) describes. Sassou's third project was to establish himself as the political master of the country, ruling without any organized or coherent opposition. In the days of the "legitimate" one-party state this task might have been more straightforward. In an era that demands at least the pretense of electoral legitimacy, however, it is considerably more complicated. To achieve this, Sassou had to follow a convoluted political path, along which the tactics frequently shifted, to give him a facade of legal legitimacy. Ultimately, he established an electoral authoritarian regime.

The international partners who mattered most to Congo, roughly in order of their significance, were France, Congo's immediate neighbors, the IFIs, the European Union, the United States, and the Organization of African Unity. France mattered both for security and financial reasons, whereas Congo's immediate neighbors mattered only for security reasons. The IFIs, the EU, and the United States only mattered because of the financial aid or debt relief that they might offer; and recognition by the OAU counted mainly for reasons of public legitimacy.

Sassou achieved international recognition for his regime following a successful incrementalist approach. Only four days after returning to

Brazzaville, and two after having himself sworn in as president, Sassou attended a regional security summit in Luanda hosted by Angolan president José Eduardo dos Santos, whose troops had been critical to Sassou's military victory. Besides dos Santos and Sassou, Gabon's Omar Bongo and the DRC's new president, Laurent-Désiré Kabila, were also present. An agreement signed at the meeting "formally committed all four leaders to a regional security pact under which they [would] not allow armed rebel factions to shelter on their soil" (Economist Intelligence Unit, *Country Report: Congo,* no. 1, 1998: 12). This first foreign trip not only formalized the sympathy of Congo's three key neighbors, but began the process of conferring international legitimacy. Two weeks later Sassou attended a meeting of the African, Caribbean, and Pacific (ACP) states of the Lomé Agreement held in Libreville. At this meeting, Sassou sagely agreed to hand over about a dozen French, Belgian, and Russian nationals who had been detained in Congo on charges of mercenary employment by the Lissouba regime (*Marchés Tropicaux et Méditerréens,* "Libératon de tous les étrangers détenus à Point Noire," 14 November 1997: 2464). This wise move showed him to be a leader of forbearance and tact with his European partners. The following week Sassou was off to yet another, more distant summit—the Organisation Internationale de le Francophonie (OIF) meetings held in Hanoi. This venue exposed him to a wider set of potential supporters, including representatives of France and Canada.

Of course, the international partner that mattered most was France, and the support of the French presidency was evident in the help that Sassou's forces received during the war. Likewise, the president–director general of Elf-Aquitaine had clearly signaled Elf's satisfaction with Sassou's victory on the very next day after Sassou's inauguration as president.[7] Sassou's only remaining task with regard to France was to gain the recognition of opposition French prime minister Lionel Jospin and the rest of the French government. By stressing his commitment to the rule of law and a return to democratic rule as soon as possible, Sassou gradually won over the rest of the French government. When Sassou visited France in December 1997, he dined with President Chirac. Significantly, he also met with Prime Minister Jospin and Cooperation Minister Charles Josselin (Economist Intelligence Unit, *Country Report: Congo,* no. 1, 1998: 13), who were persuaded to recognize Sassou's regime out of solidarity with their president, the practical need to get aid flowing back into Congo's shattered society, and perhaps their recognition that Lissouba had behaved autocratically and sparked the war that had returned Sassou to power.

Other international actors followed the French lead in recognizing the Sassou regime. In February 1998, the EU's representative in Congo "declared that the national forum's adoption of a three-year preelection transition period satisfied the democracy criteria for structural adjustment aid" (Economist Intelligence Unit, *Country Report: Congo*, no. 2, 1998: 10). Five months later, the IMF extended its first "postconflict recovery" credits to Congo, signaling that the regime had been accepted by the donor countries (Economist Intelligence Unit, *Country Report: Congo*, no. 4, 1998: 11). Throughout 1998, various foreign countries reopened their diplomatic missions in the country, as did major international organizations, including the WHO, the FAO, the UNDP, Unicef, and the EU. Sassou deflected international criticism that his regime had come to power by force of arms by launching an international effort calling for the arrest of Lissouba and Kolélas on charges of genocide. By the end of 1998, virtually all of Congo's foreign partners were again doing business with the regime more or less regularly. The United States did not reopen its looted embassy, but it accorded an ambassador who operated from the US embassy in Kinshasa.

In gaining the right to speak exclusively for the Congolese nation on the international stage, Sassou secured a traditionally fatherly role. The metaphor of family—if *extended* family—is also relevant to Sassou's diplomatic dealings in the early post-1997 war months. Sassou began the process of international recognition with the presidents of neighboring countries and with French president Chirac. His personal relationships with these leaders were so deep and long-standing that they were virtually of a familial nature. His daughter married Gabonese president Bongo.

Sassou achieved physical mastery over the territory of Congo during yet another long and bloody civil war (December 1998 to November 1999). Recall that when Sassou retook power in October 1997, he had few forces loyal to him in the southern one-third of the country, all of the territory south of Brazzaville. In these areas, the Angolan army controlled the larger towns (including Pointe Noire) on behalf of the new Congolese regime. Naturally, Sassou aspired to establish his own control over these areas since the Angolan presence could not be permanent.[8] Accordingly, Sassou's army and police commanders gradually moved into the southern regions of the country during the early part of 1998. Many of those recruited to the local police were Cobra militiamen who preyed upon the local populations, committed countless assaults, including rape, and extorted money from the local citizens.[9] In response, members of the Cocoye and Ninja militia groups retaliated, for instance, killing three policemen and an administrative official in the Bouenza town of Mouyondzi in April 1998; in May 1998, former pro-Lissouba fighters seized control of the Moukoukoulou dam in Bouenza for several weeks, cutting off electricity to Pointe Noire (Economist Intelligence Unit, *Country Report: Congo*, no. 3, 1998: 9). In September 1998, ten former Ninjas carried out an attack on a train that had departed from Brazzaville in the Pool region, about 25 miles southeast of the capital (Economist Intelligence Unit, *Country Report: Congo*, no. 4,

1998: 9). Whereas the government described such incidents as banditry, the local populations typically saw them as acts of resistance.

These sporadic events led to all-out warfare again in mid-December 1998 when several hundred Ninja militia began infiltrating the southern suburbs of Brazzaville. Government forces, including the Cobras, and elements of the army using heavy weapons, answered with devastating strength. These forces were supported by occupying Angolan forces and, allegedly, those of other African states. Some 200,000 residents of Bacongo and Makélékélé were pushed out of their homes as government forces took control of the neighborhoods and systematically looted the houses. The refugees fled into the surrounding Pool region, into the northern parts of Brazzaville, and some went across the river to the DRC (Amnesty International 1999: 11; Economist Intelligence Unit, *Country Report: Congo*, no. 1, 1999: 9–10). Some of those fleeing tried to escape along so called *couloirs humanitaires* (humanitarian corridors) set up by the progovernment forces. Along these exit routes, hundreds of young males were killed on suspicion of collaborating with the Ninjas, and virtually all were threatened and looted of their belongings; there were also many instances of sexual violence against women, though this horrifying indignity was not as systematically used as it has been in some other settings (Bazenguissa-Ganga 2001: 71–74).[10] Many thousands returned to southern Brazzaville along the same routes in May 1999, at which time they faced somewhat less harsh treatment (73).

The opposition militia groups also committed grievous human rights offenses against pro-regime "militants" and members of northern population groups. Some even took advantage of the case to victimize individuals belonging to the very ethnoregional groups that they putatively defended (Bazenguissa-Ganga 2001: 79–85). At least one new militia group arose during 1998, leading up to the war of 1998–1999, the Nsilulu. This group is loyal to a charismatic and mysterious cult figure named Frédéric Bitsangou, alias Pasteur Tata Ntoumi.[11] The Nsilulu are inculcated with a strong messianic streak and are sometimes convinced that they possess magical powers, causing them to be fearless—but ineffectual—in combat. This new group, along with the remnants of the Ninja and Cocoyes, were responsible for terrible exactions against the civilian population. The Bitsangou phenomenon strongly recalls the cult of those who followed Matsoua and the N'Zambie Bougie sect, both discussed in Chapter 3.

Despite the fact that all sides had dirty hands in the war of 1998–1999, there can be no doubt that the ultimate victors, the governmental forces of Sassou, were responsible for a majority of the deaths. Even if many of the killings were spontaneously conducted by undisciplined militiamen, there was a political purpose behind them: to demonstrate definitively that Sassou would master control over all Congolese territory without negotiating with his enemies. The two choices given to the population were sub-mission to Sassou's rule or death.

Although countless killings took place throughout the Pool and Nibolek regions of southern Congo, one episode has become infamous, the so-called Affaire des Disparus du Beach de Brazzaville (Fédération Internationale des Ligues des Droits de l'Homme 2004; Amnesty International 2003: 4). Following an agreement between the governments of Congo, the DRC, and the UNHCR in May 1999, several thousand Congolese refugees in the DRC returned home across the Congo River via ferry. Of these refugees, several hundred men were arrested by Congolese authorities upon their return between 5 and 14 May 1999, and some 350 of them disappeared, never to be seen again. Since that time, the Fédération Internationale des Ligues des Droits de l'Homme has pursued this case on behalf of the families of the victims, initially in Congolese and French courts, and later before the International Court of Justice. Several high-ranking Congolese officials have been implicated in the affair. Congolese police chief Jean François Ndengue was briefly arrested in December 2001 while passing through Paris (Fédération Internationale des Ligues des Droits de l'Homme 2004: 6). Other officials implicated include former interior minister Pierre Oba; Norbert Dabira, inspector general of the Congolese Army; and General Blaise Adoua, the former head of Sassou's presidential guard. This incident demonstrated that not all of the killing in the war of 1998–1999 was carried out by unregulated, undisciplined militia fighters.[12]

While the fighting ended in the capital by May 1999, it continued spo-radically in the Nibolek regions for several more months. During these months, the governmental forces gained the upper hand and dealt blow after blow to the opposition militias, which fragmented into ever smaller groups. Finally, several officers from the Cocoye and Ninja militias signed a cease-fire agreement with government commanders in Pointe Noire on 16 November 1999 in a move that "amount[ed] to little more than a surrender" (Economist Intelligence Unit, *Country Report: Congo,* no. 1, 2000: 8). On 29 December, all of the leading commanders signed a more definitive peace agreement that effectively ended resistance for the time being (Economist Intelligence Unit, *Country Report: Congo,* no. 2, 2000: 9). The fact that Pasteur Ntoumi and the Nsilulu were not part of these agreements is notable—these political forces had not yet submitted to Sassou's will. There have been subsequent flare-ups of violence in Congo's Pool region, though these have not brought into serious question Sassou's ability to maintain control.

Sassou's final fatherly project was to make himself the quasi-permanent political master of Congo. Unlike the two roles discussed above, this one was completely incompatible with a competitive democratic system. Sassou deployed the tried and true techniques used by autocrats, and adapted them to the need for electoral legitimacy required by the contemporary political environment. The results show him to be an extraordinarily skilled political operative, given that his ethnic base is relatively small and his record of political reconciliation and economic success modest. Among the classic methods he used to dominate Congo's political scene, four are particularly salient: the neutralization of his main potential political rivals; a "divide and rule" strategy toward the (largely potential) opposition; the manipulation of fear in the general population; and some superficial efforts at public reconciliation aimed at winning over the fainthearted and "normalizing" political processes in the country.

Sassou's neutralization of his main political opponents was greatly facilitated by their own behavior in 1997. There were only three other political figures in the country with enough standing within the southern ethnoregional groupings to unite a majority that might have defeated Sassou electorally: Lissouba, Kolélas, and possibly Milongo. Lissouba's botched arrest attempt at the start of the 1997 war made it legitimate for Sassou to later exclude him from a return to political life. Had Kolélas not joined the same war in September 1997, just before Sassou's triumph, Sassou would have had to deal with him politically. His choice to become Lissouba's prime minister at the eleventh hour forced him to flee the country and made it legitimate for Sassou to prevent his return. Sassou later tried both former leaders in absentia on multiple charges in trials in 1999 and 2000; they were both condemned to death for "attempts at assassination" and "crimes against humanity" at these proceedings. Sassou and his ministers systematically condemned the two for genocide against northern elements of the population, a particularly weighty charge only three years after the real genocide in Rwanda. For good measure, the constitution of January 2002 (Article 58) stipulates that candidates for the presidency must be living within the national territory for twenty-four months before any election. Compared to the other two political figures, Milongo would have been a long shot in the elections of 2002, but he withdrew his candidacy two days before the elections and appealed to his compatriots to boycott the poll.[13] By 2005 Sassou felt secure enough in power and confident enough in the opposition's marginalization to arrange an amnesty for Kolélas, following the death of his wife, so that he could return to Brazzaville.

A second strategy of political mastery used by Sassou was the classic divide and rule approach. The exclusion of the major opposition figures, just discussed, was the first step. The follow-up was to identify potential defectors from within the opposition camps and then offer them major government posts that allowed them to benefit financially. When opposition figures accepted these overtures, they were instantly discredited as potential leaders of a united anti-Sassou opposition. This strategy effectively prevented the emergence of ethnoregional or political party leaders. Two members of Sassou's post-1997 war cabinet are good examples. Martin Mberi, who served as Sassou's minister of transport from 1997 to 2001, had been one of Lissouba's closest advisers, the influential Bembé who had organized the former president's first militia group; Michel Mampouya, meanwhile, was a prominent Lari and member of the MCDDI with close ties to Kolélas. Mampouya accepted the industry and mining portfolio and kept it until after the elections of 2002.[14] Sassou similarly manipulated the Vili-Kouilou constituency of Thystère-Tchicaya by appointing François-Luc Macosso, the second-ranking politician of the RDPS, as the mayor of Pointe Noire.[15] The temptation to take posts offered by Sassou was strong since most individuals of political potential realized, entirely correctly, that Sassou was destined to remain in power.

Sassou complemented these overtures to political opposition figures with more general reconciliation efforts aimed at the larger educated classes, and even the general population. The first of these efforts was the "National Reconciliation Forum" staged by Sassou's loyalists in January 1998. Following the war of 1998–1999 and the launching of a discussion of a new constitution in 2000, Sassou mounted a putatively much deeper reconciliation effort through the Orwellian-named Dialogue Nationale Sans Exclusive (DNSE) in early 2001. The nominal purpose of the dialogue was to permit broad discussion of a draft constitution drawn up by the transitional legislature. The real purposes were to provide a facade of legitimacy to the formal process of selecting new political leaders. The DNSE began with meetings in each of Congo's ten regions, plus Brazzaville, during March 2001, known as the "decentralized" debate.[16] The discussions at the regional DNSE meetings were of matters of real public interest such as the insecurity caused by the presence of too many arms in society, the need to get the nation's schools functioning again, the urgency of improving public health, and so on. Discussion of serious political matters, however, was scant. All of the discussions of the constitution itself were on the fine points of the document, and none challenged the draft constitution's profoundly presidentialist orientation. Each of the regional dialogues was presided over by one of Sassou's ministers, and the discussions were hardly open or frank.[17] Congo's political opposition of the day regarded the whole exercise as a farce, designed to legitimate the forthcoming elections,[18] and most boycotted. In any case, the participants in the regional dialogues were mostly selected by the local Sassou loyalists in charge of organizing them. Predictably, the dialogue at the national level that took place in April did not challenge the draft constitution in any significant way, much less Sassou's right to organize the elections as he wished (Economist Intelligence Unit, *Country Report: Congo,* July 2001: 11–12).

The final method by which Sassou controlled the population and assured the electoral result that he desired in the polls of 2002 was through the manipulation of public fear. Like Charles Taylor of Liberia in the elections of 1997, Sassou sent thinly veiled messages to the population that their real choice was between his own election as president or a return to civil war. The messages were received and understood. A surprising number of individuals in Brazzaville indicated in 2001 that they preferred for Sassou to be elected because that event would signal a return to peace and "normal" life in the country. A great many people just wanted to be able to send their children to functioning schools in safety, and get on with similar aspects of their lives.[19] Meanwhile, most Congolese perceived that Sassou would not give up power without another fight, which few relished. The majority also perceived that Sassou had the virtually unequivocal backing of both the French government and the regime in Angola, whose troops still occupied strategic points in the country. Finally, Sassou's own vigorous political activity showed that he indeed wanted to maintain power at all costs. Sporadic clashes between his military forces and opposition forces during the 2000–2002 period served as a reminder that fighting could resume at any time, as it in fact did, in Pool, following the announcement of the presidential elections in 2002.

The March 2002 elections, in which Sassou was confirmed in power, were of exceedingly low quality (Economist Intelligence Unit, *Country Report: Congo,* April 2002: 14–15), but it did not matter. All of the major opposition figures were either banned from the elections or boycotted them because of irregularities in the preparations. Sassou prevailed with 89 percent of the votes in the first round. The preparation for the elections had been rushed, and few believed in the fairness of the registration procedures, not to mention tabulation process. The large and visible role of France in organizing the elections, and the lack of a neutral electoral commission, thoroughly undermined any illusion that the poll reflected the will of the Congolese people. The lopsided results of the legislative elections, in which Sassou's coalition of parties won about two-thirds of the seats, only confirmed that the process had been manipulated to produce the desired result.[20] Turnout in some opposition strongholds was as little as 15 percent (Economist Intelligence Unit, *Country Report: Congo,* July 2002: 16–17). Some well-known opposition politicians, including Milongo and Thystère-Tchicaya, did get elected to the Assembly. No one could doubt, however, that Sassou had proved himself the master of the Congolese political class in the elections of 2002 or that little stood in the way of him serving at least one seven-year term before again facing serious political opposition.

■ Sassou the "Family Man"

As Schatzberg (2001) suggests, African rulers have often used the metaphor of family to describe and understand their relationships with their own citizens. Like other authoritarian African rulers of his kind, Sassou often uses the rhetoric of national unity in his public statements and equates national unity with that of a family. His language in his annual Message to the Nation on 1 January 2003 was typical: "I say to you again this evening: my engagement for peace and national unity is without ambiguity. It is the foundation of my political action. I will never tire of [this mission]. I will fight always, with my heart and soul, for the consolidation of peace and the consolidation of the unity of our people."[21]

The reality of Sassou's rule has been something altogether different, depending upon a much narrower meaning of the family concept. Namely, Sassou has relied heavily on ethnic and regional constituencies as major bulwarks of his regime. In turn, he has had to patronize them with access to power and wealth. Perhaps surprisingly, the networks of power that he has built since retaking control in 1997 have been more narrowly "northern" than those of the one-party era. At the very center of power, a number of key officials from Sassou's own hometown (Oyo) and even his own family are found.[22] Also occupying key posts far in excess of their demographic weight in the country are other Mbochi figures and members of Sassou's clan. To the extent that Sassou has shared power with those from other regions, there has been a marked preference for those from other northern regions besides Cuvette: Cuvette Ouest, Sangha, and Likouala. During the 1998 to 2002 period, he also made special efforts to woo the population of the neighboring Plateaux with key appointments from that region.

During the transitional period before the elections of 2002, Sassou relied particularly heavily on northern cadres to support his regime. A strong majority of the seventy-five members of the Conseil National de la Transition (CNT) came from the north. This outcome was not surprising since neither UPADS nor the MCDDI participated in the National Reconciliation Forum that selected the CNT (Economist Intelligence Unit, *Country Report: Congo,* no. 2, 1998: 7). The CNT proved to be an embarrassingly compliant rubber stamp for the decrees Sassou issued during this period.

Perhaps the best loci to trace the dominance of Mbochi and northern cadres in Sassou's post-1997 regimes are his successive cabinets. An ethnoregional analysis of the cabinet that Sassou put in place on 2 November 1997 at the start of his second presidential incarnation illustrates the point well. That cabinet had thirty-three total members, of which sixteen were from the four northern regions and three others were from Plateaux, in the center.[23] It featured only six ministers from Pool, four from the Nibolek regions, and three from Kouilou, all holding minor posts. Of the four ministers holding special honorary status as "ministers of state," only one (Paul Kaya) was from the south. All of the key ministries were held by Mbochis: interior (Pierre Oba), foreign affairs (Rodolphe Adada), and information

(François Ibovi); oddly, there was no official minister of defense, but the post was implicitly held by Sassou himself. The Mbochi leader of the Cobras, Jean Marie Tassou, got the ministry of energy and hydrology. One other important office—minister of finance and budget—was given to Mathias Dzon, a Téké, partly as a reward for Téké support for Sassou during the war. Among the southerners appointed to the cabinet of November 1997, they were of two political stripes: they were either former Sassou loyalists from his first regime who had not joined with the 1992–1997 rulers, like Jean-Baptiste Taty-Loutard (who took the petroleum ministry),[24] or feckless politicians such as Martin Mbéri, who many thought was a spy for Sassou inside the Lissouba camp. Another northerner, Firmin Ayessa, was put in charge of organizing the forthcoming National Reconciliation Forum.

The cabinet reshuffle of 12 January 1999 only increased the percentage of northerners in the cabinet from fewer than 50 percent to an even 60 percent (fifteen of twenty-five). The most important change was that Sassou handed the defense ministry to one of his most loyal fellow Mbochis, Justin Lekoundzou Itihi Ossetoumba. On this occasion Sassou also expelled from the cabinet the most prominent southerner, the independent and intellectually gifted Paul Kaya. The only significant remaining southerner was Isidore Mvouba, from Pool, the head of the president's office (chief of staff). This cabinet would remain in place until the executive and legislative elections of 2002, after which Sassou formed a new team.

Sassou's lopsided victories in the elections, discussed above, gave the president the opportunity to make his cabinet more ethnically and regionally balanced. The new National Assembly of 2002 was far more balanced than the old CNT, and thus he had a wider legislative group from which to choose. His actual behavior was to follow a tried and true formula of African ethnoregional dictators: to put most or all of the key posts in the hands of regional loyalists, while giving minor posts to the representatives of other regions and ethnic groups.[25] Sassou's August 2002 cabinet, however, was much stingier toward non-northerners than the African norm. The enlarged cabinet of thirty-four members had only three from Kouilou (including Pointe Noire), two from Niari, and two from Pool (not including Brazzaville). These are the three largest constituencies in Congo aside from Brazzaville itself. Once again, all of the key posts in terms of either security or finance were controlled by northerners, especially Mbochi representatives: defense, Sassou himself, with General Jacques-Yvon Ndolou (Mbochi) as deputy defense minister; interior and security, Oba (Mbochi); finance, Roger Andely (Mbochi); foreign affairs, Adada (Mbochi); administration and decentralization, François Ibovi (Mbochi); mines and energy, Philippe Mvouo (Mbeti, from Cuvette Ouest); planning and territorial development, Pierre Moussa (Mbochi); and justice and human rights, Jean-

Martin Mbemba (Téké). The only southerners with significant posts were Isidore Mvouba (Lari), who served as a de facto prime minister (*Marchés Tropicaux et Méditerréens,* "Composition du nouveau gouvernement Congolais," 23 August 2002: 1808), and Taty-Loutard (Vili) retaining the hydrocarbons ministry. Meanwhile even most of the minor posts were held by other northerners including agriculture (Jeanne Dambenzet, Cuvette), civil service and reform (Gabriel Entcha-Ebia, Sangha), forestry and environment (Henri Djombo, Likouala), higher education (Henri Ossebi, Mbochi), and so on. It is striking that Sassou's cabinet remained so heavily northern- and Mbochi-dominated after his electoral successes.

Sassou also replaced senior-level civil servants from the south with his own loyal northern cadres soon after taking power. Illustrative of this pattern was the replacement of Ange-Édouard Poungui, Sassou's last prime minister before the transition of 1991. Poungui, a native of the Bouenza region, was serving as the national director for the Banque des États de l'Afrique Centrale (the regional bank controlling the CFA franc) at the end of the Lissouba regime. When he returned from a trip abroad in early 1998, the Sassou regime sacked him, confiscated his passport, and replaced him with Pacifique Issoïbéka, another Mbochi (Economist Intelligence Unit, *Country Report: Congo,* no. 2, 1998: 9). Four other senior civil servants from Niari had already been sacked and indeed imprisoned without charge in November 1997 (9). Most lower-level civil servants were allowed to return to their posts, as long as they were not directly implicated in the politics of the previous regime.[26]

Northern and Mbochi dominance in the postdemocratic Congolese army is somewhat hard to document but at the same time widely acknowledged. At the highest levels of army leadership, the pattern is clear. Upon his return to power, Sassou immediately brought back all of the northern officers who had been sidelined by Lissouba (Moukoko 1999: 125; *Marchés Tropicaux et Méditerréens,* "Securité: Nominations aux postes-clés," 21 November 1997: 2539). Sassou put northern officers in charge of five of the country's eight military zones (Economist Intelligence Unit, *Country Report: Congo,* no. 1, 1998: 9). He appointed General Yves Mutondo Mungonge, from Likouala, as his chief of staff soon after seizing power. In January 1999, shortly after the start of the 1998–1999 war, Sassou replaced him with Brigadier General Jacques Yvon Ndolou, another northerner who later became minister of defense. Although Sassou's military representatives have claimed that the integration of former militiamen into the army forces was neutral and open to all,[27] no one takes this claim seriously. Virtually all southern Congolese aver that former Cobra militiamen were gradually integrated into the army, whereas militiamen from the other groups were not. A larger number of former Cobras were taken into the reorganized gendarmerie, as well as into the police forces of southern cities (Economist Intelligence Unit, *Country Report: Congo,* no. 3, 1998: 9). Some junior officers who abstained from the fighting during the war of 1997 were allowed to retain their posts if they occupied technical posts and if the regime did not consider them a security risk. In these cases, however, they retained limited access to arms and intelligence.[28] The army now appears to be much more uniformly northern than it was before 1991, though the claim would be impossible to document.

■ Sassou the "Provider"

A large percentage of Congolese would be offended by the notion that Sassou is a provider of economic sustenance to the people of his nation. But this is not what Schatzberg (2001) was suggesting when he included food—and eating—in his list of central metaphors that explain how power is maintained in African states. Rather, he demonstrated ably that an important tool for African rulers is the control and distribution of economic resources in their territories. As a result, he claimed, citizens of the states in middle Africa (at least) associated the right and ability to "eat," in the large sense of thriving economically, with access to power.

Sassou's behavior since his return to power in 1997 has reinforced this enduring politico-cultural African tradition in Congo. A different set of policies and behaviors, in particular those that would have promoted a vibrant private sector, might have undermined this culture. But Sassou has shown no interest in pursuing any such policy. In fact, even the limited steps taken by Lissouba to create a meaningful private sector economy were reversed. One might wonder how Sassou has been able to maintain such a centralization of state control over the economy when the country is one of the most indebted (per capita) in the world and, as a result, nominally still under structural adjustment. The answer is that the Sassou regime has played a game with the IMF in which it pretends to be serious about reform but never undertakes any real policy changes. The idea that such behavior is possible will come as no surprise to those who have absorbed the fact that numerous African regimes have played this game for over twenty years, never instituting serious reforms (Van de Walle 2001).

The 1998–2002 economic record of the Sassou regime was unimpressive, and the modest successes that the regime enjoyed depended entirely on periodic rises in world oil prices. For instance, Congo's 7.5 percent jump in GDP in 2000 resulted specifically from a near tripling of world oil prices in 1999–2000. Overall, income from petroleum revenues rose from US$1.1 billion in 1998, to US$1.53 billion in 1999, to US$2.3 billion in 2000 (Economist Intelligence Unit, *Country Report: Congo,* various years). Despite this windfall, the average annual growth of GDP for 1998–2000 was still only 3.0 percent, as it was for the entire 1998–2002 period, even though 1997 was a low "baseline" year because of the war. Meanwhile, the population was growing at an annual rate of some 2.6 percent in the same period, so that there was no appreciable growth in average incomes.[29] At the same time, Congo's foreign debt remained virtually static at about US$5 billion, with the government not using rising petroleum incomes to pay down the debt.

One reason for the Sassou regime's undistinguished economic record, despite rapidly rising oil revenues, was a perpetuation of large-scale corruption in Congo. Both the IMF and World Bank criticized the Sassou regime heavily for its high level of corruption and the opacity of its spending habits (*Africa Confidential,* "Caught Out," 21 July 2004; *Africa Confidential,* "Changing Regimes," 20 January 2006; Gourmelon 2004: 86–87). *Africa Confidential* ("A Shining Example," 17 December 2004: 8) had the following to say about the government's management of the state-owned oil company, Société Nationale des Pétroles du Congo (SNPC): "Up to 13 percent of each oil cargo has gone missing, swallowed up in advance payment loans from oil traders involving annual interest charges of 140 percent, as well as other costs related to 'layering'—adding complex, untraceable transactions involving offshore accounts, shadowy traders, and front companies." Few doubt that the Sassou regime skims a substantial portion of the country's petroleum revenues off the official payments both for personal enrichment of loyalists and for buying off would-be opponents.

The policies of the Sassou regime that might have improved the standards of living of the Congolese people were among the worst in Africa. The UN's Economic Commission for Africa (ECA) developed one measure of these policies, the "Expanded Policy Stance Index." The measure "covers three broad areas of policy performance: macroeconomic policies, poverty reduction policies, and institution-building policies" (Economic Commission for Africa 2003: 53). In its annual report for 2003 (54), the ECA assessed the policies of twenty-nine different African countries on these three issues. Of the countries surveyed, Congo finished dead last, just below such low performers as Guinea, Chad, and Zimbabwe (finishing next to last). This miserable performance translated into such tangible results as reduced access to clean water, frequent cuts in the electricity service (to the lucky homeowners and businesses with access to electricity at all), nonpayment of government salaries, a disgraceful level of public health services, rising rates of HIV infection, and rapidly falling levels of public literacy (Gourmelon 2004: 116–119). Even in the official budget, to which the government adhered only notionally, a huge percentage of state expenditures went for security and nonsocial spending. In 2003, about 42 percent of recurrent government expenditures went either to the military or to "sovereign" expenses (i.e., the presidency, territorial administration, or foreign affairs) (121). A large percentage of the spending for health, education, and the provision of other public services was paid out to civil servants, mostly working in the capital, and not to the actual providers of these services. The quality of life in Brazzaville ranked dead last in the world according to one UN study (cited in Gourmelon 2004: 132).

Among those who received the least provision in post-1997 Congo are women. The political disempowering of women and their socioeconomic marginalization have gone hand in hand since Sassou's rise. In fairness to Sassou, Congolese women never broke the fundamentally paternalistic nature of politics in Congo, neither under the Marxist-Leninist regime, nor under the competitive regime of Lissouba. Since there were only *two* women (of 125 members) in the Congolese National Assembly elected in 1993, one cannot condemn Sassou for the fact that only eight gained power in the poll of 2002. Yet one must observe that he seems to have no interest in the kind of bold experiment undertaken by Museveni in Uganda in terms of empowering women. Moreover, Sassou's economic policies (and non-policies), as well as his neopatrimonialist practices, have fallen hardest on women. With the decline of the public schools, families have had to choose which of their children to educate at their private expense. This has created a discrepancy between the female rate of illiteracy (over 50 percent) and that of men (only about 20 percent). Moreover, Congolese women suffered horribly during the country's civil wars, not only through hugely increased rates of physical assault, but also through the loss of men in their familial support networks (Gourmelon 2004: 110–111).

While Sassou was failing to engage in serious economic reforms or to overhaul the dysfunctional civil service, he undid some of the limited decentralization that Lissouba had achieved between 1992 and 1997. Most notably, he did away with the local election of mayors, restoring the practice of central government appointment. The practice allowed him to reward friends like Emmanuel Yoka, from Sassou's hometown of Oyo, with the mayoralty of Brazzaville, or divide the opposition, as he did by appointing Macosso in Pointe Noire. The few meager sources of revenue available to local and municipal governments gained from 1992 to 1997 were taken back by the central government after the 1997 war or destroyed along with private businesses that failed after 1997.[30] In a survey of decentralization in Africa (Ndegwa 2002: 3–4, 12), the results show that Congo had one of the most highly centralized governments and bureaucracies of the thirty countries studied. In the case of Congo, this result was no accident, since Sassou very much wanted to control the ability of the Congolese to "eat" and to make the luxury of doing so at his pleasure.

■ The Stagnant Politics of the Postelectoral Period

Following the manipulated elections of 2002, the opposition to Sassou's regime became weaker and even more fractious than it had been before. The three parties formally opposing the Sassou regime controlled a total of only twelve seats in the 137-seat National Assembly (Clark, forthcoming). Thystère-Tchicaya's RDPS also won six seats, but the former mayor of Pointe Noire had made an agreement in 2000 to cooperate with Sassou's government. This arrangement allowed the erstwhile opposition figure to become the president of the National Assembly and thereby add to the putative legitimacy of the ruling regime. The tiny opposition forces in Parliament, which also included Claudine Munari, did not manage to coordinate either among themselves or with the sizable contingent of independents to have influence on policy or to challenge Sassou's political dominance.

The opposition in exile carried on with its efforts to draw attention to the illegitimacy of the Sassou regime, but without effect. Former presidents Yhombi-Opango and Lissouba, several former prime ministers including Kolélas and Poungui, and countless former cabinet officials tried in vain to have the international community hold Sassou to account. Meanwhile, a younger generation of Congolese opponents of Sassou also sought to organize abroad. Most notably, a group of some two hundred exiled opposition figures gathered in Rouen, France, in June 2003, to organize protests against international support for the Sassou regime. The meeting was organized by Raymond-Timothée Mackitha, president of the Front Uni des Républicains Congolais (FURC), and the economist Paul-Guyvish Matsiona.[31] Their efforts had no more effect that those of similar opposition groups in Europe that oppose virtually every undemocratic regime in Africa. With the passing of the 2002 elections, moreover, they lost the focus that the call for a fair poll had previously provided. In October 2005, Sassou permitted Kolélas to return to Brazzaville to bury his recently deceased wife. Kolélas subsequently remained quiet, suggesting that he had a tacit agreement with Sassou not to challenge openly the latter's regime. Sassou's act of generosity toward his former political rival thus had the salutary effect, from his point of view, of enervating a potentially formidable opponent.

Sassou's biggest achievement following the election was the agreement reached between Pasteur Ntoumi and the Congolese government in March 2003. The agreement was negotiated on Ntoumi's behalf by Daniel Mahoulouba, seconded by the shadowy "Dr. Gozardio," said to be the younger brother of Ntoumi (*Jeune Afrique l'Intelligent,* "De guerre lasse," 23–29 March 2003: 26). Isidore Mvouba, the de facto prime minister and senior ranking representative from the Pool region, served as the government's chief negotiator and signed on behalf of the government. Also important on the government side in the negotiations was Minister of Commerce Adélaïde Moundélé-Ngollo, another Pool native (*Jeune Afrique l'Intelligent,* "L'Adieu aux armes?" 4–10 May 2003: 11–12). Some two thousand of the Nsilulu fighters were demobilized in the early months following the peace accords (Economist Intelligence Unit, *Country Report:*

Congo, no. 3, 2003: 12). Since the accords of 2003, there have only been acts of banditry and some low-grade violence.[32]

The terms of the accord were lopsided in favor of the government, revealing that the rebels were largely beaten, exhausted, and lacking in practical support from the local population.[33] For his part, Ntoumi promised to order a halt to hostilities against government forces and infrastructure; he promised to disarm his fighters and turn over their arms; he pledged to allow the free circulation of people and goods in the region; and finally, he agreed to accept the authority of state representatives in Pool, including the redeployment of the armed forces in the region. For its part, the government offered amnesty to the rebels and pledged to "maintain security in the region," implying that it would prevent government forces from preying upon the local population. It further agreed to engage in the "reinsertion" of the former rebel soldiers into civilian life or into the armed forces; finally, the government emphasized that it would include Pool in its general reconstruction plans for the country.

Since the 2003 accords, Ntoumi's political status has been ambiguous. Despite the accords, he has refused to appear in Brazzaville, reportedly out of fear for his personal safety. In 2005, however, he announced that he would form a political party that would present candidates for the eight seats left vacant in Pool during the 2002 elections. Rumors circulated frequently that Ntoumi would come to Brazzaville and even take up a cabinet post in Sassou's government before the 2007 elections. Although this did not occur, Ntoumi did finally register a political party, the Conseil National des Républicains, with the Brazzaville authorities in January 2007. It remains uncertain how much of a political following the mysterious leader actually has, however; the countless acts of banditry carried out by the remnants of his militia in the Pool region have alienated a large percentage of his would-be Lari supporters.

While Sassou's regime pursued a carrot and stick approach with Ntoumi, it simultaneously tried to restore order to the army. Although little is publicly known about the post-2002 Congolese army, it is clear that Sassou made a serious effort to get the military reorganized and to "reprofessionalize" the ramshackle forces. He has also sought to bring them more reliably under civilian control. Significant reforms were announced after the elections in December 2002. The most important was the appointment of Charles Richard Mondjo as the chief of staff of the armed forces.[34] General Mondjo, an Mbochi and only a colonel at the time of his appointment, was a surprise because two generals from Likouala were then thought to be in line for the position (Economist Intelligence Unit, *Country Report: Congo,* April 2003: 15). New officers were simultaneously made chiefs of staff of each branch of the armed forces, and new inspectors general were appointed. The formerly powerful General Gilbert Mokoki was given charge of the gendarmerie. The clearest fact about the Congolese armed forces is that they remained dominated by officers from the north, and most of the key positions were held by officers from the Cuvette region. General Mondjo remained in office as chief of staff through 2007, suggesting that Sassou approved of his efforts to restore military order.

With the army under secure civilian control, and the opposition neutered, the most important politics of the 2002–2007 period was *internal* to the ruling regime. This political pattern harkened back to the 1970s and 1980s, when ethnic and clan-oriented factions within the PCT jockeyed for position and patronage. The political contest between a hardline Mbochi faction and a more conciliatory faction dominated Congolese political life virtually from the moment that the 2002 elections ended (Clark, forthcoming).[35] The Mbochi faction, as the name suggests, includes those of Mbochi ethnicity close to Sassou for many years, including such figures as Rudolph Adada, Pierre Oba, Florent Ntsiba, Justin Lékoundzou and François Ibovi, all members of post-2002 cabinets. This group took a hard line on the Nsilulu rebellion and sought to keep political space in Congo firmly under the control of northerners close to the president. Another faction, at one point referred to as the "Katangais," favored negotiation with the rebels and more political openness. Ethnically, this faction includes several non-Mbochi northerners, especially a group from Likouala region, including Forestry Minister Henri Djombo and Generals Yves Mutondo and Léonard Essongo. It also includes all of the prominent southerners in the regime, notably PCT secretary general Ambroise Noumazalaye, the powerful Isidore Mvouba, and ministers such as Moundélé-Ngollo.

The future of the PCT itself soon emerged as the main point of contention between these two factions of the regime. The liberal, more progressive faction, led by the president himself, wanted to organize a party conference to "refound" the party and merge it with the other parties in the Forces Démocratiques Unies (FDU) coalition (Economist Intelligence Unit, *Country Report: Congo,* January 2007: 12). This would have broadened the reach of the party, and brought in prominent political figures from the center and south of the country. The hardline faction, led by Lékoundzou, resisted this move, seeking to maintain the PCT as a smaller party dominated by northerners. Because the factions were so much at odds, a potential party conference was perpetually delayed, month after month, beginning in early 2003 when the idea was first mooted. Despite the president's public preferences on this issue, and despite the fact that Sassou had "created a sense of inevitability" about a refounding of the PCT, Lékoundzou and the hardliners seized the initiative by organizing a conference of like-minded party loyalists in October 2006 (13). When this party conference proved to be well attended by PCT loyalists in apparent defiance of the president, Sassou sent two key cabinet loyalists, Emmanuel Yoka and Pierre Oba, to negotiate with them. The conference was then suspended, and a "unified" party conference of both factions was reconvened in December. By that time, however, the hardliners had the momentum behind them and Sassou actually had to withdraw the proposal to refound the party. The Congolese president apparently did not want to force the issue of the refounding on the eve of the 2007 legislative elections, though the move would have potentially broadened his political base (13–14).

The episode over the reformation of the PCT reveals interesting contradictions in the nature of post-multiparty politics in Congo. On the one hand, it does demonstrate that the president cannot have his way on every single political issue. This suggests that the regime is not a purely personalist regime, authoritarian though it is. On the other hand, the episode demonstrates that Sassou is a prisoner to some of the very antidemocratic politicians on whose support he has depended. Namely, the clique around the president wants to control the country for their personal gain, rather than for the public's interest. Their tactics reflect the antidemocratic political culture that has permeated the country's entire history. More specifically, the group operates as an ethnoregional mafia, controlling the army and the key political institutions of the country to the advantage of this subnational constituency.

As with all Congolese regimes since the 1970s, petroleum revenues were the economic bulwark of the post-2002 Sassou regime. Indeed, the rentier nature of the country's political economy was reinforced by rising oil revenues during this period. The "mafia" that now runs Congo has rewarded itself generously with the fruits of the country's petroleum endowment.[36] Beyond that, however, the entire political opposition and even the general population are to some degree politically immobilized by the oil-generated income that Congo has enjoyed in recent years. Had Congo's economy stagnated after 2002, perhaps its politics might have been more contested. As it happened, though, oil prices rose rapidly throughout this period, and export revenues soared right along with them. Congo's export earnings climbed steadily upward from US$2.29 billion in 2002 to US$5.86 billion in 2006, an increase of more than 150 percent over the five-year period (Economist Intelligence Unit, *Country Report: Congo,* April 2007: 5).[37] Largely due to rising oil income, government revenues nearly tripled in the same period, going from 675 billion CFA francs in 2002 to 1,921 billion CFA francs in 2006 (Economist Intelligence Unit, *Country Report: Congo,* April 2003: 20; Economist Intelligence Unit, *Country Report: Congo,* April 2007: 18). These rising revenues were paralleled by rising government expenditures and, notably, the civil servants regularly—though not systematically—received their pay again beginning in 2003. This income received by the functionaries trickled down, as those lucky enough to receive their salaries started small enterprises, hired masons to repair their homes, consumed more in local markets, and so on. As a result, the Congolese economy grew by an average of 4.7 percent per year during the 2002–2006 period (Economist Intelligence Unit, *Country Report: Congo,* April 2007: 5).

The Sassou regime continued to engage in the kind of game with the IFIs that it had in an earlier period. Namely, the regime professed an earnest desire to make real economic reforms, but its efforts perpetually proved to be half-measures, temporary accommodations, and deceitful sleight of hand in financial affairs. Owing to prior financial opacity and indiscipline, Congo was under an IMF "staff-monitored program" at the time of the 2002 elections. Anxious to get debt relief and financial breathing space, Sassou regime worked hard to demonstrate a measure of financial discipline and transparency during 2003 and 2004 (Clark, forthcoming). The regime was finally rewarded with a three-year US$84.4 million "poverty reduction and growth facility" (PRGF) for the country in December 2004. This agreement cleared the way for the elimination or rescheduling of some US$3 billion of Congo's US$6 billion international debt (US Department of Energy 2005; Economist Intelligence Unit, *Country Report: Congo,* January 2005: 12–13). At the time, this was a major breakthrough for Sassou.

By October 2006, however, the Congolese government was out of compliance with this agreement "owing to spending overruns and lack of progress in the implementation of structural reforms" (Economist Intelligence Unit, *Country Report: Congo,* April 2007: 16). The government had not properly carried out the audits of the oil sector that it had repeatedly promised, nor had it stuck to its planned annual budgets. In particular, little of the unanticipated spending went for social services and poverty reductions, the areas that the World Bank had targeted for "investments." What can explain the government's anxiousness to accommodate the IFIs in the earlier period and its indifference to them only two years later? The key to this puzzle is, again, rising petroleum revenues. These rising revenues allowed Congo's foreign reserves to escalate dramatically from a scant US$35 million at the end of 2003 to over US$1.8 billion by the end of 2006 (23). With so much money in the bank by the end of 2006, the Sassou regime no longer needed to feign interest in the efforts of the IFIs to reduce poverty, liberalize the economy, or shine any light on the shadowy activities of the state-operated SNPC.

In step with Congo's economic revitalization following the end of civil war and the rise of world oil prices, foreign investment flowed steadily into the country. Aside from new investments in the petroleum sector to keep up production, major new foreign investments were made in the areas of hydroelectricity, metals, gemstones, and forestry products. A Canadian company (MagAlloy) has been undertaking a major project involving the production and refinement of potash and magnesium in southern Congo since exploration began in the late 1990s.[38] In the area of electricity production, the most notable project was the Imboulou hydroelectric dam on the Lefini River, 130 miles north of Brazzaville. The dam, constructed and partly financed by the Chinese, promises to double Congo's hydroelectric energy production when it is complete (Economist Intelligence Unit, *Country Report: Congo,* April 2007: 22).

In foreign relations, all Sassou needed to do in the postelectoral period was to solidify the good relations with all of the allies identified above, France in particular. After the 2002 elections, Chirac, who had been friends with Sassou since the 1980s, took greater pains than ever to support Sassou. The powerful Dominique de Villepin, both as foreign minister and prime minister, was also entirely solicitous of Congolese needs. According to one French journalist, this was partly because Sassou had uncovered documents suggesting that de Villepin had been bribed by Lissouba (Harel 2006: 78–79). Whatever the reasons, French leaders were remarkably generous to Sassou after 2003. The resolution of a dispute between Total-Fina-Elf and the Congolese government in July 2003 cleared the last unresolved Franco-Congolese issue from the Lissouba era (Clark, forthcoming). In 2003–2004, Chirac helped Sassou clear his debts with the African Development Bank, provided 920,000 euros in military assistance, took steps to impede judicial actions against the regime in the "Beach" case, and defended the Sassou regime against the criticisms of the World Bank (Harel 2006: 79–85). This last action was critical for the regime after Sassou had run afoul of former World Bank president Paul Wolfowitz. Sassou had come to Wolfowitz's attention after running up a massive hotel bill in New York during the UN General Assembly's opening session in 2005. When this came to Wolfowitz's attention, he investigated, and found that Congo had not lived up to its transparency agreements with the World Bank on the oil sector.[39] Wolfowitz was inclined to halt further debt relief until Sassou addressed corruption in his government and made an honest accounting of oil revenues, but Sassou was protected from these pressures by Chirac personally. In 2005, Congo was the recipient of the second largest amount of French aid of any country in the world (following Nigeria) at US$582 million.[40]

Sassou also continued to cultivate cordial relations with his immediate neighbors. In particular, the Sassou regime maintained its very friendly relations with that of dos Santos in Angola. Once the crisis in the Pool region, stimulated by the elections, was controlled, Angolan troops were able to return home in December 2002. Sassou showed his gratitude to dos Santos by cooperating in the effort to control the rebels of the Frente de Libertação do Enclave de Cabinda. Sassou also worked hard to maintain good relations with the DRC despite some tensions caused by the inevitable problem of refugees from each Congo taking up residence across the river.

Most significantly, Congo signed a peace and security agreement with Angola and the DRC on 15 January 2003 in which the three countries pledged to cooperate on security (Economist Intelligence Unit, *Country Report: Congo,* April 2003: 9). Finally, the last potential regional opponent of Sassou disappeared with the ouster from power of Ange-Félix Patassé in the CAR in March 2003. Patassé had empathized with Lissouba during the 1997 war (Clark 1998b: 33) and had subsequently experienced poor relations with the Chirac government. With the assumption of power of François Bozizé in Bangui, Sassou's Congo was surrounded by cooperative newcomers (also including Joseph Kabila) or old friends on all sides. On the broader diplomatic front, Sassou was so fully rehabilitated that he was elected to serve as head of the African Union for 2006.

Finally, Congo rekindled the flame of an old affair with China in the period after 2003. Congo had enjoyed close relations with China during the 1970s, when China competed with the Soviet Union to win friends among the Afro-Marxist regimes of that period. China's thirst for foreign oil, however, and its uncritical respect for the "sovereign rights" of African dictators created a new and practical basis for the renewal of old relationships (Harel 2006: 227–234). In 2003 China became the leading buyer of Congolese exports, primarily petroleum, and it has maintained this position ever since. Meanwhile, China has risen in the ranks of Congo's import suppliers, moving from fourth in 2002 to second in 2005 (Economist Intelligence Unit, *Country Report: Congo,* various issues). Perhaps most important, China has become a major source of foreign investment in Congo, especially in the hydroelectric energy sector, but in petroleum, as well; notably, China's Sinopec signed an important exploration and production agreement with Congo in March 2005 (US Department of Energy 2005). There is little doubt that Chinese political support, investments, and loans at critical moments serve to further bolster Sassou's regime, and shield it against pressures from the West to improve human rights, liberalize the economy, and shed light on the shadowy financial activities of the SNPC.

■ Conclusion

Just as Congo's democratic experiment of 1992 to 1997 need not have failed, Congo was not predestined to a return to authoritarianism after the war of 1997. Sassou might have made different choices than those he did; he might have gradually put Congo back on the path of competitive politics. He might also have taken a myriad of steps to begin changing the country's political culture: he might have made serious efforts to control corruption in the government; he might have elevated the status of women in the polity and society; he might have launched a real debate over how to stimulate economic development; he might have tried to create a more multiethnic, republican national military; he might have tried to generate real reconciliation among the country's ethnoregional groups and their leaders at another national conference, like that of 1991.

Instead, Sassou acted opportunistically to stay in power for as long as possible. He found this easiest to do by taking advantage of the authoritarian political culture that Congo had accrued over many decades. He reinforced that political culture and made any future efforts at democratization all the harder. He chose this path because he was afraid to face fair political competition for power in his own country and because he lacked the courage and patriotism to recognize that the stakes ôf political change in Congo exceed the fortunes of any individual.

Unlikely though the eventuality is, Sassou could still end his second stint in power in a positive way. First, he might allow a freer, more competitive presidential election to take place in 2009. Second, he might give up power peacefully after the end of either his first or second term. Meanwhile, he still might begin to undertake any of the steps suggested above. Although his personality and experience make such outcomes unlikely, Sassou has the freedom to act patriotically if he so chooses. In the longer term, Congo will have another chance to test the waters of competitive democracy whatever Sassou does. When the moment comes, outside observers will be able to judge whether the exhilarating but, finally, bitter experiences of the 1991 to 1997 democratic experiment had any impact on the country's political culture and ability to produce better leaders for the future.

■ Notes

1. On the concept of electoral authoritarianism, see Schedler (2002 and 2006), and for a discussion of the range of different "hybrid" regimes between liberal democracy, on the one hand, and forthright authoritarianism, on the other, see Levitsky and Way (2002).

2. Freedom House annually ranks all states of the world on a scale of 1 to 7 in the areas of "political rights" and "civil liberties," with 1 being the best score and 7 the worst.

3. This was reported on the Freedom House website at www.freedomhouse.org, accessed 16 September 2006.

4. A well-known French Catholic priest in Brazzaville, Père Christian de la Bretèche, described Sassou and his followers to me as "a mafia," and this characterization was not different from that expressed to me by many other Congolese, educated or otherwise, during my visits to the country. Interview on 10 June 2002, in Brazzaville.

5. On the concept of "critical junctures" for national societies, see Villalón and Huxtable (1998).

6. I wish to emphasize the reinforcement in these values of the political elite because a significant number of respondents during interviews in 2001 and 2002 told me that political culture at the village level was far more open and democratic.

Although I cannot judge the validity of this claim, I was struck by the number of individuals who made it. Among others, a vice-rector of Marien Ngouabi University made this point to me in an interview on 4 June 2002 in Brazzaville.

7. See Chapter 8 of this volume. On the visit of the Elf president, see Economist Intelligence Unit, *Country Report: Congo,* no. 1, 1998: 14.

8. The Angolan military presence did, however, last much longer than might have been expected. When I visited Loubomo (Dolisie) in March 2001, I noted the presence of armed soldiers wearing the insignia featuring the Angolan flag on their uniforms. Local residents confirmed for me that the soldiers were indeed Angolans.

9. Interviews with several local residents of Loubomo in March 2001. Also see Amnesty International (1999: 10).

10. One of those fleeing Makélékélé was a personal friend who told me his own harrowing tale. Although none of his family was assaulted or injured, they were robbed of their possessions. When they returned to their home in May 1999, they found it completely looted; their family dog had been shot by Cobra looters.

11. In Kikongo, "tata" means "uncle," and "Ntoumi" means "messenger" or "envoy." The implication is that Bitsangou is a messenger from God.

12. For a recent analysis of these events, see Harel (2006: chapter 6).

13. There is some controversy over Milongo's motives in, first, launching a campaign and then in withdrawing at the last moment. More than one source in Brazzaville told me that Milongo's life was threatened by Sassou's supporters. Others maintained that Milongo realized he had no chance of electoral success and withdrew to deny Sassou the legitimacy of having stood in a more competitive election.

14. When I visited Brazzaville in 2001, Mampouya was living in the Meridien Hotel. Some claimed he was afraid to mingle with the locals in Bacongo for fear of his physical safety because he was working for Sassou. Mampouya did win a seat in Parliament in 2002, though most of the population of his constituency boycotted the elections. Kolélas subsequently excluded Mampouya from the MCDDI after his return to Congo in 2005.

15. Thystère-Tchicaya was bitter about this appointment of his deputy as mayor of Pointe Noire, as was evident in an interview with me on 23 September 2006 in Miami.

16. As part of my participation in a mission of the International Foundation for Elections Systems (IFES) preelections assessment exercise, I was able to attend meetings of the DNSE in Pointe Noire, in Loubomo, and in Brazzaville. The rest of the analysis here is based on notes from my observations at these meetings.

17. I was struck by the presence of many individuals wearing T-shirts sporting Sassou's face and carrying such slogans as "Sassou-Nguesso: Intiateur du Dialogue National Sans Exclusive" ("Initiator of the Inclusive National Dialogue").

18. For instance, the IFES team met with a group of nine opposition figures from the MCDDI, UPDA, and the RDD on 30 March 2001 in Brazzaville. The nine were unanimous on this point.

19. This was an important theme of individuals with whom I spoke in Brazzaville in 2001, women in particular, but politically detached males as well. On the subject of fear in the population, also see Eaton (2006).

20. For a more positive view, see US Department of State (2003). The State Department report is based on the observations of the international monitors, including the International Francophonie Organization, the EU, and the African Union. The conclusions of these organizations were based much more on the events of election day than on the sociopolitical context of the elections.

21. *Le Semaine Africaine,* "Message à la nation du president de la République à

l'occasion du nouvel an 2003," no. 2395, 2 January 2003: 5.

22. The most prominent of his own family members to play highly visible roles in his recent governments have been Sassou's cousin, Pierre Oba, minister of interior and then minister of security and police in successive cabinets, and Sassou's uncle, Emmanuel Yoka, head of the president's office after August 2002. François Ibovi, successively minister of communication and minister of administration and decentralization, is also allegedly a cousin of Sassou.

23. This analysis is drawn mainly from *Marchés Tropicaux et Méditerréens,* 7 November 1997: 2429. Also see Economist Intelligence Unit, *Country Report: Congo,* no. 1, 1998: 10–11. These regions represent only about one-quarter of the country's population.

24. Numerous sources in Brazzaville explained to me that it did not really matter who nominally ran the apparently critical "Ministère de Hydrocarbures" because in fact all petroleum revenues were routed directly through the president's office.

25. On this pattern of ethnoregional balancing under Mobutu Sese Seko of Zaire, see Clark (1995); on the composition of the August 2002 cabinet in Congo, see *Marchés Tropicaux et Méditerréens,* "Composition du nouveau gouvernement Congolais," 23 August 2002: 1808–1809, and Economist Intelligence Unit, *Country Report: Congo,* July 2002: 5, 13–14.

26. This information was related to me in several interviews in 2001 and 2002 in Brazzaville and Pointe Noire.

27. For instance, this was the claim of then-colonel Charles Mondjo, the *commandant de zone* for Pointe Noire, whom I interviewed with an IFES team on 24 March 2001. Mondjo was subsequently named chief of staff of the FAC.

28. This was reported to me in an interview with a colonel from the Pool region in Brazzaville on 4 June 2002. He reported that he, and most other officers from Pool, had refrained from fighting in the 1997 war, and that this accounted for his ability to return to army service.

29. Average GDP growth figures are from Economist Intelligence Unit, *Country Report: Congo,* various years, and the population growth figures are from the CIA World Factbook, www.cia.gov/cia/publications/factbook/geos/cf.html, accessed 30 September 2006.

30. This became clear to Mayor Macosso once he had assumed power in Pointe Noire and found himself virtually without revenues (Diboto 2006).

31. *Afrique-Express* online newsletter, "Des opposants en exil dénoncent le soutien international au Président Sassou Nguesso," no. 272, 17 June 2003, www.afrique-express.com/archive/CENTRALE/congo/congopol/272 opposantsenexil.htm, accessed 17 March 2007.

32. Kolélas's return to Brazzaville in 2005 was accompanied by a bloody clash between government forces and some Ninja supporters, but the fighting only lasted for a brief period before order returned. Economist Intelligence Unit, *Country Report: Congo,* January 2006: 14–15.

33. The short text of the agreement can be found at www.ne-kongo.net/pool /butsiele/avril03/accord-ntoumi.htm, accessed 15 March 2007.

34. This is reported in Economist Intelligence Unit, *Country Report: Congo,* April 2003: 15, where Mondjo's given name is misreported as "Norbert Richard." Mondjo's name is also misreported in *Africa Confidential,* "Brazzaville Breakdown," 30 April 2004.

35. This analysis is distilled from *Africa Confidential,* "Who's Who in Sassou's Congo," 14 June 2002; Economist Intelligence Unit, *Country Report: Congo,* July 2003: 6 and 13; and Economist Intelligence Unit, *Country Report: Congo,* October 2003: 12.

36. Of course, no one knows what percentage of the recent oil revenues have been diverted by state officials. Enterprising Congolese opponents of the regime have been able to underscore ably the financial benefits of holding public office in Congo, however. One website features photographs and descriptions of the properties that have been built or acquired by present and former barons of Sassou's post-1997 regimes. These properties include luxurious apartments and businesses in Europe, as well as elaborate mansions in Congo itself. The website is at http://congo-biensmalacquis.over-blog.com, accessed May 2007. The French journalist Xavier Harel (2006: 15, see also 35–36) claims that US$1 billion of petroleum revenues "mysteriously evaporated" between 2003 and 2005, citing an audit of the firm KPMG.

37. Congo's rising petroleum revenues were chiefly due to escalating world oil prices. The average price per barrel of oil rose from US$23.78 in 2002 to US$58.30 in 2006 (in constant 2006 dollars), according to http://inflationdata.com/inflation/Inflation_Rate/Historical_Oil_Prices_Table.asp, accessed April 2007. Congolese oil production actually peaked in 2000, at approximately 280 million barrels per day (bpd), and thereafter dropped to a rate of about 240 million bpd in 2005 and 2006. See US Department of Energy (2005); and Economist Intelligence Unit, *Country Report: Congo,* April 2007: 6.

38. For background see Derrick (2006: B322). Updates on the project can be found in Brown (2004: 40–43) and at the MagAlloy website at www.magindustries .com/business/magalloy.php, accessed 14 February 2007.

39. See Tony Allen-Mills, "Congo Leader's £169,000 Hotel Bill," *Sunday Times,* 12 February 2006, and Tom Gjelten, "Wolfowitz Corruption Push Clashes with Debt Relief," *Morning Edition,* National Public Radio, 12 April 2007, available at www.npr.org.

40. See the OECD website www.oecd.org/dataoecd/42/0/23704506.gif, accessed 20 June 2007; the bulk of this large sum apparently went for debt relief.

Acronyms

ACP	African, Caribbean, and Pacific (Group of States)
ACR	African Contemporary Record
AEF	Afrique Equatorial Française
ANC	Assemblé Nationale Congolaise (Congolese National Assembly)
AND	Alliance Nationale pour la Démocratie (National Alliance for Democracy)
ANP	Armée Nationale Populaire (National People's Army)
AU	African Union
BDP	Botswana Democratic Party
CAR	Central African Republic
CFA (franc)	Communauté Financière Africaine (African Financial Community)
CFCO	Chemin de Fer Congo–Océan (Congo-Ocean Railway)
CFD	Caisse Française de Développement (French Development Fund)
CONOSELA	Commission Nationale d'Organisation et de Supervision des Élections Législatives Anticipées (National Commission for the Organization and Supervision of the Anticipated Legislative Elections)
CNR	Conseil National de la Révolution (National Council of the Revolution)
CNT	Conseil National de la Transition (National Transitional Council)
CSC	Confédération des Syndicats Congolais (Confederation of Congolese Unions)
CSR	Conseil Supérieur de la République (High Council of the Republic)
DNSE	Dialogue Nationale Sans Exclusive (Inclusive National Dialogue)
DRC	Democratic Republic of Congo (Congo-Kinshasa)
ECA	Economic Commission for Africa

EIU	Economist Intelligence Unit
EU	European Union
FAC	Forces Armées Congolaises (Congolese Armed Forces)
FAO	Food and Agricultural Organization
FF	French franc
FIDH	Fédération Internationale des Ligues des Droits de l'Homme (International Federation of Leagues of Human Rights)
FDU	Forces Démocratiques Unies (United Democratic Forces)
FLEC	Frente de Libertação do Enclave de Cabinda (Front for the Liberation of the Enclave of Cabinda)
FURC	Front Uni des Républicains Congolais (United Front of Congolese Republicans)
GAP	Groupement Aéroporté (Airborne military unit)
GPES	Groupement pour le Progrès Economique et Social (Grouping for Social and Economic Progress)
HDI	Human Development Index
IFES	International Foundation for Elections Systems
IFIs	International financial institutions (World Bank and International Monetary Fund)
IMF	International Monetary Fund
JMNR	Jeunesse de la MNR
MCDDI	Mouvement Congolais pour le Développement et la Démocratie Intégrale (Congolese Movement for Development and Comprehensive Democracy)
MNR	Mouvement National de la Révolution (National Movement of the Revolution)
MSA	Mouvement Socialiste Africaine (African Socialist Movement)
NEC	National Electoral Commission
OAU	Organization of African Unity
OIF	Organisation Internationale de le Francophonie (International Francophone Organization)
PCT	Parti Congolais du Travail (Congolese Labor Party)
PPC	Parti Progressiste Congolaise (Congolese Progressive Party)
PPP	purchasing power parity
PR	proportional representation (electoral system)
PRGF	Poverty Reduction and Growth Facility
PRI	Partido Revolucionario Institutiónal (Revolutionary Institutional Party) (Mexico)
RDA	Rassemblement Démocratique Africain (African Democratic Rally)
RDD	Rassemblement pour la Démocratie et le Développement (Rally for Democracy and Development)

RDPS	Rassemblement pour la Démocratie et le Progrès Social (Rally for Democracy and Social Progress)
SAPs	structural adjustment programs
SFIO	Section Française de l'Internationale Ouvrière (French Section of the Workers' International)
SMD	single-member district (electoral system)
SNPC	Société National des Pétroles du Congo (National Petroleum Company of Congo)
UDDIA	Union Démocratique pour la Défense des Interêts Africains (Union for the Defense of African Interests)
UNDP	United Nations Development Programme
UNESCO	United Nations Educational, Scientific, and Cultural Organization
UNHCR	United Nations High Commissioner for Refugees
UPADS	Union Panafricaine pour la Démocratie Sociale (Pan-African Union for Social Democracy)
UPSD	Union pour le Progrès Social et la Démocratie (Union for Social Progress and Democracy)
URD	Union pour le Renouveau Démocratique (Union for Democratic Renewal)
URFC	Union Révolutionnaire des Femmes du Congo (Revolutionary Union of Congolese Women)
WHO	World Health Organization

References

Achikbache, Bahjat, and Francis Anglade. 1988. "Les villes prises d'assaut: Les migrations internes." *Politique Africaine* 31 (October): 7–14.

Adekanye, J. Bayo. 1995. "Structural Adjustment, Democratization and Rising Ethnic Tensions in Africa." *Development and Change* 95: 355–374.

Africa Contemporary Record. Various years. New York: Holmes and Meier.

Ake, Claude. 1998. "Globalization, Multilateralism, and the Shrinking Democratic Space." In *Future Multilateralism: The Political and Social Framework,* ed. Michael Schecter. New York: Macmillan.

Allen, Chris. 1989. "Benin." In *Benin, the Congo, Burkina Faso,* ed. Chris Allen et al. London: Pinter.

Almond, Gabriel A., and Sidney Verba. 1963. *Civic Cultures: Political Attitudes and Democracy in Five Nations.* Princeton: Princeton University Press.

Amnesty International. 1999. "Republic of Congo: An Old Generation of Leaders in New Carnage." 25 March. amnestyUSA.org.

———. 2003. "Republic of Congo: A Past That Haunts the Future." 9 April. amnestyUSA.org.

Amphas, Mbow M. 2000. *Political Transformations of the Congo.* Durham, UK: Pentland.

Andereggen, Anton. 1994. *France's Relationship with Sub-Saharan Africa.* Westport, CT: Praeger.

Apter, David, and Carl Rosberg, ed. 1994. *Political Development and the New Realism in Sub-Saharan Africa.* Charlottesville: University of Virginia Press.

Azevedo, Mario J. 1999. "Ethnicity and Democratization in Congo and Chad (1945–1995)." In *State Building and Democratization in Africa,* ed. Kidane Mengisteab and Cyril Daddieh, 125–156. Westport, CT: Praeger.

Babu-Zalé, René, et al. 1996. *Le Congo de Lissouba.* Paris: Harmattan.

Baniafouna, Calixte. 1995a. *Congo démocratie: Les déboires de l'apprentissage,* vol. 1. Paris: Harmattan.

———. 1995b. *Congo démocratie: Les références,* vol. 2. Paris: Harmattan.

Bates, Robert H. 1999. "The Economic Bases of Democratization." In *State, Conflict, and Democracy in Africa,* ed. Richard Joseph, 83–94. Boulder, CO: Lynne Rienner.

Bayart, François. 1991. "La problématique de la démocratie en Afrique noire: La Baule, et puis après?" *Politique Africaine* 43 (October): 3–20.

———. 1993. *The State in Africa.* London: Longman.

Bazenguissa-Ganga, Rémy. 1994. "Ninja, Cobra et la milice d'Aubeville: Sociologies des pratiques de la violence urbaine à Brazzaville." In *Urban Management and Urban Violence in Africa,* ed. Isaac O. Albert et al., 115–122. Ibadan: IFRA.

——. 1997. *Les voies du politique au Congo: Essai de sociologie historique.* Paris: Karthala.

——. 1998. "Instantanés au coeur de la violence: Anthropologie de la victime au Congo-Brazzaville." *Cahiers d'Études Africaines* 38, nos. 2–4: 619–625.

——. 1999. "The Spread of Political Violence in Congo-Brazzaville." *African Affairs* 98: 37–54.

——. 2001. "Les violences contre les civils au Congo entre 1998 et 2000." In *Une guerre contre les civils: Réflexions sur les pratiques humanitaires au Congo-Brazzaville (1998–2000),* ed. Marc Le Pape and Pierre Salignon, 59–91. Paris: Karthala.

Beblawi, Hazem. 1987. "The Rentier State in the Arab World." In *The Rentier State,* ed. Hazem Beblawi and Giacomo Luciani, 49–62. London: Croom Helm.

Belmont, Katharine, Scott Mainwaring, and Andrew Reynolds. 2002. "Institutional Design, Conflict Management, and Democracy." In *The Architecture of Democracy,* ed. Andrew Reynolds, 1–11. Oxford: Oxford University Press.

Bembet, Christian Gilbert. 1997. *Congo: Impostures "souveraines" et crimes "démocratiques."* Paris: Harmattan.

Berkeley, Bill. 2001. *The Graves Are Not Yet Full: Race, Tribe, and Power in the Heart of Africa.* New York: Basic.

Berlin, Isaiah. 1969. "Two Concepts of Liberty." In *Four Essays on Liberty,* Isaiah Berlin. London: Oxford University Press.

Bernault, Florence. 1996. *Démocraties ambiguës en Afrique Centrale, Congo-Brazzaville, Gabon: 1940–1965.* Paris: Karthala.

——. 1998. "Archaïse colonial, modernité sorcière et territorialisation du politique à Brazzaville, 1959–1995." *Politique Africaine* 72 (December): 34–49.

Birmingham, David. 1981. *Central Africa to 1870: Zambezia, Zaire and the South Atlantic.* Cambridge: Cambridge University Press.

Bitadys, Benjamin Bilompbot. 1998. "Le jeu d'Elf au Congo." *Le Nouvel Afrique Asia* 101 (February): 5.

Boko, Sylvain H. 2002. *Decentralization and Reform in Africa.* Norwell, MA: Kluwer Academic.

Boudon, Laura. 1997. "Burkina Faso: The 'Rectification' of the Revolution." In *Political Reform in Francophone Africa,* ed. John F. Clark and David E. Gardinier, 23–39. Boulder, CO: Westview.

Boulaga, F. Eboussi. 1993. *Les conférérences nationales en Afrique Noire: Une affaire à Suivre.* Paris: Karthala.

Braeckman, Colette. 1992. *Le dinosaure: Le Zaïre de Mobutu.* Paris: Fayard.

Bratton, Michael, and Nicolas Van de Walle. 1997. *Democratic Experiments in Africa: Regime Transitions in Comparative Perspective.* Cambridge: Cambridge University Press.

Brown, Robert. 2004. "Kouilou Magnesium Project—Set for Success: Solution-Mining Carnallite in the Republic of Congo." *Light Metal Age* 62, no. 4 (August): 40–43.

Bruel, Georges. 1935. *La France Equatoriale Africaine: Le Pays, les Habitants, la Colonisation, les Pouvoirs Publics.* Paris: Larose.

Bustin, Lunda. 1975. *Under Belgian Rule: The Politics of Ethnicity.* Cambridge, MA: Harvard University Press.

Callaghy, Thomas. 1984. *The State-Society Struggle: Zaire in Comparative Perspective.* New York: Columbia University Press.

——. 1987. "Absolutism, Bonapartism, and the Formation of Ruling Classes: Zaire in Comparative Perspective." In *Studies in Power and Class in Africa,* ed. Irving L. Markovitz. New York: Oxford University Press.

Chazan, Naomi. 1988. "Ghana: Problems of Governance and the Emergence of Civil Society." In *Democracy in Developing Countries: Volume Two, Africa*, ed. Larry Diamond, Juan J. Linz, and Seymour Martin Lipset. Boulder, CO: Lynne Rienner.

———. 1994. "Between Liberalism and Statism: African Political Cultures and Democracy." In *Political Culture and Democracy in Developing Countries*, ed. Larry Diamond. Boulder, CO: Lynne Rienner.

Chipman, John. 1989. *French Power in Africa*. Oxford: Basil Blackwell.

Clark, John F. 1993. "Socio-Political Change in the Republic of the Congo: Political Dilemmas of Economic Reform." *Journal of Third World Studies* 10, no. 1 (spring): 52–77.

———. 1994a. "The Constraints on Democracy in Sub-Saharan Africa: The Case for Limited Democracy." *SAIS Review* 14, no. 2 (summer–fall): 91–108.

———. 1994b. "Elections, Leadership and Democracy in Congo." *Africa Today* 41, no. 3 (3rd Quarter): 41–60.

———. 1995a. "The Anglophone-Francophone Rivalry and Rwanda's Crises." Presented at the 38th Annual Africa Studies Association Conference, Orlando, FL, 5 November 1995.

———. 1995b. "Ethno-Regionalism in Zaire: Roots, Manifestations and Meaning." *Journal of African Policy Studies* 1, no. 2: 23–45.

———. 1997a. "The Challenges of Political Reform in Africa," In *Political Reform in Francophone Africa*, ed. John F. Clark and David E. Gardinier, 23–39. Boulder, CO: Westview.

———. 1997b. "Congo: Transition and the Struggle to Consolidate." In *Political Reform in Francophone Africa*, ed. John F. Clark and David E. Gardinier, 62–85. Boulder, CO: Westview.

———. 1997c. "Petro-Politics in the Republic of Congo." *Journal of Democracy* 8, no. 3 (July): 62–76.

———. 1997d. "Political Change and Social Contestation in the Republic of Congo: Sources and Analyses." *International Journal of African Historical Studies* 30, no. 3: 601–606.

———. 1998a. "Democracy Dismantled in the Congo Republic." *Current History* 97, no. 619 (May): 234–237.

———. 1998b. "Foreign Intervention in the Civil War of the Congo Republic." *Issue* 26, no. 1: 31–36.

———. 1998c. "National Conferences and Democratization in Francophone Africa." In *Multiparty Democracy and Political Change*, ed. John M. Mbaku and Julius O. Ihonvbere. Aldershot, UK: Ashgate.

———. 2000. "Congo-Brazzaville." *Africa Contemporary Record, 1992–1994*, vol. 24, B223–231. New York: Holmes & Meier.

———. 2001. "Explaining Ugandan Intervention in Congo: Evidence and Interpretations." *Journal of Modern African Studies* 39, no. 2: 261–287.

———. 2002a. "The Neo-Colonial Context of the Democratic Experiment of Congo-Brazzaville." *African Affairs* 101, no. 403 (April): 171–192.

———. 2002b. "Republic of Congo: Uneasy Peace and Gradual Economic Reform." *Africa Contemporary Record, 1994–1996*, vol. 25, B228–249. New York: Holmes & Meier.

———. 2002c. "Resource Revenues and Political Development in Sub-Saharan Africa: Congo Republic in Comparative Perspective." *Afrika Spectrum* 37, no. 1: 25–41.

———. 2005a. "The Collapse of the Democratic Experiment in the Republic of Congo: A Thick Description." In *The Fate of Africa's Democratic Experiments*, ed. Leonardo A. Villalón and Peter VonDoepp, 96–125. Bloomington: Indiana University Press.

———. 2005b. "Petroleum Revenues and Political Development in the Congo Republic: The Democratic Experiment and Beyond." In *Resource Politics in Sub-Saharan Africa,* ed. Matthias Basedau and Andreas Mehler, 121–144. Hamburg: Institute for African Studies.

———. 2006. "Rwanda: Tragic Land of Dual Nationalisms." In *After Independence: Making and Protecting the Nation in Post-Colonial and Post-Communist States,* ed. Lowell W. Barrington, 71–106. Ann Arbor: University of Michigan Press.

———. 2007. "Political Liberalization and Military Intervention in African States: Democratic Legitimacy and Military Restraint." *Journal of Democracy* 18, no. 3 (July): 141–155.

———. Forthcoming. "Congo-Brazzaville." *Africa Contemporary Record, 2003–2004,* vol. 29. New York: Holmes & Meier.

Clark, John F., and David E. Gardinier, ed. 1997. *Political Reform in Francophone Africa.* Boulder, CO: Westview.

Clark, John F., and Bruce A. Magnusson. 2005. "Understanding Democratic Survival and Democratic Failure in Africa: Insights from the Divergent Democratic Experiments in Benin and Congo." *Comparative Studies in Society and History* 47, no. 3 (July): 552–582.

Cohen, Abner. 1974. *Two-Dimensional Man: An Essay on the Anthropology of Power and Symbolism in Complex Society.* Berkeley: University of California Press.

Colton, Timothy, and Cindy Skach. 2005. "The Russian Predicament." *Journal of Democracy* 16, no. 3 (July): 113–126.

Comaroff, John L., and Jean Comaroff, ed. 1999. *Civil Society and the Political Imagination in Africa: Critical Perspectives.* Chicago: University of Chicago Press.

Conner, Walker. 1994. *Ethnonationalism: The Quest for Understanding.* Princeton: Princeton University Press.

"La constitution de la République du Congo." 1992. *Afrique Contemporaine* 162 (2nd trimester): 35–59.

Coppedge, Michael. 1994. "Venezuela: Democratic Despite Presidentialism." In *The Failure of Presidential Democracy: The Case of Latin America,* ed. Juan J. Linz and Arturo Valenzuela, 322–347. Baltimore: Johns Hopkins University Press.

Coquery-Vidrovitch, Catherine. 1972. *Le Congo au temps des grandes compagnies concessionaires, 1898–1930.* Paris: Mouton.

———. 1997. *African Women: A Modern History.* Trans. Beth Gillian Raps. Boulder, CO: Westview.

Coulon, Christian. 1988. "Senegal: The Development and Fragility of a Semidemocracy." In *Democracy in Developing Countries,* ed. Larry Diamond, Juan J. Linz, and Seymour Martin Lipset. Boulder, CO: Lynne Rienner.

Crook, Richard, and James Manor. 1998. *Democracy and Decentralization in South Asia and West Africa.* Cambridge: Cambridge University Press.

Cumming, Gordon. 1995. "French Development Assistance to Africa: Towards a New Agenda?" *African Affairs* 94 (1995).

Dahl, Robert A. 1971. *Polyarchy: Participation and Opposition.* New Haven: Yale University Press.

———. 1997. "Development and Democratic Culture." In *Consolidating the Third Wave Democracies,* ed. Larry Diamond et al. Baltimore: Johns Hopkins University Press.

Davis, John U., and Aboubacar B. Kossomi. 2001. "Niger Gets Back on Track." *Journal of Democracy* 12, no. 3 (July): 80–87.

Decalo, Samuel. 1981. "People's Republic of the Congo." In *Marxist Governments: A World Survey,* vol. 1, ed. Bogdam Szajkowski. London: Macmillan.

———. 1990. *Coups and Army Rule in Africa: Motivations and Constraints,* 2nd ed. New Haven: Yale University Press.

Decalo, Samuel (with Virginia Thompson, and Richard Adloff). 1996. *Historical Dictionary of Congo,* 3rd ed. Lanham, MD: Scarecrow.

———. 1997. "Benin: First of the New Democracies." In *Political Reform in Francophone Africa,* ed. John F. Clark and David E. Gardinier, 43–61. Boulder, CO: Westview.

Derrick, Jonathan. 1995. "Benin: Peaceful Revolution Paves the Way for Democracy and Bankruptcy." *Africa Contemporary Record, 1989–1990,* vol. 22. New York: Holmes & Meier.

———. 2006. "Republic of the Congo: Democratic Transition Consolidates Sassou-Nguesso's Victory." *Africa Contemporary Record, 2001–2002,* vol. 28, B311–B322. New York: Holmes & Meier.

Devey, Mariel. 1997. "L'amélioration du cadre macro-économique: des résultats compromis." *Marchés Tropicaux et Méditerréens* 6886 (June): 6–16.

Diamond, Larry. 1992. "Economic Development and Democracy Reconsidered." In *Reexamining Democracy: Essays in Honor of Seymour Martin Lipset,* ed. Larry Diamond and Gary Marks. Newbury Park: Sage.

———. 1999. *Developing Democracy: Towards Consolidation.* Baltimore: Johns Hopkins University Press.

Diamond, Larry, Juan J. Linz, and Seymour Martin Lipset, ed. 1988. *Democracy in Developing Countries: Volume Two, Africa.* Boulder, CO: Lynne Rienner.

Diamond, Larry, et al., ed. 1997. *Consolidating the Third Wave Democracies.* Baltimore: Johns Hopkins University Press.

Diboto, Daniel Lobé. 2006. "Interview with François-Luc Macosso, Mayor of Pointe Noire, 1997–2002." www.congopage.com/article.php3?id_article=3918, accessed 9 September 2006.

Dimoneka, Erasme. 1997. "Anatomie et crise des partis-ethnie." *Rupture* 9 (1st trimester): 25–36.

Dorier-Apprill, Élizabeth. 1996. "Jeunesse et ethnicités citadines à Brazzaville." *Politique Africaine* 64 (December): 73–88.

Eaton, David. 2006. "Diagnosing the Crisis in the Republic of Congo." *Africa* 76, no. 1: 44–69.

Economic Commission for Africa. 2003. *Economic Report on Africa 2003: Accelerating the Pace of Development.* Addis Ababa: ECA.

Elazar, Daniel J. 1997. "Contrasting Unitary and Federal Systems." *International Political Science Review* 18, no. 3 (July): 237–251.

Elgie, Robert, ed. 1999. *Semi-Presidentialism in Europe.* Oxford: Oxford University Press.

———. 2005. "Variations on a Theme." *Journal of Democracy* 16, no. 3 (July): 98–112.

Eller, Jack, and Reed Coughlan. 1996. "The Poverty of Primordialism: The Demystification of Ethnic Attachments." *Ethnic and Racial Studies* 16, no. 2.

Englebert, Pierre, and James Ron. 2004. "Primary Commodities and War: Congo-Brazzaville's Ambivalent Resource Curse." *Comparative Politics* (October): 61–81.

Fatton, Robert. 1992. *Predatory Rule: State and Civil Society in Africa.* Boulder, CO: Lynne Rienner.

Fédération Internationale des Ligues des Droits de l'Homme. 1998. "Entre

Arbitraire et Impunite: Les droits de l'homme au Congo-Brazzaville" (April). www.fidh.org/rapports/congo.htm.

———. 2004. "République du Congo: Affaire des 'Disparus du Beach' de Brazzaville." Report no. 400 (July). www.fidh.org/.

Fernandez, Damian. 2000. *Cuba and the Politics of Passion.* Austin: University of Texas Press.

Forrest, Joshua B. 2005. "Democratization in a Divided Urban Political Culture: Guinea-Bissau." In *The Fate of Africa's Democratic Experiments,* ed. Leonardo A. Villalón and Peter VonDoepp. Bloomington: Indiana University Press.

Fottorino, Eric. 1990. "France-Afrique: Les liaisons dangereuses: La démocratie à contrecouer." *Le Monde dossier. Sommet Franco-African à la Baule.* www.lemonde.fr/dossier/africa/1003.htm.

Frank, Philippe. 1997. "Ethnies et partis: le cas du Congo." *Afrique Contemporaine* 182 (2nd trimester): 3–15.

Friedman, Kasja Ekholm, and Anne Sundberg. 1994. "Ethnic War and Ethnic Cleansing in Brazzaville." Unpublished manuscript.

Frye, Timothy. 2002. "Presidents, Parliaments, and Democracy: Insights from the Post-Communist World." In *The Architecture of Democracy,* ed. Andrew Reynolds, 81–103. Oxford: Oxford University Press.

Fukuyama, Francis. 1993. *The End of History and the Last Man.* New York: Harper Perennial.

Galloy, Martine Renée. 1997. "The Electoral Process and Women Parliamentarians: Identifying the Obstacles of the Congolese Experience." Paper presented at the Africa Leadership Forum, Accra, Ghana, 27–29 January.

Galvan, Denis. 2001. "Political Turnover and Social Change in Senegal." *Journal of Democracy* 12, no. 3 (July): 51–62.

Gardinier, David. 1997a. "Gabon: Limited Reform and Regime Survival." In *Political Reform in Francophone Africa,* ed. John F. Clark and David E. Gardinier, 145–161. Boulder, CO: Westview.

———. 1997b. "The Historical Origins of Francophone Africa." In *Political Reform in Francophone Africa,* ed. John F. Clark and David E. Gardinier, 9–22. Boulder, CO: Westview.

———. 2000. "France and Gabon Since 1993: The Reshaping of a Neo-Colonial Relationship." *Journal of Contemporary African Studies* 18, no. 2: 225–242.

Gaulme, François. 1994. "France-Afrique: Une crise de cooperation." *Études* 380 (January): 41–52.

Gauze, René. 1973. *The Politics of Congo-Brazzaville.* Translated, edited, and supplemented by Virginia Thompson and Richard Adloff. Stanford: Hoover Institution Press.

Gazibo, Mamoudou. 2005. "Foreign Aid and Democratization: Benin and Niger Compared." *African Studies Review* 48, no. 3 (December): 67–87.

Geertz, Clifford. 1973. *The Interpretation of Cultures: Selected Essays.* New York: Basic.

Gervais, Myriam. 1997. "Niger: Regime Change, Economic Crisis, and Perpetuation of Privilege." In *Political Reform in Francophone Africa,* ed. John F. Clark and David E. Gardinier. Boulder, CO: Westview.

Ghai, Yash Pal. 2002. "Constitutional Asymmetries: Communal Representation, Federalism, and Cultural Autonomy." In *The Architecture of Democracy,* ed. Andrew Reynolds, 141–170. Oxford: Oxford University Press.

Giddens, Anthony. 1984. *The Constitution of Society: Introduction of the Theory of Structuration.* Berkeley: University of California Press.

Gide, André. 1994 [1927]. *Travels in the Congo.* Trans. Dorothy Bussy. Hopewell, NJ: Ecco.

Gil, Graeme. 2000. *The Dynamics of Democratization: Elites, Civil Society and the Transition Process.* New York: St. Martin's.

Glaser, Antoine, and Stephen Smith. 2005. *Comment la France a perdu l'Afrique.* Paris: Calmann-Lévy.

Gourmelon, Isabelle. 2004. "Gestion de la rente pétrolière au Congo Brazzaville: Mal gouvernance et violations des droits de l'homme." Report of the Fédération des Ligues des Droits de l'Homme (19 May). www.fidh.org.

Gray, Christopher J. 2002. *Colonial Rule and Crisis in Equatorial Africa: Southern Gabon, ca. 1850–1940.* Rochester, NY: University of Rochester Press.

Green, Daniel, ed. 2002. *Constructivism and Comparative Politics.* Armonk, NY: M. E. Sharpe.

———. 2002. "Constructivist Comparative Politics: Foundations and Framework." In *Constructivism and Comparative Politics,* ed. Daniel Green, 3–59. Armonk, NY: M. E. Sharpe.

Grosh, Barbara. 1994. "Through the Structural Adjustment Minefield: Politics in an Era of Economic Liberalization." In *Economic Change and Political Liberalization in Sub-Saharan Africa,* ed. Jennifer A. Widner, 29–46. Baltimore: Johns Hopkins University Press.

Gruénais, Marc-Éric. 1997. "Congo: La fin d'une pseudo-démocratie." *Politique Africaine* 68: 125–133.

Gruénais, Marc-Éric, Florent Mouanda Mbambi, and Joseph Tonda. 1995. "Messies, fétiches et lutte de pouvoirs entre les 'grands hommes' du Congo démocratique." *Cahiers d'Études Africaines* 137, no. 1.

Harbeson, John W., ed. 1987. *The Military in African Politics.* Westport, CT: Praeger.

Harbeson, John W., Donald Rothchild, and Naomi Chazan. 1994. *Civil Society and the State in Africa.* Boulder, CO: Lynne Rienner.

Harel, Xavier. 2006. *Afrique pillage à huis clos: Comment un poignée d'initiés siphonne le pétrole africain.* Paris: Fayard.

Haugerud, Angelique. 1993. *The Culture of Politics in Modern Kenya.* Cambridge: Cambridge University Press.

Herbst, Jeffrey. 2000. *States and Power in Africa: Comparative Lessons in Authority and Control.* Princeton: Princeton University Press.

Hermann, Margaret G., Thomas Preston, Baghat Korany, and Timothy M. Shaw. 2001. "Who Leads Matters: The Effects of Powerful Individuals." *International Studies Review* 3, no. 2: 81–131.

Hochschild, Adam. 1998. *King Leopold's Ghost: A Story of Greed, Terror, and Heroism in Colonial Africa.* New York: Houghton Mifflin.

Hollis, Martin, and Steve Smith. 1990. *Explaining and Understanding International Relations.* Oxford: Oxford University Press.

Holm, John. 1988. "Botswana: A Paternalistic Democracy." In *Democracy in Developing Countries,* ed. Larry Diamond, Juan J. Linz, and Seymour Martin Lipset. Boulder, CO: Lynne Rienner.

Horowitz, Donald. 1975. "Ethnic Identity." In *Ethnicity: Theory and Experience,* ed. Nathan Glazer and Daniel P. Moynihan, 111–140. Cambridge, MA: Harvard University Press.

———. 1980. *Coup Theories and Officers' Motives: Sri Lanka in Comparative Perspective.* Princeton: Princeton University Press.

Hsiao, Hsin-Huang, and Hagen Koo. 1997. "The Middle Classes and

Democratization." In *Consolidating the Third Wave Democracies,* ed. Larry Diamond, Marc F. Plattner, Yun-han Chu, and Hung-mao Tien. Baltimore: Johns Hopkins University Press.

Huntington, Samuel. 1968. *Political Order in Changing Societies.* New Haven: Yale University Press.

———. 1991. *The Third Wave: Democratization in the Late Twentieth Century.* Norman: University of Oklahoma Press.

Hyden, Goran. 1980. *Beyond Ujamma in Tanzania: Underdevelopment and an Uncaptured Peasantry.* Berkeley: University of California Press.

Ikounga, Martial De-Paul. 2000. *Congo-Brazzaville: Devoir de Parole.* Paris: NM7 Éditions.

Inglehart, Ronald, and Christian Welzel. 2005. *Modernization, Cultural Change, and Democracy: The Human Development Sequence.* Cambridge: Cambridge University Press.

International Foundation for Elections Systems. 1992. "Observers' Report on Election in Congo." Unpublished report.

Isaacs, Harold. 1975. *The Idols of the Tribe: Group Identity and Political Change.* New York: Harper and Row.

Jackson, Robert, and Carl Rosberg. 1982. *Personal Rule in Black Africa: Prophet, Prince, Autocrat and Tyrant.* Berkeley: University of California Press.

Janis, Irving L. 1972. *Victims of Groupthink: A Psychological Study of Foreign Policy Decisions and Fiascoes.* Boston: Houghton Mifflin.

Jones, Mark P. 1997. "Evaluating Argentina's Presidential Democracy: 1983–1995." In *Presidentialism and Democracy in Latin America,* ed. Scott Mainwaring and Matthew S. Shugart, 259–299. Cambridge: Cambridge University Press.

Joseph, Richard, ed. 1999. *State, Conflict, and Democracy in Africa.* Boulder, CO: Lynne Rienner.

Kabongo-Mbaya, Philippe. 2000. "Société civile et devenir politique du Congo-Brazzaville." In *Les Congo dans la tourmente,* ed. Rupture-Solidarité, 117–136. Paris: Karthala.

Karlström, Mikael. 1999. "Civil Society and Its Presuppositions: Lessons from Uganda." In *Civil Society and the Political Imagination in Africa,* ed. John L. Comaroff and Jean Comaroff, 104–123. Chicago: University of Chicago Press.

King, Gary, Robert O. Keohane, and Sidney Verba. 1994. *Designing Social Inquiry: Scientific Inference in Qualitative Research.* Princeton: Princeton University Press.

Kirk-Greene, Anthony. 1995. "'Le roi est mort! Vive le roi!': The Comparative Legacy of Chiefs After the Transfer of Power in British and French West Africa." In *State and Society in Francophone Africa Since Independence,* ed. Anthony Kirk-Greene and Daniel Bach, 16–33. London: Macmillan.

Kirk-Greene, Anthony, and Daniel Bach, ed. 1995. *State and Society in Francophone Africa Since Independence.* London: Macmillan.

Kizerbo, Joseph. 1972. *Histoire de l'Afrique noire.* Paris: Hatier.

Kohli, Atul. 2004. *State-Directed Development.* Cambridge: Cambridge University Press.

Kombo, Ernest. 1992. "Nécessité et urgence d'un engagement communautaire." *Telema* 3–4.

Koula, Yitzhak. 1999. *La démocratie congolaise "brûlée" au pétrole.* Paris: Harmattan.

Kounzilat, Alain. 1993. *Tribus et Ethies du Congo.* Paris: ICES.

──────. 1998. *Ninjas, Cobras et Zoulous: Les guerres congolaises.* Paris: ICES.

Kouvibidila, Gaston-Jonas. 2000. *Histoire du multipartisme au Congo-Brazzaville: Les débuts du'une crise attendee, 1992–1993.* Paris: Harmattan.

Kouvouama, Abel. 1988. "A chacun son prophète." *Politique Africaine* 31 (October).

Kowert, Paul. 2002. *Groupthink or Deadlock: When Do Leaders Learn from Their Advisors?* New York: State University of New York Press.

Krop, Pascal. 1994. *Le génocide Franco-Africain: Faut-il juger les Mitterrand?* Paris: Editions Jean-Claude Lattès.

Kuhn, Thomas. 1962. *The Structure of Scientific Revolutions.* Chicago: University of Chicago Press.

Laitin, David. 1986. *Hegemony and Culture: Politics and Religious Change Among the Yoruba.* Chicago: University of Chicago Press.

Lanne, Bernard. 1997. "Chad: Regime Change, Increased Insecurity, and Blockage of Further Reforms." In *Political Reform in Francophone Africa,* ed. John F. Clark and David E. Gardinier, 267–286. Boulder, CO: Westview.

Leites, Nathan. 1951. *The Operational Code of the Politburo.* New York: McGraw Hill.

Lemarchand, René. 1970. *Rwanda and Burundi.* London: Pall Mall.

──────. 1994. *Burundi: Ethnocide as Discourse and Practice.* Cambridge: Cambridge University Press.

Le Vine, Victor T. 1987. "Military Rule in the People's Republic of Congo." In *The Military in African Politics,* ed. John W. Harbeson, 123–140. Westport, CT: Praeger.

──────. 2004. *Politics in Francophone Africa.* Boulder, CO: Lynne Rienner.

Levitsky, Steven, and Lucan A. Way. 2002. "The Rise of Competitive Authoritarianism." *Journal of Democracy* 13, no. 2 (April): 51–64.

──────. 2005. "International Linkage and Democratization." *Journal of Democracy* 16, no. 3 (July): 20–34.

Lijphart, Arend. 1999. *Patterns of Democracy: Government Forms and Performance in Thirty-Six Countries.* New Haven: Yale University Press.

──────. 2002. "The Wave of Power-Sharing Democracy." In *The Architecture of Democracy,* ed. Andrew Reynolds, 37–54. Oxford: Oxford University Press.

Lindberg, Staffan I. 2001. "Forms of States, Governance, and Regimes: Reconceptualizing the Prospects for Democratic Consolidation in Africa." *International Political Science Review* 22, no. 2 (April): 173–199.

Linz, Juan J. 1978. *The Breakdown of Democratic Regimes.* Baltimore: Johns Hopkins University Press.

──────. 1994. "Presidential or Parliamentary Democracy: Does It Make a Difference?" In *The Failure of Presidential Democracy,* ed. Juan J. Linz and Arturo Valenzuela, 3–87. Baltimore: Johns Hopkins University Press.

Linz, Juan J., and Alfred Stephan. 1996. *Problems of Democratic Transition and Consolidation: Southern Europe, South America, and Post-Communist Europe.* Baltimore: Johns Hopkins University Press.

Linz, Juan J., and Arturo Valenzuela, ed. 1994. *The Failure of Presidential Democracy.* Baltimore: Johns Hopkins University Press.

Lipset, Seymour Martin. 1959. "Some Social Requisites of Democracy: Economic Development and Political Legitimacy." *American Political Science Review* 53, no. 1 (March): 69–105.

Lissouba, Pascal. 1997. *Congo: Les fruits de la passion partagée.* Paris: Editions Odilon Media.

"Loi électorale [of Congo]." 1992. Reprinted in Calixte Baniafouna, *Congo démocratie: Les références,* vol. 2 (1995), 112–138. Paris: Harmattan.

Longman, Timothy. 1997. "Rwanda: Democratization and Disorder: Political Transformation and Social Deterioration." In *Political Reform in Francophone Africa,* ed. John F. Clark and David E. Gardinier, 287–306. Boulder, CO: Westview.

———. 1998. "Rwanda: Chaos from Above." In *The African State at a Critical Juncture,* ed. Leonardo A. Villalón and Phillip A. Huxtable, 75–92. Boulder, CO: Lynne Rienner.

Mabeko-Tali, Jean-Michel. 2000. "Quelques dessous diplomatiques de l'intervention Angolaise dans le conflit Congolais de 1997." In *Les Congo dans la tourmente,* ed. Rupture-Solidarité, 153–164. Paris: Karthala.

MacGaffey, Wyatt. 1970. "The Religious Commissions of the BaKongo." *Man* 5, no. 1.

Magnusson, Bruce. 1999. "Testing Democracy in Benin: Experiments in Institutional Reform." In *State, Conflict, and Democracy in Africa,* ed. Richard Joseph, 217–238. Boulder, CO: Lynne Rienner.

———. 2001. "Democratization and Domestic Insecurity: Navigating the Transition in Benin." *Comparative Politics* 33, no. 2 (January): 211–230.

———. 2005. "Democratic Legitimacy in Benin: Institutions and Identity in a Regional Context." In *The Fate of Africa's Democratic Experiments,* ed. Leonardo A. Villalón and Peter VonDoepp, 75–95. Bloomington: Indiana University Press.

Magnusson, Bruce, and John F. Clark. 2005. "Understanding Democratic Survival and Democratic Failure in Africa: Insights from Divergent Democratic Experiments in Benin and Congo (Brazzaville)." *Comparative Studies in Society and History* 45, no. 3 (July): 552–582.

Mainwaring, Scott. 1997. "Multipartism, Robust Federalism, and Presidentialism in Brazil." In *Presidentialism and Democracy in Latin America,* ed. Scott Mainwaring and Matthew S. Shugart, 55–109. Cambridge: Cambridge University Press.

Mainwaring, Scott, and Matthew S. Shugart. 1997a. "Juan Linz, Presidentialism, and Democracy: A Critical Appraisal." *Comparative Politics* 29, no. 4 (July): 449–471.

Mainwaring, Scott, and Matthew S. Shugart, ed. 1997b. *Presidentialism and Democracy in Latin America.* Cambridge: Cambridge University Press.

Makonda, Antoine. 1988. "Une école 'pour le peuple'?" *Politique Africaine* 31 (October).

Mamdani, Mahmood. 1996. *Citizen and Subject: Contemporary Africa and the Legacy of Late Colonialism.* Princeton: Princeton University Press.

———. 2001. *When Victims Become Killers: Colonialism, Nativism, and the Genocide in Rwanda.* Princeton: Princeton University Press.

Mampouya, Joseph. 1983. *Le tribalism au Congo.* Paris: Pensée Universelle.

Manning, Carrie. 2005. "Assessing Adaptation to Democratic Politics in Mozambique: The Case of Frelimo." In *The Fate of Africa's Democratic Experiments,* ed. Leonardo A. Villalón and Peter VonDoepp. Bloomington: Indiana University Press.

Manning, Patrick. 1988. *Francophone Sub-Saharan Africa, 1880–1985.* Cambridge: Cambridge University Press.

Marcus, Richard. 2005. "Elections and the Legitimization of Autocracy in Madagascar." In *The Fate of Africa's Democratic Experiments,* ed. Leonardo A. Villalón and Peter VonDoepp, 153–174. Bloomington: Indiana University Press.

Martin, Guy. 1995. "Continuity and Change in Franco-African Relations." *Journal of Modern African Studies* 33, no. 1.

Martin, Phyllis. 1972. *The External Trade of the Loango Coast, 1576–1870: The Effects of Changing Commercial Relations on the Vili Kingdom of Loango.* Oxford: Clarendon Press.

———. 1995. *Leisure and Society in Colonial Brazzaville.* Cambridge: Cambridge University Press.

———. Forthcoming. *Catholic Women of Congo-Brazzaville.* Bloomington: Indiana University Press.

Massengo, A. Moudileno. 2001. *Genealogie d'un chaos: Congo-Brazzaville.* Paris: Harmattan.

Massengo, Gualbert-Brice. 2000. "L'economie pétrolière du Congo: Les effets pervers de la monoressource économique dans les pays en développement." Ph.D. dissertation, Université de Provence-Aix-Marseille I.

Mbaku, John M., and Julius O. Ihonvbere, ed. 1998. *Multiparty Democracy and Political Change: Constraints to Democratization in Africa.* Aldershot, UK: Ashgate.

McClintock, Cynthia. 1994. "Presidents, Messiahs, and Constitutional Breakdowns in Peru." In *The Failure of Presidential Democracy: The Case of Latin America,* ed. Juan J. Linz and Arturo Valenzuela, 286–321. Baltimore: Johns Hopkins University Press.

McGowan, Patrick. 2003. "African Military Coups d'État, 1956–2001: Frequency, Trends, and Distribution." *Journal of Modern African Studies* 41, no. 3: 339–370.

Mehler, Andreas. 2005. "Central African Republic: The Shaky Foundation and Limited Achievements of a Democratic Transition." In *The Fate of Africa's Democratic Experiments,* ed. Leonardo A. Villalón and Peter VonDoepp. Bloomington: Indiana University Press.

Menga, Guy. 1993. *Congo: La transition escamotée.* Paris: Harmattan.

Mengisteab, Kidane, and Cyril Daddieh, ed. 1999. *State Building and Democratization in Africa: Faith, Hope, and Realities.* Westport, CT: Praeger.

Mkandawire, Thandika. 1999. "Crisis Management and the Making of 'Choiceless Democracies.'" In *State, Conflict, and Democracy in Africa,* ed. Richard Joseph, 119–136. Boulder, CO: Lynne Rienner.

Mokoko, Jean-Marie. 1995. *Congo: Le temps due devoir.* Paris: Harmattan.

Moore, Barrington. 1966. *The Social Origins of Dictatorship and Democracy: Lord and Peasant in the Making of the Modern World.* Boston: Beacon.

Morgenthau, Hans. 1946 [1974]. *Scientific Man Versus Power Politics.* Chicago: University of Chicago Press (Midway reprint, 1974).

Morgenthau, Hans, and Kenneth W. Thompson. 1985. *Politics Among Nations: The Struggle for Power and Peace,* 6th ed. New York: Knopf.

Morris, Morris D. 1979. *Measuring the Condition of the World's Poor: The Physical Quality of Life Index.* New York: Pergamon.

Moukoko, Philippe. 1999. *Dictionnaire Général du Congo-Brazzaville.* Paris: Harmattan.

Mundt, Robert J. 1997. "Côte d'Ivoire: Continuity and Change in a Semi-Democracy." In *Political Reform in Francophone Africa,* ed. John F. Clark and David E. Gardinier, 182–203. Boulder, CO: Westview.

Ndegwa, Stephen N. 2002. "Decentralization in Africa: A Stocktaking Survey." World Bank Africa Region working paper series. Washington, DC: World Bank.

Newbury, Catharine. 1988. *The Cohesion of Oppression: Clientship and Ethnicity in Rwanda, 1860–1960.* New York: Columbia University Press.

Nsafou, Gaspard. 1996. *Congo: De la démocratie à la démocrature*. Paris: Harmattan.

Obenga, Théophile. 1985. "Les rois-dieux au royaume Loango." *Revue des Sciences Sociales* 3 (July–September).

———. 1998. *L'histoire sanglante du Congo-Brazzaville (1959–1997): Diagnostic du'une mentalité politique africaine*. Paris: Présence Africaine.

O'Donnell, Guillermo. 1973. *Modernization and Bureaucratic-Authoritarianism: Studies in South American Politics*. Berkeley: Institute of International Studies.

O'Donnell, Guillermo, Philippe C. Schimitter, and Laurence Whitehead, ed. 1986. *Transitions from Authoritarian Rule: Comparative Perspectives*. Baltimore: Johns Hopkins University Press.

Okoko-Esseau, Abraham. 1995. "The Christian Churches and Democratisation in the Congo." In *The Christian Churches and the Democratisation of Africa*, ed. Paul Gifford. Leiden: E. J. Brill.

Olowu, Dele, and James S. Wunsch, ed. 2003. *Local Governance in Africa: The Challenges of Democratic Decentralization*. Boulder, CO: Lynne Rienner.

Onuf, Nicholas. 1998. "Constructivism: A User's Manual." In *International Relations in a Constructed World*, ed. Paul Kowert, Vendulka Kubálková, and Nicholas G. Onuf. Armonk, NY: M. E. Sharpe.

Ossebi, Henri. 1998. "De la galère à la guerre: Jeunes et 'Cobras' dans les quartiers Nord de Brazzaville." *Politique Africaine*, no. 72 (December): 17–33.

Ottaway, Marina. 1999. "Nation Building and State Disintegration." In *State Building and Democratization in Africa*, ed. Kidane Mengisteab and Cyril Daddieh, 83–98. Westport, CT: Praeger.

Ottemoeller, Dan. 1999. "Three Schools of Democracy in Africa." *African Studies Review* 42, no. 3 (December): 63–66.

Ould-Mey, Mohameden. 1998. "Structural Adjustment Programs and Democratization in Africa: The Case of Mauritania." In *Multiparty Democracy and Political Change*, ed. John M. Mbaku and Julius O. Ihonvbere. Aldershot, UK: Ashgate.

Pereira, Luiz Carlos Bresser, José Maria Maravall, and Adam Przeworski. 1993. *Economic Reforms in New Democracies: A Social-Democratic Approach*. Cambridge: Cambridge University Press.

Pigasse, Jean-Paul. 1998. *Congo: Chronique du'une guerre annoncée*. Paris: Éditions ADIAC.

Plattner, Mark. 1998. "Liberalism and Democracy: Can't Have One Without the Other." *Foreign Affairs* 77, no. 2 (March–April): 171–180.

Pourtier, Roland. 1998. "1997: Les raisons d'une guerre 'incivile.'" *Afrique Contemporaine* 186 (2nd trimester): 7–32.

Powell, G. Bingham. 2000. *Elections as Instruments of Democracy: Majoritarian and Proportional Visions*. New Haven: Yale.

Power, Timothy J., and Mark J. Gasiorowski. 1997. "Institutional Design and Democratic Consolidation in the Third World." *Comparative Political Studies* 30, no. 2: 123–156.

Przeworski, Adam. 1988. "Some Problems in the Study of the Transition to Democracy." In *Transitions from Authoritarian Rule: Comparative Perspectives*, ed. Guillermo O'Donnell, Philippe C. Schmitter, and Laurence Whitehead. Baltimore: Johns Hopkins University Press.

Przeworski, Adam, et al. 1997. "What Makes Democracies Endure?" In *Consolidating the Third Wave Democracies*, ed. Larry Diamond et al., 295–311. Baltimore: Johns Hopkins University Press.

———. 2000. *Democracy and Development: Political Institutions and Well-Being in the World, 1950–1990*. Cambridge: Cambridge University Press.

Putnam, Robert D. 1993. *Making Democracy Work: Civic Traditions in Modern Italy*. Princeton: Princeton University Press.

Quantin, Patrick. 1997. "Congo: Transition démocratiques et conjoncture critique." In *Transitions démocratiques africaines: Dynamiques et contraintes (1990–1994)*, ed. Jean-Pascal Daloz and Patrick Quantin, 139–191. Paris: Karthala.

Radu, Micahel, and Keith Somerville. 1989. "The Congo." In *Benin, the Congo, Burkina Faso: Politics, Economics and Society*, ed. Chris Allen et al. London: Pinter.

Reefe, Thomas Q. 1981. *The Rainbow and the Kings: A History of the Luba Empire to 1891*. Berkeley: University of California Press.

Reno, William. 1998. *Warlord Politics and African States*. Boulder, CO: Lynne Rienner.

Reynolds, Andrew, ed. 2002. *The Architecture of Democracy: Constitutional Design, Conflict Management, and Democracy*. Oxford: Oxford University Press.

Robertson, Lawrence. 1997. "The Constructed Nature of Ethnopolitics." *International Politics* 34 (September): 265–283.

Robinson, Pearl T. 1994a. "Democratization: Understanding the Relationship Between Regime Change and the Culture of Politics." *African Studies Review* 37, no. 1.

———. 1994b. "The National Conference Phenomenon in Francophone Africa." *Comparative Studies in Society and History* 36, no. 3 (July): 575–610.

Rodney, Walter. 1966. "African Slavery and Other Forms of Social Oppression on the Upper Guinea Coast in the Context of the Atlantic Slave Trade." *Journal of African History* 7, no. 3.

Ross, Michael L. 2001. "Does Oil Hinder Democracy?" *World Politics* 53, no. 3 (April): 325–361.

Rupture-Solidarité [collective editors]. 2000. *Les Congo dans la tourmente*. Paris: Karthala.

Samuels, Richard J. 2003. *Machiavelli's Children: Leaders and Their Legacies in Italy and Japan*. Ithaca: Cornell University Press.

Sartori, Giovanni. 1994. "Neither Presidentialism nor Parliamentarism." In *The Failure of Presidential Democracy: Comparative Perspectives*, ed. Juan J. Linz and Arturo Valenzuela, 106–118. Baltimore: Johns Hopkins University Press.

Saul, John S. 1997. "'For Fear of Being Condemned as Old-Fashioned': Liberal Democracy vs. Popular Democracy in Sub-Saharan Africa." *Review of African Political Economy* 24, no. 73 (September): 339–353.

Sautter, Gilles. 1966. *De l'Atlantique au Fleuve Congo: Une géograhie du sous-peuplement*. Paris: Mouton.

Schaffer, Frederic. 1998. *Democracy in Translation: Understanding Politics in an Unfamiliar Culture*. Ithaca: Cornell University Press.

Schapera, Isaac. 1970. *Tribal Innovators: Tswana Chiefs and Social Change, 1795–1940*. New York: Humanities Press.

Schatzberg, Michael. 2001. *Political Legitimacy in Middle Africa: Father, Family, Food*. Bloomington: Indiana University Press.

Schedler, Andreas. 2002. "The Menu of Manipulation." *Journal of Democracy* 13, no. 2 (April): 36–50.

———, ed. 2006. *Electoral Authoritarianism*. Boulder, CO: Lynne Rienner.

Schraeder, Peter J. 2000. "Cold War to Cold Peace: Explaining US-French Competition in Francophone Africa." *Political Science Quarterly* 115, no. 3: 395–419.

Shils, Edward. 1957. "Primordial, Personal, Sacred, and Civil Ties." *British Journal of Sociology* 7: 113–145.

Simiyu, Vincent. 1988. "The Democratic Myth in the African Traditional Societies." In *Democratic Theory and Practice in Africa,* ed. Walter O. Oyugi et al. Portsmouth, NH: Heinemann.

Simon, David J. 2005. "Democracy Unrealized: Zambia's Third Republic Under Frederick Chiluba." In *The Fate of Africa's Democratic Experiments,* ed. Leonardo A. Villalón and Peter VonDoepp. Bloomington: Indiana University Press.

Sinda, Martial. 1978. *André Matsoua: Fondateur du Mouvement de Libération du Congo.* Paris: ABC Press.

Smith, Zeric Kay. 2000. "The Impact of Political Liberalization and Democratization on Ethnic Conflict in Africa: An Empirical Test of Common Assumptions." *Journal of Modern African Studies* 38, no. 1 (March): 21–40.

———. 2001. "Mali's Decade of Democracy." *Journal of Democracy* 12, no. 3 (July): 73–79.

Snyder, Jack. 2000. *From Voting to Violence: Democratization and Nationalist Conflict.* New York: Norton.

Solnick, Steven L. 2002. "Federalism and State-Building: Post-Communist and Post-Colonial Perspectives." In *The Architecture of Democracy,* ed. Andrew Reynolds, 171–205. Oxford: Oxford University Press.

Soni-Benga, Paul. 1998. *Les Dessous de la guerre du Congo-Brazzaville.* Paris: Harmattan.

Stretton, Hugh. 1969. *The Political Sciences: General Principles of Selection in Social Science and History.* New York: Basic.

Suleiman, Ezra N. 1994. "Presidentialism and Stability in France." In *The Failure of Presidential Democracy,* ed. Juan J. Linz and Arturo Valenzuela, 137–162. Baltimore: Johns Hopkins University Press.

Sundberg, Anne. 2000. "The Struggle for Kingship: Moses or Messiah—Ethnic War and the Use of Ethnicity in the Process of Democratization in Congo-Brazzaville." In *Ethnicity Kills?* ed. Einar Braathen, Morten Boas, and Gjermund Saether. New York: St. Martin's.

Takougang, Joseph. 1997. "Cameroon: Biya and Incremental Reform." In *Political Reform in Francophone Africa,* ed. John F. Clark and David Gardinier, 162–181. Boulder, CO: Westview.

Thornton, John K. 1983. *The Kingdom of Kongo: Civil War and Transition, 1641–1718.* Madison: University of Wisconsin Press.

Tonda, Joseph. 1988. "Marx et l'ombre des fétiches: Pouvoir local contre *ndjobi* dans le nord-Congo." *Politique Africaine* 31 (October): 73–83.

———. 1998. "La guerre dans le 'Camp Nord' au Congo-Brazzaville: Ethnicité et ethos de la consommation/consumation." *Politique Africaine* 72 (December): 50–67.

Toulabor, Comi. 1995. "'Paristroika' and the One-Party System." In *State and Society in Francophone Africa Since Independence,* ed. Anthony Kirk-Greene and Daniel Bach, 106–120. New York: St. Martin's.

Turner, Thomas. 1997. "Zaire: Flying High Above the Toads: Mobutu and Stalemated Democracy." In *Political Reform in Francophone Africa,* ed. John F. Clark and David Gardinier, 246–264. Boulder, CO: Westview.

United Nations Development Programme. 1998. *Human Development Report 1998.* New York: Oxford University Press.

———. 1999. *Human Development Report 1999.* New York: Oxford University Press.

United States Department of Energy. 2005. "Country Analysis Briefs: Congo-Brazzaville." www.eia.doe.gov/emeu/cabs/congo.html.

United States Department of State. 2003. "Congo: Country Reports on Human Rights Practices." www.state.gov/g/drl/rls/hrrpt/2002/.

Valenzuela, Arturo. 1994. "Party Politics and the Crisis of Presidentialism in Chile: A Proposal for a Parliamentary Form of Government." In *The Failure of Presidential Democracy: The Case of Latin America,* ed., Juan J. Linz and Arturo Valenzuela, 91–150. Baltimore: Johns Hopkins University Press.

Vallée, Olivier. 1988. "Les cycles de la dette." *Politique Africaine* 31 (October): 15–21.

Van de Walle, Nicolas. 1999. "Globalization and African Democracy." In *State, Conflict, and Democracy in Africa,* ed. Richard Joseph, 95–118. Boulder, CO: Lynne Rienner.

———. 2001. *African Economies and the Politics of Permanent Crisis, 1979–1999.* Cambridge: Cambridge University Press.

Vansina, Jan. 1969. "The Kingdom of the Great Makoko." In *Western African History,* ed. Daniel F. McCall, Norman R. Bennett, and Jeffrey Butler. New York: Praeger.

———. 1973. *The Tio Kingdom of the Middle Congo, 1880–1892.* London: Oxford University Press.

———. 1990. *Paths in the Rainforest: Toward a History of Political Tradition in Equatorial Africa.* Madison: University of Wisconsin Press.

———. 1994. *Living with Africa.* Madison: University of Wisconsin Press.

Vengroff, Richard, and Lucy Creevy. 1997. "Senegal: The Evolution of a Quasi-Democracy." In *Political Reform in Francophone Africa,* ed. John F. Clark and David E. Gardinier, 204–222. Boulder, CO: Westview.

Vengroff, Richard, and Alan Johnston. 1989. *Decentralization and the Implementation of Rural Development in Senegal: The View from Below.* New York: Edwin Mellen.

Verschave, François-Xavier. 1998. *La Françafrique: Le plus long scandale de la République.* Paris: Stock.

———. 2000. *Noir silence: Qui arrêtera la Francafrique?* Paris: Editions Arènes.

Villalón, Leonardo A., and Phillip A. Huxtable. 1998. *The African State at a Critical Juncture: Between Disintegration and Reconfiguration.* Boulder, CO: Lynne Rienner.

Villalón, Leonardo A., and Abdourahmane Idrissa. 2005a. "Repetitive Breakdowns and a Decade of Experimentation: Institutional Choices and Unstable Democracy in Niger." In *The Fate of Africa's Democratic Experiments,* ed. Leonardo A. Villalón and Peter VonDoepp, 27–48. Bloomington: Indiana University Press.

———. 2005b. "The Tribulations of a Successful Transition: Institutional Dynamics and Elite Rivalry in Mali." In *The Fate of Africa's Democratic Experiments,* ed. Leonardo A. Villalón and Peter VonDoepp, 49–74. Bloomington: Indiana University Press.

Villalón, Leonardo A., and Peter VonDoepp, ed. 2005. *The Fate of Africa's Democratic Experiments.* Bloomington: Indiana University Press.

VonDoepp, Peter. 2005. "Institutions, Resources, and Elite Strategies: Making Sense of Malawi's Democratic Trajectory." In *The Fate of Africa's Democratic Experiments,* ed. Leonardo A. Villalón and Peter VonDoepp. Bloomington: Indiana University Press.

Von Mettenheim, Kurt, ed. 1997. *Presidential Institutions and Democratic Politics:*

Comparing Regional and National Contexts. Baltimore: Johns Hopkins University Press.

Wagret, Jean-Michel. 1963. *Histoire et sociologie de la République du Congo (Brazzaville)*. Paris: Pichon and Durand-Auzias.

Waltz, Kenneth. 1959. *Man, the State, and War: A Theoretical Analysis*. New York: Columbia University Press.

Weissman, Fabrice. 1993. *Election presidentielle de 1992 au Congo: Entreprise politique et mobilisation électorale*. Bordeaux: CEAN.

Weldon, Jeffrey. 1997. "The Political Sources of Presidencialismo in Mexico." In *Presidentialism and Democracy in Latin America*, ed. Scott Mainwaring and Matthew S. Shugart, 225–258. Cambridge: Cambridge University Press.

Westebbe, Richard. 1994. "Structural Adjustment, Rent Seeking, and Liberalization in Benin." In *Economic Change and Political Liberalization in Sub-Saharan Africa*, ed. Jennifer A. Widner, 80–100. Baltimore: Johns Hopkins University Press.

Whitehead, Laurence. 1986. "International Aspects of Democratization." In *Transitions from Authoritarian Rule*, ed. Guillermo O'Donnell, Philippe Schmitter, and Laurence Whitehead, 3–46. Baltimore: Johns Hopkins University Press.

Whitehouse, Bruce. 2007. "Exile Knows No Dignity: African Transnational Migration and the Anchoring of Identity." Ph.D. dissertation, Department of Anthropology, Brown University.

Widner, Jennifer A., ed. 1994. *Economic Change and Political Liberalization in Sub-Saharan Africa*. Baltimore: Johns Hopkins University Press.

Wiseman, John. 1990. "Review of *Benin, the Congo, Burkina Faso: Politics, Economics and Society* by Chris Allen et al.," *African Affairs* 89, no. 357 (October).

World Bank. 2000. *The World Development Report*. New York: Oxford University Press.

Woungly-Massaga. 1974. *La révolution au Congo: Contribution à l'étude des prob-lèles politiques d'afrique centrale*. Paris: F. Maspero.

Yates, Douglas. 1996. *The Rentier State in Africa: Oil Rent Dependency and Neocolonialism in the Republic of Gabon*. Trenton, NJ: Africa World Press.

Yengo, Patrice. 1998. "'Chacun aura sa part': Les fondements historiques de la (re)production de la 'guerre' à Brazzaville." *Cahiers d'Études Africaines* 38, nos. 2–4: 471–503.

Young, Crawford. 1965. *Politics in the Congo: Decolonization and Independence*. Princeton: Princeton University Press.

———. 1976. *The Politics of Cultural Pluralism*. Madison: University of Wisconsin Press.

———. 1982. *Ideology and Development in Africa*. New Haven: Yale University Press.

———. 1994a. *The African Colonial State in Comparative Perspective*. New Haven: Yale University Press.

———. 1994b. "Evolving Modes of Consciousness and Ideology: Nationalism and Ethnicity." In *Political Development and the New Realism in Sub-Saharan Africa*, ed. David Apter and Carl Rosberg, 61–86. Charlottesville: University of Virginia Press.

———. 1994c. "In Search of Civil Society." In *Civil Society and the State in Africa*, ed. John W. Harbeson, Donald Rothchild, and Naomi Chazan, 33–50. Boulder, CO: Lynne Rienner.

————. 1999. "The Third Wave of Democratization in Africa: Ambiguities and Contradictions." In *State, Conflict, and Democracy in Africa,* ed. Richard Joseph, 15–38. Boulder, CO: Lynne Rienner.

Young, Crawford, and Thomas Turner. 1985. *The Rise and Decline of the Zairian State.* Madison: Wisconsin University Press.

Zartman, I. William, ed. 1995. *Collapsed States: The Disintegration and Restoration of Legitimate Authority.* Boulder, CO: Lynne Rienner.

Zartman, I. William, and Katharina R. Vogeli. 2000. "Prevention Gained and Prevention Lost: Collapse, Competition, and Coup in Congo." In *Opportunities Missed, Opportunities Seized: Preventive Diplomacy in the Post–Cold War World,* ed. Bruce W. Jentleson. Lanham, MD: Rowman and Littlefield.

Index

299

About the Book

Why did the democratic experiment launched in the Republic of Congo in 1991 fail so dramatically in 1997? Why has it not been seriously resumed since then? In tackling these complex questions, John F. Clark provides a thorough analysis of more than fifteen years of Congolese politics.

Clark explores a series of logical hypotheses regarding why democracy failed to take root in Congo, moving from political culture to economic performance, ethnoregional identities, French foreign policy, the role of militias, and institutional design. He also discusses the country's present "electoral authoritarian" regime. His conclusions shed light not only on the nature of Congolese politics, but also on the utility of the scientific approach to understanding the social world.

John F. Clark is associate professor of international relations at Florida International University. His publications include *The African Stakes of the Congo War* and *Political Reform in Francophone Africa* (coedited with David Gardinier).